DR. TONY HYMAN'S

I'll Buy That Too!

How to Make Easy Money Selling "Junk" Found around Your Home and Neighborhood

by

Dr. Tony Hyman

Treasure Hunt Publications
Shell Beach, California

A Division of Collectors' Clearinghouse

© H. A. Tony Hyman

1992

Treasure Hunt books are available at discount
with bulk purchase for business or promotional use.
Custom editions can be created to fill your specific needs.
Please call our Promotions Department at (805) 773-6777.

Previous books on buying and selling by Dr. Hyman:
The Where To Sell Anything and Everything Book
Where To Sell Anything and Everything by Mail
Cash For Your Undiscovered Treasures
I'll Buy That!

Books on tobacco collectibles by Dr. Hyman:
The World of Smoking and Tobacco at Auction
Handbook of American Cigar Boxes

Treasure Hunt Publications
PO Box 3028
Shell Beach, CA 93448

Covers:
Steve Gussman
North Hollywood
0 9 8 7 6

ISBN: 0-937111-02-3

Our readers have been
making money for 12 years...
a lot of money.

If you want
to make money
with one item or a thousand...

read the next few pages.

They show you how to use this book to
put dollars in your pocket.

You will be more successful
if you read and follow directions
than if you do not.

Table of Contents

Table of Contents

This book is written for people who want to make money by paring down their own possessions or by finding other people's things and reselling them.

I'll Buy That Too! can put money in your pocket. It can do other things for you, but its prime purpose is to help people who want to sell something get fair value for what they have. The following are the most often asked questions.

Who should read this book?
Isn't this for antique dealers?

This book is for everyone who wants to make money. The things you will learn in this book can be done by anyone, whether you are age 18 or 80, whether you are an antique dealer or not.

You can make money selling things you already own. Many readers also make additional money reselling things they buy from yard sales and flea markets run by people who have not read this book. Many of our readers are able to go into shops and spot things they can sell for higher prices to people inour book.

We are not trying to turn you into an antiques dealer or picker. We are giving you the information you need to protect yourself, and to make money with what you own. If you would like to become a successful part time antique dealer with a minimum of effort, **I'll Buy That Too!** is probably the single most important book you can own.

I'll Buy That Too! is written for the total beginner, but is used by the top editors, columnists, auctioneers, and dealers in America.

I'm 80 years old. Can anyone do this?

This is nothing more than a little reading, writing a few letters, and perhaps having a few items copied on a Xerox© machine. People of any age who can read, write, or talk on a telephone can do this. This book was written and designed by an older person to be easy to read and use by other older people. No one needs this book more than people over 50 because they own the best stuff, and make the most mistakes. **I'll Buy That Too!** is easy to use by anyone who wants to be get fair treatment and prices.

Of course it takes a little effort. But it's worth it.

"We are both in our 70's. We made so much money selling off the things we had accumulated over the years, that now we shop at flea markets looking for things we can resell to people in your book."

Mr. & Mrs. Joseph Christ, Indiana

How do I turn my "trash into cash"?

Five simple steps are all it takes.

1: Find an item to sell.
2: Identify a buyer.
3: Contact the buyer.
4: Agree to a price.
5: Ship the item.

It's easy. Anyone can do it. Keep reading. We'll show you how.

How can this book help me?

I'll Buy That Too! does many things, but two are most important.

FIRST: It tells you what is collected. Reading it will help you avoid mistakes when deciding what to keep, what to sell, what to give away, and what to discard.

SECOND: It give you the name and address of a buyer (in some cases, many buyers) who are willing to buy antiques and collectibles. Inside these pages you will meet approximately 1,000 people and institutions who are top buyers... people ready to pay you cash for good items.

I'll Buy That Too! brings you reliable, knowledgeable buyers who can identify what you have, determine its current market value, and buy it from you at a fair price. Many have volunteered to help you dispose of it in other ways.

No other book does that for you, but *I'll Buy That Too!* doesn't quit there. Besides helping you find something to sell and a buyer for it, it teaches you how to evaluate codition, prepare an accurate description and negotiate a price. Once you've sold your item *I'll Buy That Too!* tells you how to ship what you have sold.

How do I find an item I can sell?

Most people buy *I'll Buy That Too!* with a specific item or items in mind that they'd like to sell. This book has a detailed index at the back of the book. Look up your item. Try looking it up under what it is, what it does, what it is made of and where it was made. The index contains many things you'd expect, toys, dolls, tools, coins, and other categories we all know are collected, but there are many things that may surprise you. Read the entire index.

Take 20 minutes to read the entire index.

Read the index with a red pen or pencil. Every time you come across something you might own, make a mark to remind you to come back there. If you're not sure, mark it anyway. Most people find something they own listed. You'll be amazed how many things you own or have seen at local yard sales and flea markets.

You now have the *I'll Buy That Too!* advantage. You know what buyers want.

Who are the buyers in your books?

They are private collectors, universities and other institutions, and specialty dealers who are ready and eager to buy things. They are selected for experience, knowledge, scholarship, fair pricing, and willingness to share information with amateur sellers.

For twelve years we have been bringing you the most accessible, helpful and varied selection of buyers possible. These are the people to whom I go when I have something to sell. Many of these people I know personally. Others have been recommended or added on the basis of other information. No one paid a fee to be in this book, but some buyers and sellers have sent 5% "thank you" checks because they were so pleased with the transactions they were able to arrange through our book.

When we produce a new directory, we work to locate top people who have reputations for fair dealing with amateur sellers. Readers report that our buyers frequently surprise them by paying much more for an item than they thought it would bring.

It's very popular these days to be cynical about honesty, and to assume that everyone is crooked. Fortunately, that's simply not the case. The world is full of honest, knowledgeable, helpful people. We've tried to help you find some of them.

Why not have a yard sale?

Great idea, as long as you sell things appropriate to a yard sale: children's clothing, modern kitchen items, and newer house-hold do-dads. If your item is fifteen or more years old, be cautious about selling it at a yard sale. Some items should never be sold at yard sales without first making certain you don't have something worth more than you think. These include: Disney items, electric guitars, briar pipes, advertising, hardback books from before 1950 with dust jackets, fishing tackle, fountain pens, perfume bottles, wrist watches, balloon tire boy's bicycles, plastic radios, tin cans, carnival glass, baseball cards, Indian items, children's games and toys, pocket knives, dolls, artwork signed in pencil, and just about anything related to TV or movies.

A Hollywood homeowner asked $15 for his yard sale perfume bottle, saying "I know bottles are collectible." The man who bought the $15 bottle drove two blocks to a gas station where he phoned our expert in perfume bottles. He asked her for an offer on the $15 bottle. "Would you take $4,000?" came the reply. In a few minutes, one seller got $15 for the bottle and another got $4,000. Which seller are you? It's up to you. *I'll Buy That Too!* gives you the power to be the smart one.

Antique dealers are around the corner. Why not sell to them?

You can. It's often convenient to do so. For a fairly high portion of your goods, it is probably the best course of action. Selling this way, you can expect from 10¢ to 20¢ on the retail dollar depending on the desirability of the item. Goods that won't resell easily will bring 1¢ to 5¢ per retail dollar. That's not unreasonable. But don't accidently sell something valuable tossed in with more ordinary goods .

You could take the rarest Indian spear point into every dealer in America, and almost no one would recognize what you have. Few would pay you the $10,000+ you'd get by dealing with an expert in Indian stone. Dealing with an expert in Indian stone will require a phone call, a letter, and perhaps a Xerox© copy or sharp photo. It will take you 20 to 30 minutes.

Selling your spearpoint to the antique dealer around the corner will also take about a half hour. No phone calls. No letters. The local dealer may pay you only a few dollars, however. From the dealer's point of view that's a fair price, as s/he doesn't know what exactly your item is and doesn't have a quick market for it. As a result, the risk is greater. The more risk they take, the less they can afford to pay. One of the advantages of dealing with experts is they know what you have and what a fair price is. As a result, they can usually pay more.

Many things are suitable for you to sell to local flea market dealers. I encourage you to do so. But don't sell to them unless you know exactly what you are doing. Remember, it was a Long Island *antique dealer* who sold the $66,000 dish for $2; It was a Southern *antique dealer* who sold the $22,000 Stickley table for $440 at his auction. It was a Western NY *antique dealer* who sold the $43,000 cast iron bank for $125 at his auction. You can visit any antique shop in America and find one or more good things priced too low because the dealer doesn't know what it is or what an expert will pay for it. No one can know everything!

Will you get cheated?

There is some indication you gain a measure of legal protection by dealing with experts. If you ask a dealer in dolls what she will pay you for your railroad lantern, and then accept the $10 she offers for your $250 lantern, you have no recourse later. She made an offer and you accepted it. Neither of you knew what you were doing.

If, however, you present yourself to an expert, identify yourself as an amateur seller and request a fair offer based on the expert's knowledge of the market, and he offers $10 for a $250 item, you may have grounds for legal action. Experts may not use their expertise to knowingly cheat you if you have established a relationship of trust between you, and are asking them, in essence to be your advisor. Fair does not mean the highest imaginable price. Depending on the hobby, payment of 40% to 70% of market is viewed as "fair." The higher the value, the higher the percentage.

Over the past twelve years, we have no indication from our readers this has been a problem. **I AM NOT A LAWYER. THIS IS NOT LEGAL ADVICE.**

Why no pictures and prices in this book?

I'll Buy That Too! is not a pictorial price guide. It's more useful than a price guide in a very important way. A price guide gives you a "dollar value" based on what the author of the guide thinks the item is worth. his opinion is based on visiting shops and reading auction reports. The more rare the item, the less likely a price guide will be accurate. You could probably look at every book in your local library and not find a picture of what you want to sell, unless you're very lucky. Hundreds of millions of items have been manufactured. No book can picture or price them all. The more rare your item is, the less likely it is to be listed or pictured in a price guide.

Some specialty price guides in fields like comics, political buttons, phonograph records, tokens, radio premiums, and *PEZ©* dispensers to name a few are comprehensive, and can help you establish relative rarity for your item, but they do not help you turn it into cash. Not one of the seven most valuable things sold by my readers last year was listed in a price guide. That didn't keep readers from getting as much as $55,000 for what they had.

Just like the value of gold and the stock market goes up and down constantly, so does the "value" of antiques and collectibles. Two years ago, a man shopping in a New England bookstore discovered a rare Edgar Alan Poe 1827 paperback in a pile of equipment catalogs. He paid $15 and resold it for $198,000 at auction. When that some book resold at auction a month ago, its price had dropped to under $150,000. What's the "value" of that book?

Price Guides do not help you sell your item. *I'll Buy That Too!* is better than a price guide because it tells you how to get money for your item. *I'll Buy That Too!* was written to put cash in your pocket. It was also written to help collectors, who I think are very special people. See the box on page 16.

How do I find out what my item is worth?

Easy. Sell it. Worth is established when someone takes cash from their pocket and puts it into yours. It's a hard concept for some people to understand, because we're so used to seeing prices on everything in stores. An item that is not for sale has no monetary value. What you can get is "an estimate of how much money it might bring if sold." Don't confuse that estimate with value or with how much money you actually will get. That estimate has little meaning if it is more than a few months old and did not come from an expert in the type of item you are researching. Value will also change depending on whether it is wholesale or retail and whether it is being determined for insurance, replacement, IRS, estate or divorce settlement, or bequest.

If it really makes you happy, go find a price guide in your local bookstore or public library and try to look up your item. If you are lucky enough to find *your exact item* in a price guide, you have a rough estimate of what its value was about six months before the price guide was printed. On items worth less than $100, this may be all you need or care to know. You can sell these items to local antique dealers if willing to accept the discount I wrote about on page 7. People who sell good items worth $300 or more based on price guide values are highly likely to get less money than they could by bargaining with experts.

What is my item worth?

No book can tell you what your item is "worth."

Price guides are designed to be read and used primarily by flea market and general line antique dealers. These guides assume their readers have a great deal of previous knowledge. As a result they are confusing for amateurs (like you) to interpret and you will usually do so incorrectly.

Amateurs often assume the value listed for an item similar to theirs is also the value of their item. This belief can cost you money.

Prices given in books are often misleading, and occasionally wildly inaccurate. Items have sold for 50 times listed value. They routinely sell for less.

The more rare an item, the less likely it is to be listed in a price guide, and the more likely the "value" will be inaccurate if it is.

When dealing with second hand goods, seldom are two items identical. Your item could sell for more or less.

The amount of money you will get for your item depends on how, where, why, by whom and to whom it is sold.

There are no answers to value until you sell. Something is "worth" what someone is willing to pay. Items from the 1960's are often "worth" more than items from the 1760's.

The people in this book are buying. If you're not selling, please don't waste their time.

I don't really want to sell what I have. Can I ask people in this book for an estimated value?

Some buyers will give free appraisals. Most do not appraise items that are not for sale. Many buyers are too busy to be bothered by readers who only want free information. There are many legal, ethical, and moral questions involved. I wrote this book for people who want to make money, not for the idly curious.

One listee voiced a common complaint. "We're a small company. We don't have the time to spend with people who are not really selling."

I understand that many of you would like an estimate first, so you can decide whether you want to part with your item. "I'd take a million dollars for just about anything I own, but would I take $50 when I'd like it to be $250?" That's a question only you can answer. You need to give thought to what your expectations are before you begin.

If what you want is an appraisal so you can insure what you own, many of the people in this book are qualified to do appraisals for you. A few will do it for free, some will do it for a fee. In either case, make it clear what you want when you contact someone. $20 is a fair price to pay for a verbal appraisal or for an informal written one for a simple item. You'll usually pay more for formal appraisals or work on obscure items.

Most buyers prefer not to be contacted if you're not selling or are unwilling to pay for an appraisal. If you do contact them frivolously they'll quit making themselves available to the serious sellers.

Do not ask experts what things are worth just so you know how much to charge a friend or relative. That is dishonest.

How do I find a buyer?

The antique/collectible market is "the law of supply and demand" at work. To sell something for a fair price, the key factors are how many are available and how many people want them.

Many items are salable, but only to a tiny handful of people. There are about 1,000 serious collectors of tin cans, maybe 200 collectors of Annalee© dolls, only 60 who want license plates from Canadian Indian reservations, and less than five willing to buy photographs of 19th century funerals.

You can make money if you can get into that inner circle of buyers. We've made that easy by finding them for you. That's what *I'll Buy That Too!* is all about. To find a buyer, go back to the index and find the items you have marked. The page numbers tell you where you might find a buyer. Turn to the pages listed.

Each page contains a number of separate entries for buyers. Each buyer's entry contains information about what they want to buy as well as their name and address. Each entry begins with bold type indicating the main category of things they buy. Read the entire entry all the way through because entries contain other information such as what the buyer wants, doesn't want, what they've written, particularly useful books, and more. Their entry also indicates whether they make offers or not. Since **most people do make offers, we only note those who do not.** Many entries contain specific information on how to best sell to that particular buyer.

Entries are your key to making money.
Read as many of them as you can.

It can be worth more money to look up your item in several categories. For example, an art glass cigar box with a label depicting nude women playing poker in a railroad car would be desirable to buyers of art glass, cigar boxes, labels, advertising, nudes, card playing, gambling and railroads. Consider all possibilities, since some of those people will pay more than others.

Before you contact a buyer, read the buyer's entry carefully. If the entry reads "No tribbles," don't ask about selling your "tribble." If it reads "Tribbles will be considered," don't bother asking about your tribble unless it is old, scarce, and in fine condition.

Before you contact your buyer, check the **update** page of *I'll Buy That Too!* You will find it on page 308. If we have learned of a buyer who has moved, died, or otherwise changed status since the previous printing, we provide that information to purchasers of later printings. If you learn of a listee who has moved or died, please inform us. As a thank you, we'll send you a free update sheet listing all changes reported since the last printing.

check your possessions thoroughly

Any object you own might be sold because of

What it is (a perfume bottle, pocket knife, etc.);
Who made it (Hires Root Beer, American Flyer, Winchester, etc.);
Where it was made (Salem bottles, NY guns, New Orleans art, etc.);
When it was made (books before 1700, dolls from the 1950's, etc.);
What it is made of (ivory, glass, paper, etc.);
What it was used for (poker chips, prison money, Holy cards, etc.);
Where it was sold (Adirondacks souvenirs, Alaska postcards, etc.);
What it is shaped like (dog figurines, monster toys, etc.);
Who painted it (Vargas paintings, comic art by Barks, etc.);
Who owned it (celebrities, gangsters, U.S. Presidents, etc.).

How do I contact a buyer?

More than half our buyers provide their phone number. Never call collect unless the buyer specifically said you may. Some buyers have a free 800 number. These 800 numbers are not advice lines and should be used only if you are actually selling.

Phone calls are fast, easy, and able to get the most information to the buyer with the least effort. Selling something worth $50 up? Use the phone.

An important reason for using the telephone is to give the buyer the opportunity to ask questions about your item, so call only when the item you wish to sell is right by the phone. Some buyers and sellers are deaf or have physical handicaps that make telephoning inconvenient. Others prefer the slower pace and lower cost of writing. If you'd rather write a letter, make certain you include all the information requested by the buyer in his entry. Don't forget to include your Stamped Self Addressed Envelope.

Contacting buyers by mail is as easy as filling in the blanks thanks to Dr. Hyman's exclusive form letter, called a SELL-A-GRAM. Using SELL-A-GRAMS is easy. All you have to do is answer the questions and fill in the blanks. SELL-A-GRAMS tell buyers you are one of our readers, and entitled to special attention. You may Xerox© the SELL-A-GRAM as many times as you need. If you have additional SELL-A-GRAMS made at a copy center, ask them to copy it onto yellow paper. Marketing psychologists say colored paper gets faster attention.

SELL-A-GRAM
from a reader of Tony Hyman's *I'll Buy That Too!*

TO:
_____
_____
_____
_____

FROM:
_____
_____
_____
Phone: (_____)

I have the following item:

Remember to include the (1) shape, (2) colors, (3) dimensions, and (4) all names, dates, and marks. Re-read pages 10-14 and and any text or entry notes for selling what you have.

It's condition is:

List all chips, repairs, cracks, dents, fading, scratches, rips, tears, creases, holes, stains, and foxing. Note any missing pages, parts, or paint.

CHECK ONE

- ☐ The item is for sale for $_____ plus shipping.
- ☐ The item is for sale. I am an amateur seller and would like you to make an offer.
- ☐ The item may be for sale if the price is sufficient. Would you like to make an offer?
- ☐ The item is not for sale, but I am willing to pay a fee to learn its value.

To assist you to evaluate the item, I am enclosing a:
☐Sample ☐Photocopy ☐Photo ☐Tracing ☐Sketch ☐Rubbing ☐Nothing

This is to certify that, to the best of my knowledge, the item is genuine and as described. Buyer has a 5 day examination period during which the item may be returned for any reason.

Signature:_____ **Date:**_____

☐ Answer Requested (SASE enclosed).   ☐ No answer needed.

BUYER'S RESPONSE:

1986 Treasure Hunt Publications, Box 3028, Shell Beach, CA 93448

TREASURE 🗝 HUNT

To make money by mail, you need
[1] a good description, [2] a photo or photocopy,
and [3] a self addressed stamped envelope (SASE).

If I write to a buyer, what do I include?

This book contains many pages of tips on how to describe things. Use the Table of Contents to find them. Also, many listees will tell you how to describe what they buy. A good description starts with what it is and, if necessary, what it was used for. Give its size, color, shape and identify the material from which it is made. Give any names, dates, model or serial numbers, maker's mark, signatures, and other characteristics which may be important. Provide as much much of an item's history as you know.

Include your phone number in your letter. Buyers often prefer to call about valuable items.

No matter what you sell, condition is important. Few people want to buy soiled, stained, damaged, or broken anything. Some items are never purchased damaged. But there are a few collectibles that can put money in your mailbox even if damaged or incomplete. These are usually mechanical devices such as phonographs or television sets that can be cannibalized for parts. Items in less than perfect condition will usually bring 50% or less of what items that are like new will bring.

If you don't describe condition accurately,
the buyer will return your item, costing you
and the buyer time, money, and wasted effort.

Photos are an important part of the description. Most amateurs do not take Polaroid© photos well enough to send them as part of the description. Polaroids© can be very useful if you use a tripod or set your camera on a table while you shoot. Many buyers request a photocopy.

What is a photocopy?

A photocopy is a copy made with a Xerox© type machine. Photocopy machines are a seller's best friend. Whenever possible, make a Xerox© copy of what you have to sell. It is the cheapest and easiest method of describing most items. Objects such as knives, small dolls, even pistols, will photocopy well. It is a particularly effective way to describe china patterns.

Copy machines are available in many businesses, banks, and libraries. Fees are a modest 4¢ to 25¢. Color photocopies are available at some copy centers, but for most items you'd like to sell are an unnecessary expense.

What is an SASE? /3/

Your Name
Your Address

If you ask someone for information or an offer, take a long "business size" #10 envelope, address it to yourself, put a stamp in the corner. This is a Self-Addressed Stamped Envelope or SASE. Include it with your SELL-A-GRAM or letter. Use a long envelope because many buyers will send you two or more pages of information, which won't fit well into smaller envelopes. When writing to Canada, send two loose U.S. stamps, instead of an SASE. If requesting photos be returned, put two stamps on your SASE if it took two to send your original letter.

If you do not include an SASE, you are telling buyers not to bother answering your letter if they are not interested in what you have to sell. "If my help isn't worth an envelope and stamp to the seller," said one expert, "it's not worth my time and money either."

Never ask for free information or appraisals without including an SASE. Our buyers have promised to eventually answer your inquiries if you include an SASE. They are under no obligation to answer mail that does not. If an answer isn't important to you, **please include a note or check the SELL-A-GRAM box reading "no reply needed."** Otherwise, include an SASE.

How much is something worth? How do I set a price?

When I sell, I almost never set a price. I ask the buyer to set the price. I recommend you do the same. I've been involved with antiques and collectibles for forty years and know that experts are better able to set a price than I am. I make more money on rare items by asking for offers. I wouldn't know a rare gun from a common one. So I ask an expert in guns who I can trust to give me honest info and a fair price. One reader offered one of my listees an item he thought to be worth $300. The buyer/listee paid $1,700 in cash plus another $1,700 in items from his store, a good example of why I suggest you ask for offers. Whether you ask for an offer or not, however, you should be prepared for the fact that many items are not worth as much as you think.

I'll Buy That Too! brings you many of the nation's top experts, men and women who write price guides, edit newsletters, and are officers in collectors' clubs. Many listees have been at their hobbies for 20 years or more, and keep up with daily market fluctuations. They, better than you or I, know what your item is worth.

What is to keep them from cheating you and telling you your $5,000 watch is worth $5? Honesty, for one thing. Reputation for another. The world of collectibles is a small one. Word gets around fast, and dishonest people seldom stay in business long. You have the best defense of all, you can say no. Requesting an offer does not oblige you to sell at the price offered.

Some people feel there is a conflict of interest in having the same person evaluate and set the price. To some extent there is, but I feel I get fair prices when dealing with honest people. And I'm confident that I'm many dollars ahead of selling at a yard sale, flea market, or local auction.

No dealer is dishonest if he pays the price you set. He is at fault if you ask him for a fair price and he lies to you. Offers help protect you. Even dealing with experts, it is advisable when selling items worth $1,000 or more to get more than one offer. Another buyer may want it for his own collection, or have an immediate customer, so can afford to pay more. Do not try to start a bidding war.

Naturally the publishers of *I'll Buy That Too!* can't guarantee private transactions between two people over whom we have no control. But hundreds of thousands of transactions have taken place based on our previous three books and we've received less than a dozen letters of complaint...most very minor.

How do I get an offer for something?

Describe what you have very carefully to the appropriate expert. Include a photograph (snapshot or Polaroid©) or photocopy (Xerox©). Tell the buyer whether you are an amateur seller or an antique dealer. Ask the buyer what you have and what s/he will pay for it.

You don't need to know an item's "value" to get a fair price. You don't even have to know what your item is. The midwestern lady who got $10,000 for her Japanese sword had no idea what she owned, nor did the woman in Los Angeles who got $55,000 for Indian medals she had looked at only once in 30 years. An Ohio teenager was surprised when his cigar box full of arrowheads put $10,000 in his pocket when he asked our expert to look at them.

How do I set my price when buyers insist?

A few experts no longer make offers, even to amateur sellers. These buyers are usually marked with NO OFFERS at the end of their entry. These are usually people who feel they have been treated dishonestly by amateurs. They believe amateurs are "fishing for free information, don't really want to sell, and have outrageous expectations about the value of their objects."

Setting your own price isn't easy. If it were, antique dealers wouldn't make so many mistakes. There are no shortcuts to pricing. You must study, study, study. That's one reason you should not abuse the good will of those still willing to help. Setting your own price means you will have to spend time in the library. You will need to read antiques magazines and two or three different price guides, and a specialty guide if one exists. This is time well spent, because most of the people who will not make offers are dealing in fields where some items are very valuable and difficult for an amateur to tell from their less valuable counterparts.

Price guides make fascinating reading. Many of the people in *I'll Buy That Too!* have written useful and interesting guidebooks to the relative scarcity of items in their hobby: comic books, pin back political buttons, Disney, PEZ© , cigar boxes, pottery, western artifacts, labels, postcards, pottery, radio premiums, radios. Every antique and flea market dealer should buy and read them.

You must be careful of pricing lamps, quilts, tin cans, perfume bottles, fountain pens, fishing tackle, pop culture, pocket knives, dolls, and toys among other things.

How much will a dealer or collector pay?

A dealer usually pays from 30% to 75% of an item's full retail value. It depends on how much money the dealer has, how anxious he is to add your item to his inventory, and how quickly he thinks your item will resell. The more expensive the item you sell, the higher percentage of retail value you should get.

Collectors tend to pay more, 60% to 100% or more of retail value. They, too, pay more for expensive items. One collector explained:

"If I'm offered a common item, worth only $5 or $6 dollars, I'm rarely interested in paying more than a dollar or two for it, if I buy it at all. I don't want to tie up money or space with minor items. When someone offers me a $100 item, I'm willing to pay full value or even more. If it's a very rare item, I'd rather overpay and make certain I get it."

High value items are much easier for you to sell than low value items. Items have low value because "everyone who wants them has them," and the demand is low. It is almost impossible, for example, to sell a $20 tin can today, but you can sell a $1,000 tin can in less than five minutes. A $2 cigar box will find no takers, a $200 box should sell quickly if you know the right buyer.

How important is condition?

In determining value, nothing is more important than condition. Some collectibles lose 40-50% of their value with their first scratch or dent. Stains, tears, fading, foxing, thin spots, runs, nicks, water damage, writing, brittleness, are all "bruises" that affect value. Except in very rare china and glass, chips and cracks are often "fatal," making value drop to almost nothing. A low or medium quality item in only fair condition almost never has a buyer.

Collectors are Important People!

Collectors are important people. If it were not for them, a great deal of our cultural heritage would be lost forever.

Private industry has little interest in its past. Libraries and museums don't have the money. Colleges don't have the time. Historical societies don't have the staff.

Collectors do it for love, spending their own time and money to learn about the way things were. When you sell to collectors, you are helping preserve a slice of American history.

I personally have a lifetime interest in the history and artifacts of the cigar industry. Many readers have given me cigar related items free because the item had special meaning to the giver or their family and they know that I and other collectors will help preserve both the item and its story.

Every little scrap of information found in letters, photos, and catalogs is important to collectors.

When you sell to a collector, your memento of the past is preserved for future generations to enjoy.

Three keys to value: condition, condition, and condition

Selling to Canadians

There are some excellent buyers in Canada. Make certain if you sell to a Canadian, however, that you request payment with a check in U.S. funds drawn on a U.S. bank. Many Canadian collectors maintain accounts for this purpose. If the buyer cannot write a check on a U.S. bank, ask for payment in U.S. funds by International Postal Money Order. These can be cashed at no charge at full value at any U.S. post office. If you are sent a Canadian bank check, it can cost you as much as $7 in charges to cash at your bank. If drawn in Canadian money, you will also lose on the exchange rate.

Many times you can sell lesser items to local flea market and second hand and antique dealers. They will pay you very little for them, and rightly so. They're worth very little.

Amateur sellers are notorious for overestimating the quality of condition. As a result, some dealers and collectors will ask to see the item before they make a final offer. This is particularly true of buyers of paper goods like post cards, trade cards, match covers, sheet music, and stamps. Paper dealers want to see what you have, because very small variations in condition mean substantial difference in price. For example, paper money worth $50 in very fine condition might be worth only $5 in circulated condition. Post cards with creases, or match covers with their strikers removed, are worth little or nothing.

A few other buyers, notably of watches, will also request an item be shipped prior to final payment. When you do this, protect yourself by insuring any package containing something worth more than $100. If it is a valuable item, send it Registered Mail or "return receipt requested" which requires the recipient's signature.

I'll Buy That Too! gives you access to many of the most helpful, interesting, and knowledgeable people in the world of collectibles. Please don't abuse them.

CAUTION

Although we have confidence in our buyers, and know many of them personally, it is advisable to always be cautious about letting people you don't know into your home. This caution applies to salesmen, delivery men, and others as well.

never send things without prior permission

Guidelines for successful packing

Always use sturdy boxes. You can buy boxes at most post offices, stationery stores, and packing companies, but heavy duty boxes can often be obtained free from book stores. Don't ship anything, even shoes, in shoe boxes

If an item is easily breakable, double boxing (one box inside another) is advised. Write your name and the addressee on the inside box as well. When packing breakables, never let two items touch. Wrap each item separately in styrofoam sheeting, bubble bags, or clean paper. Don't leave lids on cookie jars, sugar bowls, and the like. They are likely to chip if you do.

Never pack your item in direct contact with newsprint. Newsprint smears, and can damage clothing and ruin items like Wedgwood and other porous chinas. Wrap in tissue, paper towel or plain paper, then use newspaper.

Flat items should be put between two sheets of cardboard approximately one inch bigger on all sides than what you're sending. Put the grain of the two pieces of cardboard at right angles. Your package will be less likely to bend.

Ship by First Class Mail or by private carrier. Do not use parcel post. The difference in price between parcel post and 1st class is so small, the few pennies you save aren't worth it. If your package weighs under two pounds, you can ship anywhere in the U.S. for about $3.

Consider using Registered Mail. For between $5 and $10 in addition to postage your item receives special handling in transit. It can also be insured up to $25,000 and must be signed for by the addressee. All this for the one fee! Anything that can not be replaced should be sent Registered Mail.

There are some special rules for Registered Mail, however, so check with your Post Office, before you wrap. The most important differences are:
>   You must use a clean box with no printed advertising.
>   The box must show no signs of damage.
>   Address and return address must be written on the box. You may not use labels.
>   Each seam of the box (where it was assembled) must be covered with brown paper tape. No matter how strong it is, plastic tape is not allowed.

Always insure what you mail. $500 worth of insurance on a 1st class package can be purchased for about $5. Insurance on Registered mail costs much less, because of the strict security under which Registered Mail is handled.

Follow these guidelines and common sense, and you'll do fine!

How do I ship all this stuff I sell?

What you ship belongs to you until the buyer agrees to accept it. It if arrives broken, you've lost a sale and your item.

Buyers can often give you tips on packing. Chances are, many similar items have been shipped to them in the past. If your item is very heavy, bulky, or large, the buyer will often pick it up or make arrangements to have it professionally picked up and packed. This is usually true of jukeboxes, slot machines, radios, TV sets, and the like. If your item sells for thousands of dollars, the buyer may want to personally pick it up, unless it's small and easy to ship, like a watch.

Most packing is easy, but do not pack complicated and expensive items, such as lamps, yourself. Care in packing can be the difference between a happy transaction and a disappointing one.

Many towns have franchised "packing stores" which can pack the more difficult items for you. They are convenient, but expensive. Since the buyer normally pays for packing and shipping, it is best to discuss this with the buyer before using professional services.

If you have sold many items, and will be packing more than a few boxes, packing supplies, tape, boxes, styrofoam, and bubble wrap are all available from stores which sell these items to the commercial market. Depending upon the size of your town and its Yellow Pages, you'll find them listed under "Packing Supplies," "Paper," or "Boxes and Cartons." If it's hard for you to get around, you can order these supplies with a credit card and they will be delivered to you.

Why didn't I get an answer to my inquiry?

Either [1] you didn't include an SASE or [2] your item was not useful to collectors and the person hasn't had time to respond or [3] your item is not what the person you wrote is looking for, [4] your letter got lost in the mail or [5] they're out of town, sick, or some other situation. Remember, you're writing to real people. They have lives to lead too. Many of us have families, travel, work long hours, and the like.

Regrettably, I myself am not always able to get to my collecting mail as quickly as I'd like. I'm backed up about 400 routine letters now. These are from people who didn't send SASE's or who have asked for specific information that I haven't had time to look up yet. I've answered every letter that offered something good. If you have something good, you'll always get an answer from any collector.

Why haven't I been paid for what I sent?

I've only been asked this question a couple times in a dozen years.

If you sent something without asking permission to send it, you haven't been paid because sending something unasked for through the mail makes it a gift. The person who receives it is not required to pay for gifts, or even acknowledge them.

If you sent it through to mail to a buyer because they specifically said in a letter or phone call that you could, or their entry in this book specifically gives you permission to send approvals, then they are obliged to pay you or return your stuff. If they do not, ask them why. It's your money, call and ask. Maybe it's lost. You should report all unsatisfactory dealings to us.

Can I buy from people in the book?

Most of them will sell items. Ask.

How often do you update?

We do an **update** every time we reprint, about three times a year. Updating consists of making address adjustments, and removing entries of people who have died or quit. We do an all new **edition** approximately every 30 months. Each new **edition** has a new title. A revision or an update does not.

Can I hire Dr. Hyman?

Dr. Hyman's schedule does not leave him time to assist individual sellers who have only a few items. He is occasionally available to help disburse significant collections, a service for which he charges a substantial fee. He does free appraisals of signs, cigar boxes, and tin cans by mail.

You can get his advice at no charge when he is a guest on radio or TV talk shows. Dr. Hyman has made more than 900 radio and television guest appearances. Call your favorite radio or TV talk show and ask them to have him as a guest so you can talk to him on air. Your request carries more weight than you think. Ask them to book Dr. Tony "Trash into Cash" Hyman. His agent's number is (805) 773-0117.

Some shows you might listen to

Larry King: c/o Pat Piper, MBS, 1755 S. Jefferson Davis Hwy, Arlington, VA 22202
Jim Bohannon: Same as Larry King
Ray Briem: KABC, 3321 S. La Cienega Blvd., Los Angeles, CA 90016
Roy Leonard: WGN, 435 N. Michigan, Chicago, IL 60611
Jim Eason: KGO-AM, 900 Front Street, San Francisco, CA 94111
Dan Steele, WHP, Box 1507, Harrisburg, PA 17105
Cathleen Dunn or Gordon Hinkley, WTMJ, 720 E. Capitol Dr., Milwaukee, WI 53212
Paul Gonzalez, WFLA, 801 E. Jackson St., Tampa, FL 33602
Bill Murphy, WTSP-TV, 11450 Gandy Blvd., St. Petersburg, FL 33702
Oprah Winfrey, c/o WLS-TV, 190 North State St., Chicago, IL 60601

You can find your favorite station listed in the telephone book. Dr. Hyman's advice on air has been worth as much as $55,000 to callers! What's your call worth?

Do you discount your books?

If you would like to order a few additional copies of **I'll Buy That Too!** as gifts, **there is a coupon on the very last page of this book that offers hefty savings.** If ordering for a store, we give even bigger discounts in lots of 12.

Do you care what happens to readers?

We sure do! We love hearing about your successes. If you tell us about odd things you sold, valuable things you sold, very old things you sold, or anything else with an interesting story, **we'll send you a free copy of our next edition** (or send a copy of this one as a gift anywhere you'd like) if we use your story on radio or advertising. We are particularly interested in items you thought of as having little value that turned out to be worth a great deal. In the unlikely event that you have a bad experience with a listee, please tell us about that as well.

furniture, rugs and lamps

You can sell big

heavy things like furniture, lamps and rugs through the mail.

Furniture, lamps and rugs exist in great variety, and many have been reproduced or copied. As a result, each piece must be seen to be evaluated. Because these items can be worth hundreds, even thousands or tens of thousands, of dollars, the fuss of taking a picture is justified.

Photos should be 35mm slides or prints. If you don't own a 35mm camera, ask a friend to take them for you. You should send buyers close ups of details, such as inlay and drawer pulls. If this is not possible, telephone the buyer and discuss your item over the phone. Be prepared to answer specific questions about colors, dimensions, type of wood, etc.

Make certain when selling large or heavy items that you and the buyer agree who has responsibility for packing and shipping. This cost is normally born by the buyer.

In cities there are "packing stores" which can ship almost anything. Most packer/shippers will come pick up items for a fee. Look under "Packaging Service" in the local Yellow Pages.

If you are elderly, have trouble getting around, or live outside a big city, request the buyer to have large items picked up as part of the sale.

tony hyman

Furniture

★ **Entire estates including furniture and accessories from the American colonial period**, art, or important collections of toys, dolls, guns, decoys, miniature lamps, art glass, advertising, or other specialties. Your estate or collection must have a value in excess of $50,000 to be handled by this important firm. No interest in minor collectibles, limited edition plates, or common items.
> James D. Julia Auctioneers
> PO Box 80
> Fairfield, ME 04937
>   (207) 453-7904   Fax (207) 453-2502

★ **Heavily carved or decorated American fur-niture made between 1820-80** including fancy Empire, Gothic revival, American Renaissance, rococo, etc., especially furniture made by Belter, Roux, or Meeks. Also **gas chandeliers and** *Argand Astral* **lamps.** This prestigious dealer does not make offers so research is in order since many of these pieces can be very valuable. Send her a photo of the furniture plus a copy of every label or maker's mark you can find. She will help an amateur seller if you're really *selling* and not fishing for free appraisals.
> Joan Bogart
> Box 265
> Rockville Centre, NY 11571
>   (516) 764-0529

★ **Furniture and accessories from the Arts & Crafts or "Mission" period.**   Oak furniture, light fixtures, and metalwork by L. & J.G. Stickley, Gustav Stickley, Roycroft, Limberts, Lifetime, Charles Stickley, Rohlfs, Stickley Brothers, and Dirk Van Erp, especially unusual pieces, custom made pieces, and items inlaid with silver, pewter or copper. Also textiles, various publications, and catalogs from these firms. "If you have any doubts, please call. I will be glad to help."
> Robert Berman
> Le Poulaille
> 441 South Jackson St.
> Media, PA 19063
>   (215) 566-1516

★ *Roycroft* **furniture and accessories** including **lamps,** waste baskets, clocks, frames, art, pottery, china, glassware, and all books and paper ephemera associated with the *Roycroft* company or its founder, Elbert Hubbard. When you write, make certain to honestly state whether the item is for sale or whether you are seeking identification and appraisal. Please give the source of the item for sale and include any stories or history.
> Tom Knopke
> House of Roycroft
> 1430 E. Brookdale Pl.
> Fullerton, CA 92631
>   (714) 526-1749

★ **Adirondack and other rustic furniture.** "I'll buy rustic furniture made of roots, twigs, antlers, diamond willow, or birch bark, and hickory furniture from the *Old Hickory Company*. Dealers must price their goods, but I will help amateur sellers set a price on what they have, as long as their letter includes a photo and a complete description, including all damage."
> Barry Friedman
> 22725 Garzota Drive
> Valencia, CA 91355
>   (805) 296-2318

★ **Twig furniture.** "I'm interested in any type of rustic or Adirondack furniture. This includes pieces by Old Hickory and Twig furniture. The wilder the style, the more I will want it. As always the better the condition, the more I will pay. If you have any doubts, call."
> Robert Berman
> Le Poulaille
> 441 South Jackson St.
> Media, PA 19063
>   (215) 566-1516

★ **Wicker furniture and luggage.** "I'll consider any good condition old wicker, but am most interested in Bar Harbor Victorian characterized by curled arms and an open weave that you can see through. Pieces can be in any color, but natural is usually best. **Wicker luggage** can have either leather or brass trim, but should be in fine condition, inside and out, suitable for resale. Give the dimensions, status and color of the lining, condition of the wicker, hardware, and the leather trim.
Joan Brady
834 Central Ave.
Pawtucket, RI 02861
(401) 725-5753

★ **Designer furniture from the 1940's and 50's** by Herman Miller, Knoll, Eames, Nelson, Gilbert Rohde, Frank Lloyd Wright, Heywood Wakefield, Noguchi, Thonet, and other national and international designers. Most pieces are signed on the bottom. Primarily interested in bent plywood chairs, tables, couches, and case pieces and chrome furniture by Wright.
Frank Novak
7386 Beverly Blvd.
Los Angeles, CA 90036
(213) 683-1963 Fax (213) 683-1312

★ **Folding chairs.** "I'm interested in everything dealing with folding chairs, including photographs of chairs in use in lodges, churches, picnics and other events. Interested in some chairs only to add to collection. Must have a photo or photocopy of offered photos, catalogs, or chairs. Particularly want folding chairs with advertising on the back.
Richard Bueschel
414 N. Prospect Manor Ave.
Mt. Prospect, IL 60056
(708) 253-0791

Rugs

★ **High quality rugs and tapestries.** Oriental, Chinese, and European rugs. American Indian rugs, and large hooked rugs are all of interest if of sufficient quality and condition. Interested in art deco, art nouveau, and arts and crafts rugs and textiles, as well. Worldwide interest in fine tapestries, textiles, embroideries, and weavings as well as paisley and Kashmir shawls. A good clear color photograph is important. Make certain to mention wear or stains. Appraisals and offers are made *only* after actually seeing your rug. Gallery open by appointment only.
Renate Halpern Galleries
325 E. 79th Street
New York, NY 10021
(212) 988-9316

★ **Oriental rugs.** Claims "highest prices paid" for Oriental rugs of all types: antique, used, old.
David Tiftickjian, Jr.
260 Delaware Ave.
Buffalo, NY 14202
(716) 852-0556

★ **Rugs with advertising logos or images** such as Buster Brown, *Coca-Cola*, etc.
Charles Martignette
PO Box 293
Hallandale, FL 33009
(305) 454-3474

★ **Greenfell hooked mats/rugs.** "I'll buy any tightly hooked textile, mat, or rug labeled "Greenfell Labrador Industries" as long as it is in excellent condition. These always depict Northern scenes like polar bears, igloos, Eskimos, etc. Please send dimensions and a photo. Dealers are expected to price their goods, but amateurs may request an offer."
Barry Friedman
22725 Garzota Drive
Valencia, CA 91355
(805) 296-2318

Lamps

★ **Lamps and lamp parts of all types from all periods.** Buys a wide range of wall, floor, and table lamps from the Betty lamps of the 1700's right through to the 1950's. Will buy kerosene, whale oil, electric, *Aladdin*, organ, marriage, student, desk, and other lamps. Also interested in *Tiffany* and other high quality leaded and painted lamps. This major Western dealer can be very helpful to amateurs with just about any type of lamp to sell. **Especially wants *Aladdin* lamps and parts** including galleries, chimney cleaners, bug screens, flame spreaders, wick cleaners, wick raisers, finials, and anything else made by *Aladdin*. Also buys parts from other lamp makers. If you have lamps or parts for sale, please note whether they are brass or nickel plated and give all numbers and wording. A photo is very helpful if asking for an offer.
Richard Melcher
1206 Okanogan St.
Wenatchee, WA 98807
(509) 662-0386

★ **Lamps and light fixtures from the early 1800's to the early 1940's** are wanted by this veteran lighting restoration dealer. He buys old iron, brass, or tin electric or gas fixtures, wall sconces, chandeliers, colored glass shades from fixtures, and damaged fixtures suitable for scavenging parts. He will buy inside or **outside lighting fixtures**, (including street lights) and has particular interest in those from commercial buildings as well as homes. He notes that large fixtures can be disassembled and shipped at his expense. Note all cracks or chips in glass. He is not interested in reproduction shades or in any fluorescent fixtures. He is, however, strongly interested in **catalogs from manufacturers** or retailers which depict large numbers of lighting fixtures from before 1920.
Robert Daly
Historic Lighting Restoration Sales & Service
10341 Jewell Lake Ct.
Fenton, MI 48430
(313) 629-4934

★ **Reverse painted, leaded glass, or art glass lamps** including table lamps, boudoir lamps, and floor lamps. "I am interested in buying shades, bases or parts for lamps of these types. I have a special interest in *Moe-Bridges*, *Classique Studios*, or *Phoenix Light Co*. I am also interested in buying catalogs from lamp and lighting fixture manufacturers (not retailers) before 1935." **Does not want** oil lamps, hurricane lamps, Gone With the Wind lamps, etc. No lamps after 1920's. Give all names and numbers found anywhere on the lamp or shade, and all dimensions. This long time collector prefers you to set your own price, but will make offers.
Merlin Merline
Box 16265
Milwaukee, WI 53216
(414) 871-6261

★ *Tiffany* **and other high quality glass lamps.** "I believe we are the only auction firm in North America that conducts specialty auctions for rare lamps only." Collections, large or small, of *Tiffany, Handel, Jefferson, Pairpoint,* and other quality lamps, lamp bases, and lamp shades from both large and small oil and electric lamps will be considered by this record setting auctioneer. Photos are a must. Telephone if you have a large group of lamps to sell.
James D. Julia Auctioneers
PO Box 80
Fairfield, ME 04937
(207) 453-7904   Fax (207) 453-2502

★ *Tiffany* **lamps, chandeliers, and other high quality glass lighting fixtures.** Please include photos and your phone number.
Carl Heck
Box 8416
Aspen, CO 81612
(303) 925-8011

★ *Tiffany* **lamps and grapevine picture frames.** Frames are worth from $300 - $1,500 depending upon their size and condition. Lamps bring from $2,500 up. Dawson requests a complete description of condition and return privileges if judged not to be as described. He prefers you to set the price, but will help amateur sellers if their item is for sale. No appraisals.
T. O. Dawson
2110 Noel Dr.
Champaign, IL 61821
(217) 352-7373 eves

★ **Lamps and light fixtures from the Mission or Arts & Crafts period.** Anything signed by L& J.G. Stickley, Gustav Stickley, Roycroft, Limberts, Lifetime, Charles Stickley, Rohlfs, Stickley Brothers, and Dirk Van Erp, especially unusual pieces, custom made pieces, and items inlaid with silver pewter or copper. Also catalogs from these firms. "If you have any doubts, please call. I will be glad to help."
Robert Berman
Le Poulaille
441 South Jackson St.
Media, PA 19063
(215) 566-1516

★ **Emeralite and Bellova lamps, 1909-40s,** wall, desk, table, and floor models, either green-shaded, acid etched or reverse painted models. These are found with brass or with other metal bases. Prefers signed pieces. Unsigned pieces must be heavily decorated to be of interest. Photo essential.
Bruce Bleier
73 Riverdale Rd.
Valley Stream, NY 11581
(516) 791-4353

★ **Oil lamps made in the shape of any figure,** especially those made of colored glass.
Tom Burns
109 E. Steuben St.
Bath, NY 14810
(607) 776-7942

★ **Small bedroom lamps made of art glass.**
Madeleine France
Box 15555
Plantation, FL 33316

★ **Revolving radio and TV lamps** from the 1930's, 40's, and 50's that are driven by the heat of the light bulb. These were made by *Econolite Corp, Scene In Action,* and *Rev-O-Lite* among others. "I will pay $350 for the scene in a fish bowl, and other substantial amounts for mermaids, motorcycles, snow skiiers, sailing ships, water skiiers, Santa Claus, and many others. Please call if you have one for sale."
Bill and Linda Montgomery
Box 68572
Portland, OR 97268
(503) 652-2992

★ **Lamp shades of cloth or beaded silk** from 1890-1930's that are in near perfect condition. He'd like you to send a photo, the dimensions, and your asking price.
Charles Martignette
PO Box 293
Hallandale, FL 33009
(305) 454-3474

Lamp collectors want to know if your lamp is original and complete. You should mention if it shows signs of repair or being a marriage of parts from different lamps.

Describe the quality of the finish on the base and whether the glass shows any cracks or chips. What's wrong with it?

A signature on the base or shade usually makes a lamp worth more. It can be very hard to find on some valuable lamps.

useful little things around the house

If you want to make money as a "picker"

read this chapter, and a few others, like a novel. Become familiar with the wide range of items that have value.

You can often find these items at yard sales and resell them for a profit. We have readers in their 70's who are adding to their income and having fun "shopping for cash." It's not unreasonable to expect $100 to $500+ a month in your pocket if you work at it!

If you plan to "pick for profit" you should familiarize yourself with what buyers want and are willing to pay. If they offer a wants list, send for it. Don't be afraid to ask questions, such as what books to read. In most fields, there are only one or two. Many collectors are happy to train you.

Some fields have a great deal of profit potential. Pocket knives, guitars, fishing tackle, perfume bottles, modern dolls, cigar boxes, tin cans, bicycles, pedal cars, pop culture toys and games, briar pipes, watches, radios, mystery books, and electric trains are all items you should get a working familiarity with, since they often sell at yard sales for far less than you can make reselling them to our buyers.

Fountain pens are another collectible often greatly undervalued. There is great profit in buying them at 25¢ to a few dollars and reselling to experts at five to ten times as much or more.

Don't buy items for resale unless certain you are fairly certain to turn a profit.

tony hyman

Kitchen Items

★ **Figural cookie jars** are wanted by Chicago's only shop devoted exclusively to kitchen counter novelties. Wants figural ceramic jars and jar tops, but nothing cracked or repaired. Jars that aren't figural aren't of interest. She also buys **figural salt and pepper shakers**. She declares a photo to be essential, plus wants you to describe all markings on the bottom of jars or salt sets. Make certain to mention every chip! Prefers you to price. Charges $10 per jar to do appraisals for insurance or estate purposes.
  Mercedes DiRenzo, Jazz'e Junque
  3831 N. Lincoln Ave.
  Chicago, IL 60613
    (312) 472-1500

★ **Figural cookie jars.** "I'll buy amusing, colorful jars in the shape of various people and animals, usually dating before 1950. Especially want those depicting fairy tales, nursery rhyme and cartoon characters such as Li'l Audrey or the Pearl China chef. I do not buy jars if they have any damage at all." This collector wants a photo or good description.
  Kier Linn
  11433 Rochester Ave., #303
  Los Angeles, CA 90025
    (213) 477-5229

★ **Fancy or unusual nutcrackers,** big or small, made of iron, brass, wood, or any other material. A sketch or photocopy is suggested. Include dimensions, colors, and all writing or marks.
  C.J. Davis
  E. 4400 English Point Rd.
  Hayden Lake, ID 83835

★ **Deco era teapots and pitchers.** "I'll buy solid color deco era teapots and pitchers that exemplify the wonderful streamlined, geometric designs of the late art-deco/moderne period." Makers to look for include *Hall, Fiesta, Riviera, Harlequin,* and others. Especially interested in *Hall* teapots. Not interested in items with gold trim or other decoration. No damaged items, no matter how small the damage. Please include a good description and sketch or photo.
  Kier Linn
  11433 Rochester Ave., #303
  Los Angeles, CA 90025
    (213) 477-5229

★ **Cast iron muffin pans,** gem pans, popover pans, and maple sugar molds in unusual patterns and shapes. Also interested in old catalogs, etc., which list multi-sectioned baking or muffin pans. Buys *any* cast iron item marked *Griswold.* Will pay $300+ for *Griswold* #13, 50, and 2800 pans. If you're a dealer, send for his wants list.
  David "the Pan Man" Smith
  Box B
  Perrysburg, NY 14129
    (716) 532-5154

★ **Early kitchen items made of cast iron** or of wood which has been folk carved or decorated are wanted by this important dealer.
  Louis Picek
  Box 340
  West Branch, IA 52358
    (319) 643-2065

★ **Iron pans and broilers in odd or decorative shapes,** including pans for muffins, popovers, rolls, and maple sugar molds. Roll pans shaped like hearts bring $100 and up, while those like fruits and vegetables are worth $150. Pans made by *GF Filley* start at $75. Cast iron broilers look like strange frying pans with grid work, slots, and holes. Not interested in reproductions (they have rough surface and grind marks) or in tin pans of any type. Trace your pans or photocopy.
  David Smith
  Box B
  Perrysburg, NY 14129
    (716) 532-5154

★ *Griswold* **cast iron pots and pans,** including skillets, lids, Dutch ovens, etc. Any items marked as being made by *Griswold* are likely to be of interest.
  Alan Stone
  Box 500
  Honeoye, NY 14471
    (716) 229-2700

★ **Glass knives** are wanted in any configuration or color, especially with original painted decoration in original box. Values run from $25 to $100 or more. Send Xerox© copy and describe color. She edits a quarterly newsletter about glass knives.
  Adrienne Escoe
  Box 342
  Los Alamitos, CA 90720

★ **Novelty figural salt and pepper shakers related to water.** She'll buy fish, frogs, ducks, penguins, seals, umbrellas, bridges, mermaids, sailors, firemen, fishermen, pirates, boats, lighthouses, shells, lobsters, crabs, alligators, seagulls, pelicans, dinosaurs, watermelons, sea serpents, and more! Generally doesn't want sets with chips or repairs, unless they are very rare. "Pictures are the only way to describe things. I have several thousand sets and it's impossible to know whether I have it without seeing a picture." (Photocopies would probably be fine). Likes you to set the price, but will make offers. Editor of the quarterly news letter of the Novelty Salt & Pepper Shakers Club, she also issues catalogs of salt and peppers.

> Sylvia Tompkins
> 25C Center Drive
> Lancaster, PA 17601
> (717) 569-9788

★ **Russian samovars** from before 1930. Please send picture with descriptive information and a statement of condition. He needs to know the size, shape, type of metal, markings, condition, and whether there are any additional matching pieces. He prefers that you price what you have. Also interested in any written material on samovars, especially catalogs.

> Jerome Marks
> 962 Sibley Tower Bldg.
> Rochester, NY 14604
> (716) 546-2017

★ **Unusual condiment sets.** These combination salt, pepper, and mustard sets are wanted if they are unusual and figural. Wants pieces without chips or repairs, but will consider slightly damaged goods if the piece is extremely unusual. Especially likes German sets, and those related to water. A picture is important.

> Sylvia Tompkins
> 25C Center Drive
> Lancaster, PA 17601
> (717) 569-9788

★ **Ceramic or chalk figural string holders,** in wall or counter style. Wants figures of fruits or people (full figure or face) including Indians, Chinamen, Black mammys, Black men, animals, cows, dogs, cats, or birds. Does not want apples, pears, Dutch girls, or chefs.

> Emma Kretchek
> 5726 Terrace Park Dr.
> Dayton, OH 45429
> (513) 434-9126

★ **Toasters.** "I'll buy old or unusual electric toasters in good, non-corroded condition, as long as there are no pieces missing. I am especially interested in very old or very unusual toasters, porcelain models and ones with toast racks. Prices vary greatly, according to rarity, but mint condition examples and ones with original boxes bring the best prices. Toasters do not have to work to be desirable. I am not interested in pop-up toasters unless they are very unusual. Please call or write if you have specific questions." Give the maker's name and model number. A sketch is helpful, but a photo is best. An accurate description of condition is essential. Toasters bring from $10 to $100+ for the very rare ones.

> Joe Lukach
> 7111 Deframe Ct.
> Arvada, CO 80004
> (303) 422-8970

★ **Hand can openers.**

> Craig Dinner
> Box 4399
> Sunnyside, NY 11104
> (718) 729-3850

★ **Tin can openers.** Will consider wall, counter, or hand operated kinds, but he wants old ones (1810-1940), not modern openers. There are more than 1,200 patents for can openers! Give all information that is stamped on the opener.

> Joe Young
> Box 587
> Elgin, IL 60123
> (708) 695-0108

★ **Jadite green (a milky light green) or delphite blue (a similar blue) kitchen ware.** Wants bowls, reamers, canisters, salt and peppers and "anything else." A wide range of items, often in a variety of shapes, were made. Green pieces start at $4, with rare pieces reaching $100, whereas the blue is much more scarce with most pieces starting around $75. Tell what piece you have, its size, whether it is marked on the bottom (most weren't), and the condition, indicating any flakes or chips in the rim and base, and the condition of the painted decoration on canisters, salts, etc.

> Steve Kelley
> Box 695
> Desert Hot Springs, CA 92240
> (619) 329-3206

★ **Kitchenware by the *Shawnee Pottery Co.*** is wanted, but only their gold trimmed (with flower decals) cookie jars, creamers, pitchers, and teapots. Most pieces are marked *Shawnee* or MADE IN USA. This small popular company operated between 1937 and 1961.

> Van Stueart
> Rt. 3 Box 216
> Nashville, AR 71852
> (501) 845-4864

★ **Hand operated egg beaters, cream whips, and glass bottomed mixers** are wanted, if they are American made and before 1920. Buys either rotary or dasher (up and down) type, wall or table style. Cast iron beaters are particularly desirable, especially those with "Flat fold" beaters. There are a great many beaters he'll buy, and quite a few he won't. No beaters with plastic handles or stainless steel dashes. No "*A&J* hand held rotary egg beaters, *Ladd* hand beaters, no *Ekco* or *Maynard* brand beaters, nor butter churns (except *Dazey* models 10, 20, or 30). "No electric beaters," he says, but is willing to make exception for pre-1920 beaters in excellent condition. Nearly all had dates and maker's marks to help you describe them. A photo is requested, but "even a pencil sketch or outline will help." Include all dates and everything printed. Describe condition accurately, including the glass. "I pay a premium for original labels, containers, or pamphlets accompanying desirable mixers. The more nearly perfect an item, the higher its value to me."

> Reid Cooper
> PO Box 900868
> San Diego, CA 92190
> (619) 286-1563 eves

★ **Tunbridge ware** is attractive woodware with geometric or mosaic designs, or with embedded pictures created with cut woods of different colors. She buys boxes, candlestick holders, tea caddies, etc. made in Tunbridge. These pieces are rarely marked. If in doubt, send a good photo or a Xerox© copy of the patterned portion of the item.

> Lucille Malitz
> Lucid Antiques
> Box KH
> Scarsdale, NY 10583
> (914) 636-3367

★ **Twentieth century plastic items.** "Don't donate your old plastic dishes to a thrift shop, I'll buy 'em" says this veteran collector and one of the few people we've found, who care about *Bakelite* and other kitchen plastic.

> [1] **Dishes**, singles or sets, especially serving pieces, sugars, creamers, etc. Look for *Branchell, Color-Flyte, Arrowhead, Russel Wright Ideal Ware*, others;
> [2] **Salt and peppers**, especially boxed sets of figurals or geometrics;
> [3] **Character mugs** of people or animals, especially *Dennis the Menace* by *F&F*;
> [4] Funny Face, Big Pitcher, and other characters, such as *Tony the Tiger*;
> [5] *Soaky* Bubble Bath, other figural bottles;
> [6] **Cookie jar** figurals in plastic.

Give dimensions, colors, and maker, as well as a piece count and statement of condition.

> Mary Anne Enriquez
> 651 So. Clark
> Chicago, IL 60605
> (312) 922-1173

★ *Melmac©* is wanted, but generally only in sets. He's looking for "heavy colorful stuff" like *Arrowhead, Brook Park, Colorflyte, Russel Wright*, and others. Wants to know the maker and condition of what you have, including whether or not you have the original box and paperwork. Dealers are to price their goods.

> "Melmac Mack"
> 443 W. 21st St.
> New York, NY 10011-2968

★ **Older fruit (canning) jars with unusual closures or in unusual colors** other than aqua or clear. Colors wanted include amber, brown, deep green, and shades of cobalt blue. Is willing to pay to $400 for a pint size jar embossed *Cadiz Jar* with a glass screw top. Also want pre-1960 **advertising**, promotional brochures, letterheads, signs, paperweights, etc., from jar and bottle manufacturers, including **wood-canning jar boxes** or box ends, which generally bring $10-30. Give the size, color, and report *exactly* on what is embossed on the jar. Note all cracks, chips, dings, or unwashable stains.

> Tom & Deena Caniff
> 1223 Oak Grove Ave.
> Steubenville, OH 43952
> (614) 282-8918

Cookbooks

★ **Cookbooks published as advertising** by various companies pre-1930, especially those from before 1900. Love to find pre-1920 *JELL-O* cookbooks. Also **fund raising cookbooks** from before 1940. Also buys pre-1920 grocer's catalogs, pre-1920 cooking magazines, reference books and bibliographies of cookbooks. **Unusual cookbooks** of any vintage including those assembled by movie stars, famous artists, etc., are also sought. Also wants **historical information concerning commercial food companies.**
  Roberta Deal
  Box 17
  Mecklenburg, NY 14863

★ **Hard and soft covered cookbooks**, especially soft cover advertising recipe books published by various food companies, such as *JELL-O, Rumford* baking powder, etc., especially fine condition ones from before 1900. Will pay $50 each for the 1930's *JELL-O* cookbooks based on the OZ books by Frank Baum. The founder of the Cook Book Collectors Club, and editor of its newsletter, does not want appliance company recipe books, diet books, or other modern health cookbooks such as heart and cholesterol related cook books. As with all books for sale, sellers should give complete bibliographic information. Sellers must price the books they offer.
  Col. Bob Allen
  Cook Book Collectors Club of America
  PO Box 56
  St. James, MO 65559
    (314) 265-8296 anytime

★ **Spiral bound church, community, or privately published cookbooks.** Will buy singles, collections, or multiple copies of the same title. Please indicate the sponsoring organization and the number of recipes. Mention the quantity you have, the original retail price, and the price you want for them all wholesale. Helen publishes cookbooks and a newsletter for recipe collectors.
  Helen Jump
  PO Box 171
  Zionsville, IN 46077

★ **Spiral bound church, community, charity, fundraiser, ethnic and other privately published cookbooks** with limited distribution.
  Bob Roberts
  Box 152
  Guilderland, NY 12084

★ **Cookbooks and related pamphlets** from before 1950. State condition and price or just ship for immediate offer.
  Alan Levine
  Box 1577
  Bloomfield, NJ 07003

★ **Cookbooks and commercial booklets in any language.** Especially wants early out-of-print items, including **hand written cookbooks**. Also wine, candy, chocolate, baking and specialty cooking books and booklets. Give standard bibliographic information on books. Condition is very important, and wants books to have tight bindings. Please don't ask for free appraisals unless you are actually selling your books.
  Kay Caughren
  284 Purdue Ave.
  Kensington, CA 94708
    (415) 524-8859

Standard Bibliographic Information

Title, author, publisher, place and date(s) of publication,
number of pages, illustrator, and approximate number of illustrations.

Give the condition of (1) the binding, (2) the spine, (3) the pages, and
(4) the dust jacket. Note bookplates, writing, and other damage.
A photocopy of the title page will save lots of writing.

Silverware

★ **Sterling and silver plated flatware**, especially made by *1847 Rogers, Community*, and *Holmes & Edwards*. Also all old "grape" patterns. Send the information on the back of your silver, and a Xerox© if you don't know the name of the pattern. An SASE will get you a pattern guide. Particularly interested in more unusual pieces such as pie forks, punch ladles, ice tongs, sardine forks, etc. "We do not want monogrammed, damaged or worn silver except large serving pieces or very rare patterns." A 30 year veteran of buying through the mail.
    L.C. Fisher
    Silver Exchange
    Route 8, Box 554 (Hwy 190 East)
    Huntsville, TX 77340
       (409) 295-7661

★ **Sterling silver flatware, holloware, jewelry** and novelty items, such as goblets, mint julep cups, trays, etc., especially in old elaborate patterns. **Will also buy unusual pieces of old silver plate**, such as tea services, large trays, and elaborate epergnes (multi-branched centerpieces holding dishes, trays, or candles). You should take photos of larger pieces, and make Xerox© copies of flatware. Everything must be in fine condition, cautions this 22 year veteran dealer. She is not interested in silver coins.
    Helen Cox
    As You Like It Silver Shop
    3025 Magazine St.
    New Orleans, LA 70117
       (800) 828-2311   Fax (504) 897-9310

★ **Victorian figural silverplate napkin rings.** Wants small figural napkin rings. Describe your rings to her well, including all markings, and "I'll probably know what you have."
    Sandra Whitson
    PO Box 272
    Lititz, PA 17543
       (717) 626-4978

★ **European sterling silver and silverplate** from companies like Christophle, Buccellatti, Puiforcat, etc. Buys and sells.
    Russ Burkett
    Box 4231
    Mission Viejo, CA 92690
       (714) 364-3844

★ **Gold or sterling silver open salt dishes,** American or European, in any size, with or without glass liners, as long as they are in fine condition. Describe well, and include your asking price if you can.
    Monica Murphy
    Savannah's Antiques
    1419 Fern
    New Orleans, LA 70118
       (504) 866-2221

★ **American and European open salt dishes in glass, sterling, or silver plate** if rare and unusual. No common or repro salts are wanted. Johnson is author of *5000 Open Salts*, available with a price guide for $52 postpaid.
    Patricia Johnson
    Box 1221
    Torrance, CA 90505
       (213) 373-5262

★ **Silverplated flatware.**   Advertises "immediate cash."
    Vintage Silver
    33 LeMay Court-D
    Williamsville, NY 14221
       (716) 631-0419

★ **Sterling spoons with "cute" Negro figures.** Will pay up to $150 for enameled spoons.
    Elijah Singley
    2301 Noble Ave.
    Springfield, IL 62704
       (217) 546-5143 eves

★ **Silver spoons with advertising** on them. Either sterling or plate.
    W.T. Atkinson
    1217 Bayside Circle W.
    Wilmington, NC 28405

★ **Souvenir spoons** from before 1930, especially those with hand engraving.
    T.K. Treadwell, Tower House Antiques
    4201 Nagle Rd.
    Bryan, TX 77801
       (409) 846-0209

★ **Sterling silver souvenir spoons of Cuba or Puerto Rico**, especially with enameled bowls. "Will pay well" for a spoon from Tampa with cigar shaped handle. Xerox©. NO OFFERS.
    Frank Garcia
    13701 SW 66th St., #B-301
    Miami, FL 33183

china and pottery

The first step in selling china is to ask

yourself, "Would I want to buy this china and use it?" No one wants chipped, stained, or damaged items.

Our buyers are pattern matching services who buy for resale. From their point of view, the best china was bought by your great grandmother, packed away, and never used. That's what brings the most money when they sell it...and when you sell it to them.

When offering china for sale, you must make an inventory of how many pieces you have. List how many of each type item (plates, cups, saucers, etc.) you have.

Unless your china dates before 1860, do not list any pieces that have cracks or chips. You should note all crazing, knife scratches and pattern wear on listed pieces.

Some pieces are harder to find and as a result worth more. Serving pieces always bring more than ordinary table settings, especially pieces with lids.

If you don't know the pattern name, send a Xerox© of the front and back of a small plate and indicate the color of the maker's marks. Photocopies are better than photographs for describing what you have unless you are able to take 35mm close up photos or slides.

tony hyman

China

★ *Wedgwood, Royal Doulton, Lenox* china. Also wants *Castleton, Coalport, Franciscan, Spode, Gorham, Pickard, Royal Worcester, Minton,* and *Flintridge* china. No giftware. Ives offers a free pamphlet *On Caring for your China* if you send her a business size SASE.

Jacquelynn Ives
China Match
219 N. Milwaukee St.,
Milwaukee, WI 53202
(414) 272-8880

★ **Discontinued English and American china patterns** in perfect condition, produced by *Castleton, Franciscan, French Haviland, Lenox, Spode, Minton, Pickard, Royal Doulton, Royal Worcester, Syracuse, Wedgwood,* etc. "We buy sets or incomplete sets consisting of ten pieces or more. For patterns in demand we buy outright; others are listed in our computer system and customers notified as to availability and prices. They do not want to buy Japanese china or *anything* that is imperfect. Roundhill personally collects 100+ year old museum quality *Worcester* products. He prefers you to set the selling price, but will make offers.

J.Warren Roundhill
Patterns Unlimited WTS
Box 15238
Seattle, WA 98115

★ *Royal Doulton, Royal Worcester, Minton* and other fine china and stoneware. This 12 year veteran matching service also **buys most fine crystal** in popular patterns.

Freda Bell
China Match
9 Elmford Rd.
Rochester, NY 14606
(716) 426-2783

★ *Noritake* china in Azalea pattern. Also *Noritake's* scenic Tree in the Meadow pattern and all raised gold patterns by *Noritake.* No chips, cracks, or worn gold or paint. Provide all info on back of pieces.

Ken Kipp
Box 116
Allenwood, PA 17810
(717) 538-1440

★ *Haviland* china for resale. Buys sets or single unusual pieces. Especially wants jardiniers, claret jugs, unusual tea or toast sets, free form salads, syrup jugs, spoon trays, tea caddys, lemonade sets, and other unusual pieces. No individual saucers, however. If your Limoge china isn't marked *Haviland,* she doesn't want it. Pieces must be in mint condition with no wear or scratches. Give the pattern name on the backstamp, a Xerox© copy, and note the colors. Eleanor has 22,000 pieces in stock and has a computerized search service to help customers find other dishes.

Eleanor Thomas
Auld Lang Syne
7600 Hwy 120
Jamestown, CA 95327
(209) 984-DISH

★ *Haviland* china in Butterfly pattern, especially unusual pieces for a personal collection. Must have fluted edges. Nothing damaged.

Sheldon Katz
211 Roanoke Ave.
Riverhead, NY 11901
(516) 369-1100

★ **Obsolete sets and pieces of fine English dinner china** including *Aynsley, Coalport, Lenox, Minton, Oxford, Paragon, Rosenthal, Spode, Royal Albert, Royal Crown Derby, Royal Doulton, Royal Worcester, Shelley, Wedgwood,* and some patterns in *Elite* and *Haviland.* Also buys and sells other popular patterns made by **American, French,** and **German makers.** Margaret does business worldwide and will make offers for items she can use. Items *must* be in excellent condition. If you wish things appraised, their appraisal fee is refundable if they buy your dishes.

Margaret Roe
Old China Patterns Unlimited
1560 Brimley Rd.
Scarborough, Ontario M1P 3G9, CANADA
(416) 299-8880

See the next page for help in dating your Haviland china.

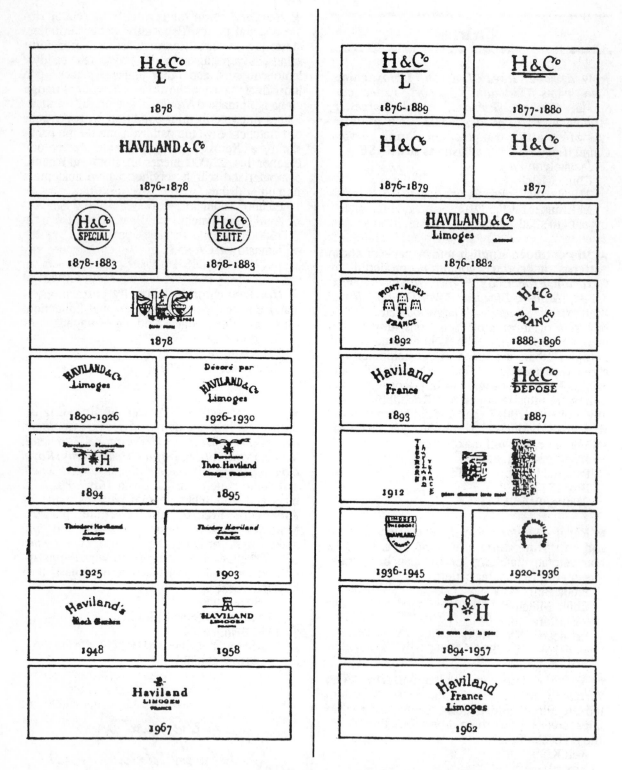

Courtesy of Eleanor Thomas.

★ *Wedgwood* **china in discontinued patterns.** Buys sets or individual pieces, but only in mint condition. "I don't give appraisals on other people's china, so please set the price you want." Include a photocopy if you don't know the name of your pattern.
  Rosemary Evans
  Vintage Patterns
  9303 Mc Kinney Rd.
  Loveland, OH 45140
  (513) 489-6247

★ *Wedgwood* **commemorative ware transfer print china.** Earthenware or bone china plates, trivets, tiles, etc., that contain American scenes, calendars, views of historic places, children's topics, or scenes from literature. "We mainly want items of American interest, but will also buy some Canadian and Australian scenes." These pieces almost always bear backstamps marked JOSIAH WEDGWOOD & SONS, WEDGWOOD, ETRURIA or ETRURIA & BARLASTON. Calendar tiles from the 1870's and 80's are worth up to $200, and tiles honoring the Washington Light Infantry and President Garfield are worth in excess of $400 each. "It's hard to give advice as to what we don't want. People are better off to inquire by giving a good description, photo, description of the back markings and sending a Xerox© of their tile. Some items will have to be seen before we can make an offer."
  Benton & Beverly Rosen
  Mansion House
  9 Kenilworth Way
  Pawtucket, RI 02860
    (401) 722-2927 winters
    (508) 759-4303 summers

★ **Sets or pieces of French, American, or English china and stemware** especially pieces by *Haviland, Castleton, Franciscan, Oxford, Royal Doulton, Lenox, Spode, Syracuse,* and *Wedgwood.* Wants **stemware** by *Cambridge, Duncan, Fostoria, Heisey, Imperial, Lenox, Rock Sharp,* and *Tiffin.* List only the perfect pieces, and give the measurements of all serving pieces. She does not buy German or Japanese china. Medley has been a dealer for 20 years.
  Laura Medley
  Laura's China & Crystal
  2625 W. Britton Rd.
  Okla. City, OK 73120
    (405) 755-0582

★ **Sets or pieces of German, Bavarian, Czechoslovakian, and Austrian china** in fine condition. Companies stocked include *Johann Haviland, Bavarian, Heinrich, Fronconia, Meissen, Rosenthal Thomas, Royal Heidelberg, Krautheim,* and many more. China need not be old, just discontinued. They also purchase **some French patterns,** but want no French *Haviland,* Japanese china, or English china. "We buy no china with cracks, crazing, or chips, or china with the color in a pattern worn off, although we will accept pieces with a slight amount of gold wear. We ask that anyone wishing to sell would send us a colored Xerox© of a six inch or eight inch plate. Copy the front for the design and the back so we can see the hallmark. We also need a good color photo of a plate and a cup. The cup should be photographed in silhouette so we can see the shape of the handle and if the cup is footed or flat. We will quote a fair purchase price for any items we can use. If we cannot use what you have, we will try to tell you how you can sell it in your locality."
  Joan Nackman
  56 Meadowbrook
  Ballwin, MO 63011
    (314) 227-3444

★ *Royal Doulton* **"logo china"** from hotels, restaurants, ships, railroads, airlines, and private companies of all types.
  Diane Alexander
  20834 San Simeon Way #70-C
  North Miami Beach, FL 33179
    (305) 770-4422

★ **Pottery by the Buffalo Pottery Company.** Also wants catalogs and other Buffalo Pottery Company ephemera.
  Thomas Knopke
  1430 E. Brookdale Pl.
  Fullerton, CA 92631
    (714) 526-1749

★ **Fine crystal.** David runs a restoration service which repairs glass, crystal, porcelain, bisque, and figurines. He also buys damaged and undamaged figurines, *Hummels,* china and crystal for resale.
  David Jasper
  Rural Rte. 3, Box 330
  Sioux Falls, SD 57106
    (605) 361-7524

★ **Buffalo Pottery or Buffalo china.** "I'll buy almost any marked piece."
Seymour Altman
8970 Main St.
Clarence, NY 14031
(716) 634-4488

★ *Deldare* **ware** made by the Buffalo Pottery Company. No damaged pieces, please.
Jerome Puma
78 Brinton St.
Buffalo, NY 14214
(716) 838-5674

★ *Warwick* **china, especially portrait items.** Include a photo with your complete description, and he'll return it. Promises to answer every letter regarding the work of this fine American china maker. Prefers you to set the price wanted, but "amateurs should still write."
Jeff Mauck
142 N. 19th St.
Wheeling WV 26003
(304) 277-2356

★ **Cowboy theme dinnerware.** Sets or single pieces of pictorial pottery or china dinnerware which features cowboys or brand marks. Makers include *Wallace, Red Wing,* and *Tepco*.
Frank Novak
7386 Beverly Blvd.
Los Angeles, CA 90036
(213) 933-0383   Fax: (213) 683-1312

★ **Eggcups.** If you have a fine eggcup to sell, the *Eggcup Collectors Corner* may be your best source of information. Sample copies cost only $5 and will give you insights into cups and their prices and a bibliography. When you order your sample, tell Joan why you want one and she'll pick an appropriate issue. Members of the club share buy and sell information.
Joan George
67 Stevens Ave.
Old Bridge, NJ 08857

★ *Goss* **china** especially pictorials, cottages, busts, animals, military commemoratives and foreign crests.
Jeanne Goss Spaulding
1325 West Ave.
Hilton, NY 14468

★ **Any plate, bowl, vase or other china marked** *Clarus Ware*. "We also buy old pieces of *Pope Gosser China Ware* and want any vase, bowl, plate, or other china signed AST VAN HISE.
C.W. & Hilda Roderick
27858 TR 31
Warsaw, OH 43844
(614) 824-3083

★ **White House china** and other items from the White House, including Presidential Christmas cards and gifts given as souvenirs of a White House visit.
H. Joseph Levine
6550-I Little River Turnpike
Alexandria, VA 22312
(703) 354-5454

★ **Pictorial Souvenir china** with views of various towns, streets, and places of interest. Especially interested in pictorial china with New England views, but all are considered. Indicate what the scene is, where the item was made, and whether there are any cracks or chips. Gary publishes *Antique Souvenir Collectors News,* the marketplace for antique souvenirs.
Gary Leveille
Box 562
Great Barrington, MA 01230
(413) 528-5490

★ **G.A.R. china, mugs, and spoons.** "I'll buy any pieces marked G.A.R. (Grand Army of the Republic)."
Don McMahon
385 Thorpe Ave.
Meriden, CT 06450

★ *Wheelock* **souvenir china.** Bill buys this German made blue and green scenic souvenir china.
Bill Copeland
2 Clifton Park Court
Melrose, MA 02176

★ **Oyster plates**. Nothing damaged, please.
Sheldon Katz
211 Roanoke Ave.
Riverhead, NY 11901
   (516) 369-1100

★ **Series Ware** by *Royal Doulton* includes hundreds of shapes and patterns of pitchers, mugs, plates, and other useful, but highly decorated items. This popular transfer ware with a hand-painted look includes a wide variety of themes such as motoring, golfing, fishing, and coaching. Value is dependent on the rarity and desirability of the form and the image. There have been four books written on *Doulton* Series Ware, so you can get information at your local public library. If your item is for sale, call Ed, who lectures frequently in the U.S. and England, and has edited price guides to *Royal Doulton*. **Also buys figurines, figural bottles, red animals, and character jugs by** *Royal Doulton* (see his listings in this book under Animals, Whiskey, and Figurines for more information). **He is not interested** in buying dinnerware, and does not do pattern matching.
Ed Pascoe
Pascoe & Co.
545 Michigan Ave.,
Miami Beach, FL 33139
   (800) 872-0195   Fax (305) 532-8543

★ **Presidential and patriotic English urns, vases, mugs, etc.,** with American historical motifs, pictures of political figures, battles, or famous events. May be any type of china by any maker. A delft teapot advocating "No Stamp Act" would bring $5-6,000.
Rex Stark
49 Wethersfield Rd.
Bellingham, MA 02019
   (508) 966-0994

★ *Clarice Cliff Bizzare Ware.* This English hand painted pottery is decorated with fanciful, geometric, and floral themes. Most pieces are marked, often with the name of the artist, but usually "Clarice Cliff" or "Bizzare." Does not want transfer patterns, only painted ones such as Crocus, Fantasque, Delecia, Caprice, Ravel, and many others. A photo or Xerox© is very important as the company made so many patterns, they're almost impossible to know which you have without seeing it.
Darryl Rehr
11433 Rochester Ave. #303
Los Angeles, CA 90025
   (213) 477-5229

★ *Coors* **pottery and porcelain.** "I'll buy any dinnerware made by the Coors Company of Golden, CO. Decalware made in the *Thermo Porcelain* line is of particular interest, as are malted milk jars, **figurines,** art pottery, and advertising items the *Coors* folks made for other companies. Among desirable figures are monks, turkeys, buffaloes, clown banks, and vases especially those more than 10" tall. *Coors* items made for the 1939 Colorado State Fair are among my favorite finds as well. I do not buy pharmaceutical or industrial items common ashtrays, *Coorsite*, or things made by HF Coors. If you want to sell, I'll need to know what you have, its size, color, markings, and condition. It's helpful if you price, but not essential."
Jo Ellen Winther
8449 W. 75th Way
Arvada, CO 80005
   (800) 872-2345 days (303) 421-2371 eves

Packing china for shipment is not as hard as you might think, but does require care and proper care. Never allow two pieces to touch. Ask your buyer for packing instructions.

Pottery

★ **American art pottery of all types.** "I'll buy pottery from *Fulper, Paul Revere, Rookwood, Grueby, Dedham, TECO, Tiffany, Clewell, Marblehead, Saturday Evening Girls, Newcomb College, George Ohr, Van Briggle, Cowan, Grand Feu, Losanti, New Orleans Art Pottery, Robineau,* and other quality American art pottery. I'll **also buy good quality European pottery** such as *Martin Bros, Moorcroft,* and others." Especially likes large and unusual pieces, and has been known to consider damaged pieces if they are important. "If you have any doubts, phone me and I will be glad to be of assistance."
Robert Berman
Le Poulaille
441 South Jackson St.
Media, PA 19063
(215) 566-1516

★ **American art pottery , especially *Van Briggle* before 1913.** A variety of fine pottery will be considered, including *Rookwood* that is artist signed, *North Dakota School of Mines* pottery "with good color contrast," *Hylong, Newcombe,* decorated *Marblehead,* and the like. But his primary interest is in pre-1913 *Van Briggle,* the man, the company, and the pottery. Wants company records and catalogs, as well as paintings and pots signed by Van Briggle. Will even accept damaged pre-1913 pieces "if priced accordingly." Is not interested in undated *Van Briggle* or in *ND School of Mines* that is plain. Describe the size, shape, colors, glaze quality, bottom markings, and condition. Scott is a former president of the American Art Pottery Association and author of *The Collector's guide to Van Briggle,* available from him for $35 and a *Van Briggle Price Guide* for $6.50. He does appraisals for a fee, and expects you to price your own goods.
Scott Nelson
Box 6081
Santa Fe, NM 87502
(505) 986-1176

★ *Stangl* **pottery.** "We especially want *Stangl* toby mugs with ashtray hats, *Stangl* birds and animals, flower pots, and flower ashtrays. We want "rainbow ware," and dripply blue, green, orange, and yellow artware. Also the following dinnerware patterns: Fruit, Fruit and Flowers, Country Gardens, Country Life, Blueberry, Garden Flower, Thistle, Town and Country, Chicory, Yellow and Blue Tulip, Wild Rose, and all Christmas patterns. We don't want brown stains, chips, or cracks, but minor flaws are acceptable."
Bob and Nancy Perzel
Popkorn Antiques
PO Box 1057
Flemington, NJ 08822
(908) 782-9631

★ **American art pottery, especially *Weller* and *TECO.*** "*TECO* pottery is one of my favorites. I'll buy geometric and organic vases with square or built in handles. Sculptural leaves and plant forms, usually in matte finish with green tones, but also brown, yellows, grays, etc. This is often highlighted in a black/gray gunmetal color. I am also a strong buyer of *Weller* vases with raised figures, lizards, snakes, nudes, etc. *Weller* also comes in strong geometrics. Colors are rose, pink, blue, gray, yellow, brown and matte green, often mixed, often veined with gunmetal. Normally signed. I buy a great deal of *Weller,* including many of their other lines." He also buys a wide range of other art pottery including *Grueby, Saturday Evening Girls, Newcomb College, University of North Dakota, Jervis, American Art Clay, Fulper, George Ohr, Arequipa, California Faience, Chelsea Keramic, Clewell, Clifton* (large vases only), and many more. Strongly suggested you take a picture since the form and color of pottery determines value. When you send your photo, write down carefully all the marks you find on the bottom of your pottery.
Gary Struncius
PO Box 1374
Lakewood, NJ 08701
(800) 272-2529

★ **Spongeware, stoneware, and redware pottery and crockery.** Note all markings on the sides and bottoms, please, if you'd like this important dealer to evaluate what you have. These are often incised with the name of the maker or user, and their city and town, as well as the size of the container. Minor damage and cracks are acceptable in very rare pieces, but you must note all damage, no matter how small. The decoration is the key to value, so photos are essential.

Louis Picek
Main Street Antiques and Art
Box 340
West Branch, IA 52358

★ **Stoneware pottery.** "I'll buy pre-1900 stoneware pottery crocks, jugs, pitchers, flasks, churns, and bottles with cobalt blue decoration, especially those depicting birds, animals, people, flowers, buildings, flags, or dates. I also buy pottery marked "Robinson Clay Products," "Old Sleepy Eye," or with elongated (stretched out) numbers on the bottom. I do not buy *Red Wing* pottery." Please send a photo, dimensions, and list of any defects in the first letter. Dealers are expected to price their goods, but he will help amateur sellers. "Nobody answers faster."

Barry Friedman
22725 Garzota Drive
Valencia, CA 91355
(805) 296-2318

★ **Stoneware crocks and jugs with blue decorations.** Especially likes pottery with clear incised markings from NY, NJ, OH, PA, and New England. "I'll pay top dollar for unusual forms decorated with people, animals, ships, trees, houses, strong blue florals, etc. Dated pieces are particularly desirable. I pay from $100 to as much as $10,000 for the right items." He emphasizes that he is interested **only** in stoneware that is blue decorated. No browns or whites. Needs to know the size of the piece in quarts or gallons if marked, in inches if not. Take a photo or make a good sketch of the decoration because the more unusual the decoration, the more he pays. Mention the darkness of the blue. Also buys inkwells, flasks, and unusual small items made of blue decorated stoneware. He will help amateur sellers determine what they have.

Richard C. Hume
1300 Northstream Parkway
Point Pleasant, NJ 08742
(908) 899-8707 eves

★ **Redware plates, bowls, and other pieces.** When describing, mention all marks on the bottom and take a photo or make a sketch of the pattern, indicating what part of the pattern is yellow or green. Make certain you note if there are any cracks or chips.

Richard C. Hume
1300 Northstream Parkway
Point Pleasant, NJ 08742
(908) 899-8707 eves

★ **Italian pottery (Majolica)** of all types, such as flower pots, vases, dinnerware, bottles, lamps, plaques, tiles, dishes, figurines, wall pockets and what have you. "The pieces are all hand-painted in bright colors, often on a white background. There are literally hundreds of types and styles of decorations, using fruit, flowers, people, mythical and religious themes, architecture, etc, but always in bright reds, blues, yellows, greens, and rose (usually all of the above!). Many are reproductions of pieces created during the Renaissance, others are more modern and look like souvenirs. Whether you have one or one-hundred, I am interested in all types if they are marked MADE IN ITALY on the bottom. Sometimes the markings identify the region where they were made, such as GUBBIO, DERUTA, ASSISI, etc." This buyer says a photo is "very helpful," but at the very least, give the dimensions, patterns, colors, and marks, along with a statement of condition. The price you'd like is "helpful" but not required.

Denise Sater
PO Box 591
Maytown, PA 17550
(717) 426-2957

★ **Majolica pottery.** Interested in all 19th century Majolica pieces from any country. Claims to pay top dollar for this bright colored pottery. Asks you to send a photo.

Rick Kranz
702 W. Olive
Stillwater, MN 55082
(612) 430-3016

★ **Majolica.**
Joan Bogart
Box 265
Rockville Centre, NY 11571

Glass

★ **Many kinds of glassware and china** are sought by Tom, a veteran collector and one of the country's largest auction firms specializing in post-Victorian glass. He buys outright or accepts on consignment for auction:
   [1] **Carnival glass** especially pitcher sets, tumblers, whimsies, opalescent pieces, and common items in rare patterns and colors. He encourages you to contact him with one item or a giant collection since there are many valuable pieces that only an expert will recognize;
   [2] **Victorian pattern glass** in a variety of pieces, colors, and patterns;
   [3] **Cameo glass vases,** plates, urns, other items made by *Phoenix Glass Co.*;
   [4] **RS Prussia china** decorated with scenes, portraits, or pearlized florals;
   [5] *Noritake* **china** with geometric designs;
   [6] **Nippon china humidors** and large high relief "blown out" vases depicting birds, animals, or figures;
   [7] **Mandarin red glassware** by *Fenton Glass Company*.
Include your phone number if the piece is for sale. Tom has a reputation for being slow to respond, but *very* helpful with amateur sellers nationwide. Phone him midweek if you think you have something good.
   Tom Burns Auction Service
   109 E. Steuben St.
   Bath, NY 14810
   (607) 776-7942

★ **Antique and 20th century art glass.** This well known auctioneer conducts cataloged specialty auctions of art glass, so can handle collections and fine individual pieces of *Daum Nancy, Steuben, Galle, Tiffany* and other art glass, as well as collections and fine pieces of *Wedgwood* and other fine porcelain.
   James D. Julia Auctioneers
   PO Box 80
   Fairfield, ME 04937
   (207) 453-7904   Fax (207) 453-2502

★ **Early American glass in** *Willow Oak* pattern in amber, blue, or Vaseline colors.
   Audrey Buffington
   2 Old Farm Rd.
   Wayland, MA 01778
   (508) 358-2644

★ **Antique Bohemian glass goblets, beakers,** and other types of drinking vessels. "I'll buy colored or clear glass with wheel engraved landscape scenes, portraits, animals, spa scenes, religious themes, etc. In addition to wheel engraved items, I'm seeking pieces decorated with transparent or opaque enamels, overlays, gilt work, cutting, paintings, etc. Cameos are particularly desirable." Not interested in any other glass. He notes, "There are many, many reproductions of this glass. It takes a trained eye to tell the difference." Common, and not desirable, pieces include deer and castle, deer and pine trees, and bird and castle. Later pieces are simple and the engraving lacks detail in the animals. You must send a close up photo of this potentially valuable glass and note every chip, flake, or crack. Dealers are expected to price their goods, but he will make offers to amateur sellers. You must include an SASE if you wish your photos back.
   Tom Bradshaw
   325 Carol Drive
   Ventura, CA 93003

★ *Fostoria* **glass and memorabilia** are wanted by the founder of the *Fostoria* Glass society in Southern California. "I'll buy dealer signs, dealer catalogs from before 1940, postcards, displays, trade cards, calendars, magazine ads (but 1924 to 1931 only), and any other *Fostoria* Glass Company memorabilia that's in mint condition." His glass wants are more restricted as he only buys frosted or clear **Victoria** (pattern #183) and rare pieces of pattern #2412 called **Colony.** He is not interested in common Colony glassware or other *Fostoria* patterns, but finding a Victoria oil lamp is high on his list. "All items must be in mint condition or don't bother."
   Gary Schneider
   7301 Topanga Canyon Blvd #202
   Canoga Park, CA 91303
   (818) 998-4588 or (818) 702-9967

★ **Glass toothpick holders** in mint condition. There are numerous patterns she is still seeking. Make a Xerox© or photo of your holder if you don't know the name of its pattern, and describe the color as best you can. There are many reproduction holders, so she'll have to examine yours before making a final offer. Judy is founder of the Toothpick Holder Collectors Society and published their newsletter for 20 years.
   Judy Knauer
   1224 Spring Valley Lane
   West Chester, PA 19380
      (215) 431-3477

★ **Antique glass paperweights,** 1845-1900. "I will buy fine French (Baccarat, Clichy, St. Louis), American (New England Glass Company, Sandwich), English, and Bohemian paperwieghts. I am looking for millefiori, flowers, sulphides, fruit and animals." Among the most valuable are large 19th century French paperweights by Pantin which contain a lizard on rocky ground with flowers and plants around it. These can be worth as much as $50,000 but have been widely copied and the copies are worth as little as $50. It takes an expert to tell the difference. Other paperweights have also been copied, often including fake dates and wear. "**I don't want** china paperweights, Italian copies, plain glass, weights with photos, mottos, or advertising, and no weights with air bubbles as part of the design." A close up color photo of your weight is important and should be accompanied by a good description. "I don't mind surface wear and nicks, but cracks in the glass are not acceptable." Include an SASE if you want photos returned. "I will make offers to amateur sellers, but dealers are expected to price their goods."
   Tom Bradshaw
   325 Carol Drive
   Ventura, CA 93003

★ **Antique glass items** including paperweights, art glass, glass pens, canes, and whimsies.
   Stanley Block
   Box 51
   Trumbull, CT 06611
      (203) 261-3223

Do not overlook the colored glass of 1910-1940, as a few pieces are quite valuable. Covered butter dishes in most depression glass patterns, for example, will bring you $75 - $200 each.

Be careful pricing carnival glass, which ranges from $10 to $10,000. Work with the buyer when it comes to pricing, as rarities are very hard for you to recognize.

★ **Depression glass** in various makers, colors, and patterns.
   Nadine Pankow
   207 S. Oakwood
   Willow Springs, IL 60480
      (312) 839-5231

★ **Carnival glass** is wanted "in any amount and any color." Prefers you to price, but may help amateurs who are actually selling.
   Dick Hatscher
   142 Walnut Hill Rd
   Bethel, CT 06801
      (203) 743-1468 eves

★ **Carnival glass.** "I'll buy one piece or a collection, in any colors." Appreciated if you price what you have.
   W.J. Warren
   38 Mosher Dr.
   Tonawanda, NY 14150
      (716) 692-2886

Household Miscellany

★ **Arts and crafts period lamps and accessories** made by Van Erp, Roycroft, Limberts, Stickley, and others. Lamps are often copper and colored glass. He also buys their furniture, which tend to be massive square oak pieces, often with dark finishes, visible pegs and hinges, and simple unornamented lines. Many people call it "mission oak." Send a photo or call if you think you have one of these pieces, as some can be quite valuable.
David Rago
PO Box 3592 Station E
Trenton, NJ 08629
(609) 585-2546

★ **Accessories from the Mission or Arts & Crafts period** including light fixtures or metalwork by L & JG Stickley, Gustav Stickley, Roycroft, Limberts, Lifetime, Charles Stickley, Rohlfs, and Dirk Van Erp, especially unusual pieces, custom made pieces, and items inlaid with silver, pewter or copper. Also catalogs from these firms. "If you have any doubts, please call. I will be glad to help."
Robert Berman
Le Poulaille
441 So. Jackson St.
Media, PA 19063
(215) 566-1516

★ **Accessories and personal items made of early thermoplastic, often mistakenly called "gutta percha."** "I'll buy any small themoplastic items made between 1850 and 1900, including photo cases, picture frames in shapes other than rectangular, mirrors with figural scenes or unusual geometric designs, vanity sets (other than those rimmed in metal), desk sets, wall plaques, boxes of all types, clocks with this early plastic as part of the decoration, jewelry, and other items, from religious objects to door knobs. Please send a photo or Xerox, along with a description of color, condition, and the price you'd like." Amateur sellers may request offers.
Mike Semegran
3711 West 230th Street, #207
Torrance, CA 90505
(213) 373-0464

★ **Art deco accessories** "that compliment my collection of radios." Ed is interested in a wide range of distinctive deco items, so give him a try for items like clocks, picture frames, and lamps. If you are the original owner, he'd appreciate the item's history. He prefers you to set your price but will make offers *if* you intend to sell.
Ed Sage
Box 1234
Benicia, CA 94510
(707) 746-5659

★ **Electric clocks covered with colored mirrors.** Wants 1930's clock brands like *GE, Telechron*, and *Seth Thomas* covered with blue, peach, or green mirrors as long as the mirrors are not cracked or damaged. It's OK if the clock doesn't work. Give the brand, model, dimensions, and the color of the glass.
David Escoe
PO Box 342
Los Alamitos, CA 90720

★ **Items of banded agate.** Will purchase pens, button hooks, snuff boxes, and small decorative items made entirely or mostly of banded agate. Give dimensions and condition.
Stanley Block
Box 51
Trumbull, CT 06611
(203) 261-3223

★ **Gold bearing quartz items.** Masculine items made from or decorated with gold bearing quartz: matchsafes, cane handles, watch fobs, watches, etc. Not much interest in jewelry, unless exceptional. Xerox© or photo is best.
Sandra Whitson
PO Box 272
Lititz, PA 17543
(717) 626-4978

★ **Indian motif sterling silver** items made for men, such as desk sets, clothes brushes, match safes, etc., made by Unger Bros. Only limited interest in women's items and jewelry by Unger.
Sandra Whitson
PO Box 272
Lititz, PA 17543
(717) 626-4978

★ **Thermometers and thermostats**, pre-1940, especially ornate Victorian desk or mantle types. "I buy just about every *non advertising* one I can locate," but outdoor and decorative models are particularly prized, and can bring more than $100 each. "I have the largest antique thermometer collection in the world but am always looking for more." Thermometer ephemera and catalogs are sought. **No commercial, industrial, clinical, advertising or "cutsey" thermometers are wanted.** Give the maker, condition and whether it has mercury or red liquid in the bulb. "all the items bought are placed in the American Thermometer Museum in Sacramento."
Warren Harris
6130 Rampart Drive
Carmichael, CA 95608
    (916) 487-6964

★ **Decorative and figural light bulbs.** Wants all unusual light bulbs including neon bulbs (a metal image inside the bulb glows when lit), Christmas bulbs (figural or bubble type), unusually shaped bulbs, and those made of colored glass (not coated) that have a standard base. Also wants display devices for bulbs and **wired artificial Christmas trees.** Prices range from $10 to as much as $600 for a Statue of Liberty bulb. A boxed set of Disney's Snow White and the Seven Dwarfs bulbs will bring $600. Santa bulbs are worth from $15-$150. Does *not* want Paramount brand Disney character lights or old utility, auto, or industrial light bulbs. Photo or sketch required. "I will beat any legitimate offer if it's a bulb I want."
Joseph Kimbell
708 Bay Street
San Francisco, CA 94109
    (415) 346-8273

★ **Glass fire grenade bottles** in any color if embossed with a brand name and "fire grenade." He is particularly interested in finding those with the name of a railroad. He does not want glass bulb grenades from the 1940's filled with carbon tet. List the color, size, and all defects.
Larry Meyer
4001 Elmwood
Stickney, IL 60402
    (312) 749-1564

★ **Early and unusual floor and desk fans.** Buys electric fans from before 1915 (check your patent dates). Very interested in fans not propelled by electricity, such as wind-up, heat engine, water power, battery powered, etc. Some interest in ceiling fans, but does not want fans by *G.E.* or fans made in the 1920's or later.
Kevin Shail
30 Old Middle Rd.
Brookfield, CT 06804
    (203) 775-7017

★ **Desk, ceiling, or pedestal fans** that are antique or unusual, especially mechanical fans not powered by electricity. Wants brands like *G.E., Westinghouse, Emerson, Peerless, Diehl* and others, but especially those made before 1920 or with unusual mechanisms. These early fans are usually cast iron and brass. Also wants literature, catalogs, ads and other information about fans and the companies that made them. Has no interest in steel fans made after 1940. Include the brand, nameplate information, dimensions of the blades, number of blades, and what the various parts are made of, if you can. When describing condition, indicate whether your fan operates. Michael is the President of the American Fan Collectors Ass'n and editor of its quarterly newsletter.
Michael Breedlove
Antique Fans of Indiana
15633 Cold Spring Ct.
Granger, IN 46530
    (219) 272-1231

★ **Vacuum cleaners** that are hand powered. "I pay well for information leading to the location of unusual and scarce items, and am prepared to travel anywhere. I pay in cash immediately without fuss or bother for the right items. I am happy to buy single items or entire collections."
Peter Frei
Box 500
Brimfield, MA 01010
    (800) 942-8968   (413) 245-4660 in MA

★ **Flashlights.** Antique flashlights, advertising, and catalogs are wanted, especially anything early marked *Eveready*.
Bill Utley
7616 Brookmill
Downey, CA 90241
    (213) 861-6247

★ **Wooden picture frames.**
Craig Dinner
Box 4399
Sunnyside, NY 11104
    (718) 729-3850

★*Weller* **flower frogs.** "I buy *Weller* frogs. How do you tell a *Weller* frog? Pottery flower frogs with bees, butterflies, frogs, fish, women, lily pads, etc. sitting on top a base are probably *Weller* if they are colored with greens, beiges, white, and muted orange, basic *Weller* colors."
Susan Cox
800 Murray Dr.
El Cajon, CA 92020
    (619) 447-0800 days

★ *Cowan* **ceramic flower frogs** in art deco style featuring dancing ladies. Values range from $100-$500 depending on the figure, colors, condition. Note all markings if you can.
William Sommer
9 West Tenth St.
New York, NY 10011
    (212) 260-0999

★ **Small hand painted American boxes.**
Louis Picek
Main Street Antiques
Box 340,
West Branch, IA 52358
    (319) 643-2065

★ **Gadgets.** "I'll buy interesting old small mechanical devices such as:
    Pocket size calculators;
    Miniature cameras;
    Optical devices;
    Personal check protectors;
    Pocket typewriters or sewing machines;
    Combination pen-pencil-rulers;
    Adding machines, and
    Everything else that whirs, buzzes, clanks, or just looks interesting."
Darryl is particularly interested in typewriters and adders, paying $1,500+ for important pocket typewriters." A photo is generally a good idea, and your description should include condition. Will respond promptly to all offers.
Darryl Rehr
11433 Rochester Ave. #303
Los Angeles, CA 90025
    (213) 477-5229

★ **Pocket items** designed to fit in the pocket and to be carried and used. Wants "mechan-ically interesting functional things" not just pretty things. "The items I like are usually made before 1930, so modern plastic stuff is of little interest." His wants include:
    Mini books (less than 4") on practical topics;
    Tool and gadget knives;
    Trick or special purpose knives;
    Folding cups, silverware, and tools;
    Vest pocket flashlights;
    Handwarmers;
    Lighters, compacts, and other pocket items
        that are combined with other tools;
    Pocket typewriters or sewing machines;
    Optical devices, sundials, etc.
    Scientific devices;
    Things that look like pocket watch but aren't;
    Any device that says "pocket" on it.
Send a photocopy, a description of any damage or other problems, and a copy of any writing.
B.H. Axler
PO Box 1288
Ansonia Station, NY 10023

★ **Strap type watch fobs picturing machinery or advertising products.** No lodge, American Legion, or VFW, and similar fobs. He'd like you to tell him how much wear it shows and the name of the stamper, usually found at the bottom. No fakes or modern fobs.
Albert Goetz
1763 Poplar Ave.
South Milwaukee, WI 53172
(414) 762-4111

★ **Stanhope viewers** are small objects with a peep hole and tiny pictures inside. They come in a wide variety of shapes and materials including alabaster urns, crucifixes, pens, and letter openers and Don will consider all types.
Donald Gorlick
Box 24541
Seattle, WA 98124
(206) 824-0508

★ **Unusual Stanhopes.** Stanhopes are objects with tiny holes which show a picture when you look inside. Wants rings, sewing items, figurals, pipes, and naughty ones. Does not want Stanhopes in crucifixes, rosaries, or pens.
Lucille Malitz
Lucid Antiques
Box KH
Scarsdale, NY 10583
(914) 636-3367

★ **Lithopanes** are figures and scenes viewed through transparent porcelain. Like Stanhopes, they are found in a wide variety of objects. Don wants them all *except* steins or cups, which are the most commonly found form.
Donald Gorlick
Box 24541
Seattle, WA 98124
(206) 824-0508

★ **Lithopanes (porcelain transparencies)** in any size or shape, colored or uncolored, used in a lamp, plaque, stein, cup, etc. Describe the object and the picture, and give any letters or numbers appearing on either or both.
Laurel Blair
Box 4557
Toledo, OH 43620
(419) 243-4115

★ **Human hair wreaths.** Serious collector wants to buy wreaths made of human hair, either framed or unframed. Send photograph and / or description with your asking price.
Monica Murphy
Savannah's Antiques
1419 Fern
New Orleans, LA 70118
(504) 866-2221

★ **Eyeglasses, spectacles, and lorngnettes,** but only old, rare, and unusual. Not interested in any common eyeglasses or in buying them for their gold content. "I only want the exotic or pre 1850, with unusual lenses, frames, or history." A photocopy machine works well on most glasses. Describe all writing on frames.
W.H. Marshall
727 SW 27th St.,
Gainesville, FL 32607
(904) 373-0556

★ **Canes.** Especially likes dual purpose, container, weapon, gadget, and fancy carved canes made with ivory, gold, or silver. "Any cane or walking stick that does something, or has something enclosed or attached to the shaft for purposes other than support is of interest, as are well executed hand-carved canes." Describe the tip of the cane and indicate whether it gives any evidence of having been shortened. Is there a hole in the shaft? What materials?
Arnold Scher
1637 Market St.
San Francisco, CA 94103
(415) 863-4344

★ **Canes and walking sticks** that are carved into figures, in either wood or ivory.
Bruce Thalberg
23 Mountain View Dr.
Weston, CT 06883
(203) 227-8175

★ **Antique and unusual padlocks.** "We'll buy padlocks of all kinds and types, odd shaped, cast iron, brass, figural, *Wells Fargo*, *Winchester*, railroad, miniature, and many others." Xerox© copy helpful. Indicate whether it has a key.
Joe and Pam Tanner
Tanner Escapes
Box 349
Great Falls, MT 59403

Cast Iron

★ **Cast iron doorstops and other items** such as figural bottle openers, figural lawn sprinklers, figural paperweights, figural pencil holders, match holders, string holders, windmill weights, horse weights, shooting gallery targets, and fire-marks. Include your phone number.
Craig Dinner
Box 4399
Sunnyside, NY 11104
(718) 729-3850

★ **Cast iron doorstops and windmill weights.** No reproductions or modern pieces.
Louis Picek
Main Street Antiques
Box 340
West Branch, IA 52358
(319) 643-2065

★ **Cast iron lawn sprinklers, doorstops, windmill weights, shooting gallery targets** and other figural cast iron. Does not want reproductions, damaged and repaired items, or items with new paint. He is also not interested in "small shooting gallery targets such as ducks and birds." Please include color photo, phone number, and general price range you'd like.
Richard Tucker
Argyle Antiques
PO Box 262
Angyle, TX 76226
(817) 464-3752

★ **Antique pressing irons of all kinds** including sad irons, polishing irons, hat irons, fluters, goffering irons, charcoal irons, alcohol irons, gasoline irons, boxed sets of irons, miniature and toy irons, and all iron related items such as postcards, trade cards, advertising giveaways by iron companies, and the like. Single items or entire collections wanted. Describe the condition. A photo is a good idea. Trace your iron and give the height. You price. NO OFFERS.
Carol Walker
The Iron Lady
501 N. 5th St.
PO Box 68
Waelder, TX 78959
(512) 665-7166

★ **Miniature sad (flat) irons.** Wants irons smaller than 4", nothing bigger. No electric iron, no matter how early.
George Fougere
67 East St.
North Grafton, MA 01536
(508) 839-2701

★ **Cast iron jewelry boxes,** particularly those that are silk lined. Please price for resale. "I also buy **woodburned glove and jewelry boxes** for resale. Please give a thorough description.
Linda Gibbs
10380 Miranda Ave.
Buena Park, CA 90620
(714) 827-6488

Pest Traps

★ **Traps of all types and sizes from fly to grizzly bear.** Wants fly, mouse, rat, mole, gopher, glass minnow traps, and spring operated fish traps. Wants anything unusual in any material including plastic, wood, wire, cast iron, glass, cardboard, and tin. Is especially fond of old and unusual mouse traps. He also buys patent models, books, catalogs, and advertising (pre 1940) related to traps. Does not want rusty or broken traps unless odd 19th century items. Send a picture or drawing, a good description, and an SASE and he promises to answer.
Boyd Nedry
728 Buth Dr. NE
Comstock Park, MI 49321
(616) 784-1513

★ **Rare and unusual traps and trap guns.**
Ron Willoughby
1072 Route 171
Woodstock, CT 06281
(203) 974-1226

★ **Glass flytraps or flycatchers,** especially early or unusual ones. Will consider interesting traps in other materials. Also advertising and paper ephemera related to early flytraps.
Maris Zuika
Box 175
Kalamazoo, MI 49004
(616) 344-7473

Knives

★ **Pocket, hunting, and military knives.**
Brands to look for include: *New York Knife,
Canastota, Remington, Wabash, Winchester,
Honk Falls, Napanoch, Henry Sears, Shapleigh,
Union Cut, Keen Kutter, Bingham, American
Knife, Bridge, Capitol, Case, Cattaraugus,
Phoenix, James Price, Platts, Press Button,
India Steel Works, Wallkill, Walden, Van Camp,
Union Razon, Standard, Zenith, Northfield,
Crandall*, and others. "This is only a small list-
ing of the many good brands to be found. I love
large bone handled U.S. made knives." **Non col-
lectible knives include** *Ambassador, Atco,
Camco, Colonial, Executive, Frontier, Hit,
Ideal, Klien, Richards, U.S.A., Pakistan*, and
Sabre. It is best to Xerox© knives with the
blade(s) open. Write down everything found on
the blades and handles. Describe the handle material as best you can. Stapp is an advisor on
knives for one of the popular price guides.
> Charles Stapp
> 7037 Haynes Rd.
> Georgetown, In 47122
> (812) 923-3483

★ **Knives less than 1" long,** especially multi-
bladed with pearl, sterling, stag, or horn handles.
As much information as possible, including
number of blades, maker, condition, etc. Old
knives only; no new items or reproductions.
Says he also "buys and trades swords and razors."
> Jim Kegebein
> Box 60669
> Sunnyvale, CA 94088
> (408) 749-9175   Fax (408) 749-1094

★ **Unusually shaped figural pocket knives**
shaped like objects such as dogs, cats, hats,
baseball bats, lady's legs, etc., from the 1800's
or early 1900's. Value depends upon the shape,
condition and maker. "Knives in unusual shapes
made by *Remington, Winchester,* and *Case* may
be worth several hundred dollars. I am also interested in any old advertising signs, pinbacks,
postcards, etc., related to the cutlery industry.
Please phone or write." Give the maker's name,
shape, number of blades, and material from
which the handle is made. NO OFFERS.
> John Baron
> 2928 Marshall Ave.
> Cincinnati, OH 45220
> (513) 751-6631

Pens & Pencils

★ **Unusual quality fountain pens,** pre-1940,
by makers such as *Eversharp, Waterman, Swan,
Dunn, MacKinnon, Laughlin, Shaeffer, Chilton,
Wahl, Moore, Camel* and many others. Some of
these can be worth several hundred dollars. She
also buys old quill cutters, stylus pens, and glass
pens. **Advertising related to pens** is also wanted, including signs, trade catalogs, repair manuals, and spare parts. Also wants packaged pow-
dered ink. Give maker's name, model, color,
and length of your pen. Describe the pen point
and all decorations on the pen. Best to photocopy. Pens will have to be inspected before
final price offered. No unbranded pens, *Wear-
ever, Esterbrook,* ball points, or magazine ads.
She will send a guide to help you describe pens.
> Mrs. Ky
> Box J
> Port Jefferson Station, NY 11776

★ **Fountain pens.** "Quality old pens, not junk
or common stuff," says this 22 year veteran.
> C. Ray Erler
> Box 140, Miles Run Road
> Spring Creek, PA 16436

★ **Inkwells,** either U.S. or foreign, figural or
traveling, whether made of pottery, glass, or
wood. Especially would like one made by
Tiffany. No desk sets or fountain pens.
> Eli Hecht
> 19 Evelyn Lane
> Syosset, NY 11791

★ **Pencils with advertising.** Wants unusual and
older unsharpened pencils. No pens.
> Susan Cox
> 800 Murray Dr.
> El Cajon, CA 92020
> (619) 447-0800 days

★ **Pencil sharpeners.** Wants small hand held
figural pencil sharpeners made of metal, celluloid or Bakelite in Germany or Japan during the
1930's and 40's. No bronze color sharpeners
from Hong Kong depicting antiques. Give the
shape, condition, country of origin, size, condition of the blade, and price.
> Martha Crouse
> 4516 Brandon Lane
> Beltsville, MD 20705

Perfume

★ **Perfume bottles with glass stoppers.** Wants art glass bottles, large department store display bottles, and samples. Give the brand of perfume and photocopy the bottle. No *Avon*.
Annette Chaussee
1530 Kenland Ct.
Colorado Springs, CO 80915
(719) 597-4000

★ **Perfume bottles, decanters, and vases with silver overlay.** Describe all markings and give dimensions and colors.
Arnold Reamer
Timepiece Antiques
Box 26416
Baltimore, MD 21207
(301) 944-6414 (301) 486-8412

★ **Perfume bottles made of blown or cut art glass**, singles or matching sets. Wants fine beautiful bottles including those with atomizers. Some important makers include *DeVilbiss, Daum Nancy, Galle, Baccarat, Webb, Moser, Czechoslovakian, Lalique*, and *Steuben*. Also English scents, bottles with sterling overlay, and figurals. Also **Sterling silver dresser sets, hair brushes, mirrors and other boudoir items.** NO OFFERS. No *Avon*.
Madeleine France
Past Pleasures for the 20th Century Woman
Box 15555
Plantation, FL 33316
(305) 584-0009

★ *DeVilbis* **atomizers,** with or without original bulb, tube, and cord. Describe the size, colors, and condition. A detailed sketch or close up photo is essential. "I prefer you write rather than phone."
Bruce Bleier
73 Riverdale Rd.
Valley Stream, NY 11581
(516) 791-4353

★ *California Perfume Company* (CPC) **products made between 1886 and 1929,** especially *Natoma Rose* fragrances. He also wants CPC products marketed as *Goetting and Company, Savoi Et Cie, Gertrude Recordon, Marvel Electric Silver Cleaner*, and the *Easy Day Automatic Clothes Washer*. Dick **does not want anything with *Avon* on the label,** although he will answer specific questions about *Avon* if you include a Self Addressed Stamped Envelope. Please give a complete description of the item you have for sale, including its condition and whether or not it has its original box. Is there a label and/or a neck band? Are there cracks or chips? Photocopy is helpful. Dick's collection is open to the public by special arrangement.
Dick Pardini
3107 N. El Dorado St.
Stockton, CA 95204
(209) 466-5550 7am to 11pm

Many perfume bottles other than Avons are worth over $100. Research is suggested before you price them.

★ *Avon* **bottles** remain a popular collectible, but there are few people buying *Avons* except rarities through the mail. Western World Publishing offers six bi-monthly issues of *Avon Collectors Newsletter*, 20 pages of articles and FOR SALE ads for $14.50. Your subscription includes club membership and free classified advertising for a year. They also publish *Avon 8*, the lavishly illustrated basic price guide to *Avon* collectibles for $20.95.
Western World Publishing
Box 23785, Dept. T
Pleasant Hill, CA 94523

Shaving & Bath

★ **Straight razors with fancy handles** made of gold or sterling silver. Also razors with figural handles, multiple blades, fancy etching on the blade, or with fraternal emblems or advertising on the handle. Handles may be made of horn, mother of pearl, or multi-colored celluloid. Rare razors will be considered even if damaged. Also **razor and cutlery advertising** and memorabilia, catalogs, trade cards, etc., including oversize displays.

   William Campesi
   Box 140
   Merrick, NY 11566
     (516) 546-9630

★ **Straight razors with handles of sterling, rough bone, mother of pearl, or aluminum.** Celluloid or pressed horn razors with several characters are also wanted. Good razors generally bring from $50-75, with some higher, some less. Please provide all information found on the blade or handle. He does not want plain handled razors from Solingen, Germany. Make Xerox© copies with the blade(s) open. Indicate the material from which the handle is made.

   Charles Stapp
   7037 Haynes Rd.
   Georgetown, In 47122
     (812) 923-3483

★ **Safety razors and accessories.** This 20 year veteran collector wants to buy odd safety razors and advertising for razors including posters, magazine ads, and signs. He'd love to find more oversize store display razors. He's not interested in shaving mugs or brushes if they're normal size, but would like oversize display ones. Give all colors and metals and note "all writing on the items. A good clear photo is best," he says, but photocopies will suffice.

   Cary Basse
   6927 Forbes Ave.
   Van Nuys, CA 91406
     (818) 781-4856

★ **Razor blades and blade sharpeners.** "I'll buy U.S. or foreign blades, in singles, packages, or on cards as well as interesting advertising signs, posters, and displays related to razor blades." Describe your sharpener carefully, pointing out all damage, and noting any words or numbers on it.

   Cary Basse
   6927 Forbes Ave.
   Van Nuys, CA 91406
     (818) 781-4856

★ **Unusual eye cups.**
   W.T. Atkinson
   1217 Bayside Circle W.
   Wilmington, NC 28405

★ **Women's powder compacts,** from before 1950. All types of attractive compacts are wanted, as long as the condition is good and the compact complete. Unusual, art deco, and precious metals are preferred. Most others are less than five dollars.

   Bird In the Cage
   118 King St.,
   Alexandria, VA 22314
     (703) 549-5114

Quilts & Textiles

★ **Graphically artistic pre-1940 quilts** especially those pre 1900. Cotton, wool, and silk quilts all have value if made well. Solid color materials and small calico patterns are the most desirable. Large patterns cut into small pieces usually make the quilt of no interest. Most desirable colors are blue/white, red/white, red/white/blue, red/green, and pre 1900 earth tones. Yellow, orange, hot pink, and purple usually make a quilt less desirable. Children's size quilts are best if they do not have children's subject matter. All quilts should be in mint condition, with at least six stitches per inch, preferably more. No holes, tears, stains, thin spots when held to light, fading, soft from too much washing, and no patched repairs. A photo is very desirable. Herb says he will pay $5,000 for an 1840-60 album quilt, $15,000 for an 1840-60 Baltimore album quilt, and $600 up for navy blue and white quilts in excellent condition. **Herb does not make offers.**

Herbert Wallerstein Jr.
Calico Antiques
611 Alta Drive
Beverly Hills, CA 90210
(213) 273-4194   FAX: (213) 273-1921

★ **Patchwork quilts made by African-Americans,** especially unusual or improvisational quilts. Provide a full photo of the quilt, a statement of condition, and all the information you can about its history. It is probably a good idea to discuss the value of the item with Eli before setting a price. "I'll also buy **fabric sample books,** especially of printed cottons."

Eli Leon
5663 Dover St.
Oakland, CA 94609

★ **High quality hand woven textiles and tapestries** from anywhere in the world.

Renate Halpern Galleries
325 E. 79th Street
New York, NY 10021
(212) 988-9316

Xerox lace and unusual material patterns.

★ **Handmade lace from 1500-1900.** Does not want Battenberg, lace known to be machine made, ordinary crochet and tatting. "Unless you are a lace scholar or have access to important reference books on lace, the best thing is to Xerox© as much of the piece as possible. From that I can often tell whether a full appraisal is warranted or if it is a piece I might like to buy." She prefers sellers to set the price, but will assist genuine amateurs to identify what they have if it's for sale. Produces an interesting newsletter for lace fanciers for $20 a year. She warns that a great deal of valuable lace is trashed each year because people don't take the time to inquire.

Elizabeth Kurella
Lace Merchant
Box 222
Plainwell, MI 49080
(616) 685-9792

★ **Linens from grandma's attic** including:
[1] **Table linens** especially with large napkins, lace, or handwork;
[2] **Lace hankies;**
[3] **Embroidered pictures, samplers,** etc.;
[4] **Lace curtains** or panels, of fine quality;
[5] **Lace collars and lace yardage** from before 1940;
[6] **Pillow cases or sheets** with hand embellishment or lace before 1925;
[7] **American arts & crafts** embroideries or printed fabrics;
[8] **Anything unusual** from before 1930 in weaving, embroidery, or lace.

No hand towels, plain linen, Damask, damaged goods, or items made after 1960. If interested in buying your items, he will request you ship on approval. Photos or Xerox© photocopies useful.

Paul Freeman
Box 2251
13 Circular Ave.
Pittsfield, MA 01201
(413) 442-1854

★ **Embroidered items and stitchery.** Also buys quilt tops, crazy quilts, and other handmade items. Send good photo or photocopy.

Linda Gibbs
Heirloom Keepsakes
10380 Miranda
Buena Park, CA 90620
(714) 827-6488

★ **Quilting and patchwork patterns, books and tools** from before 1950. Also wants vintage fabric, cloth scraps, patterned feed sacks, and other material useful for old style quilting.
> Judy Speezak
> Box 2528 Rockefeller Cntr Station
> New York, NY 10185

★ **Indian pattern blankets** made by *Beacon, Buell, Candelario, Capps, Esmond, Hamilton, Oregon City, Pendleton*, and *Racine (Badger State)*. "I'm writing a book on these blankets and am buying blankets, catalogs, and promotional advertising pieces, especially swatch books. I prefer all material to be priced, but will make offers to people who are not dealers. I answer calls and letters promptly." A photo or Xerox© is a must, and you are requested to list all flaws, holes, etc., in your first letter. Because blankets are often washed improperly, shrunk, and therefore undesirable, dimensions are a must.
> Barry Friedman
> 22725 Garzota Drive
> Valencia, CA 91355
> (805) 296-2318

★ **Fabrics from the 1940's and 1950's.** If you have at least three yards of any floral or tropical patterned fabric, and it's in perfect condition, it could find a buyer here.
> Leda Andrews
> 2110 Staples Ave.
> Key West, FL 33040

★ **American sewing machines from before 1875,** especially rare early treadle machines with low serial numbers for which he will pay from $1,000-$10,000. Small hand operated machines in the shape of animals are of particular interest. Also photographs of sewing machines in use before 1890. Tell him the maker and the serial number as well as the condition. If there is no name, send a photograph. No *Singers, Wheeler & Wilson, Willcox & Gibbs*, or machines which you recognize. No oak-cased treadle machines. No machines with chrome or nickle plated fly wheels or high serial numbers.
> Carter Bays
> 143 Springlake Rd.
> Columbia, SC 29206
> (800) 332-2297

Clothing & Accessories

★ *Levis, Lee,* and *Wrangler* **jeans and jackets** for resale. "I'll buy all pre-1970 *Levi Strauss* jeans and jackets and some older *Wrangler* and *Lee* jeans and jackets. The *Levis* he wants all have a small red tag on the front pocket [jackets left, pants right] which spells out LEvis. That capitol "E" makes these called "Big E" items, and they are a hot fad item in various markets at this time. Jackets from 1920-1949 bring $500 to $1,500; if heavily worn, still $100 to $300. Others jackets, with two front pockets, bring from $25 to $500. Does not want *Levis* with tags of any color other than red. Pants with waists larger than 34" are not of interest either. If you have a red Big E *Levis* tag in one of your front pockets, and want an immediate cash offer, describe condition carefully noting stains, holes, wear, the condition of the leather ID tag, the serial number on the back pocket leather id tag would be helpful. Also buys advertising signs or figures from these same companies.
> David Bailey
> Bailey's Antiques & Thrift
> 2580 La-i Road
> Honolulu, HI 96816
> (808) 734-7628

★ **Vintage Hawaiian shirts, 1930-1955.** The label, size, coloration, and pattern are important, as is the material, so include all that when you write. Shirts can be made of cotton, rayon, or silk. A silk shirt with a fish pattern (his personal favorite) could bring as high as $500. Most are considerably less, but well worth your time. "I'm willing to answer questions and provide information to people who are not sure if their shirts are old enough." A photo or Xerox© is helpful.
> Evan Olins
> Flamingo's
> 75-5744 Alii Drive
> Kailau-Kona, HI 96740
> (808) 329-4122

★ **Men's and women's clothing and accessories, 1900-1940.** Want average sizes in good condition. Very interested in old warehouse stock and in rayon yardage.
> The Way We Wore
> 2238 Filmore St.
> San Francisco, CA 94115
> (415) 346-1386 11am-7pm

★ **Hawaiian shirts made before 1960**
David Bailey
Bailey's Antiques & Thrift
2580 La-i Road
Honolulu, HI 96816
 (808) 734-7628

★ **Vintage clothes made before 1950** such as beaded sweaters and **beaded purses and bags,** evening gowns, prom dresses, men's tuxedos and hats, etc. Also buys **parasols** and **piano shawls**. No damaged or stained items as items are purchased for resale in her 2,000 sq.ft. shop. Price your goods when possible.
 Bird In the Cage
 118 King St.
 Alexandria, VA 22314
 (703) 549-5114

★ **Alligator and crocodile handbags and luggage.** In addition to fancy leather bags, she wants designer luggage by *Hermes, Chanel,* and *Vuitton.* Everything must be in resale condition. Send measurements and sketch or photo. Describe condition inside and out including handles and hardware. Give the color of the bag and lining, and any special features. **Also wants some unusual vintage purses** suitable for resale. Use Xerox© copier when appropriate.
 Joy Horvath,
 12 Belair Road
 Norwalk, CT 06850
 (203) 847-9035

★ **Women's spiked or high heeled shoes** in excellent condition from the 20's through the 60's. Please send photos, shoe size, and the height of the heels.
 Charles Martignette
 PO Box 293
 Hallandale, FL 33009
 (305) 454-3474

★ **Clothing worn by famous people,** such as US Presidents, first ladies and entertainers.
 Paul Hartunian
 127B East Bradford Ave
 Cedar Grove, NJ 07009
 (201) 857-7275

★ **Hand painted ties** from the 1930's and 40's. Easy to Xerox©.
 Barry Pener
 9254 High Dr.
 Leawood, KS 66206

★ **Neckties by Dali.** "Will pay well."
David Wilcox
Box 11203
Indianapolis, IN 46201
 (317) 359-9342 (Leave message)

★ **Ladies hand fans** from 1600 to 1900 are wanted in ivory, mother of pearl, tortoise shell, horn, or wooden sticks with painting or decor on silk, lace, paper, or chicken skin. All origins are sought: French, German, English, American, Chinese, Viennese, and Spanish, but only in good to mint condition. Send Xerox©.
 Monica Murphy
 Savannah's Antiques
 1419 Fern
 New Orleans, LA 70118
 (504) 866-2221

★ **Antique fancy buttons.** Wants those with metal pictures, Oriental, pearl, *Bakelite*, etc. The way to tell whether she wants your buttons is to ask two questions before contacting her:
[1] Are there holes showing in the button? If yes, she doesn't want it.
[2] Is it fancy or unusual? If so, she wants it. She does not want shirt buttons or ordinary plastic buttons with visible sewing holes. Almost all the buttons she buys are shank type. Please price your buttons for resale. Xerox© copies or approvals are suggested.
 Barbara Bronzoulis
 Barbara's Button Bracelets
 1931 Laurel Hill,
 Kingwood, TX 77339
 (713) 358-1518

Clothing is bought for resale. Stained or torn clothes are not wanted. Describe the style, color, material, size, and label. Designer label clothes are particularly desirable.

watches and clocks

Readers have found their watches worth

far more than they thought. One lucky reader bought a watch at a yard sale for $10 because he thought it was "curious looking." One of our buyers paid $4,500 for that watch!

In most cases, watch buyers will want to inspect your timepiece themselves before making final offer.

Send watches and jewelry via Registered US Mail, insured. This is a very safe way to ship, and will require the recipient to sign for the package.

To describe a watch or clock, answer as many of the following as you can:

[1]   What does it look like?
[2]   What name is on the dial?
[3]   What name is on the movement [internal mechanism]?
[4]   Does it say how many jewels?
[5]   What is the size of the case?
[6]   What is the case made of?
[7]   Is the case decorated or engraved?
[8]   Is there a label inside the case?
[9]   Is there a serial number?
[10] How is it wound or activated?
[11] Do you have the key and weights?
[12] Is it presently running?

Be cautious about selling watches locally. It is unlikely your local jeweler is expert in the pricing of old watches, even though he sells new ones. There is a great deal of money at stake, and you many put five or ten times as much money in your pocket when you deal with international experts.

tony hyman

Watches

★ **Vintage wristwatches and better antique pocket watches,** especially *Patek Philippe, Cartier, Rolex, Vacheron & Constantin, Audemars Piguet, E. Howard, Hamilton, Reed,* and *Illinois.* Also wants chronographs, watches that chime, enamels, phases of the moon, calendar watches, historical watches, gold cases, character watches, sports watches, oddly shaped watches, both U.S. and foreign. Exceptional prices paid for fine and rare vintage wristwatches and pocket watches, running or not. Call toll free if you have a watch to sell or know someone who does. "We pay a $ignificant finder$ fee for leads on large collections, estates, or accumulations." Not buying *Timex,* electronic, or inexpensive watches made after 1965. Describe your watch according to instructions on previous page. Ask for his wants list.
Miles Sandler
Maundy International
PO Box 13028 TH
Overland Park, KS 66212
(913) 383-2880 for info about watches
(800) 235-2866 toll free for selling

★ **High quality and collectible watches** by *Patek Phillipe, Rolex, Cartier, Tiffany, Audemars* and types of watches like chronographs, repeaters, alarm, doctor's watches, two time zone, and rectangular faces made between 1870 and 1960. **Also advertising items relating to watches.** Irv deals in watches from rare to common. Buys parts, cases, boxes, movements, dials, bands, from all *Rolex, Patek* or *Cartier* watches. If you are thinking of auction, Irv says, "We will buy any piece of interest at 95% of anticipated net sellers hammer proceeds." Irv promises: "Fair prices, next day payment, postage refunded, and free appraisals," adding "I will come to you if what you have is very valuable or if you have many good pieces." Describe metal, shape, details, all names and numbers, as indicated on previous page. Irv offers a priced wants list.
Irv Temes
American International Watch Exchange
113 N. Charles St.
Baltimore, MD 21201
(301) 882-0580 for info about watches

★ **Wrist and pocket watches,** both men's and women's, in gold, silver, or gold fill. Pocket watches may be in other metals if they date before 1940. Doesn't matter whether running or not. Describe all markings and give dimensions.
Arnold Reamer
Timepiece Antiques
Box 26416
Baltimore, MD 21207
(301) 944-6414 or (301) 486-8412

★ **Racing stopwatches, pocket watches, dashboard clocks, and schoolhouse clocks** with the name of a horse, horse race, carriage company, or automobile manufacturer on the face. Also sterling silver clock cases, with or without clocks. Also leather cases for car clocks that clip over the dashboard of a carriage. "When in doubt, please write, or send on approval for an immediate response."
Donald Sawyer
40 Bachelor St.
West Newbury, MA 01985
(508) 346-4724 days

★ **Watches and clocks with cartoon characters or product advertising on the face.** Any pre-1975 items that are mint in their original box are particularly desirable. "I'll pay $1,000 for a mint in the box 1934 Ingersoll Tom Mix pocket or wrist watch." Wants to know whether the face is round or rectangular, any wording on the face or back of the watch, defects (including scratches), the condition of the box (if any), and whether or not it is working. Don't overwind!
Maggie Kenyon
Maggie's Place
One Christopher #14G
New York, NY 10013
(212) 675-3213

★ *Hamilton* **"electric" wristwatches.** "I'm particularly interested in those with odd and asymmetrically shaped cases." An electric watch specialist and repairman, he also wants parts, movements, **advertising materials, catalogs,** and most anything else related to the *Hamilton Electric* watch, particularly dealer's stock, early prototypes, and calendar models. No *Hamilton Electronic* watches, or watches marked "Swiss." Only American made pre-1970 electric watches.
Rene Rondeau
120 Harbor Dr.
Corte Madera, CA 94925

Clocks

★ **American wall and mantle clocks** from the 1700's through the arts and crafts movement of the early 20th century. "I'll buy, sell, or trade a wide range of clocks, but my specialties are weight driven calendar and regulator clocks that hang on a wall. I also buy interesting, unusual, and better grades of shelf (mantle) and other wall clocks of the 1800's. Especially like to find clocks with multiple dials or faces, in either plain or fancy cases." Some of the many names to look for include *Simon-Willard, E.N. Welch, Howard, Ithaca, Waterbury, Seth Thomas, New Haven*, and other early Connecticut makers. Bruce is well versed in clocks of all types so can be helpful to the amateur seller. "If I'm offered something I can't use, I try to refer folks to someone who might like to buy it. Early electric clocks don't interest me much, but I may be able to give readers some help in identifying or evaluating them." Provide a full description . Bruce says, "For my own collection, I like to find ones that are a little out of the ordinary." Some interest in **European clocks with porcelain dials, or with fine cases with gilt, inlay, or marble.**
> Bruce Austin
> RIT, College of Liberal Arts
> Rochester, NY 14623
> (716) 223-0711 eves

★ **Grandfather clocks made in America.** "I want tall floor clocks made in the United States, especially in Pennsylvania. I generally don't buy them myself, but I screen clocks for one of the world's expert buyers of good clocks. If you have something good in the way of an old tall case clock, we will put you in touch with the buyer." **No European tall clocks.**
> Old Timers
> Box 392
> Camp Hill, PA 17001-0392
> (717) 761-1908

★ **Novelty and animated clocks,** running or not. Want clocks with swinging cats' tails, rolling eyes, etc., by *Lux, Keebler,* and others.
> Ed Kazemekas
> 35 Riverview Circle
> Wolcott, CT 06716
> (203) 879-1814

★ **Fine European clocks.** Buys a wide variety of high quality clocks including:
> [1] French, English and German tall case;
> [2] Wall clocks from 1600 to 1900;
> [3] Fancy inlaid, gilded, or bronze cases;
> [4] Musical clocks of any type;
> [5] Porcelain, Meissen, and Sevres cases;
> [6] Skeleton clocks with works that show;

and many other unusual, highly decorated, or artistic types of clocks, dials, and/or cases. This company wants European, not American clocks of any kind! They want a clear photo and a description of the case, including dimensions, where and when you got it, and anything you know about repairs, internal or external. Mention names on the dial. Give your phone and best time to call. Does not return photos.
> Fraser Cameron, Ltd.
> PO Box 27162
> Minneapolis, MN 55427
> (612) 926-6609   fax (612) 949-1177

★ *Howard Miller* **clocks** from the 1950's and 60's. These are usually metal or metal and wood and marked on the back (and sometimes the front). Photo or sketch is helpful.
> Frank Novak
> 7386 Beverly Blvd.
> Los Angeles, CA 90036
> (213) 683-1963   Fax (213) 683-1312

★ **Winking eye clocks.** "I'll buy any good specimens of these 19th century figural cast iron clocks which wink their eyes as the hands go around. Made in CT during the 3rd quarter of the 19th century by *Bradley and Hubbard*, they bring $1,000 up in fine condition and paint. Take photos from more than one angle or phone me with the item in front of you."
> Gregory "Dr. Z" Zemenick
> 1350 Kirts, #160
> Troy, MI 48084
> (313) 642-8129   or   (313) 244-9426

★ **Advertising clocks** made by Baird.
> Jerry Phelps
> 6013 Innes Trace Rd.
> Louisville, KY 40222
> (502) 425-4765

★ **Clocks, pocket watches** and better quality wristwatches.
> Robert Kolbe's Clock Repair,
> 1301 So. Duluth,
> Sioux Falls, SD 57105
> (605) 332-9662

★ **Old wall and shelf clocks.** This husband - wife team buy a wide range of 18th and 19th century shelf and wall clocks, but are especially interested in the following:

[1] **Victorian shelf clocks.** Want ornate ones, with hanging teardrops, busts (such as Jenny Lind), cherubs, side mirrors, etc.;

[2] **Reverse painting on glass pillar and scroll clocks** about 36" high with free standing wooden pillars and curved scroll ("swan's neck") tops;

[3] **Steeple or beehive shelf clocks,** *but only if the veneer is nearly perfect.* "These are plentiful with poor veneer. I want those in beautiful condition."

[4] **Any American carved clocks.** "I'm a pushover for clocks with carved columns or splats, with eagles, fruit baskets, etc.," says Ken.

[5] **Clocks by Eli Terry or any of his sons.**

[6] **Seth Thomas clocks.**

[7] **French, German, and English clocks from the 18th and 19th century.** "Some excellent 20th century German clocks were made in Mission style, but no matter how good the clock, we don't buy 20th century."

[8] **Coo-coo clocks if very old, very heavily carved, and in perfect condition.** "I'm afraid I'll open a floodgate if I mention I'm interested in coo-coos, because there are so many junk ones around. I only want those that are very early, and very ornate...no souvenir clocks. Sending a photo a must."

[9] **Black Forest trumpeter clocks.** These are chiming clocks, like coo-coos, but instead of a bird have a man who plays a tune on a trumpet. "These are valuable, and we'll travel to pick yours up if it's a nice one."

"We buy clocks with walnut or cherry cases. We buy spring driven clocks but especially like to find older weight driven clocks. We buy clocks with wooden works only if in running condition," say the owners, "but there are a few exceptions, so it's worth inquiring."

"We are *not* interested in oak clocks or metal figural clocks, no matter who is depicted. We don't buy any 20th century clocks, oak gingerbread kitchen clocks, electric clocks, or mission (arts and crafts) clocks. Nor do we buy *Lux* or *Keebler* novelty clocks with rolling eyes or swinging tails. We also do not buy plain ogee clocks (rectangular veneered clocks with fronts that look like picture frames). We almost never buy clocks that have undergone restoration or modification".

"My wife and I think of ourselves as a clock adoption agency. We look for nice items in need of a good new home. We don't want to spend lots of time with the clocks. We prefer to buy them in nearly perfect condition."
Old Timers
Box 392
Camp Hill, PA 17001
(717) 761-1908

"SCHOOLHOUSE"   "BEEHIVE"

VICTORIAN "MIRROR –   "STEEPLE"   WALNUT "TEARDROP"
SIDES WITH CHERUBS"

"CARVED COLUMN"   "GINGERBREAD"   "PILLAR AND SCROLL"

jewelry

Diamonds are often mistaken for glass

in old jewelry. So are emeralds, rubies, and many precious and semi-precious stones. Stones used to be cut very differently than popular today. One reader showed me a two and a half carat diamond he bought at a yard sale for a quarter. Have you ever sold one in a box of junk jewelry?

Jewelry buyers want to know what your item is made from and what it looks like. Answer the following:

[1] Is it silver, gold, brass, plastic, or a material you do not recognize? Describe the color of your item and any names, numbers, or markings.

[2] If there are stones, what color are they? How many of them are there?

Dimensions are helpful. Many items of jewelry can be copied on a Xerox© machine. It is a very good way of describing hatpins, brooches, pins, and some bracelets.

Be prepared to ship your jewelry with a five day return privilege. Buyers usually want to inspect jewelry before they commit to buy. Get payment first, before you ship, but be willing to give the money back if they are not happy for any reason with what you send.

When mailing items worth more than $500, send them Registered Mail. For between $5-$10 you can mail with near certain safety throughout the U.S. with insurance as high as $25,000. The recipient signs for Registered Mail.

tony hyman

Jewelry

★ **Hatpins and hatpin holders** and related objects such as pincushion dolls from before 1930. "Especially interested in plique-a-jour hatpins for which I'll pay up to $350 or more if artist signed. I also like sterling hatpins marked "C.H." and will pay $45-$110. Always interested in vanity or figural hatpins such as compacts, pin-holders, perfume tops, thimble with needle, etc., especially if Art Nouveau design atop 12" pin stems. My special want is a hatpin hinged on the top ornament which opens to reveal a teeny nude baby and I would pay up to $500 for a perfect one on a long pin. I also want to buy **figural hatpin holders** by *Royal Bayreuth, RS Prussia* (red mark only), *Oriental, Schafer & Vater* (S&V), others." Mrs. Baker is the author of books on jewelry and an encyclopedia of hatpins available for $79 postpaid. She founded the International Club for Hatpin Collectors. An SASE brings information about the club or available books. She wants the history of your hatpin, and whether it has any flaws. Will make offers to amateurs only after inspection.
>   Lillian Baker, "The Hatpin Lady"
>   15237 Chanera Ave.
>   Gardena, CA 90249
>   (213) 329-2619

★ **Tassie cameos.** Very rare and hard to find, they are named after James Tassie of Scotland who, in the 1700's, invented glass cameo molds, used by *Wedgwood* to make the cameo decorations on their pottery. Tassie cameos are most often hung in picture frames. "I want those made of marble dust with gold colored paper wrapped around it. These are most often of mythological characters. Also want the molds they were made from, if signed by Tassie or his son. Will pay premium prices. Send a photo and/or description."
>   Monica Murphy
>   Savannah's Antiques
>   1419 Fern
>   New Orleans, LA 70118
>   (504) 866-2221

★ **Plastic or metal *Hummel* jewelry** from 1940's in shapes similar to their figurines. She buys both painted and unpainted jewelry.
>   Sharon Vohs-Mohammed
>   Box 14192
>   Tallahassee, FL 32317

★ **Old and antique jewelry** especially
>   [1] **Karat gold pieces**, particularly signed art nouveau and art deco designs;
>   [2] **Sterling silver items** signed by *Unger Brothers* or *Kerr*, mostly art nouveau brooches featuring female faces;
>   [3] **Designer costume jewelry** signed by *Coro, Trifari, Mariam Haskell, Hattie Carnegie*, or *Eisenberg Original*
>   [4] *Georg Jensen* jewelry;
>   [5] **Silver puffed heart fancy charms.**

Describe your items completely, or make a Xerox© copy. If you know the item's ownership history, please give it. Note all markings.
>   Arnold Reamer
>   Timepiece Antiques
>   Box 26416
>   Baltimore, MD 21207
>   (301) 944-6414 or (301) 486-8412

★ **Antique jewelry**, 17th to 19th century, 8K to 22K gold, any type of stones. Especially wants earrings, but also complete suites, hair and mourning jewelry, cameos (shell or stone), seed pearls, miniature ivory portraits, tiaras, tortoise shell jewelry, fine hair combs, Berlin ironwork jewelry..."anything worn from head to toe." She requests photo and/or description with your asking price, and pledges "will pay for rarity."
>   Monica Murphy, Savannah's Antiques
>   1419 Fern
>   New Orleans, LA 70118
>   (504) 866-2221

★ **Old jewelry before 1930**, garnets, blacks jets, cameos, rings, **lockets**, **charms**, filigree beads, glass beads, and glass buttons. Can be broken and need repair. "I look for all unusual items of clothing, jewelry, and accessories." Xerox© suggested.
>   Linda Gibbs
>   10380 Miranda Ave.
>   Buena Park, CA 90620
>   (714) 827-6488

★ **Gold scrap.** "I buy all marked and unmarked gold and silver rings, wedding bands, and scrap" says this giant dealer in medals, who advises you may ship whatever you have for his offer.
>   Rich Hartzog, World Exonumia
>   Box 4143 BID
>   Rockford, IL 61110
>   (815) 226-0771

comic books

Comic collectors are very fussy folks.

Every tiny crease, tear, wrinkle, misprint, and off center or rusty staple affects the value of comic books. Severe grading standards are suggested in comic book price guides, and collectors follow them fairly closely.

If you have comics for sale, it will be worth your while to get Overstreet's *The Comic Book Price Guide.* It is comprehensive, easy to use, and the reference used by nearly all collector's and dealers. You can purchase the latest edition at bookstores ($15-20) . The library can obtain it for you through interloan.

The Comic Book Price Guide contains current "prices"for nearly every American comic book. You will also find pages of ads from comic dealers. Dealers and our buyers generally pay from 30% - 70% of prices quoted in Overstreet, although that range varies according to the dealer's finances, customer wants, and that month's market.

Collectors and dealers will usually request that you send your items for inspection prior to payment. Since the value of comics is so tightly linked to condition, this is a reasonable request.

Ask your post office for "return receipt requested" which costs about $1. Always include a list of what you are sending and keep a copy of the list for yourself. Cautious sellers Xerox© the covers of what they send, since the creases on the cover are like a fingerprint and can identify *your* comic should it be necessary.

tony hyman

Comic Books

★ **Comic books,** 1935-1970, especially super-hero, Western, science-fiction, humor and funny animal, and movie or TV related. Particularly looking for the following companies: E.C., Dell, Marvel & DC [before 1970], Fawcett, Fiction House, Quality, and Harvey. Also buys **Classics Illustrated,** both originals and reprints. The comics most wanted are "Timely Titles" including *Captain America*, *Marvel Mystery*, *Mystic*, *All Winners*, *Human Torch*, *Sub-Mariner, USA,* and *Young Allies.* He will pay up to $1,000 for early issues of *Marvel Mystery.* He does not want comics newer than 1970 or any comics, no matter how old, without covers. When writing or calling, give the title, publisher, and issue number (usually found on the cover, inside front cover, or first page). Describe condition including cover gloss, creases, stains, tears, tape, and damage to the spine. Note loose or missing pages, bends, and folds, as well as browning of the pages. All inquiries answered if you include an SASE.
Joe Hill
Phoenix Enterprises
RD #1, Box 423
Erin, NY 14838
(607) 796-2547 eves

★ **All comic books in fine condition 1900-69,** *Big Little Books* 1932-1950, and Sunday comics 1929-59 *but nothing brittle or damaged.* Also original comic book or comic strip art. Pays in U.S. dollars and bank drafts.
Ken Mitchell
710 Concacher Dr.
Willowdale, Ontario M2M 3N6
CANADA

★ **All 10¢ comic books,** for which he claims to have "unlimited funds" to pay 50%-100% of price guide figures. Send a list of titles and issue numbers with a brief description of condition. No comics which sold for more than a dime originally. Also **comic strip original art** for daily or Sunday strips. This chain of comic book stores has six Illinois outlets.
Gary Colabuono
Moondog's
1201 Oakton St., #1
Elk Grove Village, IL 60007
(708) 806-6060 or (800) 344-6060

★ **Comic books** from the 1940's, 50's and 60's with the work of the "EC gang" of Johnny Craig, Reed Crandall, Jack Davis, Wally Wood, George Evans, Al Feldstein, Frank Frazetta, Basil Wolverton, Graham Ingels, Bernie Krigstein, and Harvey Kurtzman. "I'm also a big fan of the comic book artists Simon & Kirby, especially their post war work. Other illustrators whose work I want to buy include Matt Baker, Steve Ditko, Will Eisner, Lou Fine, Bob Powell, Alex Raymond and Alex Schomburg. Does not want EC's, but does want all other comic book appearances of these artists. Geoff deals in movie memorabilia. Send $2 each for his long catalogs of **inexpensive movie memorabilia for sale** in the bad girl, Western, and science fiction/horror genres.
Geoffrey Mahfuz
PO Box 171
Dracut, MA 01826
(508) 452-2768

★ **Flip books** from any period, in any style or size. These are small booklets whose pictures move like a movie when the pages are flipped. Wants all kinds, including cartoons, photos of real people or animals, "how to" instructions, product advertising, sexy, or artistic abstractions. Especially seeking two rare hardcover books from the 1920's, *Santa Claus Play Pictures* and *Mother Goose Play Pictures,* which had pages to be cut out and assembled into flip books, and would pay $200 for them. He is not interested in the *Big Little Books* which sometimes had flip illustrations in the upper corner, nor does he want the recent reproductions by Merrimack or Shackman & Co. A Xerox© of the cover is suggested, along with a brief description of the action. Give the dimensions, whether it is color or black and white, cartoons or photos, etc.
Jeff Jurich
1220 Hudson St.
Denver, CO 80220

★ **Full color comic sections from Sunday newspapers,** 1900-1940 in good or better condition. Value depends on several factors. Write or phone giving the city, newspaper, date, number of pages, and comics included. Free appraisals.
Al Felden
8945 Fairfield St.
Philadelphia, PA 19152
(215) 677-0657

★ **Pre 1968 comic books,** *Better Little Books* and *Big Little Books*. Twenty year vet dealer.
   Hugh O'Kennon
   2204 Haviland Dr.
   Richmond, VA 23229
     (804) 270-2465

★ **Sunday comic sections,** 1930-60. Prefers to purchase runs of several years. "A few odd sections are not needed." He especially wants the color comics from the Saturday issues of the Chicago or the NY *Journal American*, 1934-64.
   Claude Held
   Box 515
   Buffalo, NY 14225

★ **Sunday and daily adventure comic strips, 1930-60** such as *Tarzan, Prince Valiant, Flash Gordon, Terry and the Pirates, Steve Canyon, Casey Ruggles, Captain Easy,* and *Dick Tracy*. No single dailies, humor strips or torn items.
   Carl Horak
   1319 108th Ave.
   SW Calgary, Alberta T2W 0C6 CANADA

Most comic art sells for $50-$2,000, but comic art has sold for more than $50,000.

Value depends on the age, artist, subject matter, and condition.

Work of Carl Barks and Richard Outcault is very popular.

Original Comic Art

★ **Original artwork for comic strips and cartoons, 1920-1950,** especially animation cels from Disney, Warner Bros, etc., for which this 25 year veteran has paid as much as $12,000. Jerry also buys original art from comic strips and magazines cartoons. Information he wants includes title, artist, description, the year, and any documentation you might have. In your description of condition, note any yellowing, folds, tears, cracked or missing paint, paste overs, etc. He does not want reproductions from newspapers or magazines; nor does he buy posters or prints of any type. Museum Graphics publishes a bimonthly newsletter and price list, available for $2 a year.
   Jerry Muller
   Museum Graphics
   Box 10743
   Costa Mesa, CA 92627
     (714) 540-0808

★ **Comic strip art by any noted cartoonist.** Dennis issues an illustrated annual catalog.
   Dennis Books
   Comic Character Shop
   Box 99142
   Seattle, WA 98199
     (206) 283-0532 eves

★ **Original art** used in creating comic books and strips. Xerox© what you have.
   Charles Martignette
   PO Box 293
   Hallandale, FL 33009
     (305) 454-3474

pop culture and other toys

Talk about junk with outrageous value

and you're probably talking about pop culture toys and ephemera.

"Pop culture" refers to a broad range of toys and advertising ephemera associated with the world of cartoons, TV, comics, the movies and other popular entertainment. It's all that trash most people threw away.

To sell toys and other pop culture, provide the following information:
[1] What it is, its size, color, and the material from which it is made;
[2] Names, dates, and numbers embossed or labeled on the toy;
[3] The condition, including missing parts, pieces, or paint. Be certain to describe all repairs or repainting;
[4] If box and instructions are included and in good condition.

Some buyers want additional info. Bank buyers want you to trace around the bank base, and to be careful in describing paint color and condition.

Vehicle buyers want the size, color, and the material from which the tires and wheels are made. Electric train buyers want serial numbers of engines, and the type and color of cars.

Photos and Xerox© copies are important since a great many of these banks, vehicles, dolls, robots, and other toys are worth $100+ and a surprising number can bring you $1,000 or more.

tony hyman

Pop Culture

★ **Americana and pop culture of all sorts** is wanted by Ted Hake the longest established mail dealer and auctioneer of pop collectibles. Ted buys:
- [1] **Political and other pin back buttons;**
- [2] **Premiums from radio/TV or cereal;**
- [3] **Disney** characters pre 1970;
- [4] **Animation art** from Disney and other cartoons;
- [5] **Battery or wind up toys** especially those related to pop culture characters;
- [6] **Television related toys,** games, lunch boxes, etc., from 1950's and 60's;
- [7] **Singing cowboys** and other western film heroes memorabilia;
- [8] **Robots and space toys;**
- [9] Items directly related to the **U.S. Space Program;**
- [10] **Elvis Presley** pre-death items;
- [11] *Beatles* and other famous rock and roll personalities;
- [12] **Movie posters,** lobby cards, etc.;
- [13] **Toys of the 1960's** like *GI Joe, Capt. Action, Batman,* etc.;
- [14] "Just about any item from a famous character or personality."

Wants to know the material your item is made from, its size, any dates you can provide, and general condition. Offers made only after inspection. Hake has written four books on pin back buttons. No reproductions and no political items after 1968.

Ted Hake
Hake's Americana
Box 1444
York, PA 17405
(717) 848-1333 days

★ **Comic character pin back buttons, 1896-1966,** from the earliest *Yellow Kid* to all comic strip and comic book characters since then. This *Star Trek* actor (Chekov) will pay as much as $500 for rare buttons like the *Flash Gordon* Movie Club or *Washington Herald Mickey Mouse.* Upon request he'll send you an illustrated wants list. Include your phone number.

Walter Koenig
Box 4395
North Hollywood, CA 91607

★ **Items depicting pre-1960 comic characters,** superheroes, fictional detectives, movie heroes and villains are purchased by this well known dealer:
- [1] **Toys and pin back buttons;**
- [2] **TV games, premiums, and ephemera;**
- [3] **Radio and cereal premiums;**
- [4] **Buttons from various radio "clubs",** worth up to $500;
- [5] **Movie Posters,** especially from serials, cartoons, and adventure movies;
- [6] **Store stand-up figural displays;**
- [7] **Memorabilia associated with heroic characters** such as *Tarzan, Batman, Superman, Flash Gordon, Captain Midnight,* and the *Green Hornet.*

"Does not want 1970s *Batman*, modern *Dick Tracy,* beat up lobby cards, coverless comics, or other junk...just rare collectibles, please." "I want a very wide range of pop culture toys and pay more than anyone for the top range items." He warns, "There are so many repros and fakes now that I will no longer buy something sight unseen. Unmarked rings worth 2¢ and $1,500 can look quite similar to the inexperienced. I pay more! If you want to sell to me it has to be on my terms. You must write first, providing a full description of the item and its condition." If Rex is interested he will request that you ship for his inspection. Rex pays postage both ways on items he does not buy. "I have bought and sold this way for 18 years," he adds, pointing out numerous awards he has won for dealer integrity. **Rex does not want Hopalong Cassidy and other 1950's cowboys, nor does he buy lunchboxes, common items, or anything damaged. Do not contact him with anything but perfect rare items.**

Rex Miller
Rte. 1 Box 457D
East Prairie, MO 63845
(314) 649-5048 (10 to 10)

★ **All comic character toys and collectibles from the 1930's and 40's,** made of any material from cardboard to cast iron, especially Disney-ana, radio premiums, and all **children's play suits** from western heroes to sailor suits. No Halloween costumes. There are also many pieces of **comic character related sheet music** Ralph is seeking.

Ralph Eodice
Nevermore
161 Valley Rd.
Clifton, NJ 07013
(201) 742-8278

★ **Pop culture treasures**, especially made of paper, including:
   [1] **Comic books** 1890's-1980's, but only hero comics after 1963;
   [2] **Sunday comics** 1890's-1959;
   [3] **Original comic strip art**;
   [4] **Walt Disney** books and anything else pre-1960;
   [5] *Big Little Books* 1933-1950;
   [6] **Movie magazines** 1920-1945;
   [7] **Television collectibles** 1948-1970;
   [8] **Radio and cereal premiums** and giveaways pre-1960;
   [9] **Song magazines** 1929-1959 such as *Hit Parader* and *400 Songs;*
   [10] **Popular music magazines** 1920-1959 including *Downbeat* and *Billboard*;
   [11] **Pulp magazines** 1930-49 except love, Westerns, and crime magazines.
Wants nothing in poor condition. Ken has been in business 25 years, and pays Americans in U.S. dollars and drafts for quick payment.
Ken Mitchell
710 Concacher Dr.
Willowdale, Ontario M2M 3N6
CANADA
   (416) 222-5808

★ **Radio premiums from children's adventure programs** such as *The Lone Ranger, Jack Armstrong, Tom Mix, Sky King, Sgt. Preston, The Shadow, Doc Savage, Buck Rogers, Dick Tracy, Radio Orphan Annie,* etc. Also **cereal boxes offering premiums** from the 30's through the 60's. Tom buys **superhero action figures, space adventure items, and Disney.** He wrote the four volume book on Disney collectibles and will buy *anything* **related to Disney** that is not pictured in one of his price guides, especially *Mickey Mouse* items from the 1930's including *Mickey* with teeth, celluloid *Mickey*, wood and bisque *Mickeys* and any Disney wind-up toy. He also wants Disney Studio Xmas cards, **character watches** and odd popular culture items in original boxes. If your item is for sale, Tom says "I will not jeopardize my reputation by underpaying and making someone mad. But sellers must understand how much even small blemishes reduce the value of an item." Tom prefers items to be priced, and makes offers only on items he can see in person.
Tom Tumbusch
3300 Encrete Lane
Dayton, OH 45439
   (513) 294-2250

★ **Robots and space toys** made of tin before 1965, either windup or battery operated. "I'll pay $2,000 for *Mr. Atomic* and $750 for the *Robby Space Patrol* vehicle. Condition is important with these toys, so I'll pay an extra 10% for any toy in its original box." Also buys tin wind-up **comic character toys** made in the USA or Europe, whether working or not, and any **Disney toys** especially celluloid toys from the 1930's. **Santa Claus toys** are also of interest.
Larry Bruch
Box 121
Mountaintop, PA 18707
   (717) 474-9202 eves

★ **Pop culture toys** including :
   [1] **Western movie/TV toys**, wristwatches, and premiums from Roy Rogers, Hoppy, Gene Autry, *Lone Ranger, Red Ryder,* etc.
   [2] **Western style cap guns** of metal;
   [3] **Disney and other comic character toys**;
   [4] **Toys from radio, television, and movie characters and superheroes**;
   [5] **Doll houses** of tin and *Renwall* plastic doll houses and accessories;
   [6] **Toy vehicles** by *Smith Miller, Tonka, Doepke, Dinky, Renwall* (plastic), *Auburn* (rubber), *Arcade, Marx,* and *Wyandotte*;
   [7] *G.I. Joe* dolls, accessories, pre-1970, in the 12" size;
   [8] **Advertising toys**.
Condition is critical and only excellent condition items are wanted. Items in original box always preferred. Detailed descriptions should include dimensions. Photo helpful. "Generous prices paid, but all offers contingent on personal inspection." Will answer all inquiries that have SASE. Calls welcome.
William Hamburg
Box 1305
Woodland Hills, CA 91365
   (818) 346-9884

★ Comic, cartoon, and pop culture characters depicted on *anything* in any form, including, but not limited to:

[1] **Lamps,** either wall or table type;

[2] **Paper dolls** but only if uncut;

[3] **Empty boxes for any toys;**

[4] **Cereal and food boxes and wrappers,** some of which are worth $100+;

[5] **Halloween costumes,** 1930-70's, but only if in original box or package;

[6] **Rubber monster masks** made by Don Post sold in *Famous Monsters* magazine;

[7] **Milk bottles depicting Disney characters,** for which he pays from $65 up;

[8] *PEZ* **and other candy dispensers** and store displays, worth up to $150 each;

[9] **Disney silverware** by Oneida, International, or Rogers, but only if you have the box, toy, or stand sold with it;

[10] *Star Wars* **toys** in original boxes;

[11] **Character dolls** of super heroes;

[12] **TV and movie monsters and science fiction creatures;**

[13] **Disney,** *Popeye,* **and** *Betty Boop* from the 1930's and '40's;

[15] *Marx* **playsets from the 1950's and 60's** such as *Gunsmoke, Ben Hur, Johnny Ringo, The Untouchables,* etc. ;

[14] **Cereal premiums,** from *Quisp, Quake, Quangaroos, Capt. Crunch, Flintstones,* and *King Vitamin.* Some are worth $50!

Condition is crucial. Make certain to note all damage and if there are missing parts. Does not buy reproductions. Make certain to mention if item is in its original box or wrapper since "that can make an item worth two to ten times as much." Photos are "very helpful."

David Welch
PO Box 714
Murphysboro, IL 62966
(618) 687-2282

★ **Pop culture toys,** including

[1] Older **comic books;**

[2] **Marilyn Monroe** memorabilia;

[3] **Elvis** memorabilia;

[4] **Disney** paper collectibles;

[5] **Non-sports cards;**

[6] Western collectibles.

This well known magazine collector/dealer has expanded into the above related ephemera. Please describe what you have fully. Items are purchased for resale.

Stan Gold
7042 Dartbrook
Dallas, TX 75240

★ **Disneyana pre-1946,** especially:

[1] *Mickey* or *Donald* painted plaster lamps;

[2] Waddle Books from the 1930's;

[3] Animation cels from before 1960;

[4] *Mickey, Minnie, Donald* costume dolls;

[5] *Vernon Kilns* ceramic statues;

[6] Tin or celluloid toys of Disney characters;

[7] Wood or porcelain figurines;

[8] Original art for WWII combat insignia.

Art from the 1950's is of interest, but nothing newer. Include dimensions, color, maker's markings, condition (mention all damage or missing parts). Dennis will make offers for items "only when I'm holding it in my hand," preferring you to set the price. Include your phone number when you write.

Dennis Books, Comic Characters
Box 99142
Seattle, WA 98199
(206) 283-0532

★ **Wind-up and battery operated toys** made in Germany, Japan, or the U.S., including comic characters, carnival items like merry-go-rounds, airplanes (no jets), and space toys. "I'll pay over $1,000 for Mr. Atomic robot or Mickey the Magician, two battery toys." He doesn't want common items like Charlie Weaver bartender, plastic toys, wind up dogs, trains, dolls, items with missing parts, or toys made in the third world. Tell this toy consultant and restorer the condition of the item and box, and whether there is any restoration or repainting.

Don Hultzman
5026 Sleepy Hollow Rd.
Medina, OH 44256
(216) 225-2668

★ **Toy robots from 1950-1972.** Wants *Mr. Atomic, Robby the Robot,* and the *Robby Space Patrol vehicle* among others. Especially in original boxes! Also buys other **German and Japanese wind-up, friction, and battery operated toys,** vehicles, and comic characters.

Chris Savino
Box 419
Breesport, NY 14816
(607) 739-3106

★ **Toy robots and** *Erector* **sets** are sometimes purchased by this specialist in toy vehicles.

Jay "The Chicago Kid" Robinson
PO Box 529
Deerfield, IL 60015
(708) 945-8691 or (708) 945-1965

★ Cereal boxes with advertisements for giveaways or the premiums themselves, if before 1970. Jerry also buys radio, TV, and movie cowboy and space premiums and pre-1960 *Crackerjack* boxes, premiums, and signs. Send for his wants list of other pop culture ephemera. No Orphan Annie decoders or manuals. NO OFFERS.

Jerry Doxey
HCR#1, Box 343
Sciota, PA 18354
(717) 992-7477

★ Cereal boxes depicting comic characters or radio show giveaways. Wants 1930-1959 boxes and the premiums they offered. A series of 1940's *Cheerios* boxes featuring Disney characters is particularly desirable as is the 1946 Atom Bomb ring box of *Kix*.

John Fawcett
RR #2, 720 Middle Turnpike
Storrs, CT 06268

★ Comic character items from the 1920's and 30's wanted, especially Disney but also *Betty Boop, KoKo the Clown, Felix the Cat, Maggie and Jiggs, Mutt & Jeff, Krazy Kat and Ignatz, Little Nemo, Barney Google*, and more. Wants figurines, masks, toys, premiums, posters, dolls, pins, original art, lamps, radios, store displays, etc. What have you?

John Fawcett
RR #2, 720 Middle Turnpike
Storrs, CT 06268

★ Radio show giveaways, membership cards, pins, photos, games, rings, toys, etc. from *Lone Ranger*, Tom Mix, *Sky King, Capt. Midnight, Charlie McCarthy*, Gene Autry, etc.

John Fawcett
RR #2, 720 Middle Turnpike
Storrs, CT 06268

★ Radio show giveaways such as rings, badges, decoders, etc. Wants *Captain Midnight, Superman, Little Orphan Annie, Buck Rogers, Howdy Doody, The Shadow, Sgt. Preston, Doc Savage, Sky King*, and other characters. Also buys the manuals from old radio, TV and cereal advertising campaigns. "Please advise what you have and what you want for it, or ship for offer."

Alan Levine
292 Glenwood Ave.
PO Box 1577
Bloomfield, NJ 07003
(201) 743-5288

★ Jimmie Allen radio show giveaways from the 1930's. "I will pay $100 each for certain Jimmie Allen wings and premium prices for other items." Since dozens of different types of wings, membership cards, and certificates were given away, it is important to make a Xerox© and indicate which sponsor's name is printed on the item. Manuals, model kits, I.D. bracelets, and "other rare and/or unusual Jimmie Allen premiums" are sought. Include your phone number when you write.

Jack Deveny
6805 Cheyenne Trail
Edina, MN 55435
(612) 941-2457

★ Monster items of all types including:
[1] Gum cards, display boxes and wrappers such as *Mars Attack, Outer Limits, Terror Tales, Spook Stories, Monster Flip Movies*, and *Flash Gordon*;
[2] Plastic model kits of Frankenstein's monster, wolfman, mummy, *King Kong, Rodan, The Munsters*, and so on, whether built or unbuilt. Will even purchase some broken models for parts, and pay up to $50 for some empty boxes;
[3] Toys and games, puzzles, novelties, and the like that feature any movie, TV, or comic book monsters or creatures. Will pay $75 for the board game, *Outer Limits*;
[4] Halloween masks of these characters, especially masks made by Don Post;
[5] Comics by Zenith, E.C., and other 10¢ publishers of monster titles;
[6] Magazines and record albums, especially *Famous Monsters,, Castle of Frankenstein, World Famous Creatures, Monster Parade* and similar titles.

"I welcome any calls or letters, and am always happy to talk with anyone who has monster items." Include where you got the item. Don't forget your phone number.

Joe Warchol
5345 N. Canfield
Chicago, IL 60656
(708) 843-2442 days
(312) 774-1628 eves

★ **Model kits of human, monster, comic, or science fiction characters** are sought. Kits were produced by *Aurora, Hawk, Revell, MPC, Multiple,* and *Lindbergh.* Any kits containing figures (not cars and boats) may be of interest as long as it is unbuilt in its original box. Will also buy empty boxes, factory promos, store displays and advertising and manufacturer's catalogs. A few items, like Godzilla's Go-Cart, can bring as much as $1,000.
   David Welch
   Box 714
   Murphysboro, IL 62966
     (618) 687-2282

★ **Children's cartoon and comic character books** such as *Big Little Books*, *Pop-Up Books, Fast Actions, Fawcett Dime Action Books, Cupples and Leon,* and other early comic reprint books from 1910's, 20's, and 30's. Also **coloring books**, *Whitman* hard cover children's books with dust jackets, *Whitman Penny Books, Nickel Books, Buddy Book*s, and any similar books published by *Salsfield, Mclaughlin, Lynn Publications, Engel Van Wiseman,* etc. "Let me know what you have and what you want for it, or ship for immediate offer."
   Alan Levine
   PO Box 1577
   Bloomfield, NJ 07003
     (201) 743-5288

★ **TV related memorabilia.** "I'll buy toys, puzzles, games, lunchboxes, etc., but specialize in all types of records and fan magazines associated with television." Wants records in all speeds, adult and children's, serious or funny, as long as it is related to television. Also TV fan type magazines like *TV-Radio Mirror, TV Fan, TV Carnival, TV Western* and the like as well as paperback books spun off from TV series. Items from before 1970 only, please. Examine your fan magazines carefully and note if they have had pictures clipped. No movie fan mags. When describing, give the date, volume and issue number and condition of magazines. Record info should include title, label, condition, and whether or not it has a sleeve.
   Ross Hartsough
   98 Bryn Mawr Rd.
   Winnipeg R3T 3P5 Canada
     (204) 269-1022

★ **Television private detective and spy memorabilia.** Wants to buy games, puzzles, toys, books, photos, gum cards, wrappers, dolls, model kits, autographs, comic books, and just about everything else you can think of from shows like *77 Sunset Strip, Dragnet, Surfside 6, Peter Gunn, I Spy, The Man from U.N.C.L.E., The Wild Wild West, Secret Agent, Hawaiian Eye, Adventures in Paradise, The Untouchables* and others. This relatively new collector dealer says he's interested in everything in good condition. Include Xerox© or good description as condition is very important. Describe the package if you still have it.
   Gary Pimenta
   64 Lakeside Dr.
   Tiverton, RI 02878

★ *Gilligan's Island* **collectibles.** "I'll buy or trade for all *Gilligan's Island* TV show items, including cast photos and videos of episodes." Especially interested in the 1965 *Gilligan's Island* bubblegum cards and the box they came in. Will also pay for video recordings of the cartoons *The New Adventures of Gilligan* or *Gilligan's Planet.* His club also produces a newsletter with classified ads for people who want to buy, sell, or trade *Gilligan* ephemera.
   Bob Rankin
   Original Gilligan's Island Fan Club
   PO Box 25311
   Salt Lake City, UT 84125

★ **Beany & Cecil memorabilia,** not only from the old *Time for Beany* of the 1950's but also from the animated TV series of the 60's. Wants a Beany cookie jar from with Beany's face, a plaster Cecil the Sea-Sick Sea Serpent lamp, program scripts and cels, kinescopes, and other items associated with the show and its creator, Bob Clampett.
   Jeff and Maria Falasca
   20159 Cohasset Street #
   Canoga Park, CA 91306
     (818) 718-8202

★ *Howdy Doody* **memorabilia** is wanted, including all items related to any character on the show. Especially seek items in original boxes. Runs *Howdy* auctions, "so will buy anything in fine condition."
   John Andrea
   51122 Mill Run
   Grander, IN 46530
     (219) 272-2337   Fax (219) 271-1146

★ *Yellow Kid* **character items.** Wants tins, buttons, dolls, paper items, "anything."
  Craig Koste
  RD #2 Box 194
  Morrisonville, NY 12962
  (518) 643-8173

★ *Yellow Kid* **memorabilia.** Wants tins, toys, buttons, postcards, ads...*anything*.
  William Nielsen
  1379 Main Street
  Brewster, MA 02631
  (508) 896-7389

★ *Mutt & Jeff* collectibles are sought, including books, comic books, figurines and dolls. Describe what you have thoroughly.
  Larry Whitfield
  Box 1330
  Duvall, WA 98019
  (206) 788-1523

★ **Tom Mix collectibles** including *Shredded Ralston* cereal boxes from the 1930's and 40's with Tom Mix markings, arcade and gum cards, postcards, unusual photos, feature films, short subjects, various radio premiums, and the 1930's Tom Mix *Ingersoll* pocket watch. This 40 year veteran is author of *The Tom Mix Book*, available from him for $24.95. Note that he **does not want** lobby cards, movie posters, newly made items, common photos, *Big Little Books*, clothing, video tapes or any material that is not in good condition. He insists that sellers price what they have.
  Merle "Bud" Norris
  1324 N. Hague Ave.
  Columbus, OH 43204
  (614) 274-4646

★ **Hopalong Cassidy collectibles.**
  Ron Pieczkowski
  1707 Orange Hill Drive
  Brandon, FL 33510

★ *Lone Ranger* items. Wants a wide range of 1930-59 items including cereal boxes, dolls, games, posters, premiums, gun sets, carnival plaster figures, books with dust jackets, autographs, and other items.
  John Fawcett
  RR #2, 720 Middle Turnpike
  Storrs, CT 06268

★ *Superman* items. Buys all unusual, rare, odd and interesting *Superman* items, particularly dating 1938-1966, but "I purchase interesting items from all years." Seeks toys, figurines, puzzles, watches, games, buttons, advertising, etc. "Please write me about any good *Superman* item because I buy duplicates and quantity." No comic books, except the free premiums. No homemade items. Give, complete description, including *every* defect, and include its color, manufacturer, copyright date and country of origin. Photo or Xerox© is appreciated. Danny has collected for 30 years and co-author of *The Adventures of Superman Collecting*.
  Danny Fuchs
  209-80 18th Ave.
  Bayside, NY 11360
  (718) 225-9030

★ *Captain Marvel, Captain Marvel Jr.,* and *Mary Marvel* memorabilia including toys, buttons, posters, comic books, mechanical items, and statues produced between 1940-1953. Also items related to similar Fawcett characters.
  Michael Gronsky
  9833 Meadowcroft Lane
  Gaithersburg, MD 20879
  (301) 926-1049

★ *Dick Tracy, Sparkle Plenty* and *Bonny Braids* collectibles. "I'm buying premiums, toys, books, paper, figures...anything!"
  Larry Doucet,
  2351 Sultana Dr.
  Yorktown Heights, NY 10598

★ **Action figures** such as *G.I.Joe, Masters of the Universe, Ninja Turtles,* various other super heroes. "Prefer still in blister pack on a card."
  Ken Clee
  PO Box 11412
  Philadelphia, PA 19111
  (215) 722-1979

★ *G.I.Joe* action figures. "I'll buy figures, uniforms, vehicles, accessories...anything in good condition whether boxed, carded or loose." Especially seeks store displays and stock, dolls, novelties, puzzles, games, vehicles, and carded stock but will buy nearly anything. Purchases both for his personal collection and for resale.
  Joe Bodnarchuk
  62 McKinley Avenue
  Kenmore, NY 14217
  (716) 873-0264 phone and fax

★ *James Bond 007*, and Ian Fleming memorabilia including first edition hard and soft cover books, magazines with articles about Bond, movie posters, record albums, toys, dolls, plastic model kits, beer cans, clothing, games, comic books, and much more. Especially wants books autographed by Fleming, the British 1st edition of *Casino Royale*, and one of the signed and numbered limited editions of *On Her Majesty's Secret Service*. Give standard bibliographic information on any books, paying attention to the condition of the dust jacket (or the covers on paperbacks). On other items, indicate whether you have the original packaging for the item or not, and if you do, describe its condition as well as that of the item itself. **He does not want** *Saturday Evening Post, Life* or *Look* magazines. Neither does he want *Signet* paperbacks after 1961 or U.S. Book Club editions.
    Gary Pimenta
    64 Lakeside Dr.
    Tiverton, RI 02878

★ *Tarzan* and Edgar Rice Burroughs memorabilia including books, magazines, and collectibles. This enormous Library collection still seeks items, such as the 1915 edition of *Return of Tarzan* with a dust jacket for which they'll pay well over $1,000. Also seeking early Tarzan movies, foreign editions, Armed Services Editions and many smaller items associated with Burroughs or any of his characters. George advises, "Don't waste your time if your items aren't in fine to mint condition, including dust jackets." Please describe what you have carefully, give a guarantee, and tell what form you'd like payment.
    George McWhorter
    Burroughs Memorial Collection
    University of Louisville
    Louisville, KY 40292
    (502) 588-8729

★ *Tarzan* books, comics and memorabilia.
    Jim Gerlach
    2206 Greenbrier
    Irving, TX 75060
    (214) 790-0922

★ *Flintstones* and Bedrock. "Anything!" says this avid collector.
    Troy Holck
    16513 Horton
    Stilwell, KS 66085

★ *Peanuts* cartoon character toys and memorabilia of all types and characters including advertising, music boxes, ceramics, jewelry, etc., as long as it is marked "United Feature Syndicate" and in fine condition. Especially wants a musical ice bucket and the *Ansi* and *Schmidt* music boxes made of wood. Not interested in *Avon*, squeak toys, or other common items, though. A picture is appreciated. This top collector and author of the price guide to Peanuts collectibles (send her $12 if you want one) cautions that you not assume the © date is the date the item was produced.
    Andrea Podley
    Peanuts Collector Club
    539 Sudden Valley
    Bellingham, WA 98226

★ *Snoopy* and *Peanuts* toys and memorabilia such as ceramics, music boxes, advertising, pins, buttons, books, magazines, toys. Especially wants a *Snoopy Says* See and Say game, *Charlie Brown's Talking Book*, and wooden Snoopy music boxes, pianos, etc. Boxes are needed for many of his toys, so don't throw one away. All items *must* be marked United Features (UFS). Freddi co-authored the price guide to Peanuts collectibles, and says, about Peanuts character items, "If I don't have it, I want it."
    Freddi Margolin
    12 Lawrence Lane
    Bay Shore, NY 11706
    (516) 666-6861

★ *Uncle Wiggily* items including books, toys, Sunday comics, puzzles, mugs, dishes, games, and "all other memorabilia." Especially Uncle Wiggily's hollow stump bungalow and stand-up figures, *Put-Together* puzzles, Marx *Crazy Car* wind-up, and decorated tin Uncle Wiggily cup.
    Martin McCaw
    1124 School Avenue
    Walla Walla, WA 99362
    (509) 525-6257

★ *Uncle Wiggily* items including toys, paper dolls, 1st edition books, comics, dishes, etc.
    Audrey Buffington
    2 Old Farm Rd.
    Wayland, MA 01778

★ *Alice In Wonderland* **illustrated books and memorabilia** including films, figurines, tins, toys, games, puzzles, posters, greeting cards, dolls, etc. Especially wants a *Beswick* china figurine of the Cheshire Cat, but encourages all inquiries. Also wants other Lewis Carroll items, including **books, letters, and personal articles associated with Carroll.** No books published by *Whitman* or illustrated by John Tenniel but would love the Alice published by *Appleton* in 1866, at least $1,000 worth!
   Joel Birenbaum
   2486 Brunswick Circle, #A1
   Woodridge, IL 60517
      (312) 968-0664

★ *Alice In Wonderland* **memorabilia** including dolls, figurines, tins, cookie jars, coffee mugs, and "anything else." Especially editions of **books in obscure languages,** or editions with lesser known illustrators like Allen, Adams, Appleton, McEune, Norfield, or Sinclair. Alice encourages you to "quote all Alice items."
   Alice Berkey
   127 Alleyne Dr.
   Pittsburgh, PA 15215
      (412) 782-2686

★ *Smokey the Bear* **ephemera.**
   Thomas McKinnon
   PO Box 86
   Wagram, NC 28396

★ *Marx* **playsets and plastic figures** from the 1950's to early 1970's. These toys came with metal buildings and loads of plastic people and accessories. Desirable boxed sets include *Gunsmoke, Wells Fargo,* the Civil War, Disneyland, *The Untouchables,* Alaska, *Ben Hur, Johnny Ringo,* and the Revolutionary War among others. Some of these, if clean and complete in original box, can be worth several hundred dollars. Rare individual parts can sometimes be worth that much. Condition is extremely important. Figures (sizes 1" to 6") that were not sold in boxed sets are also wanted.
   David Welch
   PO Box 714
   Murphysboro, IL 62966
      (618) 687-2282

★ **Comic character children's lunch boxes,** both metal and vinyl, from 1970 or before. Must have pictures depicting space, cartoon, TV, sports, western, or other kid-related themes. Condition is very important. Boxes and bottles should look as if they were only slightly used, with no rust, bad rubbing, dents, serious scratches, or names written in marker on the outside of the box. Top boxes bring over $100.
   David Welch
   PO Box 714
   Murphysboro, IL 62966
      (618) 687-2282

Some "pop culture" toys can be surprisingly valuable, so don't set prices if you don't know what you're doing.

Games & Puzzles

★ **Card and board games.** A wide range of adult and children's games are wanted, especially games that are hand made, patriotic, or have unusual themes. Strategy games, domino sets, backgammon sets, cribbage boards, early *Monopoly* games, *Mah Jongg* sets, anagrams, and playing card packs, will all be considered, especially those that are in some way unusual. Pre-1946 items preferred. Best if complete with rules, all pieces, and original box. No *Pit, Rook, Authors, Flinch, Touring,* and other common card games.

Dave Galt
302 W 78th Street
New York, NY 10024
(212) 769-2514

★ **Antique and collectible board and card games** made in the U.S. from 1840-1960's. Any game before 1860 is wanted, especially those made by Ives, Crosby, Magnus, or Adams, for which they will pay $500 and up. Other items of particular interest are baseball games before WWI, and games about TV shows, cartoon characters, space exploration and pop culture (including movies) of the 1930-1970's. They also buy **wooden jigsaw puzzles, blocks, and paper toys.** No chess, checkers, *Pit, Lotto,* anagrams, *Rook, Flinch, Autobridge, Parcheesi, Touring,* variants of *Bingo,* TV "Game show" games, or "kiddie" games like *Chutes and Ladders.* Give name, condition, size, maker, copyright date, and the degree of completeness.

Dave Oglesby & Sue Stock
57 Lakeshore Dr.
Marlborough, MA 01752
(508) 481-1087

★ **Jigsaw puzzles and board games with space theme** are bought. Only wants items from before 1966 in excellent condition. Puzzles may be jigsaw or frame type. Will pay $50 for *Lost in Space* puzzle. Pop culture, not real life space themes are wanted. Also buys greeting cards and phono record sleeves with space theme. Does not want items made after 1966, nor does he want things related to the real moon landing.

Don Sheldon
PO Box 3313
Trenton, NJ 08619
(609) 588-5403

★ **Almost any complete playable game,** especially out-of-print titles by Avalon Hill, 3M, SPI, pre-1964 Parker Bros., war games, sports games, political games, and TV related games. Include the name of the manufacturer and copyright date. Please thoroughly check the contents and note whether *anything* is missing, and how much wear is evident on the box and pieces. **Also buys gaming magazines** such as *The General, The Wargamer, The Dragon,* and *Games & Puzzles.* Please, no checkers, chess, or common children's games like *Authors.*

H.M. Levy
Box 197CC
East Meadow, NY 11554
(516) 485-0877

★ **Chess sets.** "I'll buy rare and unusual chess sets of all sorts, but primarily those with *themes* such as Disney, Watergate, etc. Will buy historical, literary, fictional, mythological, geographical." If it's out of the ordinary in theme, design, material, or whatever, give him a call. He would especially like to find the 3-D chess set from *Star Trek* in the late 1960's. No plastic or "typical wooden sets," he warns, "I'm looking for works of art or imagination." Describe the board if one accompanies your set. Provide whatever background you can about the history of the board and pieces. Describe condition of both. Photo or Xerox© copy, please.

Dennis Horwitz
425 Short Trail
Topanga, CA 90290
(213) 455-4002

★ **Figural European chess sets** with playing pieces shaped like actual people or animals. Also antique chess boards. This 30 year veteran collector also wants porcelain or bronze figurines as well as paintings and other original **art depicting chess players.**

David Hafler
11 Merion Road
Merion Station, PA 19066
(215) 839-7171

★ **Games and puzzles** from 1920-1959 with sexy or sentimental themes such as pin-ups, children and animals, parents and children, patriotism, etc. Must be in the original box.

Charles Martignette
PO Box 293
Hallandale, FL 33009
(305) 454-3474

★ **Marbles and marble related toys.** Wants old marbles including clay, china and porcelain marbles decorated with flowers, people, animals or geometric designs. He also buys Indian swirls, German swirls, clam broth, sulfides and machine made marbles if before 1940. "I'll pay up to $2,000 for colored sulfide marbles with unusual objects or people in them and up to $1,000 for porcelain or china marbles decorated with flowers, ships, birds, or people and animals." He also wants, and will pay well for, early boxed sets of marbles made by Christensen Agate Co., Peltier Marble Co., or Akro Agate. Toys related to marbles are also often of interest. He does not want *Chinese Checker* marbles and boards or any cat's-eye marbles. If you know your marble's history, tell him. Otherwise a good description should include what is on or in the marble and its diameter.

    Edwin Snyder
    PO Box 156
    Lancaster, KY 40444
      (606) 792-4816 eves

★ **Marbles and marble related items.** "I'll buy marbles with pontil marks (from where they were made), toys and games using marbles, marble bags, tournament pins and medals, boxes of marbles, and pictures, magazine ads, and postcards which depict children playing marbles." He does not buy beat-up or chipped marbles, machine made marbles, homemade games, or *Chinese Checkers.* When selling marbles, give the diameter as part of your description.

    Larry Svacina
    2822 Tennyson
    Denver, CO 80212
      (303) 477-9203

★ **Better quality marbles.** Stan is publisher of *Marble Mania Quarterly* and will make offers.

    Stanley Block
    Box 51
    Trumbull, CT 06611
      (203) 261-3223

★ **Marbles and marble related ephemera.** Will buy postcards, magazine covers or ads, trade cards, stories or calendars..."anything depicting kids playing marbles."

    William Nielsen
    1379 Main Street
    Brewster, MA 02631
      (508) 896-7389

★ **Jigsaw puzzles.** "I'll buy wooden and die-cut cardboard jigsaw puzzles and related ephemera, catalogs, prints depicting puzzlers, company records, etc." Special interest in:

    [1] Mystery puzzles, but none by Springbok, American Publishing Company, or Bepuzzled;

    [2] Puzzles picturing WWII, patriotism, celebrities, or "characters" other than Disney;

    [3] Depression era weekly puzzles: *Duo Jig, Gelco, Every Week,* and similar;

    [4] Advertising between 1880 and today, but not interested in *Dif, Campfire Marshmallows, Chase & Sanborn, Cocomalt, Lux* or *Kellogg's.* Not interested in wooden puzzles by Victory or Joseph Straus. Send long SASE for specific wants list. To sell, tell him the manufacturer, the title, size, completeness, and condition of original packaging. "I pay one price if the puzzle is guaranteed complete and has the original box and a far different price if I am buying at risk." Price what you have. NO OFFERS.

    Harry L. Rinker, The Puzzle Pit
    5093 Vera Cruz Road
    Emmaus, PA 18049
      (215) 965-1122

★ **Checkers ephemera,** primarily books about checkers or draughts, but also early handmade boards or anything unusual related to checkers. Give standard bibliographic information, and Don would like you to Xerox© any advertising in the book.

    Don Deweber, Checker Book World
    3520 Hillcrest, #4
    Dubuque, IA 52001

★ *Mah Jongg* **sets, racks, and accessories,** pre-1930. Tiles may be made of bone, bamboo, celluloid, jade, or ivory. Especially interested in jade, ivory, gold, or fine inlaid tiles and boxes. Pays $500-$1,000 and up. Does not buy partial sets unless unusual. *Mah Jongg* is also called *Ma Chuck, Pung Chow, Sparrows, Game of China,* etc. Buys *Mah Jongg* books and magazines. Also **domino sets** made of ivory or ebony and **ebony** *Pai Gow* **games.** For his offer, mail him two typical tiles (insured), a count of how many pieces you have, and a list of other items.

    Joe Scales
    3827 Los Santos Dr.
    Cameron Park, CA 95682
      (916) 677-0262

*See also section on "Games and Puzzles"
in the chapter on paper.*

Banks

★ **Cast iron mechanical banks, 1870-1920, and Japanese tin battery operated banks, 1946-1960.** Include a bottom tracing. To sell a battery toy, indicate whether it works or not and if you still have the original box. Battery banks *must* be in near mint condition. No plastic banks.
Rick Mihlheim
Box 128
Allegan, MI 49010
(616) 673-4509

★ **Still banks made of cast iron or metal** with special emphasis on unusual or rare examples in excellent to near-mint condition. Letters should include an accurate description including an estimate of how much of the original paint is still there. Carefully measure the length, width, and height. Photos are appreciated. Private collector answers all letters which include SASE.
Ralph Berman
3524 Largo Lane
Annandale, VA 22003
(703) 560-5439

★ **Mechanical banks made of cast iron, tin, or wood.** Especially any mechanical bank with its original box, packing, and receipt. Also buys painted and stenciled cast iron or tin still banks shaped like buildings. Will consider incomplete and non-working specimens, if old and genuine. No banks made after 1940, including those which say BOOK OF KNOWLEDGE on the bottom. Also buys trade cards, catalogs, and other advertising depicting mechanical banks. Send sharp photos of the bank from different angles, or telephone with the item in front of you. Greg is the former president of the bank collectors' club.
Gregory "Dr. Z" Zemenick
1350 Kirts, #160
Troy, MI 48084
(313) 642-8129   or   (313) 244-9426

★ **Cast iron or tin banks, still or mechanical.** Also buys original boxes and color trade cards for mechanical banks. No banks after 1950. Indicate any repairs, repaints, and give the dimensions. Prefers you to set the price you want.
Virginia Jensen
c/o GI School
23270 E. River Rd.
Grosse Ile, MI 48138
(313) 561-9259 eves

Miscellaneous Toys

★ **Fine old kaleidoscopes** made of wood and/or brass especially elaborate inlaid or complex instruments from the mid 19th century. No cardboard toys.
Lucille Malitz
Lucid Antiques
Box KH
Scarsdale, NY 10583
(914) 636-3367

★ **High quality kaleidoscopes** from the 1800's, made of wood and/or brass by makers such as Bush, Brewster, Carpenter, or Leach. Prefer perfect original condition brass instruments in wooden cases with the Royal seal, but will consider less. He does not buy cardboard or other inexpensive kaleidoscopes. Nothing made in the 1900's. Include your phone number and time you're home so he can phone.
Martin Roenigk
Grand Illusions
26 Barton Hill
East Hampton, CT 06424
(203) 267-8682

★ **Polyramapanoptique and megalethescopes.** If you have to ask what they are, you probably don't have one. The former are early 19th century cardboard or wooden boxes with flaps for slides, which permit viewing of hand painted or pin-pricked scenes. Megalethescopes, invented in 1860, are large wooden cabinets, often heavily carved, also devices for slides, usually seen as day/night views of the same scene in 3D. Also wants slides for them.
Lucille Malitz
Lucid Antiques
Box KH
Scarsdale, NY 10583
(914) 636-3367

★ **Cast iron bell toys,** working or not. Will consider incomplete specimens of these early toys which move and ring a bell when pulled on a string. Send clear photos taken from more than one angle, or phone with the item in hand.
Gregory "Dr. Z" Zemenick
1350 Kirts, #160
Troy, MI 48084
(313) 642-8129   or   (313) 244-9426

★ **Collections of fine tin and iron toys** are sought for cataloged specialty auctions by this well known New England auctioneer. No junk, reproductions or items made after 1940.

James D. Julia Auctioneers
PO Box 80
Fairfield, ME 04937
(207) 453-7904   Fax (207) 453-2502

★ **Antique toys** of many different types:
[1] **Mechanical banks,** pre 1920, tin or iron;
[2] Cast iron **bell toys,** circa 1890;
[3] Figural clockwork toys, in tin or iron, from the 1870's;
[4] **Political campaign toys** and banks;
[5] European **tin toys** and large boats;
[6] Colorful paper on wood boats and trains from the 1890's;
[7] Colorful **Victorian children's games** and **block sets;**
[8] **Hand painted tin clockwork toys.**

Not interested in anything after 1940, nor does he want banks marked BOOK OF KNOWLEDGE, or repainted items, or things that have been dug up. Broken mechanical banks, or toys that are in-complete may still be of interest. Give the size, condition of the metal, condition of the paint including fading, list all repairs and note if the item has been lacquered or refinished. This 15 year veteran insists you set the price wanted.

Mark Suozzi
PO Box 102
Ashfield, MA 01330
(413) 628-3241

Some mechanical banks and toys sell for more than $1,000.

A little research before you price your toys may be worth a lot of money.

★ **Antique toys** in excellent condition, including cars, carousels, and character and comic wind-ups. German and American tin toys, penny toys, nested blocks, and pop-up books. No interest in dolls or trains. List manufacturer, size, and condition. Picture desirable.

James Conley
2758 Coventry Lane, NW
Canton, OH 44708
(216) 477-7725   (216) 499-9283

★ **Old one of a kind kites from before 1940** especially those made by important inventors. Names on desirable kites include *Hargrave, Lecornu, Saconney, Conyne, Perkins, Bell,* and many others including *Barrage Kite, Target Kite,* and the *U.S. Weather Bureau.* Also wants prototype models of production kites. Also traditional kites of Europe, the Orient, Malaysia, or South America. If it's old, interesting, or unusual, she'd like to hear about it. As publisher of *Kite Lines,* Valerie says she can act as a contact person to help you sell your kite if it's something she doesn't want. Rare and important kites are scarce but the market is small. They bring from $100 to $500. Give the history of your kite if you can.

Valerie Govig
Kite Lines
Box 446
Randallstown, MD 21133
(301) 922-1212

★ **Early miniature outboard marine motors** used on model boats. Wants fuel type motors only. No electrics. Condition should be described carefully.

Sven Stau
Box 437
Buffalo, NY 14212
(716) 825-5448   or   (716) 822-3120

★ **Toy outboard motors,** either battery or wind up, alone or mounted on toy boats. "I'll buy motors by *K&O Fleetline* between 1952-1962 with names of popular manufacturers of real outboard motors." Will pay $75-$400 for your toy depending on the model. Describe decals and color.

Jack Browning
214 16th St. NW
Roanoke, VA 24017
(703) 890-5083 eves

★ **Toys run by live steam or hot air.** Also wants accessories and catalogs related to steam and hot air toys. "I'll pay from $100 to several thousand dollars for steam engines, or for boats, trucks, automobiles, trains or tractors run by live steam, whether American, English or German made. Collectible makers include *Weeden, Buckman, Union, Bing, Marklin, Carette* and others. I don't want modern steam toys made by *Wilesco, Mamod,* or *Jansen.*" Give dimensions and markings. Some *Marklin* power plants were nearly four feet tall, and can be worth as much as $10,000. "Usually I require a photo or two before I buy, since most people do not understand the technical aspects of steam toys."
Lowell Wagner
5492 Feltl Road
Minnetonka, MN 55343
   (612) 442-4036 or (612) 933-2011

★ **Model airplane engines,** made between 1930-1955, that used a miniature spark plug (often a *Champion*). These engines also had a coil, condenser, batteries, and incorporate a movable timer for spark advancement. Later engines use a glow plug and do not require electrical support once running. "It is usually necessary to see the engine to assess its condition."
Bruce Pike
RD #1, Box 291, Lot 92
Aliquippa, PA 15001
   (412) 378-0449

★ **Any sand-operated self contained toys,** including the "not very old" enclosed boxes with figures set in motion by flipping over the box. Also **small toy scales** made of tin.
Donald Gorlick
Box 24541
Seattle, WA 98124
   (206) 824-0508

★ *Schoenhut* **circus animals, games and dolls.** "I'll pay $150+ for each glass eyed animal in original or near original condition. Also want circus wagons, tents, and comic characters, but no pianos."
Harry McKeon, Jr.
18 Rose Lane
Flourtown, PA 19031
   (215) 233-4094

★ **Yo-Yo items** including displays, boxes, pins, awards and patches.
John Fawcett
RR#2, 720 Middle Turnpike
Storrs, CT 06268

★ **Mechanical puzzles.** Wants all types of mechanical and dexterity puzzles. No jigsaw puzzles. Please send a Xerox©, sketch, or clear photo.
Cary Basse
6927 Forbes Ave.
Van Nuys, CA 91406
   (818) 781-4856

★ **Sets of early wooden 9 pins or 10 pins bowling games.**
Craig Dinner
Box 4399
Sunnyside, NY 11104
   (718) 729-3850

★ **Toys made by *Fisher-Price*. Also Raggedy Ann dolls.**
Pat Wagner
5492 Feltl Road
Minnetonka, MN 55343
   (612) 442-4036

★ *Erector* **sets** by A.C. Gilbert. Will buy complete sets, parts, manuals, signs, and sales catalogs. Give model numbers, dates, whenever possible.
Elmer Wagner
256 South Pitt St.
Carlisle, PA 17013
   (717) 243-3539

Toy Guns & Soldiers

★ *Quackenbush* air guns. Send a complete description, including a sketch or photo. Will make offers, but appraisals are for a fee.
Charles Best
6288 So. Pontiac
Englewood, CO 80111

★ BB Guns. Wants American made spring-air BB guns in excellent condition. Numerous brands are wanted, although *Daisy* guns are preferred from the Plymouth, MI, factory. Does not want recently made guns, or those that are damaged, broken or otherwise in less than very good condition. You must list **everything** that is broken or missing. Is the stock, forestock, or grip broken, cracked or worn? Describe the finish on all metal and wooden parts. Include **all** names, numbers and addresses found on the gun. Indicate whether it works or not.
James Buskirk
Toy Gun Collectors of America
312 Starling Way
Anaheim, CA 92807
(714) 998-9615

★ Cap pistols. Especially interested in cast iron guns by *Kilgore, Stevens, Hubley* and *Kenton*. Premium paid for character guns such as the *Kilgore Long Tom, Big Horn, Roy Rogers, Lone Ranger* or *American*, the *Kenton Lawmaker*, the *Stevens Cowboy King*, or any of the many different models of *Gene Autry* guns made by *Kenton*. Also interested in the 1950's and 60's diecast guns. Buys any guns marked *Gene Autry, Roy Rogers, Dale Evans, Trigger, Lone Ranger, Tonto, Paladin, Alan Ladd, HopalongCassidy, Hoppy*, or *Shane*. Particularly seeks character guns made in Los Angeles by the *Schmidt Company* or by *LATCO*. Must give all identifying marks, numbers, etc., found on the guns and a complete accounting of damage or wear to the gun, finish, or handles (grips). Buys only guns in fine condition. Publishes the Toy Gun Collectors Newsletter.
James Buskirk
Toy Gun Collectors of America
312 Starling Way
Anaheim, CA 92807
(714) 998-9615

★ Cap pistols. "I'll buy cap guns, holsters and related items in good condition. I collect Western cap guns, and am not looking for new guns mint in their boxes, but rather for guns that have been played with but still work and look good. Price what you have or request my offer." Give material, maker, length, model number, of guns you'd like to sell. Welcomes letters from other collectors, as he buys, trades, and sells, and issues frequent catalogs, free if you send a long SASE.
Mark King
1504 Helena
Gallup, NM 878301

★ Toy soldiers.
Lt. Col. Wilfred Baumann
PO Box 319
Esperance, NY 12066
(518) 875-6753

★ Cap pistols made of cast iron, especially animated guns from 1800's or guns featuring movie cowboys and other pop culture heroes before 1940. A magnet *must* stick to your gun or he's not interested.
George Fougere
67 East St.
North Grafton, MA 01536
(508) 839-2701

★ Repairable lead soldiers. "I'll buy them if you have the broken pieces and you set the price wanted."
Ken Cross
6003 Putnam Ave.
Ridgewood, NY 11385

★ Toy soldiers of all types including:
[1] Dime store soldiers, 1930-50, made in USA of painted (usually khaki) lead;
[2] German composition soldiers of WWII;
[3] Boxed sets of fine British soldiers.
Make photocopies of your soldiers if you'd like a free appraisal.
Larry Bruch
Box 121
Mountain Top, PA 18707
(717) 474-9202

Toy Vehicles

★ **Metal vehicles and toys,** pre-1959, including cars, trucks, airplanes, trains, boats, and construction equipment:
[1] **Large steel toys** by *Buddy-L, Sturditoy, Turner, Kingsbury, Sonny, Keystone,* and *Structo.* Will pay $800 for 14" *Ford Buddy-L* delivery truck;
[2] *Tootsietoys* with white rubber tires or all metal wheels, pre-1940;
[3] **Old tin toy boats,** the larger the better;
[4] **Children's pedal cars** and trucks made pre-1940;
[5] **Large steel** *Smith-Miller* or *M-I-C* **trucks** made in California 1945-57;
[6] **Tin windup automotive, aviation, or comic toys,** U.S. or European, working or not. Pays $2,500 for an 8" Aunt Eppie Hogg truck in perfect condition;
[7] **English and French** *Dinky* **toys,** pre-1964;
[8] **Any metal motorcycle** longer than 8", especially *Hubley Indian* delivery cycle worth $1,500 in original condition;
[9] **Japanese scale models of U.S. cars;**
[10] **Cast iron toys** by *Hubley, Arcade, Kilgore,* and *Williams.*
Plastic, rubber, or wood vehicles are not wanted.
Larry Bruch
Box 121
Mountaintop, PA 18707
(717) 474-9202 eves

★ **Metal vehicles** including:
[1] **Pedal cars** and other vehicles;
[2] **Large steel toys** by *Buddy-L, Turner, Sturditoy, Kingsbury, Sonny, Structo* and *Keystone*;
[3] **Small cast toys** by *Dinky, Tootsietoy, matchbox* and others;
[4] **Tin or steel toy boats;**
[5] **Steel toys** by *Tonka, MIC,* and others.
Also buys **plastic factory made dealer models** of new cars from the 1950's and 60's. Please send a photo and good description. He wants you to price. NO OFFERS.
Calvin Chaussee
1530 Kenland Ct.
Colorado Springs, CO 80915

★ **Larger pressed steel toy cars and trucks** are wanted by this ten year veteran collector-dealer. "I'll buy *Smith Miller, Doepke, Tonka, Buddy-L, Keystone, Arcade* and other makes of toy vehicle including construction types, boats, airplanes, and farm tractors." To sell your vehicles, tell him [1] the maker if you can, [2] what it looks like, including what type of vehicle it is, [3] how many you have, [4] and the condition of each. Make an estimate of what percentage of the original paint is left. "I prefer not to buy rusty or damaged vehicles, but this policy is not written in stone."
Jay "The Chicago Kid" Robinson
PO Box 529
Deerfield, IL 60015
(708) 945-8691 or 945-1965

★ **Pedal cars.** "I'll buy pedal cars made after WWII in excellent original condition, and pedal cars made before the war in any condition. I will pay over $1,000 for the better examples." This relatively new collector also will buy any pedal car advertising, sales catalogs, and the like as well as photos of kids with their pedal cars. He does not want pedal cars with plastic wheel covers and/or plastic steering wheels, as they are considered too new by collectors. The *one* exception to that rule is the *Ford Mustang* pedal car which he does want. Give the name of the manufacturer and the length of the vehicle. "I will not purchase or make offers without a good clear color photo of both sides."
Frank Martin
7669 Winterberry Drive
Youngstown, OH 44512
(216) 758-4470

★ **Hard rubber toy vehicles,** motorcycles, trains, airplanes, ships, animals, **soldiers,** football and baseball players, especially by Rainbow Rubber Co. Hard rubber toys only. No vinyl. Hard rubber is painted. Vinyl is made in the color of the toy and is the same color throughout. Give the maker, size, colors, condition, and description of features. Also buys **other pre-1950 toy vehicles of all sizes, from** *Dinky* **to pedal cars.** "Photos are best."
Steve Kelley
Box 695
Desert Hot Springs, CA 92240
(619) 329-3206

★ *Dinky* toys of all types except army vehicles. Also wants to buy all types of **toy motorcycles.**
   Don Schneider
   Box 1570
   Merritt, BC, V0K 2B0 Canada

★ **Toy motorcycles** made in the U.S., Japan, Germany, France, or England of tin, cast iron, hard plastic, or rubber that function by means of wind-up, friction, or batteries, especially by *I-Y*. Also other **vehicle and comic character toys** from Japan and Germany, especially *Lehmann.*
   Chris Savino
   Box 419
   Breesport, NY 14816
   (607) 739-3106

★ **Toy farm tractors and equipment** from 1970 or older. "I'll buy the ones with real farm equipment company names like *John Deere, Farmall, Oliver, Ford, Allis-Chalmers* and the like, in plastic or metal, and will pay over $100 for some tractors. A *John Deere* Model 430 is worth $750+ in its original box and an *Oliver* Super 55 is worth $500+ in its box. Also buys other scale model toys, like outboard motors, with tractor company names, and is interested in all scale *Caterpillar* **tractor and heavy equipment toys.** Does not want repros or anything made after 1975. Give the color, size, brand, model, condition, and status of original box.
   Dave Nolt
   PO Box 553
   Gap, PA 17527
   (717) 768-3554

★ **Model race cars from the 1940's,** that ran with model airplane engines. These engines used a miniature spark plug (often a *Champion*), and had a coil, condenser, batteries, and incorporate a movable timer for spark advancement. Later engines use a glow plug and do not require electrical support once running. The cars were operated with hand held wires. Describe the car and its condition, including ercentage of original paint. Indicate the brand name of the engine and whether it is complete. "It is usually necessary to see a car to assess its condition."
   Bruce Pike
   RD #1, Box 291, Lot 92
   Aliquippa, PA 15001
   (412) 378-0449

★ **Gas powered toy cars.**
   Johnny Henard
   820 Avery Dale Drive
   Pacific, MO 63069

★ *Aurora* and *AFX* **electric race cars**, track, and accessories made after 1968.
   T. Pat Jacobsen
   437 Minton Court
   Pleasant Hill, CA 94523
   (415) 930-8531

★ *Atlas* and *Aurora* **electric race cars.** "No limit," he says, but emphasizes he wants to buy "complete collections." Like other pop culture collectors and dealers, he particularly wants items in complete sets and original boxes. Would love to find store displays and stock, but "will consider any *Atlas* and *Aurora* electric race cars you have." Photos are requested, but for large collections, phone him. "I also collect colorful **hockey related games,** preferably complete in original box, but will consider incomplete sets if the boxes are good."
   Joe Bodnarchuk
   62 McKinley Ave
   Kenmore, NY 14217
   (716) 873-0264 phone or fax

★ **Toy firetrucks and fire related toys.** This veteran collector/dealer wants U.S. made fire toys made prior to 1960. Buys all types, all sizes, all styles as long as they are in good condition. Is particularly interested in finding *Ahrens Fox* and *Bulldog Macks* and other large steel firetruck toys, some of which can be worth $700 or more. Buys toy fire stations, firemen, and other toys and games that are fire related. Requests color photos, the price you'd like, and a statement of condition. Include your phone number. Will assist amateurs to set price. No Japanese tin toys or anything made after 1965.
   Luke Casbar
   Toys for Boys
   22 Garden St.,
   Lodi, NJ 07644
   (201) 478-5535

Plastic Model Kits

★ **Plastic model kits** especially from the 1950's made by *Aurora, Bachman, Comet, Hawk, ITC, Frog, Allyn, Monogram, Revell, Strombecker,* and others. Models can be airliners, commercial ships, space, science fiction, TV, movie subjects, cars, and figures. Also manufacturers catalogs and store display models. Kits must be complete and unbuilt, with minimal damage to the box. Sealed unopened kits are best. He offers to send a copy of the grading system used by kit collectors for an SASE. He'll pay $100 for a perfect condition *Athearn* gas-powered flying model of the *Convair* XFY-1 Pogo. Bob publishes *Vintage Plastic,* the journal for kit collectors and produces *The Model Club,* a public access TV show on model building.
Bob Keller's Starline Hobbies
Box 38
Stanton, CA 90680
(714) 826-5218 days

★ **Plastic model kits** of airplanes, tanks, ships, figures, cars, buildings, or what have you *if complete, unbuilt, and in original box.* Include the manufacturer and kit number. John publishes *Kit Collector's Clearinghouse,* a bimonthly newsletter for kit collectors and is the author of *Value Guide for Scale Model Plastic Kits,* available for $30, and other model books.
John Burns
3213 Hardy Dr.
Edmond, OK 73013

★ **Plastic model car kits depicting antique cars.** Unbuilt kits from before 1970 only, please.
Henry Winningham
3205 S. Morgan St.
Chicago, IL 60608
(312) 847-1672

★ **Plastic 1/25th scale model car kits,** built or not. Also buys dealer promotional materials, model car books and magazines, if issued before 1975. Does not want anything currently available. Give the name of the maker and the model number on the box. If you have **dealer promotional models,** give the color, condition, and note whether the original box is present.
Rick Hanson
PO Box 161
Newark, IL 60541
(815) 695-5135

Electric Trains

★ **All types of old electric trains** including *Lionel, American Flyer, Ives, Marklin, Bing, Carette, Howard,* and other U.S. and foreign brands in "any amount, any condition, working or not." Is particularly interested in *Lionel* trains from the 40's and 50's, especially the pink *Lionel* trains made for girls. Give the number on the body of the engine, the color of the engines and cars, the condition, and whether or not you have the box. "I would be glad to help anybody interested in the hobby of collecting old toy trains."
Tom Ryan
234-04 Bay Ave.
Douglaston, NY 11363
(718) 423-3732

★ **Toy trains and accessories, U.S. or foreign, made between 1900 and 1970.** Will buy any maker and gauge except HO gauge trains. Items do not have to be in perfect condition to be considered. **Also buys train literature.** A wind-up *American Flyer* train with cars marked *Coca-Cola* is worth $350 in mint condition.This 40 year veteran will make offers only if you're serious about selling. Lazarus is past president of the Toy Train Operating Society and publisher of its attractive monthly newsletter. He will accept donations for the Society's exhibit at the California State Railroad Museum in Sacramento.
Hillel Don Lazarus
14547 Titus St., #207
Panorama City, CA 91402
(818) 762-3652 eves

★ **All makes of old toy trains except HO gauge and hand made scale models.** Buys Lionel, *American Flyer, Ives, Marx* and all foreign trains larger than HO. "I'll buy engines, cars, accessories, signals, and incomplete sets that are new, like new, used, and even incomplete but useful for parts, but no layouts, transformers, track, rusty junk, or other toys. This 37 year veteran hobby shop operator offers a very large price guide to trains for only $6.
Allison Cox
18025 8th Ave., N.W.
Seattle, WA 98177
(206) 546-2230

★ *Marklin* and other European toy trains and metal toys. Trains can be powered by clockwork, electricity, or live steam. Other *Marklin* toys (airplanes, boats, circus toys, and many others) were usually clockwork or live steam. The name *Marklin* appears on many; others are marked with an entwined GM. "I want anything by *Marklin* before 1950 in decent condition." Also want *Bing, Schuco, Carlyle & Finch, Carette,* and *Bassett-Lowke* trains and metal toys in very good or better condition. *Marklin* trains from the 1930's are worth from $500 to $10,000 to Ron so check carefully. "I will buy common items in excellent condition, but don't want repros, fakes, or toys with pieces missing. I'm a collector so prefer people not contact me unless they actually want to sell or trade what they have. I pay fair prices and am willing to travel to inspect collections."
Ron Wiener
Packard Bldg #1200
111 S. 15th St.
Philadelphia, PA 19102
(215) 977-2266

If toy trains interest you, join the Toy Train Operating Society.

Their Bulletin is one of the truly fine club publications.

For information write:

25 W. Walnut St., #408 Pasadena, CA 91103

★ Toy trains in all gauges and types are wanted, including electric, wind-up, floor type, etc. "Age is not the main consideration, but I want items from before World War II." I like to buy large collections, but will buy smaller units, and consider properly priced junkers, but no reproductions." Wants to know the train's gauge, maker, condition, the number of pieces and the markings on each, and whether the original boxes are there.
Jay "The Chicago Kid" Robinson
PO Box 529
Deerfield, IL 60015
(708) 945-8691 and (708) 945-1965

★ HO trains and accessories, preferably in running order, but they "don't have to be old." he says. He also buys HO railroad books and magazines.
Cliff Robnett
7804 NW 27th
Bethany, OK 73008
(405) 787-6703

★ Trains and other vehicles. Will offer on trains in any gauge, especially HO, standard, and O. Also any fine old toys, but especially steam engines, tin plate toys, and airplanes. Color photo is a must to sell to this long time dealer.
Heinz Mueller
Continental Hobby
Box 193
Sheboygan, WI 53082
(414) 693-3371

★ Electric trains by *Marx* with metal or plastic cars that have eight wheels. Especially wants complete sets in original boxes. "I'll pay $100 for *Marx* Pennsylvania RR car #53941. I also buy *American Flyer* standard (large) gauge freight cars, and prewar *American Flyer* three-rail trains and sets (1938-1942). Not interested in plastic engines numbered #400 or #490 or cars with only four wheels." When writing, give him all numbers you find on boxes or cars.
Robert Owen
Box 204
Fairborn, OH 45324

dolls and teddys

Modern plastic dolls can be worth $100+

while high quality mechanical dolls, French fashion dolls, and a few others can be worth $10,000. A half billion dollars were spent last year on second hand dolls.

Because valuable modern dolls are found all over the country, we have included new buyers and more information to help you make money.

Doll buyers want to know different things, depending on the doll. Buyers of most dolls want info like this:

[1] Length of the doll, and on older dolls, how big around the head is;

[2] Material from which the head, hair, hands, feet and body are made;

[3] Type and color of eyes (painted, button, glass) and whether they move;

[4] Whether the mouth is open and whether teeth (molded, painted, or attached) show;

[5] Marks incised into the scalp, neck, shoulders, or back of the doll;

[6] How the doll is dressed and whether the clothes seem to be original;

[7] Any chips, cracks, repainting, or other repairs;

[8] History of your doll.

A photo can be helpful, but you can often get better results faster, easier, and cheaper with a Xerox© machine.

Many fine books on dolls can help you identify your doll. You can get these through your public library. Ask the help of the reference librarian for "interloan" if you can't find one.

tony hyman

Dolls

★ **Antique and collectible dolls, primarily those with china heads.** "We are constantly looking for fine **antique** and older dolls for auction. If you are considering liquidating all or part of your collection, we can be of assistance. We are happy to visit with you to discuss packing, pricing, shipping, and selling dolls. We know how to make the sale easy, comfortable, private, and profitable for you." There is no obligation and all inquiries are handled personally and confidentially by Barbara. She does not want modern dolls made after 1940, broken dolls, plastic dolls, Japanese dolls, or other junk. Don't bother this lovely lady by fishing for free appraisals. Contact her when you're ready to sell.
　　Barbara Frasher's Doll Auctions
　　RD #1 Box 142
　　Oak Grove, MO 64075
　　　　(816) 625-3786

★ **Collections of early china headed dolls** are sought for cataloged specialty auctions by this well known New England auctioneer. No junk, reproductions, or dolls made after 1940.
　　James D. Julia Auctioneers
　　PO Box 80
　　Fairfield, ME 04937
　　　　(207) 453-7904　Fax (207) 453-2502

★ **Old dolls and their parts.** "I buy, both as a collector and as a dealer, a large variety of old dolls and their parts. I will also buy any **damaged dolls** if priced reasonably. I'm always looking for **accessories for old dolls,** such as shoes, clothing, wigs, purses, **doll carriages,** etc. I'm interested in old wooden creche-type jointed dolls for display at Christmas. Also any **cloth comic characters** such as Lulu, Tubby, Alvin, Nancy, or Sluggo and *old* Raggedy Ann or Andy dolls. I am most interested in adding to my collection of old German dolls, bisque snowbabies, and **Buster Brown china dishes** but I have no interest at all in Japanese bisque or currently made dolls."
　　Patricia Snyder
　　My Dear Dolly
　　Box 303
　　Sparta, NJ 07871
　　　　(201) 729-8087

★ **Dolls and doll accessories.** This doll museum owner buys better and unusual dolls, both antique and modern. Also buys old cotton lace, costumes, trim and material for dressing old dolls. Also wants doll props like shoes, purses, combs, opera glasses, **furniture, buggies,** etc.
　　Madalaine Selfridge
　　Forgotten Magic
　　33710 Almond St.
　　Lake Elsinore, CA 92330
　　　　(714) 674-9221

★ **Dolls, doll parts, and doll clothes.** Buys old bisque and china heads, old bodies, baby gowns, slips, bonnets, etc. "No bids. You must price."
　　Annie Nalewak, Shop 4
　　5515 So. Loop, East Crestmont
　　Houston, TX 77033

★ **Realistic ethnic costume dolls,** 6"-14" tall, with nicely sculpted adult faces only. Faces may be composition, clay, wax, or wood but bodies can be of any materials. Asian, Mid-Eastern, and Eastern European dolls *only*, especially representing peasants, dancers, musicians, and theatrical characters such as Japanese Kabuki dolls. No baby dolls, cute dolls, homemade dolls, or dolls from Western Europe, tropical Africa, or South America. Whether old or new, high quality is a must. If you wish to sell to her, a photograph is essential. Pays $50-$200.
　　Karen Kuykendall
　　Box 845
　　Casa Grande, AZ 85222
　　　　(602) 836-2066

★ **Chinese Door of Hope dolls** sold by Christian missionaries to raise funds between 1909 and 1947. **Also china or bisque headed dolls** made before 1925. Will buy doll parts, bodies, heads, and old clothes. NO OFFERS.
　　Marjorie Gewalt
　　94 E. Parkfield Ct.
　　Racine WI 53402
　　　　(414) 639-2346

★ *Skookum* **Indian dolls.** If you own an Indian doll wearing a colorful Indian pattern blanket, chances are it's a *Skookum*, and he buy perfect examples from the smallest sizes up to those five feet tall. Some dolls marked SKOOKUM and/or BULLY GOOD on the underside of the feet. He does not want *Skookums* with plastic parts. Please send a photo for offer.

Barry Friedman
22725 Garzota Drive
Valencia, CA 91355
 (805) 296-2318

★ *Vogue Ginny* **dolls** are among many sought by this active dealer. She also buys *Kathe Kruse, Chase, Madame Alexanders, Izannah Walker,* and *Steiff* character and animal dolls. She also buys **early cloth dolls,** and will consider a wide range of good looking fine condition dolls in papier mache, wood, china, or bisque, including expensive French fashion dolls, character dolls, and what have you. Also has some interest in **doll houses, and teddy bears** as well. Describe what you have thoroughly.

Valerie Makseyn
61 6th St.
Cambridge, MA 02141
 (617) 576-0796

★ **Doll houses and miniatures,** especially Schoenhut and Bliss houses for which he will pay $500-$1,500. "We are one of the oldest and most experienced companies in the dollhouse and miniatures industry," Bob says, "and we will consider buying anything in miniatures that is old and in good condition." Their catalog of new doll house parts is fascinating, and well worth the $5.50 charge!

Robert Dankanics
The Dollhouse Factory
Box 456
Lebanon, NJ 08833
 (908) 236-6404

★ **Doll houses and furniture circa 1900,** but *only* wooden houses covered with colorfully lithographed paper. Especially wants houses made by *Bliss*.

Jerry Phelps
6013 Innes Trace Rd.
Louisville, KY 40222

Teddy Bears

★ **Teddy bears that are fully jointed with glass or shoebutton eyes.** Wants pre-1920 Steiff bears in any condition and will pay $1,000+ for those larger than 20" long. Not interested in any non-jointed bears or bears made after 1940. Also Teddy Bear books, postcards, photos, trays, etc. Polly also buys **stuffed animal toys on cast iron wheels.**

Polly Zarneski
5803 N. Fleming
Spokane, WA 99205
 (509) 327-7622

★ **Mohair teddy bears with long arms and big feet** made between 1903-1915 are wanted in all sizes as long as they are fully jointed. Also wants perfume and compact bears in various colors and any unusual mohair teddy or teddy related items. Also looking for early **Steiff cats and dogs** with printed ear buttons. Also wants **Billy Possum stuffed dolls with shoebutton eyes,** President Taft's answer to Roosevelt's Teddies. All Billy Possum related items are also wanted including doll dishes and silverware, banks, and postcards. Mimi wants us to assure you that your dolls are going to a "loving home, not a dealer."

Mimi Hiscox
12291 St. Mark
Garden Grove, CA 92645
 (213) 598-5450

Special feature
Modern dolls
for play
and show

*This special bonus feature
is provided because
so many of our readers
have these dolls.
We hope the extra detail
makes you money.*

★ *Barbie* **dolls.** Wants to buy all *Barbie* dolls, fashions and accessories, 1958-1972. "Anything *Barbie* related," she says, especially prototypes, gift sets, lunch boxes, watches, ponytails, color magics, *American Girls*, and the rest of *Barbie*'s family, including Ken (introduced in 1961), Midge (1963), Rickey (1963), Skooter (1963), Skipper (1963), Allan (1965), Julie (1966), Tutti, Todd, Stacey, Casey, Francie, Twiggy, etc.). Watch for Christie, the Black *Barbie*, among many others.

Will pay $1,000 for a mint in box airplane and $500 for a MIB *Barbie* boat. She does buy porcelain and international *Barbies* too. It's worth your time to look for early *Barbie* dolls, especially for clothes and accessories in original boxes, because some were made for a very short time, or sold in very limited markets.

Some inside tips: Sleep eyes were introduced in 1964. If the knees bend, the doll was made after 1965. Rooted eyelashes come into use in 1966, talking *Barbie* family in 1968. The dolls that are easy to pose, and those with growing hair are both products of the 1970's, and too late to interest most *Barbie* collectors.

To describe a *Barbie*, you must give the name of the doll, hair color, lip color and condition. "Please," she asks, "do not send or write about *Barbies* because they say 1966 on their back. Today's dolls still say 1966 on them."

Marl offers an important clue about how to tell if your *Barbie* is old. "If it does not say JAPAN on the buttocks, I don't want it. Today's dolls say HONG-KONG, MALAYSIA, PHILLIPINES, OR TAIWAN on their behinds. Even CANADA turns up on a few dolls."

Marl buys dolls for her personal collection and for resale.

Marl Davidson, IBTT
5707 39th Street Circle E.
Bradenton, FL 34203
   (813) 751-6275

★ *Annalee Dolls*. Wants 1950's, 60's and 70's versions of these modern felt dolls with painted faces, most of which have internal wires for positioning arms and legs. All types considered, including human, animal, and holiday, especially those with embroidered tags.

Tags, more than copyright dates, are indicators of when a doll was made, although early dolls didn't always have tags, and doll owners often cut them off. Dating dolls by their tags is a job for experts, and never foolproof, as many different tags appear on the oldest dolls.

Some *Annalee Dolls* were custom made, some limited production, and others factory made in fairly large quantities, so in most cases Sue will need to talk to you or inspect the doll before giving an offer.

If you are certain your doll was made between 1950 and 1975 and not later, you may ship it for a check, but only if certain. Dolls tend to be worth $20 to $150 with a few very special ones worth more. "I'll analyze your doll and will always give you a fair price." Pictures are helpful, but "I need to know what the doll is (human or animal) and what it's doing and how it's dressed. I also need to know the height of the doll, as they come in many different sizes. Condition is important in determining price. If you think you have an early *Annalee Doll*, I'd really like you to call with the doll in front of you. Before you call, please make a careful inspection for moth and silverfish damage in the form of holes, pock-marks, etc., and for any signs of fading in the doll or costume. Also I want to know if there is evidence of glue on either of the doll's hands"

Sue is willing to train pickers who regularly shop at yard sales and flea markets.

Sue Coffee
10 Saunders Hollow Rd.
Old Lyme, CT 06371
  (203) 434-5641

★ *Cabbage Patch Kids*. There is not much premium paid for *Cabbage Patch* dolls; most sell slightly above or below their original issue price. A few rare dolls can bring $150 and up. Identifying them can be tricky and not for amateurs. To discover whether you have a rare doll means providing a great deal of information:

[1] Head mold number (from 1 to 45) impressed on the back of the neck; some dolls don't have a mold number;

[2] Hair style and color; colors are generally beige (champaign or wheat), lemon yellow blond, gold or mustard, red orange, dark brown, and rust red brown;

[3] Eye color;

[4] Whether or not is has freckles;

[5] Pull down the diaper and find the body tag, usually stitched into the doll's lower left hip; in a circle on that tag is a letter or combination of letters (UT/P/OK/PMI/IC/KT are typical) that tells what factory made the doll; you must include this information when you write;

[6] On the lower buttock is usually found a signature and sometimes a very tiny date; give the color of the signature (black, forest green, turquoise, etc.) and the date if you can read it;

[7] With the above info, send a color picture.

None of these characteristics by itself means a doll is rare; it is the combination of particular sex, hair color and style, eyes, mold number, factory mark, freckles, signature color, etc., that makes a doll desirable. Sometimes an outfit can be worth more than the doll if it is a rare or hard-to-find outfit on a mundane doll. A good many cabbage patchers are not "box fanatics" and do not believe that the box adds any value. If you're unwilling to take your doll out of the box, then you can't give the information needed (you can open the box from the end and untwist the wire holding the doll in place).

BJ, who writes a fun monthly column on *Cabbage Patch* dolls for *Collector's Companion & Exchange*, is not a buyer of them except for a select few for her own collection, but can in many cases refer you to someone who is *if you provide sufficient information and include a stamped self addressed envelope.*

B.J. Resue
130 Lori Lane
Broomall, PA 19008

★ *Nancy Ann Storybook Dolls* were created by movie actress Nancy Ann Abbott, who began by dressing dolls in movie costumes for her co-stars in the mid 1930's. These early dolls were bisque (unglazed china) dolls made in Japan, adorned with her fancy clothes, and usually marked with a sticker that said "Nancy Ann Dressed Doll."

Early dolls are marked JAPAN 1146 or 1148. Other companies used the same same doll so it's the outfit that distinguishes a Nancy Ann doll.

Demand increased to the point where she began selling them commercially, hiring out costume making as a cottage industry. With perfect timing, she moved the company to San Francisco just before WWII and began manufacturing her own dolls, as she felt the Japanese dolls were "of increasingly poor quality." These too were china, with movable arms and legs.

In 1941-42 she switched from a round sticker to a gold foil bracelet with the name of the doll on one side and the company name on the other.

Baby dolls and *Story Book Dolls* ranged from 3.5" to 7" high. Eventually, the clothes became all factory made. In 1942 she began using a new doll mold with what collectors call "frozen legs." The arms remained movable.

For a while in the mid to late 1940's, *Nancy Anns* were every little girl's dream birthday and Christmas gift, dressed in frilly dresses with lots of imported lace. They were the number one seller in the girls' toy market, and produced in very large quantities.

After the baby dolls she did a series on nursery rhyme characters. The popularity of this series led her to create many more. Variations include a short lived series of dolls of the month with a "socket head." In 1947 they introduced plastic arms while she used up supplies of bisque bodies, then converted to all plastic bodies, the earliest of which were painted to look like bisque.

In 1949, a doll was introduced with an opening and shutting eye, instead of painted, and in 1953 their eyes were changed from black to blue. At that time the back markings changed and TRADE MARK REG was added to STORY BOOK DOLL USA embossed in the plastic.

Many different series were created, such as "Around the World," "Masquerade," "Sports," "Flowers," and others, as well as famous pairs like Hansel and Gretel, the Twin Sisters, and Jack and Jill, all of which are desirable.

Other series of dolls you may find include:

Nursery rhymes, days of the week, and months of the year, the most common of her dolls.
Margie Ann is same storybook doll but dressed as little girls in suits, etc.
Audrey Ann is one particular doll, a little larger than the others (5.75"), wearing an organdy dress and white boots. It's hard to find.
Geraldine Ann was a gift set, #400, based on her movie days. It came with eight outfits and a "movie set" with a director's chair, lights, etc. It is fragile and very desirable today.
Judy Ann was marketed for a while, but a copyright conflict prevented use of the name.
Dolls marked JUDY ANN/USA are very scarce.
Muffie and Debbie, 8" and 10" hard plastic dolls, were the tops of the line, and came with many matching outfits.

She made a great many other dolls too, and most are common. Values range from $20 to $175 with a few over $500. Dolls must be individually evaluated, however, because there are so many different costumes. One series of dolls named after the days of the week was sold for a dozen years, with new costumes each year. That's almost 100 different dolls in one series!

In general, the frozen leg and plastic dolls are less valuable, but there are collectors who are glad to find certain ones. Old or new style, there are few boy dolls, so they're usually desirable.

Nancy Ann factory made furniture is rare and desirable, and recognizable only by the fabric. The bed, sofa, chairs, bassinet, dressing table, ottoman and chaise lounge often bring $100+. Even the *McCalls* pattern (#811) for making the cardboard and cloth furniture at home can be worth a good $50+ to you!

All *Nancy Ann* dolls have a hat or ribbon in their hair. They must be original and complete. A missing hat reduces the value of a doll by more than half, and "you can't put just any old ribbon in the hair. Hers were special imports."

To sell a *Nancy Ann*, you must tell whether it's plastic or bisque, has moving or frozen legs, has eyes that move or not (and their color), and the height. Make a Xerox© copy of the doll which will show the dress. If you have the original box, please Xerox© that too, since some boxes are more valuable than others.

Elaine M. Pardee
PO Box 6108
Santa Rosa, CA 95406
    (707) 538-3655   Fax (707) 537-0604

★ **Modern collectible fashion dolls** including a range of scarce collectible modern dolls:

[1] *Nancy Ann Storybook Dolls,* particularly the Black *Nancy Ann Dolls,* Topsy and Mammy, and the brown skin *Nancy Anns* with Indian Sari clothes, in either bisque or plastic. Wants others as well, but notes, "Once *Nancy Anns* are played with, or the hair is messed up, or they're a little dirty, many collectors pass them up. At one time, this factory produced 8,000 dolls a day, so most *Nancy Anns* need to be in unused condition to interest collectors."

[2] *Miss Revlons* were fashion dolls made by Ideal Toy Company in the 1950's. "These were the modern woman of the 50's," complete with girdles and nylons, little high heels, and pierced ears with pearls.

[3] Ideal fashion dolls from the 1950's, such as *Miss Clairol, Toni* and *Bonnie Braids.*Ideal Toy Company dolls are usually marked on their head with the company name, the earliest with the name enclosed in a diamond.

[4] *Hollywood* **dolls,** in either bisque or hard plastic. "The costume's the thing," she says. During the 1940's and 50's, more *Hollywood* dolls were produced than any other company, but without their costumes, these are relatively undistinguished, and are modestly prices. They are often, but not always, marked HOLLYWOOD on their back, between their shoulder blades. Look for boxes covered with Hollywood stars as it's their most distinguishing characteristic.

If you have a perfect condition doll, especially one with its original box, give length, description, and tell whether clothes are original. A Xerox© is helpful.

Sharon Vohs-Mohammed
Box 2891
Glen Ellyn, IL 60138
   (708) 858-1852

★ *Renwal* **plastic dolls and furnitures.** They are hard plastic jointed dolls ranging in height from a few inches to a foot. They are embossed "Renwall USA" and a number. Also interested in other kinds of **hard plastic furnitures and dolls that were made by Ideal and Acme.** No foreign plastic furniture or anything with broken or missing parts or costume.

Judaline McNece
11270 Sirius Way
Mira Loma, CA 91752

★ *Madame Alexander* **dolls of the 1950's.** Beatrice Alexander began making dolls in 1923. Early dolls were cloth, then composition. In 1948 she adapted WWII plastic technology to make dolls that were both sturdy and beautiful. These uniquely 1950's Alexanders were made of hard plastic, jointed at neck, shoulders and hips, and often knees, elbows, and even ankles! In the early 1960's, these hard plastic dolls gave way to squeezable vinyl dolls with rooted hair.

Lia wants to buy **hard plastic dolls with wigs glued on,** as long as they are in good condition with original clothes. There are a few basic styles of hard plastic dolls she wants:

[1] Dolls that are 14", 18", 21" or 25" high;
[2] Any 8" dolls (called *Alexanderkins*);
[3] *Cissy,* a 21" fashion doll, and its 9" high counterpart, *Cissette;*
[4] *Lissy,* 11" tall, and 16" high *Elise.*

Wants all sizes, from 8" to 21", but they must be in good condition with original clothes. As with many other types of dolls, the costume makes the doll. The same doll might have 80 or more different costumes, and a variety of hair. "Some that don't look too exciting may actually be rare and valuable because they didn't sell and were only offered for a short time."

Many, but not all, *Madame Alexander* dolls are marked on the back of their head or across their shoulders.Marks include MME ALEXANDER, ALEXANDER, or ALEX. Other Alexander dolls were not marked, and only a tag attached to the clothing stated who or what the doll represented. The 1950's dolls she seeks were generally tagged and marked.

To sell your doll, give her the information on the clothing tag, a description of the costume, and a statement of condition. Note whether you have the original box. Have the doll in hand if you call.

Lia says, "I will consider older composition or cloth *Alexander* dolls, but only if in mint perfect condition. They don't have to be in the original box, but must be like new."

Lia Sargent
74 The Oaks
Roslyn Estates, NY 11576
   (800) 421-9912 Fax (516) 621-7517

entertainment

Nearly anything associated with entertainment is worth money.

Entertainment is another aspect of pop culture that's generally popular with collectors, who seek just about anything related to being entertained. That includes radio, television, movies, theater, music, sports, racing, drinking, gambling, carnivals, magic, fairs and expositions, and Disneyland. Even sex.

If you don't find a listing in the index for the entertainment related item you own, don't give up hope. Most pop culture dealers will buy entertainment items, so read their entries.

Though valuable movie memorabilia does continue to surface, most star photos and production stills from films are of limited value. Sadly, many of the movie star autographs and signed photos are not genuine, but signed by secretaries or machines. As a result, their signatures on hand written letters and on scripts are of much more interest. Turn to the section on autographs to find additional buyers.

Posters from popular stars and important or cult films can bring in the hundreds of dollars. Poster dealers buy movie posters too.

Follow general guidelines for describing, and whenever possible send Xerox© copies.

tony hyman

Movies

★ **Kinetoscopes and peep machines from old arcades and amusement parks.** He does not buy a great many machines, instead is selectively looking for a few fine examples with historical or intrinsic value. "Amateurs can't tell one machine from another. An expert should look at all old arcade machines." Pays $7,500 for an Edison Kinetoscope from 1894. He suggests you shoot a roll of high speed 35mm film, covering all aspects of whatever machine you might wish to sell. Send him the roll and he'll process it and reimburse you for your film. That's a good deal so it's not fair to waste his time with junk or late model machines. *"It is very important for me to know where you got your machine."* Richard is author of numerous books on slot machines, trade stimulators, pinball, and arcade machines and is historical editor of *The Coin Slot*, the quarterly magazine for people who collect coin operated machines.
   Richard Bueschel
   414 N. Prospect Manor Ave.
   Mt. Prospect, IL 60056
      (708) 253-0791

★ **Professional motion picture cameras from the silent era,** 1900-1927, especially with wooden bodies and hand cranks, although some desirable cameras have metal bodies and electric motors. They range in size from small hand held to as large as suitcases. When describing, pay particular attention to the size, finish, and whether the film magazine is square or round, inside or outside the camera. There are a number of cameras that can be worth more than $1,000 to him, including the Bell & Howell #2709 and machines by Mitchell or Gaumont. No home movie or 16mm. No motion picture projectors. Wes is a member of numerous clubs, and is publisher of *Sixteen Frames*, a quarterly bulletin for collectors of early cine equipment.
   Wes Lambert
   1568 Dapple Ave.
   Camarillo, CA 93010
      (805) 482-5331

★ **Anything depicting silent movie stars** including coming attraction slides, posters, lobby cards, figurines, sheet music, pin back buttons, paper dolls, plates, especially a Star Players photo plate of Bryant Washburn and anything featuring Our Gang or Jackie Coogan. Nothing from the talkies or from later stars. No autographs or photographs from any period.
   Richard Davis
   9500 Old Georgetown Rd.
   Bethesda, MD 20814
      (301) 530-5904

★ **Movie ephemera** including posters, lobby cards, **souvenir booklets**, and standees, both American and European. "I guarantee a fast decision and faster check."
   George Theofilies
   Miscellaneous Man
   Box 1776
   New Freedom, PA 17349
      (717) 235-4766 days; (717) 235-2853 fax

★ **Movie memorabilia,** including lobby cards (especially from B movies of the 30's, 40's, and 50's), theater souvenirs, tickets, programs, photos of theaters, coming attraction pamphlets, materials sent by studios to theater owners, etc. Also wants **trade magazines** such as *Motion Picture Herald, Box Office, Showmen's Trade Review, The Exhibitor*, and others aimed at theater owners and will buy them in any condition. This 20 year veteran collector generally does not buy items made after 1960.
   Chris Smith
   26 Ridge Ave.
   Aston, PA 19014
      (215) 485-0814

★ **Paper movie ephemera 1925-1950** including movie heralds, posters, sheet music, photographs, and studio disks of film music. **Studio disks** were 78rpm for studio use only. Also interested in movie magazines 1930-1944 and in trade journals sent to theater owners.
   Buddy McDaniel
   2802 West 18th St.
   Wichita, KS 67203
      (316) 942-3561

★ **Original studio production movie scripts** with original binders or covers when possible. Not interested in Xerox© copies, TV scripts, or unproduced scripts unless by very important writers. When describing your script, indicate whether it has its cover, what draft (or the date), whether all pages are present, whether there are notations, and the name of the author.
   Grayson Cook
   367 W. Avenue 42
   Los Angeles, CA 90065
      (213) 227-8899

★ **B Western cowboy star memorabilia** from Hopalong Cassidy, Tom Mix, Ken Maynard, Roy Rogers, Tex Ritter and especially Gene Autry. "I'll buy buttons, photos, games, toy guns, radio giveaways, autographs, and most anything else that has to do with these stars of yesteryear." Dennis is interested only in the ephemera of B westerns, not the epics. He has only minor interest in paper items, and does not buy "damaged or overpriced goods."
Dennis Schulte
8th Ave., NW
Waukon, IA 52172
    (319) 568-3628 before 10pm

★ *Gone With The Wind* **items** associated with the film, the book, or its author. Wants book and Mitchell related items 1936-1965, foreign language editions of the book, movie scripts, movie posters, banners, props from the film, and all the promotional items such as dolls, games, scarfs, book ends, figurines, jewelry, nail polish, paint books, paper dolls, and more. Nothing printed after 1965. Herb has joined the ranks of collectors who will no longer do free appraisals or make offers.
Herb Bridges
Box 192
Sharpsburg, GA 30277
    (404) 253-4934

★ *Gone With The Wind* **items** associated with the film or the book such as tickets, posters, autographed books, magazines, scarfs, buttons, handkerchiefs, candy boxes, dress patterns, hair nets, bow ties, lockets and you name it. "I'd love to find a ticket to the premier," he says. He expects you to price what you have. NO OFFERS.
Robert Buchanan
277 West 22nd St., #2B
New York, NY 10011
    (212) 989=3917

★ *Gone with the Wind* **memorabilia from 1939 only** including jewelry, games, posters, music, paper dolls, press books, and the like. No reproductions, story books, fakes, copies, or junk. NO OFFERS.
Frank Garcia
13701 SW 66th St., #B-301
Miami, FL 33183

★ *Wizard of Oz* **memorabilia** from 1900 to the present, with particular emphasis on the 1900-1939 period. Is especially interested in early 1939 movie items, especially the August 1939 *Movie Life*. Also pin back buttons picturing *Oz* characters. He requires sellers to price, but says "I am open to and willing to consider all offers." Like most collectors, he says, "I am very particular about condition," so make certain you describe it completely. Tell him how much you want for shipping as well. Remember to price your goods. NO OFFERS.
Jay Scarfone
6 Westmont
Hershey, PA 17033
    (717) 533-5806

★ **Cartoon posters from silent movies.** "I buy posters featuring cartoon characters like Felix the Cat, Out of the Inkwell, and other silents, but will consider other silent movie posters as well."
Richard Davis
9500 Old Georgetown Rd.
Bethesda, MD 20814
    (301) 530-5904

★ **Comedy movie posters (and a few others).** Dennis wants original posters from movies by The Marx Brothers, W.C. Fields, The Three Stooges, Laurel and Hardy, Buster Keaton, Charlie Chaplin, and Woody Allen. He **also** wants movie material from specific films: *Psycho, Bedtime for Bonzo, 2001: A Space Odyssey, Some Like It Hot, Midnight Cowboy, Clockwork Orange,* and *The Kid From Cleveland.* Prefers American posters but will consider foreign editions. When describing posters, mention [1] folds, tears, and stains, [2] whether rolled or linen backed, and [3] if it is an original release poster. Photo desirable.
Dennis Horwitz
425 Short Trail
Topanga, CA 90290
    (213) 455-4002

★ **Movie memorabilia** including autographs of stars, promotional stills, lobby cards, and posters. This dealer is **primarily interested in buying in bulk** rather than in buying single items from private parties, unless, of course, the items were unusually good. Everything is purchased for resale.
Ralph Bowman's Paper Gallery
5349 Wheaton St.
La Mesa, CA 91942
    (619) 462-6268

★ **Movie memorabilia.** Buys posters, lobby cards, pressbooks, heralds, fan photos and other memorabilia from 1898 to 1970. Also movie **magazines** before 1950. "Please let me know what you have and what you want for it, or just ship for my immediate offer."
Alan Levine
292 Glenwood Ave.
PO Box 1577
Bloomfield, NJ 07003
(201) 743-5288

★ **Movie memorabilia** 1920-59, including posters of all sizes, inserts, and lobby cards. Also wants movie autographs and magazines. Stars of particular interest include Jean Harlow, Marlene Dietrich, Bette Davis, Errol Flynn, James Cagney, Humphrey Bogart, James Dean, and Marilyn Monroe. Condition on all material is important. Seller must give phone number.
Gary Vaughn
Box 954
Clarksville, TN 37041
(615) 552-7852 eves

★ *101 Dalmations* related items such as games, etc. "A Xerox© copy would be nice. Describe condition honestly," and give the year you bought it, if you can remember.
Michael Dyer
230 Eldon Dr. N.W.
Warren, OH 44483

★ **Movie posters, lobby cards, and still photos** pre-1950 especially from major stars like Jean Harlow, Boris Karloff, Laurel and Hardy, etc. All types of films (comedies, Westerns, Scifi, etc.) are wanted. No reprints, reissues, or magazine ads. Will buy 1950's posters from Monroe, James Dean, and John Wayne movies only. Prefers to buy in quantity. Give title of movie, releasing company, major star, size, and condition of posters.
Gene Arnold
2234 South Blvd.
Houston, TX 77098
(713) 528-1880

★ **Shirley Temple memorabilia** especially sheet music and "unusual stuff" including paper dolls and jewelry. Pays $50 for early press books featuring Shirley.
Frank Garcia
13701 SW 66th St., #B-301
Miami, FL 33183

★ **8x10 studio glosses of sexy starlets** and actresses, 1920-1990.
Charles Martignette
PO Box 293
Hallandale, FL 33009
(305) 454-3474

★ **Jeanette MacDonald and Nelson Eddy memorabilia.** Wants scrapbooks and original material. Send description and asking price.
IBT Hanson
Box 1222
Edgewood, MD 21040

★ **Humphrey Bogart and Woody Allen memorabilia.** "I want anything of interest about these two personalities." Among special wants, he lists film or video copies of early Bogart films: *Broadway's Like That, A Devil with Women, Body and Soul, Bad Sister, A Holy Terror,* and *Women of all Nations.*
Dennis Horwitz
425 Short Trail
Topanga, CA 90290

★ **Three Stooges and other comedy team memorabilia.** Frank buys and sells.
Frank Reighter
10220 Calera Rd.
Philadelphia, PA 19114
(215) 637-5744

★ **Marilyn Monroe.** Wants "anything and everything" U.S. and foreign including lobby cards, press books, sound track albums, collector plates, dolls, and the like. Will buy magazines with Marilyn on the cover if they are uncut condition. He does not want scrapbooks, new posters, or new pictures. Xerox© copies helpful.
Clark Kidder
1582 West County Hwy "N"
Milton, WI 53563
(608) 868-2376

★ *Castle* **newsreels,** 1937-1975, sound or silent, 16mm or 8mm, as long as they are complete. No shortened 50' or 100' versions are wanted. Will also buy selected titles of *Castle* space and moon flight films, and 200' or longer 8mm comedies by Laurel and Hardy or Our Gang if made before 1935. Please list film number if possible.
Art Natale, Newsreels
278 North Eleventh St.
Prospect Park, NJ 07508

Amusements

★ **Carnegie Hall memorabilia.** Seeking relics of its own past, the Carnegie Hall Corporation wants especially to find programs and stagebills from 1892-98, 1929-31, and 1944-45. Also photos of the building in construction, or any interior shots of performers or speakers on stage. Also recordings, films, and posters of events as well as any administrative records of Hall history. Any type performances wanted.
   Gino Francesconi, Archivist
   Carnegie Hall Corporation
   881 Seventh Ave.
   New York, NY 10019
      (212) 903-9629

★ **Ferris Wheel memorabilia** related to the Columbian Expo (1893) and the St. Louis World's Fair (1904), including folders, guide books, photos of the wheel (even in the background), sheet music, drawings, newspaper or diary accounts of first time riders. He will pay $1,500 for blueprints of the wheel.
   Richard Bueschel
   414 N. Prospect Manor Ave.
   Mt. Prospect, IL 60056
      (708) 253-0791

★ **Amusement park memorabilia:** catalogs, brochures, photos, tickets, stationery, sheet music, letterheads, pennants, tokens, advertisements, books, postcards, and anything else.
   Jim Abbate
   1005 Hyde Park Lane
   Naperville, IL 60565

★ **Roller coaster and amusement park memorabilia** including official or amateur photos, prints, blueprints, postcards, souvenirs, home movies, and *anything* else, no matter how small or odd that is remotely related to roller coasters or amusement parks. This long time veteran collector has ridden 230 different roller coasters, once for 9 hours straight!
   Thomas Keefe
   Box 464
   Tinley Park, IL 60477

★ **Mardi Gras souvenirs, tokens, and other ephemera** are wanted, especially pre-1900 ball invitations and colorful Carnival Bulletins originally printed in local newspapers. Hardy and his wife are always looking for photographs, postcards, early magazine articles, and other items from before 1940 which they can reproduce in their annual *Mardi Gras Guide*. Please inquire about all illustrated items and this prominent New Orleans collector will help you with pricing.
   Arthur Hardy
   Box 19500
   New Orleans, LA 70179
      (504) 488-2326

★ **Disneyland and Disney World souvenirs.** Wants licensed, marked items only.
   Mike Dyer
   230 Eldon Dr. NW
   Warren, OH 44483

★ **Disneyland souvenirs.** Dean will buy all types including ceramic figurines, guidebooks, maps, buttons, pins, coins, postcards, employee materials,etc. Items should be marked 'Disneyland.' Also will buy *Disneykins,* tiny one to two inch high plastic figurines of Disney characters sold by *Marx* in the 1950's and 60's. Also will buy anything related to **Tinker Belle.** Special wants include Disneyland items from 1955-59, a Tinker Belle glow-in-the-dark wand, and Walt Disney's autograph. Everything must be in mint to near mint condition. Items may be sent on approval or described in writing if you want an offer. He edits a newsletter devoted to pin back Disney buttons.
   Dean Mancina
   Box 2274
   Seal Beach, CA 90740
      (310) 431-5671

★ **Minstrel memorabilia of all sorts.** "I'll buy playbills, autographs, letters written by minstrels, news clippings, postcards, posters, radio and TV programs, rare book and magazine articles, recordings, and miscellaneous artifacts. I'm particularly interested in Bert Williams, Al Jolson, Eddie Cantor, Sophie Tucker, and Jimmy Durante. Has a lengthy multi-part wants list which details books, TV shows, movies, phonograph records, and other items he seeks. If you have *anything* related to minstrels or minstrel shows, give Norm a call. Norm is a professional recreator of minstrel shows and serious researcher of that entertainment.
   Norman Conrad
   Box 184
   East Walpole, MA 02032
      (508) 668-6926 eves

★ **Harry Houdini memorabilia** including book, magazine and newspaper articles, photos, handbills, pamphlets, autographs, posters, personal apparatus and belongings. Anything relating to Houdini will probably be of interest. He especially wants to find a voice recording of Houdini or copies of any of his silent movies (including home movies) except *The Man From Beyond*. If you are offering personal apparatus or effects you must explain why you know it is from Houdini. You may price or he will make offer. Standard bibliographic information when offering books. Art is a 15 year veteran collector and happy to provide free appraisals and make offers.

Arthur Moses
3512 Wosley
Ft. Worth, TX 76133
    (817) 294-2494

★ **Magic apparatus of all sorts** including all paraphernalia and props, escape devices, tokens, programs, books, and other ephemera. Has a particular interest in pre-1900 posters, original photos of Houdini, and a complete set of Houdini letters, one on each of his twelve letterheads (worth $5,000 if you have it). A complete set of Thayer Manufacturing's wooden turned devices (1910-20) is worth $12,000 to some lucky seller. No items after 1950, newspaper clippings, radio premiums, or pulp books issued by Wehman Bros. An illustrated catalog of magic books and devices is available for $5 from this veteran collector dealer.

Mario Carrandi Jr.
122 Monroe Ave.
Belle Mead, NJ 08502
    (201) 874-0630

★ **Magic memorabilia.** "I'll buy old original magic posters and lithographs, old magic playbills, programs, old magicians photos, letters, autographs, old original magic books, old magic sets, and all advertising and promotional materials to do with magic and magicians. I am especially interested in any old **Houdini memorabilia** including original old posters, playbills, programs, photos, letters, etc." Your description should include the item's approximate age, and notation of any chips, tears, stains, foxing, or other damage.

Joseph Gargano
PO Box 170
124 N. Beverwyck Rd.
Lake Hiawatha, NJ 07034
    (201) 538-2501 eves

★ **Magic posters and memorabilia.**
Ken Trombly
5131 Massachusetts Ave.
Bethesda, MD 20816
    (202) 887-5000 days (301) 320-2360 eves

★ **Houdini memorabilia** of all types, including apparatus, posters, letters and books.
Joe and Pamela Tanner, Tanner Escapes
Box 349
Great Falls, MT 59403

★ **Theatrical lighting from the gas-light era.** "I'll buy anything you have dealing with theatrical lighting, particularly gas and limelighting. I want spotlights themselves, stage lights, footlights, parts, manuals, patents, manuals, and catalogs. I will even buy photocopies of documents related to the history of their development and use." A good description includes how complete the item is, any maker's information, and a good sketch or photo. No magic lantern or cinema projectors as a rule but Lindsay will buy projector literature that has information about limelight that he can use in his research. "I would be grateful if people set the price they want." Lindsay would pay as much as $400 for a perfect condition complete spotlight from the mid 1800's.

Lindsay Lambert
324-B Somerset St. West
Ottawa, Ontario K2P 0J9, Canada
    (613) 232-7797

★ **Theater programs and souvenirs** especially items related to an anniversary such as 50th performance, 100th performance, etc. Wants pre-1920 items mostly.
D. Eliot
400 W. 43rd St., #25T-CC
New York, NY 10036
    (212) 563-5444

★ **Theatrical memorabilia related to Charles Hoyt**, whose plays always started with "A" as in *A Rag Baby, A Midnight Bell*, etc. Will buy posters, playbills, souvenirs, etc., as well as theatrical magazines, 1884-1901.
Cliff Hoyt,
Box 3
Buckeyestown, MD 21717

★ **Circus ephemera.** "I'll buy anything directly related to circuses, especially Barnum & Bailey, but other tented shows as well. I want posters, programs, photos, route books, etc."
Al Mordas
66 Surrey Drive
Bristol, CT 06010

★ **Buffalo Bill's Wild West Show.** Wants all ephemera including programs, photos, business forms, advertising, pre-1918 clippings, and miscellany of all kinds. No books. Send Xerox©.
Melvin Schulte
211 Fourth Ave., SW
Pocahontas, IA 50574

★ **Carnival, motordrome, and amusement park ephemera** is sought. Will purchase posters, handbills, route arrows, ride catalogs, show and fair promotional material, letterhead, contracts, and "anything else." "I don't want circus material," he emphasizes.
David Gaylin,
Box 9686
Baltimore, MD 21237

★ **National Orange Show, San Bernardino, CA,** 1911-1920, souvenirs and paper ephemera.
Gary Crabtree
Box 3843
San Bernardino, CA 92413

★ **Chalk carnival prizes,** especially cartoon and movie characters or figures marked *Jenkins, Rainwater, Venice Dolls,* or *Gittins.* No animals except movie or comic characters. The earliest figures were not painted on the back and have a pink cast to the plaster. When describing what you have, mention whether or not is has glitter highlights. *The Carnival Chalk Prize,* a 250 page illustrated guidebook is available from him for $15.
Thomas Morris
PO Box 8307
Medford, OR 97504
(503) 779-3164

★ **Ventriloquist's dummies,** ephemera, photos and other items related to early ventriloquism.
Vent Haven Museum
33 West Maple Ave.
Ft. Mitchell, KY 41011
(606) 341-0461

World's Fair

★ **1851 Crystal Palace memorabilia** including books, engravings, stereo cards, photos, newspapers, tickets, guidebooks, awards, and various artifacts made of paper, glass, porcelain, metal, or something else. Ron wants **all material on the building's history (1851-1937),** but is especially interested in early years.
Ronald Lowden, Jr.
314 Chestnut Ave.
Narberth, PA 19072
(215) 667-0257

★ **International expositions and fairs, 1851-1940.** The library buys print and photographic materials including reports from various governmental and official bodies relating to the construction, exhibits, awards, and demolition of expositions. Also interested in letters, sheet music, tickets, passes, award medals, maps, and photos (both commercial and non commercial). The library does not collect exposition artifacts or souvenirs. "Purchase offers are made based on the value to the collection rather than on any other consideration."
Ron Mahoney, Head of Special Collections
Madden Library
Calif. State University
Fresno, CA 93740
(209) 294-2595

★ **Worlds fair ephemera from before 1935.** "I'll buy pre-1935 tickets, official and unofficial stationery, postcard sets, badges, pin back buttons, tokens, medals, elongated coins, toys, and souvenirs. Please write or ship for offer." Hartzog does not buy single items after 1935 except unusual items. Newer pieces are wanted only in large collections. Rich runs numerous auctions and invites your consignments.
Rich Hartzog
Box 4143 BID
Rockford, IL 61110
(815) 226-0771

★ **1895 Atlanta Cotton States Exposition** memorabilia, especially medals, tokens, and postcards. Also **agriculture medals from Georgia state fairs.**
R.W. Colbert
4156 Livsey Rd.
Tucker, GA 30084

★ **1876 Centennial** collectibles such as tokens, books, textiles, trade cards, tickets, posters, broadsides, pamphlets, medals, plates, and all other souvenirs of the exposition. Describe fully, noting all damage. Will make offers only on items he requests you send on approval.
    Russell Mascieri
    6 Florence Ave.
    Marlton, NJ 08053
       (609) 985-7711   fax (609) 985-8513

★ **1904 World's Fair in St. Louis** and other U.S. expositions from 1876 to 1939. Especially want *Ingersoll* souvenir watches, clocks, banks, lamps, steins, lithopanes, hold to light postcards, large china souvenirs picturing fair scenes, ribbons, badges from judges and officials, full sets of stereo cards, photographs, complete decks of playing cards, and much more. Only "very rare and unusual items" from fairs after 1939.
    Doug Woollard, Jr.
    11614 Old St. Charles Rd.
    Bridgeton, MO 63044
       (314) 739-4662

★ **Worlds fair ephemera from 1904 or before** including china, wood, metal, textiles, paper, souvenirs, and glass. "Any and all items from a Fair from 1851 to 1904 will be considered," although he has a particular interest in 1851, 1876, 1893, 1901, and 1904 fairs. A photo is requested, especially for any "high ticket" items, and he requests that you indicate your asking price, although he will make offers on items genuinely for sale.
    Andy Rudoff
    PO Box 111
    Oceanport, NJ 07757
       (908) 542-3712

★ **1907 Jamestown Exposition memorabilia** is sought, except for postcards.
    W.T. Atkinson, Jr.
    1217 Bayside Circle W.
    Wilmington, NC 28405

★ **1909 Alaska-Yukon-Pacific Exposition** in Seattle. "Postcards and memorabilia."
    W.E. Nickell
    102 People's Wharf
    Juneau, AK 99801
       (907) 586-1733

★ **World's fair and international exposition souvenirs** from all fairs, 1851-1964. Wants toys, china, women's items, buttons, advertising booklets, cloth items, celluloid, posters, and all other decorative items. Especially interested in toys, games, puzzles, dolls, building models, and other small playthings. Send description, including size, color, and condition along with your asking price. NO OFFERS. "Photo appreciated."
    Andy and Irene Kaufman
    PO Box 383
    Manchester, NH 03105
       (603) 622-7404

★ **Paper picturing the trylon and perisphere at the 1939-40 NY World's Fair** is sought by this major NY stamp dealer, in business for 50 years. Send a Xerox© of what you have.
    Harvey Dolin
    5 Beekman St. #406
    New York, NY 10038

★ **1964 New York World's Fair.** Especially want fabrics, jewelry, toys, and unusual items.
    Dave Oglesby
    57 Lakeshore Drive
    Marlborough, MA 01752

★ **Paper ephemera from any world's fair before WWII** including award and attendance certificates, honorable mention diplomas, passes, admission or concession tickets, invitations, stationery, employee badges, and playing cards.
    William Lipsky
    1800 Market St. #260
    San Francisco, CA 94102
       (415) 821-6017

★ **Atlanta Cotton States Exposition memorabilia**, including postcards and envelopes.
    Gordon Mc Henry
    Box 1117
    Osprey, FL 34229

★ **World's fair memorabilia suitable for resale or auction.** All fairs before 1940 are wanted, especially very early ones. Rex is one of the largest mail order dealer/ auctioneers in the country. He offers a large quarterly auction catalog, and constantly needs new items. No items under $20.
    Rex Stark, Americana
    49 Wethersfield Rd.
    Bellingham, MA 02019
       (508) 966-0994

TV sets and radios

Valuable radios are impossible for amateurs to recognize

so be very careful, as radios have become a hot collectible. Radios worth thousands of dollars are discarded by people who do not realize their value.

Buyers of radios and television sets like to know the maker, model name and number and its cosmetic condition. Describe whether it is scratched, faded, dented, chipped, cracked, or the paint or veneer is peeled, etc.

Do not test very old equipment. Plugging it in may cause damage because insulation around wires deteriorates, resulting in short circuits or fire.

Examine the chassis carefully for missing parts or damage. If the chassis has blank spots where a tube or component might have originally been, tell the potential buyer.

Radios and television sets are among those few collectible items that don't have to be in perfect condition to find a buyer. Certainly, the better the condition, the better the price, but scarce radios and television sets will find buyers in almost any condition, because parts are always in demand by people who enjoy rebuilding them.

Note that two of our buyers produce periodicals which contain advertising for radios.

tony hyman

Radios

★ **Radios of many types** including crystal sets, battery operated of the 1920's, wireless sets and parts, WWI military radios, unusual cathedral radios by *Grebe* or *Ozarka*, grandfather clock style, odd shapes, and all luxury models like *Zenith* Stratosphere (pays $6,000+). Other names and models to watch for are *Marconi*, *De Forest, Leutz, Wireless Specialty, EICO, Norden Hauck, E.H. Scott, Grebe*, and *RCA Radiolas* VI and VII. Also novelty radios like Snow White and the Seven Dwarfs, Peter Pan, or Mickey Mouse. In addition, he likes radio dealer indoor and outdoor **advertising signs,** point of purchase displays, brochures, instruction books, and service manuals. Not interested in plastic radios of any kind. Don is editor of the monthly *Radio Age* for collectors of vintage electronics. Don is a collector rather than a dealer but will consider large collections.
Donald Patterson
636 Cambridge Rd.
Augusta, GA 30909
(404) 738-7227

★ **Radios of many types 1905-40,** including crystal sets, wireless receivers and transmitters, battery operated radios 1914-1928, and small electric table models 1928-35. Buys radios in wood, metal, or plastic cabinets. Especially interested in large collections of usable speakers, **tubes and parts** for radios from this period. No large console models of the 30's except those with chrome plated interiors. Also radio **magazines, catalogs, service manuals, sales literature, and advertising,** pre 1935, including novelties and radio dealer **promotional items** such as banks, toys, pin back buttons, games, postcards, and dealer promotional items. Gary publishes *Antique Radio Classified*, a monthly digest for electronic collectors.
Gary Schneider
14310 Ordner Dr.
Strongsville, OH 44136
(216) 582-3094

★ **Antique radios.** Wants WWI equipment, fancy horn speakers, crystal sets, *Atwater Kent* breadboards, *Radiola, Kennedy, Federal*, the older and the more primitive the better, working or not. Will buy **art deco and novelty radios of the 1930's.** Also wants all **WWI wireless communications equipment** from ships, planes,

and ground forces, either complete or for parts (worth from $200-$3,000 and up). Especially looking for old U.S. Navy equipment with CN prefixes. Also **pre World War II television sets** and sports transmitting equipment. No floor model radios.
Mel Rosenthal
507 S. Maryland Ave.
Wilmington, DE 19804
(302) 322-8944

★ **Pre 1930 wireless, crystal sets, and battery radios** such as *Atwater Kent, Crosley, Amrad, Deforest, Federal, Grebe, Kennedy, Firth, Paragon, Marconi, R.C.A.,* and *Zenith*. Also early vacuum tubes with brass or Bakelite base. Also *Jenkins* **scanning disc television.** Also all wireless and radio books and magazines printed before 1930. Also radio advertising, parts, relays, ear phones, horn speakers, amplifiers, batteries, meters, etc. Will pay $500 for a *Marconi* CA294, $600 for a *Marconi* 106, $800+ for a *Pacific Wireless Specialty* audio receiver, and some others to $2,000. "I do not want anything made after 1940, floor model radios, or transistor radios."
David Shanks
115 Baldwin St.
Bloomfield, NJ 07003
(201) 748-8820

★ **Unusual radios.** "We buy unusual radios from the 1930's and 40's, the more unusual looking the better." Look for novelty designs like Mickey Mouse, Charlie McCarthy, sets shaped like baseballs, bottles, ships, horses, etc. Mirrored radios in blue, peach or silver, can be worth from $1,000 to $15,000 (for a floor model *Sparton Nocturne*, model 1186). *RCA* radios made in black painted wood with chrome trim are worth $500 to $5,000. Table top radios made of celluloid, Catalin, or colored Bakelites are $200 to $10,000. Look for *Air King, Fada, Garod, Emerson, Motorola, Kadette*, and more. Will buy floor model radios, but only if unusually shaped or colored. Will also buy transistor radios by *Regency, Raytheon, Sony,* and others for $20 to $200, and novelty transistor sets shaped like hands, bottles, animals, or advertising items. If you send a photo and a SASE, we'll try to help you sell your radio if we don't want it!"
Harry Poster
Box 1883
South Hackensack, NJ 07606
(201) 794-9606 weekdays before 7pm

★ **Plastic radios** from the 1930's and 40's. Brand names to look for include *Detrola, DeWald, Addison, Crosley, Emerson, Espey, Fada, Garod, Halson, Kadette, Motorola, RCA, Sentinel, Sparton, Air King, Arvin* and others. Will also buy odd or novelty radios, including "any radio with mirrors." Radios need not work but the condition of the cabinet must be excellent. If in doubt, call him. Whether you write or call, give the brand name, model number, color, measurements, and a description of condition. No stereos, phonographs, or clock radios.
Jeff Viola
475-B Eltone Road
Jackson, NJ 08527
   (908) 928-0666 or (201) 902-3313

★ **Mirrored glass radios.** "I'm especially fond of green mirrored glass radios and forever trying to acquire *Sparton* floor model mirrored glass radios (model 1186). I'll pay through the nose if I have to." That translates to as much as $35,000 for a perfect condition peach colored glass and up to $30,000 for a perfect blue glass radio. Glass covered radios do not have to work and the glass may be cracked as "I don't turn down mirrored glass radios offered to me." He claims to outbid anybody, and points out that he will either come pick up any radio or have it professionally moved so you don't have to worry about shipping. He also buys **colorful plastic radios** of the 1930's and 40's. He prefers you to price but will make offers if you intend to sell.
Ed Sage
PO Box 1234
Benicia, CA 94510
   (707) 746-5659

★ **Radio manuals, handbooks, and sales literature** pre-1970.
Alan C. King
PO Box 86
Radnor, OH 43066

★ **Old radios, tubes, test equipment, open frame motors, generators** and other electrical apparatus, switch board meters, knife switches, **neon signs, fans,** Tesla coils, **quack medical devices,** and **electric trains** and accessories, as well as early books on radio and electrical theory and practice. Give info from the item's ID plate, and include a sketch or photo.
Hank Andreoni
504 W. 6th
Beaumont, CA 92223
   (714) 849-7539

★ **Radios with wood cabinets.** Give make and model number, condition, and price. NO OFFERS.
Alvin Heckard
RD 1, Box 88
Lewistown, PA 17044
   (717) 248-7071

★ **Microphones,** 1940-1960, but only the short stand-up desk type mikes used by broadcasters and radio stations. Especially wants to find microphones with the station or network letters still attached.
Charles Martignette
PO Box 293
Hallandale, FL 33009
   (305) 454-3474

★ **Early tube high fidelity equipment** 1947-1960 especially monaural but also some early stereo from companies such as *Dynaco, Marantz, Fisher, McIntosh, Scott, Eico, Altec Lansing, JBL,* etc. Most makes and models are wanted, working or not, complete or for parts, as well as tubes, loudspeakers, schematics, manuals and **hi-fi magazines.** Of special interest are all early *McIntosh* amps. Nothing after 1970, "but I'll buy anything relating to early audio, from broadcast equipment to home systems."
Jack Smith
288 Winter St.
North Andover, MA 01845
   (508) 686-7250

★ **Early tube high fidelity equipment** including stereo and mono amplifiers, pre-amps, tuners (especially *McIntosh, Marantz, Western Electric* and *Quad*), large old speakers (especially *Altec, JBL, Tannoy, Western Electric,* and *Jensen*). Also buys old radios, vacuum tubes, home made amplifiers and kits (*UTC, Dynaco,* and *Heath*), movie theater sound equipment (including amps, speakers, and microphones), **antique electrical, electronic, telephonic,** and **telegraphic items.** Also wants old **hi-fi magazines,** books, and other literature. He does not want "department store console stereos, television tubes, or any TV's after 1955." When you write or call, give the manufacturer's name, model number, electrical condition, cosmetic condition, and tell whether any of the original literature is included.
Vernon Vogt
330 SW 43rd Street, #247
Renton, WA 98055
   (206) 251-5420 ext 247

Television Sets

★ **Television sets made before 1941** are sought by Chase, one of the country's biggest buyers of memorabilia from TV's earliest years. "Mechanical TV's are often mistaken for early electronic junk," he cautions, "so look for 12" metal disks containing tiny holes that spin in front of a neon glow lamp. These early TV's drew their sound from radio sets, and most had no cabinets. Look for names like *Daven, Insuline, ICA, Jenkins, See-All, Western Television,* and *Shortwave Television.* The electronic era sets from 1938-41 used picture tubes and were often combined in consoles with radios. One popular early style was the "mirror in the lid" which reflected the picture from a vertical picture tube. Brands to look for include *Andrea, GE, Philco, RCA, Stewart-Warner,* and *Westinghouse.* Minimum value for an early set is $500 with many of them a great deal more. A 1939 *Zenith* television would be worth about $10,000 to me, regardless of condition," says Chase. He will also buy selected sets made from 1941-1948 which can be recognized by having a Channel 1. He will also buy early giant screen 30" sets made by *Dumont* and *CBS-Columbia's* sets with a spinning color wheel. Readers are encouraged to send for his large and informative wants list. **Interested only in items mentioned.**
> Arnold Chase
> 9 Rushleigh Rd.,
> West Hartford, CT 06117
>   (203) 521-5280

★ **Early television items.**
> Gary Schneider
> 14310 Ordner Drive
> Strongsville, OH 44136
>   (216) 582-3094

★ **Television sets** with a reflective mirror in the lid and other small screen television sets such as the RCA TRK-9 or TRK-12 ($2,000+ each), and the GE HM 171 (worth $750). Only wants sets dating from before 1940.
> Donald Patterson
> 636 Cambridge Rd.
> Augusta, GA 30909
>   (404) 738-7227

★ **Early television sets.** "I'll buy old or unusual TV's, and will pay more than $2,000 for any TV sold before 1942. Mechanical scanners such as *Baird, Western, Empire, Pilot, ICA* and more. Mirror-in-lid sets by *Pilot, Andrea, Philco, RCA, GE, Garod,* and *Zenith.* Also buy *Fada* and *Meissner* 5" kit televisions. Some values: *RCA TRK-5, TRK-9, TT-5* will bring $3,000+ each. I pay $50 to $500 for unusual 1940's TV's with 3", 7", and 10" picture tubes. Also buy early 1950 color TV's with 16" or smaller picture tubes, and color wheels, and color adapters. Will also buy unusually shaped transistor TV's such as the *Sony 8-301W, Panasonic TR-005* (flying saucer), *JVC Video-sphere* (ball). I am willing to buy an entire TV shop, attic, or estate to get one TV I want." Harry is willing to travel. He publishes an illustrated price guide to vintage TV's and radios.
> Harry Poster
> Box 1883
> South Hackensack, NJ 07606
>   (201) 794-9606 weekdays before 7pm

★ **Television literature,** including books, catalogs, and company pamphlets (whether internal or intended for the public) from before 1940.
> Harold Layer
> SFSU-AV
> 1600 Holloway Ave
> San Francisco, CA 94132

Cities where you're most likely to find early TVs: Los Angeles, New York, Chicago, Philadelphia, and Schenectady.

music and song

Guitars can have surprising value

as can other stringed instruments. Don't underestimate the value of good guitars. Some 1950's electrics will really surprise you!

Many instruments will indicate a manufacturer, and a few will have model names or numbers. Include all wording on any paper labels inside string instruments.

Your condition statement should include mention of all cracks, dents, and the like. If it is something unusual, make a sketch or take a photograph.

If you have phonograph records to sell, it is important to list the artist, song, record label, and the catalog number. Note the condition of the record, the record jacket, and its paper sleeve. Mention any tears, scuffs, owner's names, cracks, chips, or scratches on the record or the cover. Damaged records are seldom worth your time.

Most later pop records are of little value, but some rock and show tune albums are considered scarce by collectors and bring $50 or more. Rock and roll posters have become hot and may also be worth money.

Condition of records is of prime importance. Even slight damage to the track reduces value.

tony hyman

Musical Instruments

star Most string, wood, and brass musical instruments are of interest for trade or resale. For his own collection he wants instruments that are rare, very old, pretty, unique, or hand crafted. He especially wants trumpets or cornets that have extra keys, fewer keys, or keys that are in unusual positions or shapes. He buys *any* museum quality instrument. Also instruments of other cultures including African, Asian, Pacific, etc. No pianos or organs. A photo should go with a complete description, including all labels or markings.

Sid Glickman
42 Butterwood Lane E.
Irvington, NY 10533
(914) 591-5371

star **American guitars, banjos, and mandolins** by the following makers: *C.F. Martin, Gibson, Fender* (older models), *Dobro, National, D'Angelico, B&D (Bacon & Day), Epiphone* (older), *Paramount, Vega, Fairbanks, SS Stewart, Washburn, Lyon & Healy, Stromberg, Gretsch,* and *Rickenbacker.* "If you have fine condition instruments for sale **by these makers** *only* you may call us collect for an offer. Have your instrument in your hand. Be prepared to answer specific questions about condition, originality, serial number, color, and the type of case it has. Without this information, we cannot provide meaningful evaluation. *Sellers only may call collect.* All others are welcome to call for advice or information." Among instruments Jay and his team would most like to find are the *Martin* D-45 with abalone inlay, the electric *Gibson* Les Paul Standard made in 1958-59, a *Gibson* F-5 mandolin made between 1922-24 signed by Lloyd Loar, and *Gibson* Mastertone banjos made during the late 1930's. Dates and models are very important. "Another model made at the same time might be worth only 1/20 as much as these key pieces. But *all* instruments made by these makers can be worth your inquiry. Original condition matters a lot." Offers an interesting catalog of high quality new and used instruments. Wants list available.

Stan Jay, Mandolin Bros.
629 Forest Ave.
Staten Island, NY 10310
(718) 981-3226

star **Stringed musical instruments** including banjos, electric and acoustic guitars, mandolins, ukes, and violins. No ukelins or Mandolin-Harps, please. He'll buy banjos by *Fairbanks, Cole, Vega, Stewart, Epiphone, Stromberg, Gibson, Leedy, Ludwig, Baystate, Haynes, Lyon & Healy, Bacon, B&D, Studio King, Recording King,* or *Paramount.* Will buy the following brands of guitar in any condition: *D'Angelico, Gibson, Martin, Epiphone, Fender, Gretsch,* and *Rickenbacker.* "There are lots of guitars purchased for $100-$300 in the 1950's that are worth five to ten times as much today. I'll pay $1,500+ for a *Gretsch* White Falcon guitar, $2,000+ for a *Gretsch* Chet Atkins, $5,000+ for a *Gibson* Flying V electric guitar, and up to $10,000 for a mint *Gibson* Les Paul with the sunburst finish. We will consider all violins from any country, especially carved or inlaid, no matter what its country of origin." Photos of the front and back of any instrument are requested.

Steve Senerchia, The Music Man
87 Tillinghast Ave.
West Warwick, RI 02893
(401) 821-2865

star **High quality Italian violins and some of their imitators** are the prime interest of this 18 year veteran west coast dealer. Cremona school violins 1650-1750 can be worth from $2,500 to $100,000 or more, but many copies exist. Jones will consider better French instruments and your fake "Stradivarius" violins. Most of the "Strads" were cottage industry instruments or made in German factories (1850-1920), and originally sold by Sears for $9. They seldom bring over $100, but a few more valuable ones do exist. There are also many **guitars, banjos, basses, violas, mandolins,** and other stringed instruments that can be fairly valuable to Jones if you have one of better quality. It takes years of handling violins to be able to recognize originals or instruments of value. For this reason "it is difficult to buy through the mail, but not impossible." The reputation of the maker and the condition of the instrument are crucial in determining value. To sell a stringed instrument, you must describe all damage, the type and quality of finish, the bow, and give every word on the label. In many cases, he will request seeing the instrument before making a final offer. No Oriental instruments are wanted.

David N. Jones' Violin Shop
3411 Ray St.
San Diego, CA 92104
(619) 584-1505

102

★ **Fretted stringed musical instruments** such as banjos, guitars, mandolins, ukuleles, and the like. "A *Martin* D-45 guitar made prior to 1942 could be worth as much as $20,000," so instruments are worth selling properly. **Also** related memorabilia such as manufacturer's catalogs, old photos of guitar shops and players, accessories, etc. State the preservation of your instrument. Examine carefully for repairs. Look for any signs that it might not be original. Mention the type of case. Offers a monthly 8pp catalog of new and used instruments for $4 per year.

Stan Werbin,
Elderly instruments
Box 14210
Lansing, MI 48901
    (517) 372-7890 days

★ **French and Italian violins, violas, and cellos.** "I'll pay high prices for high grade quality instruments, both commercial and hand-made from anywhere in the world, but especially France and Italy. I don't want children's or school violins nor any imitations of Stradivarius, Guarnerius, or other masters." Describe the label inside the instrument. Appraisal services available.

Robert Portukalian
Violin Shop
1279 North Main St.
Providence, RI 02904
    (401) 521-5145

★ **Rare and unusual musical instruments** including harps, bagpipes, hurdi-gurdies, wooden flutes, concertinas, ethnic instruments, and all manner of brass and woodwinds, stringed instruments, and others. No keyboards. Mickie repairs instruments and will purchase good ones in "any restorable condition." Can make arrangements for consignment selling of instruments he doesn't wish to buy. This 20 year veteran conducts annual seminars on musical instrument history and performance and is available for insurance appraisals and offers. An extensive illustrated catalog may be ordered for $3.

Mickie Zekley
Lark in the Morning
Box 1176
Mendocino, CA 95460
    (707) 964-5569

★ **Drums and drum catalogs** from the early 1900's to 1970. Buys sets or single tom toms, bass drums, or snare drums, and buys uncracked **cymbals marked K.ZILDJIAN** but not those made by A.ZILDJIAN. "To save everyone effort, a thorough and complete inspection of your instrument should be done before contacting us. Check and note modifications and/or damage of any kind including scratches, cracks, peeling, bulging, holes drilled, warps of rims and shells, rust, pitting, stains, or discoloration." Information needed to evaluate your drum(s): the brand name, shape and color of the ID emblem, the diameter of the head(s), the depth of each drum's shell (not including the rims), and the color and type of finish of the drum(s) on both the outside and inside. **Does not buy** drums or drum catalogs produced after 1970, exotic or ethnic drums, or parade basses. He requests "serious inquiries only, please. Kindly keep in mind that we do not offer appraisals or estimates by mail or phone. If you are a sincere seller interested in selling your item specifically to us, we would like to hear from you. If you are planning on selling your item to another party, please do not call us. If you have no idea of the value of your item(s), I'll give you a retail price range that your item sells for in the vintage drum market and then request you quote me your wholesale asking price. I'm willing to educate sellers so they can make an informed decision and determine a fair price, keeping in mind that we must often recondition items, resell them, and make a profit." One of the world's largest dealers in collectible drums, Vintage Drum Center publishes a quarterly catalog, available to drum buyers on request.

Ned Ingberman
Vintage Drum Center
Route 1, 95B
Libertyville, IA 52567
    (800) 729-3111 extension 5 to buy or sell
    (515) 693-3101 fax

★ **Cigar box musical instruments.** Any type musical instrument made out of a cigar box. Send description and a sketch or photo. If you know any of the instrument's history, please include that information. Mention whether strings and pegs are present, the type and condition of finish, and any applied or painted decorations.

Tony Hyman
Box 3028
Pismo Beach, CA 93448
    (805) 773-6777   fax (805) 773-0117

★ **Old Jew's harps** (also called jaw harps, juice harps), especially those that are hand-forged or made of ivory, bone, silver, or gold. They must me in good condition, complete with the tongue ("twanger"). "I'll buy Jew's harp cases in any material and want literature, instruction books, etc., and would love to find instruments composed of several harps joined together."
Leonard Fox
2965 Marlin Road, Box 729
Bryn Athyn, PA 19009

★ **Brass musical instruments,** especially the unusual and obsolete. He wants "to know about all your old brass instruments since they all look the same to the untrained." Among other things, he especially wants a B-flat cornet with the bell pointing over the shoulder and a Schreiber horn with a straight up bell. He hopes to assemble a representative collection of the hundreds of brass instruments. If you regularly sell musical instruments, his informative illustrated wants list is a must.
Jonathan Korzun
1201 Williamson Rd.
North Brunswick, NJ 08902
    (201) 297-0308 eves

★ **Piano related items** including:
[1] Advertising signs, posters, and catalogs;
[2] Photos or factory and store interiors;
[3] Models of pianos and mechanisms;
[4] Tools used by piano tuners and builders;
[5] Piano trade publications.
He is not interested in magazine ads. Your description should include size and condition as well as identifying the materials from which it is made. Photo or Xerox© "very helpful" to this 20 year veteran piano tuner who says, "the history of pianos and their manufacture fascinates me." **He is not interested in buying your old piano.**
Phillip Jamison III
17 Sharon Alley
West Chester, PA 19382
    (215) 696-8449

Music Books

★ **Songbooks with oddly shaped notes.** "I'll buy singing school books with oblong, triangular, rectangular, pictorial or other shaped notes, especially pre-1860, for $25 and up in good condition. Authors of these books include Funk, Carden, Davisson, Swan, and others."
Jim Presgraves
Box 639
Wytheville, VA 24382
    (703) 686-5813

★ **Songbooks and song broadsides:**
[1] American and British **songsters (books)** 1700-1900 in paper, leather, or hard covers, including political candidate songbooks, temperance song collections, medicine company advertising songbooks, and vaudeville performer songsters, as well as circus promotional songsters;
[2] American and British **song broadsides and ballad sheets,** 1500-1900;
[3] **Hillbilly and Country and Western song folios** before 1946;
[4] **Song books of occupational groups,** miners, sailors, lumberjacks, etc;
[5] **Regional American folk song collections** from any period;
[6] **British and Irish folk song collections.**
Note that this is a fairly restrictive list of books of collected songs. He is a prominent authority, author, producer in the world of folk music and has no interest in common items or things not on this list. Full bibliographic information is required. **Please do not inquire about collections of sheet music or religious song books.**
Kenneth Goldstein
4840 Cedar Ave.
Philadelphia, PA 19143
    (215) 476-5857

Sheet Music

★ **Sheet music illustrated by E.H. Pfeiffer.** They are signed in a variety of ways including EHP, Fifer, Pfeiffer Illustrating Co., Pfeiffer Publishing Co. Has a lengthy wants list. Also buys other items illustrated by Pfeiffer. Please describe things carefully, noting all damage, tears, creases, stains, tape, etc.
> Ann Pfeiffer Latella
> 70 Mariposa Dr.
> Rochester, NY 14624
> (716) 247-2823

★ **Old popular sheet music** from 1820-1970, with pictorial covers, especially movie and show song sheets, WWI, WWII, ragtime, blues, Negro, ethnic, baseball, cartoons, musical comedy, fire, aviation, and automobile songs especially with illustrations by Homer or Nathaniel Currier. No classical or religious. **Also buys** *Downbeat, Metronome, Billboard* **and movie magazines.**
> Beverly Hamer
> Box 75
> E. Derry, NH 03041
> (603) 432-3528

★ **Sheet music** in small or large collections or accumulations. Primary interest is in popular music of the 20th century (1890-1970). Movie and show tunes are of primary interest, but "also any music that falls into any of the main collectible categories, like presidential, political, patriotic, war, transportation, cartoon, baseball, *Coca-Cola*, advertising, historical, Black related, and others with interesting cover art." Particularly likes to find music published by the ET Paull Music Company, and will pay from $10 to $300, depending upon the title and condition. **Does not want to buy classical music or sheet music designed for teaching.** "If the person wants to sell the music as a lot, I need to know quantity, condition, and the rough percentage of movie, show, and pop tunes. I also want to know the percentage of large format (11" x 14") and small format (9" x 12") music."
> Wayland Bunnell
> Clean Sheets
> 199 Tarrytown Rd.
> Manchester, NH 03103
> (603) 668-5466

★ **Bound volumes of sheet music from before 1900.** Pays $1 or more per title for illustrated ones. Those by rare publishers bring more. Prefers books with no music titles removed.
> Jim Presgraves
> Bookworm & Silverfish
> Box 639
> Wytheville, VA 24382
> (703) 686-5813

★ **Sheet music about WWI and WWII** in very good to mint condition *only*. Also wants sheet music with pictures of Frank Sinatra or Presidents of the U.S. **Also buys music by Charles K. Harris and Irving Berlin.**
> Herman Rush
> 10773 Ojai-Santa Paula Rd.
> Ojai, CA 93023

All collectors are fussy. Sheet music collectors are among the most fussy. Don't waste their time and yours by offering items in poor condition.

"Please don't describe
sheet music as
'good for its age.'

That means fair or poor condition.

In the world of sheet music
'Excellent' and 'mint'
are terms reserved for
music that has almost
never seen the light of day,
music store stock,
or publisher's remainder."

Wayland Bunnell

Phonograph Records

★ **Jazz, blues, big band, hillbilly, rock and roll, rhythm and blues, rockabilly, and celebrity records,** including 78's, 45's, and LP's. Especially jazz and dance bands from the 1920's and 30's and jug and washboard bands. Also radio transcription disks. He buys many rare, obscure, and scarce but unpopular records and will buy anything recorded on the following labels: *Autograph, Black Patti, Bluebird, Broadway, Brunswick*, and 50 others. Also most records which are marked "fox trot," "stomp," or "for dancing." No easy listening, hit records, or pop recording stars like Jolson or Crosby. If you have 78's to sell, send $2 for the *Shellac Shack's Wants List*, a 72 page booklet listing the prices they pay for thousands of records. Les is author of *American Premium Record Guide*, a popular reference work available for $16.95.

    Les Docks
    The Shellac Shack
    Box 691035
    San Antonio, TX 78269
      (512) 492-6021

★ **78 rpm recordings, 1900-1940**, including popular, classical, jazz, country and Western, and personality. Also catalogs and sheet music in those areas of interest. David especially likes to buy entire collections and will travel anywhere in the East.

    David Alan Reiss
    3920 Eve Drive
    Seaford, NY 11783
      (516) 785-8336

★ **78 rpm** "*Columbia* **Grand Opera Series**" 10" one-sided records. Also buys **LP classical** recordings, **but only** if they're part of *Mercury* records' "Living Presence Series" in stereo. Does not want damaged items or reissues. Include the label and catalog number.

    John Widmar
    3829 8th Ave.
    Kenosha, WI 53140
      (414) 654-6802

★ **Rare 78 rpm records and phonograph cylinders.** Among his wants are:
  [1] Jazz, blues, cajun and country 1925-1935;
  [2] Rock & Roll, 1948-1960;
  [3] Records before 1903 (often 7" in diameter and without paper labels);
  [4] Speeches by historical figures;
  [5] Picture records (transparent records with a picture visible under the grooves);
  [6] Advertising, promotional, and special purpose records, some of which are made of thin cardboard *[don't play them!]*;
  [7] Unusual sizes and shapes of records;
  [8] Classical and operatic records made before 1908, especially smaller than 10";
  [9] Long play 78's, marked "longer playing," "five minute record," or some such;
  [10] Puzzle, or multi-track, records;
  [11] Rare labels, of which he can supply you a long list, including names like *Black Patti, KKK, Sunshine, Marconi, Vitaphone*, and more.

He urges you to make a list of your more valuable records, using *The American Premium Record Guide* (list anything valued at $15 or more) or his wants list to help you decide which are worth listing. Include the label, number, artist, and any noticeable defects. "If you have a large collection so that making a list would be impractical, call me and we can discuss the possibility of evaluating your collection in person." A wants list is available if you send a long SASE. **He does not want** big bands, Hawaiian, popular songs, religious music, album sets, country music after WWII, home recordings, or later opera and classical, nor does he want 45's or LP records.

    Kurt Nauck
    Memory Machines
    6323 Inway
    Spring, TX 77389
      (713) 370-7899

★ **Pop American 78 rpm records, 1888-1949**, especially in quantity. Pays 10¢ - $1 apiece, less if records are not in fine condition. Buys disks, cylinders, and sapphire ball recordings at higher prices. Like to find pre-1960 versions of *Froggy Went a Courtin*, especially Victor black label version from 1926 worth $100. Some interest in **sheet music for pop music** from 1890-1925.

    Ron Graham
    8167 Park Ave.
    Forestville, CA 95436
      (707) 887-2856

★ **Recorded music.** "I'll buy collections of all 45's, used CD's, and record albums, but I don't buy 78's or any classical music or other instrumentals. Be specific in your descriptions, including label. Seller must price."
Otti Schmitt
Finders-Keepers Collectibles
7724 Hayfield Rd.
Alexandria, VA 22310
(703) 550-1454

★ **Transcription discs of old radio programs** such as *Suspense, Jack Benny, Lux Radio Theater, Bing Crosby*, newscasts, the big bands, dramas, mysteries, detective shows, kids shows, "most all categories." Discs are typically 16" and aluminum based, but may also be 10" or 12" and can be found single and double sided. Glass disks from WWII years are extremely fragile and desirable. Larry is not interested in dubs or copies of originals, nor does he want disks of advertising, public service spots, or promotions. "Not interested in most library type disks but will consider if asking price low." Prefers not to make offers.
Larry Kiner
Box 724
Redmond, WA 98073-0724

★ **Bobby Breen phonograph records and song sheets** from the late 1930's.
Ralph Eodice
161 Valley Road
Clifton, NJ 07013

"Records in mint condition are preferred by collectors, but a few rare early records have never been found in perfect condition.

If a record lists in
The American Premium Record Guide
for more than $15
some collectors may want it
even if it looks beat up."

Kurt Nauck

★ **Jazz LP's from the 1950's and 60's.** Also **jazz literature of all kinds,** any years, and "some other materials associated with jazz" such as magazines. No 45's or 78's. No music other than jazz. No records with poor condition covers. Please include your phone number.
Gary Alderman, G's Jazz
Box 9164
Madison, WI 53715
(608) 274-3527   Fax (608) 277-1999

★ **Rhythm and Blues or Rock and Roll 45s from the 1950's.** Want original recordings of groups like the *Flamingos, Robins, Wrens, Penguins*, etc. Will buy any 45's from race labels such as *Chance, Red Robin, Blue Lake, Harlem, Grand, Rockin, After Hours, Aladdin, Parrot, Flip, Allen, Rhythm, Club 51*, and *Swingtime*. No records that are reissues, bootlegged, or damaged. When writing, give the label, catalog number and condition.
John Widmar
3829 8th Ave.
Kenosha, WI 53140
(414) 654-6802

★ *Vogue* **78 rpm picture records.** Will pay $500 for *"Rum and Coca Cola."* Records must be clean and in excellent condition. Long SASE brings wants list.
John Widmar
3829 8th Ave.
Kenosha, WI 53140
(414) 654-6802

★ **Rock and roll, rhythm and blues, and country music records.** Wants 45 and 33 rpm, especially 45's with picture sleeves, odd ball items, and disc jockey radio promos. Also rock, blues, or country sheet music and magazines. No classical, big bands, opera, or polka.
Cliff Robnett
7804 NW 27th
Bethany, OK 73008
(405) 787-6703

★ **45 rpm records in quantity** in unplayed or nearly unused condition. Looking for store stock or radio station collections, but will also buy small collections if they contain desirable records. Nothing worn or scratched. Phone.
Ken Clee
PO Box 11412
Philadelphia, PA 19111
(215) 722-1979

Singers & Musicians

★ **Eubie Blake or Sissle & Blake records and other memorabilia**, especially 10" recording *Jammin' at Rudi's*.
Steven Ramm
420 Fitzwater St.
Philadelphia, PA 19147

★ **Concert Band memorabilia** from the era of **John Philip Sousa**, Patrick Sarsfield Gilmore, and Arthur Pryor. "I'll buy posters, programs, autographs, photographs, letterhead, uniforms, books, sheet music, diaries, and musical instruments that can be authenticated that they were used in the bands mentioned. Also want advertising items with Sousa's picture on it such as cigar labels, tobacco cans, shot guns, Victor records, music cylinders, etc. Would like to find autographed copies of Sousa's various books." He does not want anything related to these men that was printed after their death: Sousa's died in 1932, Pryor in 1942, and Gilmore in 1892. "Condition is very important. Sheet music should not be trimmed or repaired, post cards should not have damaged corners." Send a good description or a Xerox© copy.
Barry Furrer
491 Valley Road
Gillette, NJ 07933

★ **Big Band memorabilia from the 1930's and 40's** especially of Glenn Miller or Bunny Berigan. John buys phonograph records, home recordings, tapes of concerts or radio performances, transcription disks, autographs, photographs, newspaper articles, magazine articles, movie short subjects, home movies, posters, and sheet music if it has to do with big bands. This 30 year veteran collector will negotiate an item's value with you.
John Mickolas
172 Liberty Street
Trenton, NJ 08611
(609) 599-9672

★ **Al Jolson and his brother Harry.** "I have an extensive collection of items and music sheets, so am mostly looking for unusual items and in novelty song sheets. No common well known songs. Please, no *Mammy*."
J. Markowitz
964 Hillside Blvd.
New Hyde Park, NY 11040

★ **Elvis Presley memorabilia** from before his death, including all marked "E.P. Enter 1956" such as lipsticks, skirts, perfume, gloves, etc. Also posters and promotional items from Elvis movies, records, and appearances. Seeks a plastic guitar with pictures on it, and issues of 1950's magazines such as *Dig* and *Teen Stories* with all Elvis features. Also buys The **Beatles, Kiss, Monkee, and other rock memorabilia.** Autographs are especially desired. No phonograph records except promotional copies.
Robert Urmanic, Bob's Nostalgia
199 Brookvalley Dr.
Elyria, OH 44035
(216) 365-3550

★ **Janet Lynn memorabilia.** "I buy photos, articles, and books, from 1970 to the present," says this fan. Xerox© copies are helpful.
Alberic Gerard
Box 97
Lafayette, OR 97127

★ **Beatles memorabilia** from before their 1970 breakup. Everything is wanted, including games, toys, dolls, posters, movie related items, candid photos, concert posters and programs, tickets, and ads for merchandise or concerts. Would love to find any Beatles toy musical instruments, such as guitars and drums picturing the group, and will pay from $200-$500 for Beatles bongos and banjo. Buys common items as long as they are old and original. Wants to know where you got your item, and requests your phone number.
Jeff Augsburger
507 Normal Ave.
Normal, IL 61761
(309) 452-9376

★ **Beatles memorabilia** of all sorts including toys, dolls, games, tickets, cartoon kit, model kits, *Yellow Submarine*, Halloween costumes, wall paper, talcum powder, shampoo, ice cream wrappers, blankets, jewelry, china, toy musical instruments, fan club items, etc., especially items sealed in their original factory cartons. Also hard to find Beatles albums such as *Beatles vs the 4 Seasons* or *Yesterday & Today* with the butcher cover. "I'll pay $800 for a mint record player, and up to $500 for an unopened bottle of pomade, and $250 for a mint Kaboodle Kit." Rick also buys **Monkees!** ephemera of all types.
Rick Rann
Box 877
Oak Park, IL 60303
(312) 442-7907

coin operated machines

Slot machines can put cash in your pocket

if you have one of these popular coin-ops. "Coin-ops" is what collectors call slot machines, jukeboxes, arcade games, trade stimulators (games you play for product prizes), kinetoscopes (early flip-card "movie" machines), and other machines which are put into play by dropping a coin into a slot.

Coin-ops are made of cast iron, aluminum, plastic and wood. The oldest machines not always the most valuable.

Coin-ops are among those few collectibles which do not need to be in perfect condition to sell readily. Most collectors and dealers restore them.

If you give the make, model, and serial number, most dealers will know exactly what machine you mean. You can find this information on an identification plate along with the address of the manufacturer, patent dates, and (sometimes) the operating instructions.

Almost all collectors want a photo of older items, especially pin ball games, arcade and vending machines, and trade stimulators since unfamiliar models turn up regularly. When shooting pinball machines, include the play field in one photo and back glass in another.

When writing about a coin-op, indicate whether it works and whether parts are missing or broken. When describing pinball machines, it is important to note how much paint is peeling off the back board illustration.

Because the machines are large, heavy, and valuable, buyers will assist in making shipping arrangements.

tony hyman 👉

Mechanical Music

★ **Any pre-1930 device that plays music mechanically** including disk and cylinder music boxes, clocks and watches that play tunes, disk players, automata dolls, player organs, monkey organs, nickelodeons, horn phonographs in any condition from perfect to incomplete. Especially a barrel operated monkey organ with pipes ($2,000-$4,000), large disc music boxes that play more than one disc at a time ($10-$12,000), and cylinder music boxes with more than 175 teeth, and early musical watches. No player pianos, but most other mechanical music brings $300 up. Give measurements of any disk or cylinder. Please include your phone number with correspondence.
Martin Roenigk
Grand Illusions
26 Barton Hill
East Hampton, CT 06424
(203) 267-8682

★ **Musical instruments "that play themselves"** by motor, springs, pneumatics, or other means, including **music boxes**, roller organs, cylinder music boxes, musical bird cages, nickelodeons, and organettes. Will buy rough condition items for parts or repair. Also musical disks, cylinders, piano rolls, old photos, postcards or paper ephemera depicting anything in mechanical music. NO OFFERS.
Doug Negus
Phonograph Phunatic
215 Mason St.
Sutherland, IA 51058
(712) 446-2270

★ **Anything that makes music automatically or mechanically** such as phonographs, music boxes, player pianos, nickelodeons, organettes, and others. Also the records, discs, rolls, cobs, and anything else that plays these instruments. Also any catalog, magazine, bulletin, book, literature or advertising pertaining to these items.
Seymour Altman
Vi & Si's
8970 Main St.
Clarence, NY 14031
(716) 634-4488

★ **Antique music boxes and phonographs.** Want all types, 1850-1920, including cylinder, disc, paper roll, and cob organs. Brands like *Regina, Mira, Stella, Symphonian,* and *Kalliope* are sought. Especially interested in a *Regina Changer,* a 15 1/2 upright music box which changes automatically. He'd pay $12,000 for a nice one. Is not interested in "late miniature music boxes." He needs the brand, model, size, and condition. Pictures are most helpful.
Chet Ramsay
RD #1 Box 383
Coatesville, PA 19320
(215) 384-0514

★ **Music cylinders.** The following cylinders (early phonograph recordings) are wanted by a well known music auctioneer:
[1] Cylinders colored brown, pink, purple, white or orange;
[2] Cylinders 6" long or 5" in diameter;
[3] Blue cylinders numbered 5000 to 5750;
[4] Operatic cylinders;
[5] Cylinders with historical content.
It is a plus if the cylinders are in their original boxes, but it is not necessary. Cylinders can bring from $5 to $200 each, depending on the size, color, and condition. List the title, artist, catalog number, color, length and diameter, and note whether you have the box. If your collection is very large, so listing is impractical, phone him to make other arrangements.
Kurt Nauck
Memory Machines
1940 E. Allegro
Houston, TX 77080
(713) 468-3472   Fax: (713) 467-8623

★ **Phonographs and related memorabilia pre-1930** including cylinder and disc records, catalogs, needle tins, postcards, stereoviews depic-ting phonographs, signs and other advertising except magazine ads. Also cylinder records of speeches by Taft, Teddy Roosevelt, and other famous people, for which he pays $10-$50. Also all material related to Thomas Edison. Also toy phonographs. List make, model, and condition. Include label, artist, and title of records. SASE for offer.
Steven Ramm
420 Fitzwater St.
Philadelphia, PA 19147
(215) 922-7050

★ **Horn phonographs in any condition.** Will buy parts from machines made by the following companies: *Berliner Gramophone, National Gramophone, Universal Talking Machine*, or *Zonophone*.

    Charlie Stewart
    900 Grandview Ave.
    Reno, NV 89503
        (702) 747-1439 days

★ **Phonographs with outside horns**, complete or for parts. No Victrolas. Alvin doesn't want to be bothered unless you're serious about selling. NO OFFERS.

    Alvin Heckard
    RD 1, Box 88
    Lewistown, PA 17044
        (717) 248-7071

★ *RCA* or *Capehart* **radio-phonographs that automatically flip records over** to play the other side. Pays $500-$700 for these large complicated machines from the 1930's. "If your machine weighs less than 75 pounds, I'm probably not interested." Take a photo of the record changing mechanism or give him a call.

    Joseph Weber
    604 Centre St.
    Ashland, PA 17921
        (717) 875-4401 3-5 pm

★ **Phonographs, music boxes, and related ephemera.** Would like to hear from you regarding all disc and cylinder phonographs with outside horns, especially those with wooden horns. Also floor model wind-up phonographs in deluxe or fancy cabinets. Also antique disc or cylinder music boxes, especially those that sit on the floor. Will pay from $200 to $10,000, depending on type, style, and condition. "I am also interested in purchasing old record catalogs, posters, metal signs, *Victor* dogs, needle tins, and the like. Phonograph related paper items before 1910 are especially desirable, particularly items associated with Thomas Edison. Send descriptions and Xerox© copies.

    Kurt Nauck
    Memory Machines
    1940 E. Allegro
    Houston, TX 77080
        (713) 468-3472 Fax: (713) 467-8623

★ **Catalogs, repair manuals, and advertising for phonograph records and piano rolls** published by record and piano roll companies, 1890 to 1960. Prefers to buy collections or very early pieces. No records, magazine ads, or damaged items. Tim is past president of the Association for Recorded Sound Collections, a national club for recording historians.

    Tim Brooks
    Box 41, Glenville Station
    Greenwich, CT 06831

★ **Telegraphones and other unusual magnetic recorders, especially wire.** Not interested in *Webster* machines.

    Harold Layer
    SFSU-AV
    1600 Holloway Ave.
    San Francisco, CA 94132

Early cylinders can break or scratch easily. Avoid touching the surface of the cylinders.

Do not play them, even if you think you have the right equipment.

Coin-ops

★ **Select coin-op machines** especially early wood cabinet and cast iron machines 1885-1912, very rare pin ball machines, kinetoscopes, and 1888-1905 peep machines. Offers $20,000 for the *Fey* 1906 Liberty Bell slot machine but has only minor interest in most other slots. Pays $7,500 for an *Edison* Kinetoscope from 1894. Particularly interested in paper ephemera about coin op machines including catalogs, brochures, advertising, letterheads, and anything else historical related to coin-ops. Also photographs of store or saloon interiors which depict the machines in place, in use, or ready for use. Also *The Coin Machine Journal, Automatic Age, Automatic World, The Pacific Coin Machine Review, Spinning Reels, The Billboard* (pre-1932), and other trade magazines devoted to coin op machines. Bueschel is an editor of the quarterly *The Coin Slot* and author or publisher of more than three dozen books and guides to coin operated machines. Since thousands of dollars are sometimes involved, he wants you to shoot a roll of 1000 ASA 35mm film of your coin op, including all details and ship the undeveloped roll to him. He'll reimburse. You *must* tell him where you got your machines.
Richard Bueschel
414 N. Prospect Manor Ave.
Mt. Prospect, IL 60056
   (312) 498-9300 days

★ **Coin-ops** including jukeboxes, nickelodeons, arcade devices such as diggers and claws, view machines, coin op fans and radios, and gum, prophylactic and other vending machines. Has particular interest in **slot machines and gambling devices that pay cash rewards.** These have a minimum value of $500 with the more exotic and unusual machines bringing considerably more. Pre-1910 gambling machines made on the West coast are very desirable. Also **paper ephemera** about coin op machines including catalogs, brochures, advertising, letterheads, and anything historical. No pin ball, video arcade, or service machines like washers.
Fred Ryan
Slot Closet
Box 83135
Portland, OR 97203
   (503) 286-3597

★ **Coin-op machines** especially pre-1940 slots and jukeboxes. No solid state pinball machines. Ted publishes the monthly *Coin Machine Trader* devoted to ads and information about coin ops.
Ted Salveson
PO Box 602
Huron, SD 57350
   (605) 352-3870

★ *Gottlieb* **pinball machines,** 1948-58. He explains that most of the games from this period have wooden cabinets, trim, and legs, except those made after 1956 which have metal legs. Machines before 1948 don't have flippers and are not of interest. Will buy *Gottlieb* machines in any condition, but premium prices are paid for fine condition working machines. The backglass must me present and in good condition with little or no chipping, cracking, or paint flaking. Cabinets that have been repainted are undesirable but acceptable. Normal wear on the playing surface is expected, but severely damaged playfields make a game uncollectible. Damaged machines have some value for parts but their value is a fraction of what collectible games in fine condition command. Pays $500 for *Gin Rummy* or *Mystic Marvel* games by *Gottlieb.* "I will consider games by other manufacturers, but only if they are in very good condition. No games which have revolving reels to record scores or that have metal cabinets. "If you are in doubt, call and I will try my best to identify your game. When you describe your game, pay attention to cosmetics, missing bumper caps, lights shields missing, cracks, etc." He prefers amateurs to set the price wanted, but he will make offers if you are serious about selling.
Gordon Hasse, Jr.
Box 1543 Grand Central Station
New York, NY 10163
   (212) 996-3825 eves

★ **Table model jukeboxes.** He will buy *all* pre-1960 jukeboxes if you live close enough for him to pick them up. Only buys the small ones if they have to be shipped. Also jukebox literature, ads and parts.
Alvin Heckard
RD 1, Box 88
Lewistown, PA 17044
   (717) 248-7071

★ *Wurlitzer* and *Rock Ola* jukeboxes, working or not, especially *Wurlitzer* model 42 (worth up to $1,800) and model numbers 500 or above (which begin at $450 for a #500 and can go to nearly $12,000 for a nice condition model #950). Also **all slot machines, in any condition**, complete or not, working or not. All but the most common working machines will bring $500, many over $1,000. He advertises widely that $50,000 is waiting for the finder of a working *Fey* Liberty Bell slot machine. Will pick up machines anywhere in the U.S.
   Frank Zygmunt
   Antique Slot Machine Co.
   Box 542
   Westmont, IL 60559
      (708) 985-2742 Fax: (708) 985-5151

★ **Coin op machines** including 78 rpm *Wurlitzer* jukeboxes from 1938-48, pre-1920 penny arcade machines, pre-1910 vending machines, and all slot machines.
   Martin Roenigk
   Grand Illusions
   26 Barton Hill
   East Hampton, CT 06424
      (203) 267-8682

★ **Pre-1940** *Wurlitzer* jukeboxes with model numbers lower than 500. These machines pre-date the "plastic-and-bright-lights era" favored by most collectors. Also *Capehart* radio-phonographs and jukeboxes from the 1930's that flip records over. Pays $500-$700 for *Wurlitzer* 416 or *Capehart* C20-30. He'll buy these in any condition, but condition does affect value. Will pick up anything east of the Mississippi and arrange for shipments in the West.
   Joseph Weber
   604 Centre St.
   Ashland, PA 17921
      (717) 875-4401 3-5 pm

★ **Penny arcade games** such as grip tests, target games, kicker and catcher, Pike's Peak, and the like. Prefers penny machines.
   James Conley
   2405 Brentwood Rd.NW
   Canton, OH 44708
      (216) 477-7725

★ *Wurlitzer* jukeboxes from the 1940's. Also **paper ephemera, service manuals, and advertising related to jukeboxes** of all types. Rick publishes the monthly *Jukebox Collector Newsletter* and is author of three books about jukeboxes, including *A Complete Identification Guide to the Wurlitzer Jukebox* available from him for $15.
   Rick Botts
   2545 SE 60th Court
   Des Moines, IA 50317
      (515) 265-8324

★ **All types of coin-operated machines**, especially unusual ones.
   Marvin Yagoda
   28585 So. Harwich Dr.
   Farmington Hills, MI 48018
      (313) 851-8158

★ **Pinball machines and coin op kiddie ride animals** pre-1965.
   Don Olson
   Box 245
   Humboldt, IA 50548

★ **Coin operated scales** in any condition and in any quantity are sought by this 10 year veteran collector/dealer who also buys scale parts, literature, advertising, route books or maps, and "anything else" related to coin operated scales. Provide the brand name, model and serial number and describe the condition. Make certain to note whether the scale in complete. He does not want scales that were not coin operated.
   Bill Berning
   PO Box 41414
   Chicago, IL 60641
      (708) 587-1839

sports

If man played with it

on a team, or in any kind of
competition, someone collects it.

Championship anything brings
top prices, with Baseball Hall of Fame
player relics the most sought after of all
sports collectibles.

Baseball is king of collectible sports,
but golf and fishing continue their
meteoric rise in popularity and value of
the last few years.

Balls, gloves, bats, uniforms, belts,
trophies, medals, photos, programs...
Value depends more on the names of
the players involved than artistry or
rarity in many cases. The importance
of condition varies.

Card collectors often require near
perfection while collectors of other
items might treasure worn cracked
game bats and balls, a sign they were
used by the heroes they collect.

Sports and non sports gum cards
can be valuable but you are not
qualified to evaluate them. A mistake
can cost you $1,000 or more.
Get cards evaluated by an expert.

Right now, 50's, 60's, and 70's
players are hot. Many experts feel now
is a good time to cash in cards from
that period as they are being forged,
and the market could collapse as a
result. It's happened in other hobbies!

tony hyman

Miscellaneous Sports

★ **Sports memorabilia of all types, especially baseball**, but also football, boxing, hockey, and others. Buys programs, baseball bats, autographed balls, major league uniforms and shoes, gum cards, sports advertising, contracts, sheet music, buttons, books, scorecards, tickets, prints, films, photos, and more. Kenrich, one of the country's largest mail order sports dealers, has 23 years' experience.
Bill Colby
Kenrich Co.
9418T Las Tunas Dr.
Temple City, CA 91780
   (818) 286-3888 Fax: (818) 286-6035

★ **Baseball, football, boxing, basketball, and Olympic memorabilia** is wanted:
[1] Uniforms, trophies, and medals from
     famous athletes past and present;
[2] Baseball gum cards pre-1920;
[3] Cabinet size sports photographs;
[4] Posters and advertising display pieces
     related to sports, pre-1930;
[5] World Series (1903-11) and all star game
     programs, and press pins;
[6] Black baseball bats;
[7] Rare autograph material of now deceased
     important players;
[8] Championship boxing belts and robes;
[9] Song sheets, games, and toys related
     to sports pre-1920.
"Unique, unusual, and rare" sports equipment and other material, especially related to Hall of Fame players from the 1920's and 1930's, is sought. All items must be old, rare, and original.
Joel Platt
Sports Immortals Museum
807 Liberty Ave.
Pittsburgh, PA 15222
   (412) 232-3008

★ **Early sports memorabilia.** "I'll buy sports ephemera 1860-1970, mainly early baseball items. I want cards, pins, postcards, silks, leathers, advertising, and autographs from boxing and football as well as baseball." Describe the condition and indicate the price you have in mind.
Steve Applebaum
Box 326
Temple City, CA 91780
   (818) 286-8311

★ **Baseball, football, and boxing memorabilia** including gum cards, World Series programs, books pre-1920, display posters, baseball scorecards pre-1900, baseball equipment pre-1920, football equipment pre-1930, all uniforms pre-1960, baseball guides pre-1920, football guides pre-1930, and advertising display pieces. "Premium prices paid for 19th century baseball items." Sought after boxing items are those dealing with James J. Corbett, Jim Jeffries, and John L. Sullivan. This 30 year veteran collector offers $1,500 for an *Allen & Ginter* poster depicting 1890's baseball cards, but does not want *anything* after 1970.
John Buonaguidi
540 Reeside Ave.
Monterey, CA 93940
   (408) 375-7345

★ **Baseball memorabilia**, pre-1948: postcards, photos, games, programs, yearbooks, guides, advertising, fans, sheet music, etc. Buys autographs from early dead Hall-of-Fame players. Pictures of major league baseball players on gum and tobacco cards, programs, silks, sheet music, photographs, and advertising before 1950 are wanted by this 25 year advanced collector-dealer, but he does not buy anything after 1960. Be as accurate as possible with descriptions and include your phone number with your letter. Photocopies are helpful.
William Mastro
25 Brook Lane
Palos Park, IL 60464
   (708) 361-2117

★ **Baseball, football, and boxing memorabilia** especially autographs of dead Hall-of-Famers and other important players. Wants yearbooks of New York sports teams and programs from championship events in all three sports. Will buy tickets, pins, and advertising items which mention players or teams, but **not interested in baseball or other sports cards.** "Sellers should be willing to send the item to me, or a good photo or Xerox© for inspection."
Richard Simon Sports, Inc. Dept TH
215 E. 80th Street
New York, NY 10021
   (212) 988-1349

★ **Philadelphia Phillies memorabilia**, especially pre-1920 programs.
Gary Gatanis
3283-B Cardiff Ct.
Toledo, OH 43606

★ **Babe Ruth material.** Send photocopy to this major Eastern stamp and ephemera dealer.
> Harvey Dolin & Company
> 5 Beekman St. #406
> New York, NY 10038
>   (212) 267-0216

★ **Baseball memorabilia from the Pacific Coast League** and selected other minor leagues. Most items wanted date from the 1940's and early 50's and include programs, selected team and League year books, *P.C.L. Baseball News*, postcards of ball parks, 1947 *Signal Oil* cards, and team photos. No cards from *Mothers Cookies, Union Oil, Remar*, or 1948 *Signal* gas. Also buys programs and other ephemera associated with **non-baseball use of Gilmore Field, Gilmore Stadium and Pan Pacific auditorium.**
> Jerry Mezerow
> 442 Via Porto Ave.
> Anaheim, CA 92806
>   (714) 630-6198

★ **Notre Dame football programs and other memorabilia** from pre-1960, especially Knute Rockne and George Gipp autographs and other items. Other Notre Dame sports considered.
> Michael Tiltges
> 2040 185th St.
> Lansing, IL 60438
>   (312) 895-3222

★ **Balls** from various sports including pre-1950 leather footballs, baseballs, soccer balls, and basketballs. Looking for moderately priced old leather balls from before 1940 suitable for decorator items. Not interested in balls autographed by famous persons.
> Joan Brady
> 834 Central Ave.
> Pawtucket, RI 02861
>   (401) 725-5753

★ **Canadian sports memorabilia.** "I'll buy all items associated with **Canadian hockey** teams and players before 1960, **Canadian lacrosse** teams and players, and **Canadian basketball** teams and players. I'm particularly looking for game schedules and calendars, programs, autographed photos, gum cards, etc. If practical, a clear photocopy is best. Small items can be sent on approval as I will always refund postage."
> Michael Rice
> Box 286
> Saanichton, BC V0S 1M0, CANADA
>   (604) 652-9047 eves

★ **Old sports equipment** that is suitable for restaurant, theme, model home, and other decorative purposes, including:
>   [1] **Wooden skis and bamboo poles.** Brand name doesn't matter, and neither do bindings, as long as they are all wood and in reasonably good condition;
>   [2] **Leather football helmets;**
>   [3] **Lacrosse equipment** including sticks, balls, and leather knee pads;
>   [4] **Snow shoes,** which are preferred intact with original gut, but frames will be considered;
>   [5] **Croquet mallets** or complete boxed sets if old and paint is in good condition;
>   [6] **Cricket bats** and balls;
>   [7] **Riding equipment** including tall boots, leather whips, velveteen riding hats, English style ladies' side saddles;
>   [8] **Wicker creels** and inexpensive bamboo fishing poles, fish nets, etc.

All items should be pre-1940 and be fairly well cared for. Please give a general description of what you have, or telephone with the item in hand. "I am seeking low end decorative items, not fine expensive antiques. If what you have is very valuable, take it somewhere else."
> Joan Brady
> 834 Central Ave.
> Pawtucket, RI 02861
>   (401) 725-5753

★ **Bodybuilding ephemera.** "I'll buy anything before 1975 related to strength, body building, physical culture, weight lifting, strongmen, etc. I buy books, magazines, training courses, photos, catalogs, programs, posters, letters, figurines, trophies, medals, certificates and videos. I'd like anything by Milo Publishing Company, George Jowett, or Eugen Sandow. I am not interested in magazines after 1970, nor do I want anything that is currently in print. Please describe what you have, give its date and condition, and your price."
> William Moore
> Joe Weider Fan Club
> PO Box 732
> Tuscaloosa, AL 35402

★ **Strongmen, weightlifters, and bodybuilders.** "I'll buy magazines, photos, books, posters, sculpture, and equipment related to these fields."
> David Chapman
> 656 32nd Ave. East
> Seattle, WA 98112
>   (206) 329-7573

★ **Ephemera related to Frank Gotch**, a turn of the century wrestling champion. He wants posters, postcards, books, photographs, etc.
> Don Olson
> Box 245
> Humboldt, IA 50548

★ **Running memorabilia.** "I'll buy medals, ribbons, trophies, cards, annuals, magazines, programs, and books related to running, track & field, road races, and the Olympics." Not interested in items since 1960, but will consider reproductions of some posters and other printed material. Tell what you have and its condition. Ed is president of the Motor City Striders, has been director of numerous races, and writes for various running magazines.
> Ed Kozloff
> 10144 Lincoln
> Huntington Woods, MI 48070
> (313) 544-9099

★ **Ice skating memorabilia** including early skates, skater's lanterns, Ice Show programs, and related books, magazines, postcards, photos, autographs, etc. Send details and prices.
> Keith Pendell
> 1230 N. Cypress
> La Habra, CA 90631

★ **Old surfboards and surfing related items**, from before 1970, such as magazines, posters, stickers, patches, etc. Wants round nosed pre-1970 longboards over 9' long, but will consider "transitional" boards from 1967-1971, if unusual in some way. Not interested in pointed nose boards. Would love to find a board ridden and signed by Duke Kahanamoku. Wants to know the make and size of the board, shape, material, age, condition, and by whom it was used. Make certain to describe the fin. On foam boards, note the number, material, and thickness of the stringers.
> Wayne Babcock
> 4846 Carpenteria Ave.
> Carpenteria, CA 93013
> (805) 684-8148 days or 684-0195 eves

★ **Roller skating memorabilia.**
> Frank Zottoli
> Box 241
> Holden, MA 01520

★ **Tennis memorabilia** such as trophies, figurines, art, postcards, cartoons, tableware, trade cards, lighters, first day covers, and all sorts of other little tennis-related knickknacks from before 1940. He does *not* want to buy rackets, photos, newspaper clippings, books, autographs, or programs, but "I'll buy any quantity of other reasonably priced items if they send a photo or photocopy and price what they have."
> Sheldon Katz
> 211 Roanoke Ave.
> Riverhead, NY 11901
> (516) 369-1100

★ **Croquet ephemera.** Will buy distinctive full size mallets, pegs, wickets, table or parlor sets, books pamphlets, catalogs, photos of people playing croquet, jewelry, and other items related to the game. Please send Xerox© copies or photos, along with your description of condition. Prefers that you price what you have if possible.
> Allen Scheuch,
> 356 W. 20th St.
> New York, NY 10011

★ **Recreational and competitive horseback riding.** Wants ephemera related to Morgan horses, Arabians, saddlebred horses, polo ponies, sidesaddles, and Lippizzaners. Buys books, catalogs, prints, and tack. She would especially like to find books by or illustrated by Paul Brown and George Ford Morris.
> Barbara Cole
> October Farm
> Rt. 2, Box 183-C
> Raleigh, NC 27610

★ **Rugby and soccer memorabilia** wanted for resale. Can be either U.S. or foreign. Wants prints, cigarette cards, stamps, postcards, and paper ephemera. Also buys large items like coin operated games and strength machines with soccer or rugby themes.
> Matt Godek,
> Box 565
> Merrifield, VA 22116

★ *Flexible Flyer* sledding. Wants "anything" having to do with *Flexible Flyer* sleds, including membership cards, models, pins, advertising, company literature, and rare sleds. Thorough description, Xerox©, or photo helpful.
> Joan Palicia,
> 15 Canton Road
> Wayne, NY 07470
> (201) 831-0527

★ **Negro League memorabilia** including bats, autographed balls, gloves and uniforms. "Anything in good condition will be considered."
Robert Faro
Box 11286
Boulder, CO 80301

★ **Pool tables** and other ephemera related to pool or billiards. Wants cased custom cues, catalogs, advertising, and other items.
Time After Time,
North Ridge Plaza
5 Padanaram Rd.
Danbury, CT 06810
(203) 743-2801

★ **Pool and billiard memorabilia.** Wants interesting and unusual items associated with the game sucprints h as light fixtures, cue sticks and racks. Also buys catalogs, advertising, signs, prints and other items that are related.
Dilworth Billiards
300 East Tremont
Charlotte, NC 28203

★ **Sports equipment:** bats, gloves, catcher's gear, football stuff. "Ready to make offers."
David Bushing
342 N. Third
Libertyville, IL 60048
(708) 816-6847

★ **Loving cup trophies** from before 1950. May be awarded for sports, beauty, service, heroism, or anything else as long as they have handles on each side and are 8" high or taller. No other style trophies, and nothing after 1950.
Joan Brady
834 Central Ave.
Pawtucket, RI 02861
(401) 725-5753

★ **Pennants** of all types, sports, events, tourist spots, universities, etc. Particularly interested in larger quantities of older ones. Depending on quantity, condition, size, age and rarity he pays from $1-5 each. Doesn't want tears, moth holes, fading, cracked or missing lettering, and has no interest in pennants "made of a stiff felt-like material." Usually not interested in pennants that are printed in neon or fluorescent colors, as they are newer. Xerox©.
Curtis Sharp
147 Columbia Heights, #1
Brooklyn Heights, NY 11201

Golf

★ **Golf memorabilia pre-1930,** especially:
[1] **Unusual wood shaft golf clubs;**
[2] **Golf books, magazines, and catalogs** pre-1930;
[3] **China and pottery** with a golf motif by *Lenox, Doulton,* other fine makers;
[4] **Old golf balls** and golf ball molds;
[5] **Quality miscellaneous items** related to "the knickers era."
This 35 year veteran collector does **not** want petty jewelry, reproductions, modern ashtrays, trinkets, common wood shaft clubs and common golf bags. Frank prefers you set the price you want, but will make offers on rare items.
Frank Zadra
Rt. 3, Box 3318
Spooner, WI 54801
(715) 635-2791

★ **Old golf books, magazines, and ephemera.** No paperback reprints or post 1950 magazines.
George Lewis
Golfiana
Box 291
Mamaroneck, NY 10543

★ **Golf award medals from before WWII** and other pre-1930 golf ephemera. If it's early and in good condition, ship it insured for his top offer. Items are purchased outright or taken on consignment for his international auctions.
Rich Hartzog
Box 4143 BID
Rockford, IL 61110
(815) 226-0771 Fax: (815) 397-7662

★ **Golf memorabilia** of all sorts, including clubs, early balls, books, prints, paintings, photos, scorecards, tournament programs, china, trophies, catalogs, statues, ashtrays, desk sets... you name it, whatever it is, if it has a golf motif, he's interested. "Paying premium prices for premium pieces." Does appraisals for a fee. Will consider consignments of certain items.
Richard Regan
3 Highview Terrace
Bridgewater, MA 02324
(508) 826-3537 or (508) 279-1296 eves

Auto Racing

★ **Auto racing memorabilia.** One piece or a complete collection of anything and everything associated with automobile racing: awards, arm bands, board games, dash plaques, entry forms, flags, goggles, helmets, magazines, models (built or unbuilt), movies, photographs, paintings, passes, postcards, posters, rule books, toys, trophies, uniforms, and "any and all items that are auto racing related" If you know any history of the item, let him know when describing what you have and its condition. This ex race driver has been collecting 25 years and is willing to travel "a reasonable distance" to buy collections.
   George Koyt
   8 Lenora Ave.
   Morrisville, PA 19067

★ **Indianapolis 500** pit badges pre-1952, race tickets pre-1950, racing programs pre-1941, and all rings or trophies. Jerry will pay $300 for a 1946 pit badge.
   Jerry Butak
   242 W. Adams
   Villa Park, IL 60181
     (312) 834-3729

★ **Auto racing ephemera,** including books, programs, posters, and what have you.
   Walter Miller,
   6710 Brooklawn Pkwy
   Syracuse, NY 13211
     (315) 432-8282

★ **Auto racing before 1916,** especially items associated with the Vanderbilt Cup races or with the Long Island Motor Parkway.
   George Spruce,
   33 Washington St.
   Sayville, NY 11782
     (516) 563-4211

Horse Racing

★ **Thoroughbred racing memorabilia** including racing and breeding books, prints, photos, games, trade and tobacco cards, trophies, postcards, etc., especially early Kentucky Derby programs, glasses and anything unusual. Program from 1932 Caliente race featuring Phar Lap especially sought. All thoroughbreds will be considered. No harness horses.
   Gary Medeiros
   1319 Sayre St.
   San Leandro, CA 94579
     (510) 351-6193

★ **Dan Patch memorabilia,** especially a Dan Patch cigar box and mechanical postcard. Also wants pre-1950 **Kentucky Derby programs, drinking glasses featuring horse racing,** and turn of the century **horse racing programs.**
   Gary Gatanis
   3283-B Cardiff Ct.
   Toledo, OH 43606

★ **Trotters, pacers, and harness horse memorabilia.** This former horse trainer wants advertising signs, county fair posters, tins, buttons, and other ephemera depicting famous trotters and pacers. He generally wants them shown in harness or with their record winning time. His number one want is a *Dan Patch* coffee container. Please describe thoroughly, including an accurate description of condition.
   Donald Ackerman
   149 E. Joseph Street
   Moonachie, NJ 07074
     (201) 807-0881

Hunting & Fishing

★ **Fishing and gun ephemera** including catalogs, posters, calendars, pinback buttons, trade cards, and decorated envelopes from before 1940. He is also interested in any fishing and hunting images from before 1900, including prints, original art, and illustrated books. Will make offers only after personally inspecting what you have to sell.
Russell Mascieri
6 Florence Ave.
Marlton, NJ 08053
(609) 985-7711   fax (609) 985-8513

★ **Antique fishing tackle** including bait and fly reels, bamboo fly and bait casting rods, willow creels, wooden nets, fishing lures (especially those with glass eyes), and early tackle boxes made of leather. Wants to find brass *Snyder* bait casting reels from early 1800's. Also buys fishing equipment **catalogs and books**. Not interested in anything made in the last 20 years.
Robert Whitaker
2810 E. Desert Cove Ave.
Phoenix, AZ 85028
(602) 992-7304

★ **Fishing tackle from before 1945** including wooden lures (especially with glass eyes or made of hollow metal), high quality fresh or salt water reels, fine cased bamboo rods, and tackle boxes. "Most people can't tell good stuff from bad. I'll check it all for them," says this veteran collector. List all brand names and numbers and make photocopies of lures. Collect calls will be accepted if you have a collection for sale.
Rick Edmisten
Box 686
North Hollywood, CA 91603
(818) 763-9406

★ **Old fishing lures,** especially *Heddon* 7500 vamps, *Heddon* 100 and 150 minnows, and all frog shaped lures. Also **odd fish scalers.** When writing, include a Xerox© of your lures, and indicate their color. Give your phone number.
Thomas McKinnon
PO Box 86
Wagram, NC 28396
(919) 369-2367

★ **Antique and classic fishing tackle** and ephemera from before 1940. Wants include:
[1] **Old wood or metal lures** in good condition; metal lures must be marked with the name of the maker or patent information, but wooden lures need not be marked; **do not want** plastic lures or lures in poor condition;
[2] **Reels of all types**, especially higher quality or with unusual features; some broken or damaged reels will be considered; **do not want** reels by *Penn, Ocean City, True Temper,* or *Lawrence* nor do they want spinning reels or spin casting reels unless very unusual;
[3] **Bamboo rods; do not want** metal rods, fiberglass rods, or rods in poor condition;
[4] **Fishing paraphernalia,** creels, tackle boxes and tools; **do not want** lead sinkers;
[5] **Early fishing licenses;**
[6] **Paintings and prints** related to fishing, including calendars, advertising, and cigarette cards; **do not want** damaged artwork.
In general they do not want anything made in the Orient or made after 1940. "We will deal with experts or with novice sellers. We make offers when necessary, but prefer folks to set their own prices. You may call, *not collect,* between 9am and 10pm. When writing, include a Xerox© or photograph. Always include your phone number. Do not ship anything without our permission first."
Ed and Carolyn Corwin
c/o All-Safe
200 State Road 206 East
St. Augustine, FL 32086
(904) 797-6464 day (904) 692-2037 eve

★ **Antique and modern fishing tackle** is wanted by an "avid fisherman" who buys quality bamboo fly rods, wooden lures with glass eyes, old tackle boxes, large ocean reels, and early tackle catalogs.
Lee Pattison
113 N. 4th Street
Olean, NY 14760
(716) 373-3098

★ **Traps, set guns, alarm guns, trapping and fur company items** such as posters, calendars, catalogs, advertising, and related memorabilia from before 1940. Does not want paper items that have been trimmed.
Ron Willoughby
1072 Route 171
Woodstock, CT 06281
(203) 974-1226

Decoys

★ **Wooden decoys and calls** for ducks, geese, crow, and fish. Buys ice fishing decoys, wooden plugs, and early reels made by *Meek, Talbot, Milan,* or *KY Bluegrass* (for which he will pay $100 up). Joe quotes prices of $200+ paid for better duck calls. Also buys various hunting and fishing signs. He suggests you send photos, but may require you to send the item for inspection before he purchases it.
   Joe Tonelli
   Box 130
   Spring Valley, IL 61362

★ **Wooden decoys of all types** including duck, swan, goose, crow, owl, shorebirds, and fish. Only old wooden items are wanted, but will consider items in any condition. You must include photos.
   Art Pietraszewski, Jr.
   60 Grant St.
   Depew, NY 14043
   (716) 681-2339

★ **Early decoys of all types** are wanted by this well known auctioneer, noted for his record setting decoy sales. Many duck decoys have value in excess of $1,000 so you are encouraged to send a good photograph along with a tracing or sketch of any markings or signatures on the bottom. No decoys made after 1940 please.
   James D. Julia Auctions
   Box 830
   Fairfield, ME 04937
   (207) 453-7904   Fax: (207) 453-2502

★ **Old duck, crow, and goose calls and decoys.** "I'll buy wooden decoys and calls in any quantity." Send a note or call with the description and the price you'd like.
   Jack Morris
   821 Sandy Ridge
   Doylestown, PA 18901
   (215) 348-9561

Boxing

★ **Boxing memorabilia of all types.** "I'm the world's largest dealer in boxing memorabilia. Large stocks on hand to buy, sell, or trade." Please photograph of photocopy.
   Jerome Shochet
   6144 Oakland Mills Rd.
   Sykesville, MD 21784
   (301) 795-5879

★ **Boxing photos and autographs** from before 1920. Please photocopy what you have.
   Johnny Spellman, DVM
   10806 North Lamar
   Austin, TX 78753
   (512) 836-2889 days;   (512) 258-6910

★ **Boxing memorabilia of all types.** Private collector, who operates a gym, seeks posters, programs, tickets, films, photographs, books and magazines, and all awards from Golden Glove ribbons to Championship belts. "If you have single items or a large collection, whether it's from the earliest days or the present champs, I'd like to hear about it."
   Fredrick Ryan
   PO Box 83135
   Portland, OR 97203
   (503) 286-3597

Gum Cards

★ **Baseball and all other sports and non-sports cards** from gum, tobacco, dairy, candy and other sources. This major sports card dealer especially wants baseball cards pre-1930. Also buys **wrappers** from pre-1970 gum packs, and lots of other sports memorabilia.
Bill Colby
Kenrich Co.
9418-T Las Tunas
Temple City, CA 91780
    (818) 286-3888

★ **Baseball and other sports cards** from gum, cigarettes, or candy. Also buys all yearbooks, programs, press pins, ticket stubs, autographs. "To a lesser degree" he also buys **basketball, football, and hockey items,** especially cards 1930-1959. Give condition details.
Robert Sevchuk
70 Jerusalem Ave.
Hicksville, NY 11801
    (516) 822-4089

★ **pre-1975 non-sports cards from candy, tobacco, and other sources.** Wants *Horrors of War, Dark Shadows, Hogans Heroes, Lost in Space, Mars Attack,* etc. Also seeks unopened boxes, wrappers, original artwork, and advertising, especially for test issues of *Hee Haw, The Waltons, Green Acres* etc. "I'll pay $1,000 for the set of *Horrors of War.*" Items must be in excellent to mint condition with no creases and fairly sharp corners.
Roxanne Toser
4019 Green St.
Harrisburg, PA 17110
    (717) 238-1936

★ **Non-sports gum cards from 1930-49.** Wants cards featuring pirates, WW II, Indians and cowboys, and comic strip characters only.
Walter Koenig
Box 4395
North Hollywood, CA 9160

Bobbing Head Dolls

★ **Bobbing head sports and non-sports dolls of all types,** especially composition/papier mache dolls from the 1960's. Wants all types of dolls from all sports, but especially miniature bobbing heads about 4" tall and real player dolls. When you write, give the color of the base.
Dale Jerkins
1647 Elbur Ave.
Lakewood, OH 44107
    (216) 226-7349

★ **Bobbing head sports and non-sports dolls,** Japanese ceramic or composition models only, no plastic dolls or dolls made in Taiwan or Korea. Indicate team or character portrayed. Also give the size, color, and shape of the base. Will pay $150 for any Blackface bobbing baseball doll in perfect condition and $600 for a perfect Roberto Clemente. Also wants **sports and non sports plastic statues by Hartland.** Will pay between $100 and $700 for excellent and complete statues, depending on the character.
Chip Norris
Box 235
Leonardtown, MD 20650
    (301) 475-2951

★ **Bobbing head and nodder dolls.** Prefer people or famous characters. Special wants include the *Pillsbury Doughboy, Elsie* the *Borden's* cow, Popeye, Presidents Eisenhower and Kennedy, Maynard, Minnie Mouse, Porky Pig, and Elmer Fudd. Also want double nodder salt and pepper shakers, ashtrays, and other unusual nodders.
Roxanne Toser
4019 Green St.
Harrisburg, PA 17110
    (717) 238-1936

the vices

"The Devil has all the good songs"

was a popular 19th century saying. Today folks say the same thing about collectibles. Nearly everything associated with liquor, gambling, tobacco, sports, sex, and other recreation is collected. Religious items are of far less interest and value (although in *I'll Buy That Too!* we have the most religious item collectors we're ever had for you) .

The best advice I can give you is to check out everything, especially older advertising, pre-WWI cigarette packs, liquor bottles with the label embedded in the glass, and all mechanical devices having to do with smoking, gambling, or liquor.

Collecting briar pipes is one of the faster growing hobbies and an area with many possibilities for profit. Don't ever throw out (or pass by) briar pipes without looking to see if you have found one of the more collectible brands. Valuable briar pipes ($25 - $100) are often bought for pennies at yard sales and second hand stores.

Cigar boxes are often overlooked. Collectors want fine condition pre-1920 boxes with interesting labels. The value of boxes is $5-$75 for most, although a few can bring $150 or more.

Many collectors of tobacciana, breweriana, gambling and saloon paraphernalia are interested only in brightly colored items to decorate their walls. Others are serious historians, seeking every photo, catalog, and scrap of historical information. Help out!

tony hyman

Beer

★ **Anything with the name of a beer on it.** It's called *breweriana*, and includes glasses, coasters, trays, calendars, label collections, signs, mugs, and anything else used to promote beer. Lynn particularly wants tin signs and other display advertising from around the turn of the century. Lynn is one of the nation's foremost authorities on beer collectibles, and operator of an auction service exclusively devoted to items associated with beer. No *Billy Beer* or *J.R.* beer.
Lynn Geyer
PO Box 47177
Phoenix, AZ 85068
(602) 943-2283

★ **Beer cans** from before 1950. This 18 year veteran beer collector also wants other beer advertising signs, trays, coasters, and bottles. He is particularly interested in cans for the seven brands of the Los Angles Monarch Brewing Company (five of which will bring you over $1,000 each if you can find them). Make certain to describe condition carefully. No *Billy Beer*, *J.R.* beer, or cans with pull tab tops.
Mike Miller
PO Box 1275
La Canada, CA 91012
1-800-882-2337

★ **Pre-1965 beer and soda cans from small regional companies.** Prefers cone topped cans but also buys flat topped cans. Also buys brewery advertising, signs, trays, statues, glasses, from the same period. Especially likes to find items from the Manhattan Brewing Company owned by Al Capone and the Grace Bros. Brewing Company in California. Prices on cans from these two companies tend to start at $500. No rusty cans are wanted by this ten year veteran collector-dealer, but "some light spotting and aging is natural. I do require cans be sent before a final purchase offer is made because condition so greatly affects the value and I need to examine cans closely."
Tony Steffens
1115 Cedar Ave
Elgin, IL 60120
(800) 443-8712 Fax: (708) 742-5778

★ **Beer uniform sew-on patches from anywhere in the world.** Jim wants any patches, arm, cap, shirt, all ages, all sizes, all breweries...any sewn patch naming a brewery. He isn't interested in beer club patches. Please describe condition noting whether it is used or unused, clean or not, and indicate whether it is a "second" or has been cut from a larger patch. Photocopy helpful.
Jim O'Brien
Box 551
Aurora, IL 60507
(312) 892-8535 eves/ weekends

★ **Beer bottles with painted labels.** American breweries only. Most of these are 6, 7, or 8 ounce size, but some older ones from the 1930's are 12 oz. There are a few, very desirable, larger bottles with painted labels. He is particularly interested in finding New York bottles, especially from Buffalo, Rochester, Utica, Syracuse, Troy, Tonawanda, and New York City. Describe condition of the paint. No soft drink bottles, please, even if from breweries.
Jim O'Brien
Box 551
Aurora, IL 60507
(312) 892-8535 eves/some days

★ *Hamm's* **brewery memorabilia** including advertising, packaging and bottles, souvenirs, foam scrapers, coasters, bottle caps, kegs, glasses, signs, and so on, for all of *Hamm's* brands. These include *Buckhorn, Velvet Glove, Matterhorn, Burgie, Right Time, Old Bru,* and *Waldech*. When selling glasses or cans, it is important to include *all* writing that appears on the object. Pete wants everything he doesn't already have and says that the areas around Houston, Los Angeles, San Francisco, Baltimore, and St. Paul "are particularly saturated with *Hamm's* breweriana."
Peter Nowicki
1531 39th Ave.
San Francisco, CA 94122
(415) 566-7506

★ **Beer mugs and steins** made in the 1970's and 80's by the *Ceramate* Brazil Company. "I'll buy both the lidded and unlidded varieties of such favorites as Budman, Busch Gardens, Clydesdales, Olympics, etc."
Tony Steffens
1115 Cedar Ave
Elgin, IL 60120
(800) 443-8712 Fax: (708) 742-5778

★ **New Jersey breweriana** from the 1930's or older including calendars, signs, trays, tap knobs and inserts, coasters, labels, cans, books and misc. "I would buy some collections of general breweriana if they contained some NJ items I want." He warns amateurs not to guess at age of items, that it's better to ask and urges you not to "buy breweriana items with the thought of reselling them to make money, since the chances are you won't." This 17 year veteran collector requests that you make it clear whether you are seeking information or have the item for sale.

   Paul Brady
   Box 811
   Newton, NJ 07860
     (201) 383-7204

★ **Near beer advertising from the days of prohibition in Chicago** and items related to Chicago pre-prohibition beers and breweries like *Budweiser, Schlitz, Blatz, Old Milwaukee, Atlas, Keely, Schoenhoffen, Sieben's,* and *Manhattan.* Wants signs, beer barrels, bottles, etc.

   Michael Graham
   Roaring 20's
   345 Cleveland Ave.
   Libertyville, IL 60048
     (312) 362-4808 days

★ **Any coasters with advertising, especially for beer.** Interested *only* in U.S. coasters. "Send any quantity for my prompt fair offer by return check."

   Art Landino
   88 Centerbrook Rd.
   Hamden, CT 06518

★ **Pottery ginger beer bottles** and associated paper ephemera. Sven has an illustrated wants list of these bottles, some of which can be worth $150! He is author of *The Illustrated Stone Ginger Beer,* a limited edition available for $12.50.

   Sven Stau
   Box 437
   Buffalo, NY 14212
     (716) 825-5448 or (716) 822-3120

★ **American and foreign miniature beer bottles** especially pre-prohibition 1880-1920. The earliest are about 5" tall, filled with beer, and have a cork stopper. These are desirable if they have complete labels or the bottles are embossed. Post-prohibition bottles are smaller and of interest only if all labels are complete and in good condition. Foreign bottles must be in mint condition to be of interest. Also bottle openers with handles in the shape of mini beer bottles, wood or metal. There is a small group of post prohibition mini beers which can be worth to $100 each. They include *Old Glory, Royal Pilsen, Wagner, Spearman, Ambrosia, Nectar, Frederick's 4 Crown, Citizens, Manro, Atlantic, Pennsy* and others. Alex will pay top price forsets of mini bottles in their original box. Condition of the label is crucial so describe every scratch or discoloration. Measure exact height. Also buys bottle shaped bottle openers. No Taiwan bottles.

   Alexander Mullin
   915 Lincoln Ave.
   Springfield, PA 19064

★ **Anheuser Busch advertising and ephemera** from before prohibition.

   Vern Bauckman
   2219 Old Bridge Road
   Woodbridge, VA 22192
     (703) 590-2988 eves

★ *Budweiser* **ceramic beer steins.** "I'll buy, for top dollar, any of the early Grant's Farms steins, and various *Bud* steins from 1975 and 1976. Steins are for my personal collection and must be in mint condition."

   Joseph Venanzi
   46 Wolfpack Rd.
   Trenton, NJ 08619
     (609) 586-3414

★ *Dixie* **beer and Lexington brewery ephemera** including openers, trays, fobs, mirrors, letterheads, and what have you.

   Thom Thompson
   1389 Alexandra Drive, #5
   Lexington, KY 40504
     (606) 255-2727

Beer Steins

★ **Steins.** "I buy etched and print *Mettlachs*, colored glass steins with pewter casings/lids or fine enameling, milk glass, early blue-gray *Westerwald*, faience, figural steins or plain gray steins with painted decorations of brewery logos, any Muenchen, and anything unusual. All must have lids and be before 1920. I do not want gaudy low relief pottery souvenir steins either cream colored or gray-blue. Photo is essential, as is a complete description including any cracks, hairlines, dents chips, or color wear. Lottie is a private collector and prolific writer about steins.
Lottie Lopez
Box 885
Santa Paula, CA 93060

★ **Steins** including fine early *Mettlach*, regimental, faience, stoneware, glass, porcelain, occupational, *Royal Vienna, Meissin*, or wooden. Gary has written five books on steins; his *The Beer Stein Book* is $42 postpaid.
Gary Kirsner
Box 8807
Coral Springs, FL 33075

★ **Antique beer steins of all types,** from $10 to $10,000 except those made after WWII. This active collector/dealer will buy one or a large collection. A photo is helpful, as are all markings, measurements, and a description of what is portrayed. Don't forget to note the condition of the stein and lid. He offers free appraisals with no obligation and, if you telephone him with your stein in your hand, he can usually tell you it's wholesale and retail value over the phone. He holds regular stein auctions, writes articles and is available to give talks.
Les Paul
568 County Isle
Alameda, CA 94501
   (510) 523-7480 or fax (510) 523-8755

Whiskey & Wine

★ *Jack Daniels, Green River Whiskey,* **and Lem Motlow memorabilia,** including crockery jugs, embossed bottles, cork screws, shot glasses, lighters, and old paper advertising. Older items only.
Don Cauwels
3947 Old South Road
Murfreesboro, TN 37129
   (615) 896-3614

★ *Green River Whiskey* **advertising and other memorabilia,** including paper, signs, display bottles, watch fobs, "giveaways," counter displays, and company receipts, letterheads, etc. Will pay $150-250 for warehouse receipts or shot glasses. Clear pencil rubbings of advertising "coins" is a must, as many types exist. No *Green River* soft drink please.
Elijah Singley
2301 Noble Ave.
Springfield, IL 62704
   (217) 546-5143 eves

★ *Dewar's* **scotch figural liquor bottles made by** *Royal Doulton*. Called KingsWare by *Doulton* collectors, more than 100 different figural bottles were commissioned in the 1920's and 30's. These distinctive brown-glazed bottles feature various literary characters and English historical figures. He pays $300+ each, says this veteran *Royal Doulton* dealer, as long as the figure is not chipped or cracked. If you wish to sell yours, call with the item in front of you.
Ed Pascoe, Pascoe & Co.
545 Michigan Ave.,
Miami Beach, FL 33139
   (800) 872-0195   Fax (305) 532-8543

★ **Liquor advertising pitchers and ashtrays.** "I'll buy liquor advertising pitchers and ashtrays that are unusual and in excellent condition. I don't want the more common ones but if you are unsure of what you have, please send a sketch or photo. The mark on the bottom and the liquor company advertising are important for indentification, as is the color. I don't want any glass pitchers or glass ashtrays, only pottery, china or porcelain."
Robert & Susan Cox
800 Murray Drive
El Cajon, CA 92020
   (619) 447-0800 days

★ Ceramic *Jim Beam* type figural liquor bottles. The bottle *must* have its original stopper. Your description should include the brand name, the figure, all marks on the bottom, the dimensions, and all colors. Fred offers a price guide to of 1,500+ figural bottles for only $3.

> Fred Runkewich
> Box 1423
> Cheyenne, WY 82003
> (307) 632-1462

★ Swizzle sticks and picks made of any material, as long as the stick has a three dimensional or cut-out design, either letters, people, buildings, etc. Collections of at least 100 sticks are preferred. Sticks *must* advertise a product, place, or service. Generally pays a dime each.

> Edy Chandler
> Box 20664
> Houston, TX 77225
> (713) 531-9615 eves

★ Wine bottles with embossed oval or circular seals on the shoulder of the bottle marked with the name and vintage, especially fine wineries and vintages. "The more crude the bottle, the better." No beer, whiskey, or wine bottles that do not have shoulder ovals. Also pre-WWII paper wine labels especially 19th century European and pre-prohibition California companies. This expert wine dealer prefers loose labels but will buy important ones still on the bottle. Rene notes that "values are still relatively low for most labels, but they are appreciated."

> Rene Rondeau
> 120 Harbor Dr.
> Corte Madera, CA 94925

★ Corkscrews and wine-related artifacts from before WWII. Buys wine tasters, wine funnels, silver and porcelain wine labels, silver coolers, coasters, decanter wagons, and the like. Will also buy unusual drinking vessels, but does not want to buy glassware or cut glass decanters. Corenman is a leading buyer of corkscrews from 18th and 19th century who is seeking mechanical types, bar mounted types, and those with ivory silver, bone, or pearl handles. Modern post war types are not needed, nor does he want anything that is broken, missing parts, or has repairs. This 25 year veteran expert offers a catalog and wants list. Include your phone number.

> Aaron Corenman
> Box 747
> Los Altos, CA 94023
> (415) 948-6174

★ Corkscrews and wine related items. Collects hand held and bar mounted corkscrews that are unusual in some way. Also wants wine related items such as wine tasters, pre-1930 bottles, silver or ceramic bottle tags, bottle cradles and buckets, etc. Little interest in labels. Xerox© smaller items if possible. Describe the others. "I will answer all letters," says Joe.

> Joe Young
> Box 587
> Elgin, IL 60123
> (708) 695-0108

★ Wine. Old and rare vintages will be purchased by this well known wine dealer but only if you can guarantee the wine has been properly stored, under cool conditions away from light. The fill level and color of a wine need to be inspected prior to purchase. There must be no signs of leakage. Single bottles of rare wines are sometimes purchased, but cases or entire cellars are preferred. Single bottles of pre-prohibition wine found in walls or trunks are purchased for curiosity but are seldom worth more than a few dollars. Free appraisals are available if you supply him with brand name, type of wine, any dates, and what you know of the wine's history.

> Rene Rondeau
> Draper & Esquin Wine Merchants
> 655 Davis Street
> San Francisco, CA 94111
> Fax (415) 397-1851

★ Everything associated with saloons and speakeasies including photos of interiors and exteriors, advertising, saloon equipment catalogs, letterheads, etc. Also trade magazines such as *the National Police Gazette* pre-1919, *Fair Play, Brewers Gazette,* and others.

> Richard Bueschel
> 414 N. Prospect Manor Ave.
> Mt. Prospect, IL 60065
> (708) 253-0791 eves

★ Prohibition artifacts of all kinds, 1919-1933, related to gangster activity in Chicago and environs. Seeks relics from famous speakeasies such as *Colosimo's Cafe, Four Deuces, Red Lantern, Pony Inn, Cotton Club,* and *The Green Mill.* Also pamphlets, posters, and the like from the Anti-Saloon League, WCTU, the Prohibition Party and other groups for/against prohibition.

> Michael Graham, Roaring 20's
> 345 Cleveland Ave.
> Libertyville, IL 60048
> (312) 362-8531 eves

Pipes & Accessories

★ **Pipes of many types** including carved meerschaums, Oriental opium pipes, water pipes, rare porcelain figural pipes, early bas- and high-relief wood pipes, and selected clays. A 20+ year veteran, Ben is author of *A Complete Guide To Collecting Antique Pipes*, available for $20. Ben is a specialist in the literature of tobacco, and buys **books, magazines and pamphlets** on all aspects of tobacco culture and use, in any language, from any period.
Ben Rapaport
11505 Turnbridge Lane
Reston, VA 22094
(703) 435-8133 eves

★ **Antique meerschaum pipes, carved briar, and quality English briars** by *Charitan, Barling,* or *Frieborg & Treyer*. This 25 year collector also buys **American Indian pipes.**
Lee Pattison,
113 N. 4th Street
Olean, NY 14760
(716) 373-3098

★ **Clay pipes and clay pipe ephemera.** Especially wants faces, figurals, or political clay pipes. Prefers American pipes, but buys others. This author-historian also buys pipe molds, presses, or anything else involved in the making of clay pipes. Also wants billheads, letterheads, checks, catalogs, and other advertising before 1950 for any clay pipe maker. Has a particular interest in William Kelman, a Baltimore pipe manufacturer. Generally not interested in plain white clay pipes with no markings or decoration. Please make a photocopy of your items, indicating any markings, and tell what you know about its origin or background. Paul has produced a giant limited edition book on 19th century pipe patents which he sells for $55, a bargain if the topic interests you.
S. Paul Jung, Jr.
Box 817
Bel Air, MD 21014
(301) 676-2194

★ **Antique smoking pipes and pipe parts.** Also buys books and other publications on pipes, tobacco, and related items. Will purchase complete collections as well as individual pipes. Not interested in damaged pipes or reproductions. Give size (length and width), condition, and all other information you can provide. Primary interest is in meerschaums, but also other antique pipes, especially porcelains, and any historical or unusual items.
Frank Burla
23 West 311 Wedgwood
Napierville, IL 60540
(312) 961-0156

★ **Name brand "pre-smoked" (used) briar pipes.** Especially wants *Dunhill, Charatan, Barling, Castello* and other top European brands from 1900-1990. Among special wants, Barry lists *Barling* pipes with bent stems in any finish. When describing a pipe, include the brand name, its dimensions, shape, finish and all stampings on the pipe. If you are not familiar with standard pipe shapes, make a photocopy. Barry does **not** buy antique pipes, meerschaums, or tobacciana. Barry is a popular dealer who produces 6-8 color sales catalogs a year of used briar pipes.
Barry Levin
Levin Pipes International
RFD #1, Box 83
Craftsbury, VT 05826
(802) 586-7744

★ **High grade briar pipes.** Brand names of interest include *Dunhill, Charatan, Barling, Comoy's, Castello, Caminetto, Sasieni, Preben Holm,* and *Peterson.* "I'll buy them smoked or new, as long as they are in good looking condition, with no uneven surfaces on the rim, no tooth holes in the stem, etc. Wants collections of pipes, but will buy singles. He especially wants *Dunhills* with "ODA" or "ODB" and patent dates marked on the stem and *Peterson* pipes with IRISH FREE STATE or EIRE on the shank. Please, no "drug store pipes" like *Medico, Yellow Bole,* or *Dr. Grabow.* When offering pipes for sale, mention any writing on the pipe and its condition. There are dozens of standard pipe shapes, so if you don't know them, send a Xerox©.
Marty Pulvers
Sherlock's Haven
4 Embarcadero Center
San Francisco, CA 94111
(415) 362-1405 or 965-4773

★ **Hookah (water) pipes.** "I'll buy one hose or multiple hose hookah's made of brass, ivory, or other materials. I'm seeking antique pipes, not head shop items, common glass bongs, and other drug paraphrenalia Please send a picture and information about the pipe's background. Dealers should price your goods but I will make offers for amateurs."
Mark Rivkind
363 Bailey Court
Palm Harbor, FL 34684
(813) 787-1169

★ **Smoking accessories and other objects marked** *Dunhill* including pipes, cigarette holders, cigarette lighters, pens, etc. This disabled combat vet says, "I prefer items to be sent to me for my offer. I will refund shipping costs if my purchase price is rejected. But I would like to stress *that I do not need common items, junk, or damaged goods*. I buy only for my own collection and will pay fair prices."
C. Ray Erler
Box 140 Miles Run Road
Spring Creek, PA 16436
(814) 563-7287

★ **Humidors** made of fine glass, china, or copper. Please send a photo of what you have.
Lee Pattison
113 N. 4th Street
Olean, NY 14760
(716) 373-3098

★ **Metal tobacco jars from before 1900.** This 10 year veteran collector is interested in unusual good condition tobacco jars made of pewter, iron, lead, bronze, brass or silver. No tin cans or ceramics. He requires a clear photograph and a statement of condition. He is available to make appraisals but wants you to price your item. Some research may be in order since these can be in the multiple hundreds of dollars.
Arthur Anthony
Mystic Valley Foundry
14 Horace St.
Somerville, MA 02143
(617) 547-1819 weekdays

★ **Snuff boxes** including early American, Civil War period, and Oriental.
Eli Hecht
19 Evelyn Lane
Syosset, NY 11791

★ **Tin tobacco cans** from before 1940, especially pocket tins, tobacco lunchboxes, and cigar cans. Wants mint or very fine condition items only. Save yourself time and effort by sending a Xerox© of the top and front of your tin and describe colors and condition. SASE is a must. If you regularly pick or deal, he will send you an informative flyer listing some tins to look for.
Tony Hyman
Box 3028
Pismo Beach, CA 93448
(805) 773-6777   Fax (805) 773-0177

★ **Tin tobacco tags** and tag collections are bought, sold, and traded by this active collector, who offers a free "suggestion sheet for new collectors." He also has the remaining stock of Gary Schild's $10 book on tobacco tags.
Lee "Tagger Lee" Jacobs
PO Box 3098
Colorado Springs, CO 80934

★ *Mail Pouch Tobacco.* "I'll buy anything and everything, in any size and in any condition."
Mike Boggs
4022 Farnham
Dayton, OH 45420
(513) 252-4839 eves

★ **All Tobacco related collectibles:** "We consider tins, pipes, cigar labels, catalogs, books, cigar boxes, posters, advertising, and other tobacco related ephemera for purchase or auction. Prefer collections, but will accept individual items if value or collectible interest is sufficiently high. Fees are 10%-20% depending upon item's value. If it is something we don't want, wa may be able to suggest where you might go to sell. SASE is a must for an answer. There are often unavoidable long delays in response."
Tobacciana Auctions
2141 Shoreline Drive
Shell Beach, CA 93449

Cigars & Cigarettes

★ **Cigar boxes and all other cigar industry ephemera** including labels, advertising, photographs, counter top lighters, cigar store figures, and everything else related to cigar making, selling, and smoking before WWII. Especially want trade directories (1865-1940) listing cigar and tobacco factories. Want all materials relevant to the Cigar Maker's International Union or to Samuel Gompers, former CMIU officer. Condition is important. Tony asks you Xerox© the inside lid. Pays from $5 to $50+ for cigar boxes, with top boxes bringing $500. Send a long SASE for informative priced wants list [which includes a useful list of common boxes]. Tony wrote *Handbook of American Cigar Boxes,* an illustrated hardback available with a *Price Guide* for $14.95. He says, "I don't want cigar bands or items covered with cigar bands, so pay very little for them."
Tony Hyman
Box 3028
Pismo Beach, CA 93448
   (805) 773-6777   Fax (805) 773-0177

★ **Cigar boxes.** "I'll buy common cardboard and wooden cigar boxes from the 1950's and 60's and 70's. I'm looking for nice clean usable boxes, not collectibles, and pay from 50¢ to $3 each depending on the box. Brands I want include *White Owl, Dutch Masters, Webster, Roi Tan, King Edward, John Ruskin, Robt. Burns, El Producto, Santa Fe, Phillies, Cinco, La Corona, Brooks & Co.,* and *Red Dot,* none of which are wanted by the person above. Send a self-addressed stamped envelope with a description of the boxes available and the numbers involved. It's helpful when you give dimensions."
Judith Garlinger
14225 Garden Road
Poway, CA 92064
   (619) 679-9552

★ **Cigar store Indians.** Wants full size wooden or metal figures, especially Punch. Also wants literature related to them, especially catalogs. Take photos from more than one angle, or phone with the item in front of you.
Gregory "Dr. Z" Zemenick
1350 Kirts, #160
Troy, MI 48084
   (313) 642-8129 or (313) 244-9426

★ **Cigar bands.** Small or moderate collections of inexpensive bands are wanted by a relatively new collector. Your help in developing a collection is appreciated.
Margo Toth
c/o Up Down Tobacco Shop
1550 N. Wells St.
Chicago, IL 60610
   (312) 337-8505

★ **pre-1941 cigar bands** especially older European and Cuban bands or bands with pictures of people, animals, places, etc. No common, current, or damaged bands. Not interested in incomplete sets or large accumulations of similar bands. "I will accept receipt of the bands by mail for an appraisal with an option to purchase. It is next to impossible for a seller to list all the required data. I will not make or accept an offer without seeing them or having *every* band described individually," says this 40 year veteran.
Paul Krantz,
356 Delaware Avenue NE
Massillon, OH 44646
   (216) 833-5429

★ **Cigar band collections** especially U.S. bands prior to 1920. Good or mint condition, only.
Joseph Hruby
1511 Lyndhurst Rd.
Lyndhurst, OH 44124
   (216) 449-0977

★ **Cigarette packs, tins, and cardboard boxes** from obsolete U.S. brands of cigarettes. No cards, premiums, silks, flat 50's tins, or cigar or tobacco items. Give the Series Number found on the tax stamp. Dick is President of the Cigarette Pack Collector's Assn and editor of *Brandstand,* a monthly newsletter for cigarette collectors.
Richard Elliott
61 Searle St.
Georgetown, MA 01833
   (508) 352-7377

★ **Cigarette packs of discontinued brands.** Including tins, boxes, labels, etc. Wants U.S. brands only.
David Brame
5405 Vicksburg Lane
Durham, NC 27712

★ *Lucky Strike* collectibles of any kind. "I'll buy bridge hand cards, celebrity ads, pre-1930 magazine ads, and LS/MFT marked items."
  John Van Alstyne
  466 South Goodman St.
  Rochester, NY 14607

★ *Philip Morris* ephemera prior to 1955, including cigarette packs, tins, advertisings, signs, stand-ups, chocks, matches, buttons, and what have you. This beginning collector does not want reprints, and expects you to price what you wish to sell.
  Stuart Morrell
  8925 Laureate Lane
  Richmond, VA 23236

Insert Cards

★ Cigar and cigarette silks and flannels and items made from them are wanted by this prestigious quilt dealer. No junk. Please take a photo or make a Xerox© of your item. List how many flags and silks and their approximate size.
  Margaret Cavigga
  8648 Melrose Ave.
  Los Angeles, CA 90069
  (213) 659-3020

★ Cigarette and other insert cards. Wants 19th century U.S. cigarette insert cards, especially the *State Seal* series from *August Beck* Tobacco and the *Wellstood Etchings* from *Wm. Kimball.* This 50 year veteran also wants cards from *Brooke-Bond Tea* Company, *Van Houten Cocoa,* and the *Liebig Meat Extract Company.* He will consider Liebig cards in any language, especially menu and calendar cards. Give quantities, and send photocopy showing sample of the front and back of cards.
  Ron Stevenson
  4920 Armoury St.
  Niagara Falls, ON
  Canada L2E 1T1
  (416) 358-5497

★ Cigarette silks in fine condition. Also selected complete sets of early cigarette cards.
  Charles Reuter
  6 Joy Ave.,
  Mount Joy, PA 17552

★ Felts and silks of national flags. Will pay 10¢ to $1 each depending on rarity.
  Jon Radel
  PO Box 2276
  Reston, VA 22090

★ Cigarette and tobacco insert cards and other tobacco related paper. Wants 19th and early 20th century U.S. tobacco and cigarette insert cards, tobacco advertising trade cards, banners, counter stand-ups, hangers, posters, albums, giveaways, premiums, and cigarette slide packs. "Each item listed above must include in the printing one of these words: tobacco, cigarette, cigarros, cut plug, chewing, long cut, smoking, fine cut, scrap cut, or navy cut." Will pay $25 each and up for many early American trade cards, and $700 for the Marquis of Lorne card issued in 1879. He does not want cigar bands, cigar labels, tobacco caddy labels, reproductions or reprints, matchbooks, badly damaged items, or British or other foreign items. Give the size (vertical then horizontal), the maker, and condition. Xerox© a good idea. Items must be in at least very good condition.
  Peter Gilleeny
  36115-76 Rose Drive
  Fruitland Park, FL 34731
  (904) 728-4819

★ Cigarette and tobacco insert cards, silks, and leathers. Wants American 19th century items primarily, such as cards by *Allen & Ginter,* but buys many 20th century pieces. Does not want flannel flags. Also buys tobacco advertising trade cards and tobacco related match covers. "Please describe and price, or send on approval. I pay all postage expenses and respond within 48 hours of receipt. Condition is important as I do not collect trimmed cards, badly creased or otherwise battered items."
  William Nielsen
  PO Box 1379
  Brewster, MA 02631
  (508) 896-7389

Matches & Lighters

★   **Matchcover collections**, match boxes, salesman's sample books, pamphlets, and other match industry ephemera. Send brief description and SASE.
   Bill Retskin
   3417-A Clayborne Ave.
   Alexandria, VA 22306-1410
      (703) 768-3932

★ **Paper matchcover collections.** Dave is a long time collector of matchcovers and past president of the Sierra Diablo Club. He collects many different types of matchcovers and buys accumulations and collections. Individual covers are not worth much, but collections of pre-WWII covers are worthwhile. Dave is happy to hear from folks with questions or collections.
   David Hampton
   1395 Springhill Dr.
   Pittsburg, CA 94565
      (415) 432-6980

Matchcovers are "damaged" if torn or dirty, or if their striker has been cut off.

Collectors do not want covers if glued, taped, or stapled into a book.

★ **Match books and boxes.** "We'll buy match books and boxes if the covers are in good condition and the matches are intact. Please send a Xerox© with your asking price."
   Robert & Susan Cox
   800 Murray Drive
   El Cajon, CA 92020
      (619) 447-0800 days

★ **Matchcovers and matchboxes**, foreign or domestic. "I don't want damaged covers generally, but will consider those with *minor* damage if they're from the early 1930's or before." Wants to know approximately how many items, whether they are U.S. or foreign, whether they are used or unused, whether the covers are in an album or loose, and whether the matches are present. John is Secretary of the Rathkamp Matchcover Society.
   John Williams
   1359 Surrey Rd., Dept. TH
   Vandalia, OH 45377
      (513) 890-8684

★ **Matchcovers and matchboxes.** Wants interesting singles or entire estates. Hiller is a West Coast auctioneer who can handle large collections. The ideal condition for matchcovers is unused, open, with the staples carefully removed. No "grocery store" covers, "Thank You's," or covers not identified as to origin (like *Holiday Inn* covers that don't give a location). His favorite find would be a matchcover from the Lindbergh welcome home dinner.
   Robert Hiller
   2501 W. Sunflower, #H5
   Santa Ana, CA 92704
      (714) 540-8220

★ **Match safes.** "I buy small pocket matchsafes made of silver, brass, nickel plate, or other materials if they are in unusual shapes or if they advertise tobacco products or outlets. Xerox© what you have, rather than take photographs which show the lighter as a small blur. Prefers you to price it, understanding that almost all are worth under $100 to him, and ordinary silver matchsafes that are not figural will only bring $20-$40 depending on the pattern."
Tony Hyman
Box 3028
Pismo Beach, CA 93448

★ **Match safes.** "I'll buy figural, fancy, and unusual match safes and related items such as catalogs, advertisements, and ephemera prior to 1915. I'll take one or a collection, but interested in quality items only. I want a detailed description, including the type of material and size, and condition. Asking price helpful. Photo or Xerox© helpful." Nothing later than 1915.
George Sparacio
Box 791
Malaga, NJ
    (609) 694-4167 eves

★ **Wall model match safes made of cast iron.** No others.
George Fougere
67 East St.
North Grafton, MA 01536
    (508) 839-2701

★ **Cigarette lighters.** Will buy old or new, books, catalogs, brochures, pictures, advertising, parts lists, instruction sheets, boxes, counter displays, etc. Will pay cash, trade for other lighters, or borrow for inspection and research. "All material guaranteed safe return." Send Xerox© copy. Jack offers an interesting illustrated catalog of lighters for sale if you send $3.
Jack Seiderman
1050 NE 120th St.
Miami, FL 33161
    (305) 893-6847

★ **Cigarette lighters.** Wants to buy a wide range of quality lighters, including those made by *Ronson, Dunhill, Evans, Thorens, Negbaur, Demley, Touchtip, Art Metal Works, Parker, Cartier, Tiffany,* and *Silent Flame.* He would like to find cigarette case/lighter combinations, figural lighters, lighters in watches, and other unusual designs. Buys both pocket and table models. Will consider all lighters made from any precious metals: gold, sterling silver or platinum. Xerox© or photograph.
Richard Weinstein
C/o Authorized Repair Service
30 W. 57th St.
New York, NY 10019
    (212) 541-5618

Sexy Stuff

★ **Erotic art in all forms and formats** including statues, paintings, prints, post cards, photography, and three dimensional objects of all kinds from the days of the Roman empire up to the present. Especially seeks Oriental and European erotic bisque/porcelain figures, revolving lamps from the 50's with pin-up shades, arcade "peep" machines, and photos of all types. Also **original art for pin up calendars** or illustrations 1920-1970, especially work by **Alberto Vargas** and **George Petty**, but including Earl Moran, Gil Elvgren, Zoe Mozert, Armstrong, Alk Buell, Al Moore, and others. Also Vargas *Esquire* calendars and prints, other calendar pin ups, and some homemade erotica, including obscene letters written by private parties. Describe condition. A Photo or Xerox© copy is suggested. Include your phone number when you write.
　　Charles Martignette
　　PO Box 293
　　Hallandale, FL 33009
　　　(305) 454-3474

★ **Erotica of all types, all languages, all eras,** including girlie and pornographic magazines, hard and soft cover books, sex newspapers, typescripts and mimeos, sex comics, original erotic art, films, photos, statuary, and sexually explicit objects of all types.
　　C.J. Scheiner, Books
　　275 Linden Blvd., # B2
　　Brooklyn, NY 11226
　　　(718) 469-1089

★ **Autographed *Playboy* playmate ephemera** including covers, gatefolds, and partial pages, but the photo must be from the magazine. Items may be dedicated ("To Bill," etc.) or not, but those without dedications are preferred, and bring from $20 to $50. Autographs of other women (actresses, models, celebrities) who have appeared in *Playboy* will be considered but only if they have signed the cover or photo spread in which they appear. Xerox© what you have.
　　David Kueragas
　　McTieg Books
　　1943 Timberland
　　Clarks Summit, PA 18411
　　　(717) 587-3429

★ **Erotica of all types,** including nude photos and photo books, original art and paintings, quality Oriental and European, and three dimensional materials.
　　Ivan Gilbert
　　Miran Art & Books
　　2824 Elm Ave.
　　Columbus, OH 43209
　　　(614) 236-0002

★ *Playboy* **jigsaw puzzles and other ephemera** is wanted, but only a select list of items: puzzles (preferably in their original unopened box), posters, playing cards, square yellow ashtrays, foreign issues of the magazine, and "unique novelties." No orange ashtrays, glasses, mugs, or calendars later than 1960, and "I do not want copies of the U.S. edition of *Playboy* magazine except for issues one, two, or three."
　　David Kueragas
　　McTieg Books
　　1943 Timberland
　　Clarks Summit, PA 18411
　　　(717) 587-3429

★ **Girlie magazines published by Parliament** from the 1950's, 60's, and 70's. Also *Playboy* from the 1950's only. Buys related girlie material, calendars, and paperbacks, but nothing from the 1980's. Fine condition items only. Warren offers an extensive magazine catalog for $3.
　　Warren Nussbaum
　　29-10 137th Street
　　Flushing, NY 11354
　　　(718) 886-0558

★ **Girlie magazines published by Parliament** between 1970 and 1980. Will pay 50¢ to $2 each for good complete copies, slightly less for those with 1 or 2 pages clipped or missing (generally unsalable elsewhere). Will consider similar "under the counter" publications from that time and pay 25¢ to $1. Pays more for those with cover prices of $10 or more. "No need to write or call. No embarrassment. Just ship one or a hundred for immediate cash." No *Playboy, Oui, Hustler, Penthouse,* or *Gallery.*
　　Henry Anthony
　　2141 Shoreline
　　Pismo Beach, CA 91449

★ **Alberto Vargas illustrations**, 1918-1960. "I'll buy magazine covers, Zigfield Follies posters, and other Vargas art depicting nudes, but only his work before he began drawing for *Playboy*. He does not want *Esquire* calendars unless they have their original jackets and is not interested in any of Vargas's *Playboy* art.

David Kueragas
McTieg Books
1943 Timberland
Clarks Summit, PA 18411
    (717) 587-3429

★ **Prostitution in the U.S.** and around the world. He buys a wide variety of ephemera from anywhere, but is particularly interested in Nevada. What have you?

Douglas McDonald
Box 20443
Reno, NV 89515

★ **Burlesque, strippers, and sexy dances**. Buys photos, posters, signs and any unusual items. Likes to find 3-D picture books.

Charles Martignette
PO Box 293
Hallandale, FL 33009
    (305) 454-3474

★ **Prophylactic (condom) and feminine hygiene** vending equipment, tins, and advertising.

Mr. Condom
1725 Lincoln Ave.
Dubuque, IA 52001
    (319) 556-3633

Cards & Gambling

★ **Clay, ivory, or mother-of-pearl gambling chips** and selected other memorabilia. No plain, paper, or interlocking chips. Send a sample, rubbing or photocopy. Tell how many chips of each color. Dale wrote *Antique Gambling Chips*, available with a price guide for $19.95.

Dale Seymour, Past Pleasures
Box 50863
Palo Alto, CA 94303

★ **Poker chips and other gambling markers** made of ivory or mother-of-pearl with scrimshawed designs. Designs can be numbers, animals, birds, or other patterns and figures. Prices start at $10 and up. Especially desired are chips or markers inscribed with the words DEALER, YOUR DEAL, or picturing an Indian or a deer. These are worth $300 up depending on size, condition, and design. Does not want chips made of plastic, paper, clay, metal, rubber, or any mass production process. Send a photocopy of the chips you have to sell. If the chips are in a rack, describe the rack and indicate whether any chips appear to be missing. Note any maker's name. Strongly warns: **Do not clean your chips!** "Send Xerox© of your chip[s] first, because I must give instructions on how to pack, as these are very fragile."

Bryan Eggers
Box 3491
Westlake Village, CA 91359
    (805) 373-1586

★ **Anything concerning playing cards and card games.** Unusual playing cards including transformation cards, non-standard decks, and decks with a different picture on the face of each card. Also single cards in quantity with colorful backs and unusual jokers, Aces or court cards. Also books, magazines, and other items on the games of contract bridge, auction bridge, and whist. Will consider early or limited edition books on other card games as well as plates, figurines, and other artwork depicting card playing. Will pay $100 up for *Royal Bayreuth* china in the pattern called "Devil and the Cards." Photocopies almost essential. Include an SASE to get an answer.
Bill Sachen
927 Grand Ave.
Waukegan, IL 60085
(312) 662-7204

★ **Antique decks of playing cards** are wanted, complete with joker and box or wrapper. Wants decks before 1930, identifiable because they are 2 1/2" wide (with no box) and 2 5/8" wide if boxed. Robert is the founder of the club for antique playing card collectors, and wants new complete decks with those dimensions, but "might be interested" in open decks. Xerox© the back of one card and the face of the Joker and the Ace of spades.
Robert Harrison
582 Woodlawn Ave.
Glencoe, IL 60022
(708) 835-0842

★ **Photographs or paintings of casino interiors** showing gambling in progress.
Charles Martignette
PO Box 293
Hallandale, FL 33009
(305) 454-3474

★ **Bridge tallies.** Please send a Xerox© of any pre-1960 bridge tallies.
Fran Van Vynckt
7412 Monroe Ave
Hammond, IN 46324

★ **All types of lottery tickets** from the 1600's to the present, from any country. pre-20th century tickets are worth $3-$5 up depending on the country and age. Modern scratch off tickets newer than 1964 normally bring 5¢ each, but smaller less populated states and smaller games fetch more. Complete sets or series are desirable and also worth more. Non negotiable "sample void" scratch off tickets issued to teach people how to play games are of particular interest. Condition is important; any bends, tears or damage make 20th Century tickets worthless. Xerox© preferred.
Karen Lea Rose
4420 Wisconsin Ave.
Tampa, FL 33616-1031

★ **Scratch off type lottery tickets.** "I'll buy instant rub-off lottery tickets from the 1970's and 80's."
Bill Pasquino
1824 Lyndon Ave.
Lancaster PA 17602

Americana

Cowboys, Indians and politicians

have all contributed to the historical legacy of America.

They are often larger in the telling than in life. Their relics are uniquely American, widely collected, and with high value potential.

Many items like arrowheads require an expert's eye to filter items worth $1 from what's worth $100. A cigar box full of arrowheads rescued from the city dump brought an Ohio teen a cool $10,000. A grandfather's trunk held a bonanza of nearly $500,000 worth of Indian clothing for an Eastern couple... because they sold it right...to experts. While tourist trade pottery is of little interest, all other Indian items require inquiry.

Cowboys, whether the B-Movie type or the real thing, are popular. A set of fancy California made spurs brought $5,000 recently. Sounds like time to check the tack room.

Very early or very rare Scouting badges and medals are highly prized, with a few top national jamboree items bringing $500 to $1,000.

Sellable items can be as small as a few inches...or as large as rugs. Watch for art, weapons, symbolic items, clothing, and tools of various trades.

tony hyman

Indians

★ **Antique American Indian and Eskimo items.** "I'll buy quality items made by Indians and Eskimos: baskets, beadwork, quillwork, pottery, clothing, weapons, old Navajo rugs, blankets and if you've got a 16 foot long birch bark canoe I'll buy that too. I don't buy Indian jewelry, books, or any modern item purchased ten years ago at a trading post on the Interstate." A photo is a must, and please list dimensions and any flaws the piece has in your first letter. Dealers should price their goods as he will make offers to amateur sellers only. Will answer all inquiries promptly.
Barry Friedman
22725 Garzota Drive
Valencia, CA 91355
(805) 296-2318

★ **Museum quality American Indian relics.** "I'll buy fine baskets, pre-1900 Plains beadwork, quillwork, weapons, etc., Southwestern pots, pre-1950 jewelry, Kachinas, Navajo blankets and rugs, Northwest Coast masks and carvings, Eskimo objects, old photos of Indians, and more. Some of these items can be worth $10,000 or more. Dan does not want anything modern, small pots, or fake / reproductions of early work.
Daniel Brown
Box 149
Davenport, CA 95017
(408) 426-0134

★ **Hopi and Zuni Pueblo Kachina dolls.** "I especially want those made between 1900 and 1940. Other Indian items, dance wands, costume parts, pottery, baskets, and jewelry from Southwest Indians are also of interest." Kachina dolls can range in value from $100 to $5,000 or more, but there are many fake Kachinas., "An expert can tell the difference." He'll need a photo and all background information.
John C. Hill
6990 E. Main
Scottsdale, AZ 85251
(602) 946-2910

★ **Indian baskets and other art** are wanted.
Louis Picek
Box 340
West Branch, IA 52358

★ **Indian artifacts** including arrowheads, stone axes, celts, pipes, flint, ceremonial pieces, bannerstones, birdstones, baskets, beaded items, pottery, rugs, blankets, masks, wooden bowls, and any other Indian related items. He will pay high prices ($500-$1,000) for ancient birdstones he can use for his own collection. Please list what you have and make a drawing or Xerox©, giving all measurements. Include your home and work phone numbers. This forty year veteran holds four to six auctions a year of Indian artifacts and is always in the market for good items.
Jan Sorgenfrei
10040 S.R. 224 West
Findlay, OH 45840
(419) 422-8531 days; 384-3730 eves.

★ **Indian stone animal effigy pipes.** No interest in reproductions, but claims he'll pay from $100 to as much as $10,000 for well documented pipes. Photo advisable.
Mel Rosenthal
507 S. Maryland Ave.
Wilmington, DE 19804

★ **North and South American Indian rugs** and weavings are sought by this major rug dealer. Color photo and dimensions, please.
Renate Halpern, Halpern Galleries
325 E. 79th Street
New York, NY 10021

★ **American Indian and Eskimo,** including art, rugs, crafts, baskets, pottery, weapons, and clothing, especially old beaded buckskin moccasins. Does not buy modern Indian items. Prefers a color photo be sent with your inquiry. Prefers you price what you have to sell, but "our appraiser will suggest a value after examination."
Lynn Munger
Potawatomi Museum
Box 631
Fremont, IN 46737
(219) 833-4700

★ **Indian totems and carvings** from before 1950, including good quality items made for the tourist trade. Provide a physical description, noting all obvious signs of damage. If you know the history of the ownership of the item, please give that information as well. Photos helpful.
Edwin Snyder
PO Box 156
Lancaster, KY 40444
(606) 792-4816 eves

Cowboys

★ **Artifacts, photos, autographs, and letters of Western personalities** including both lawmen and outlaws. Has particularly strong interest in **Samuel Colt, Sam Houston and Benito Juarez.** This active Western collector seeks "historically important" correspondence from any of these men.

Johnny Spellman, DVM
10806 North Lamar
Austin, TX 78753
(512) 258-6910 eves
(512) 836-2889 days

★ **Antique cowboy regalia** such as chaps, holsters, belts, badges, saddles, hats, boots, and lassos. Also buys *Colt* and *Winchester* guns and rifles suitable for the period. Would love to find outfits with documented history tying them to a particular sheriff, marshall, or outlaw from between 1850 and 1900. Also interested in Western documents, and some gambling and saloon items. No interest in reproductions or fakes. This licensed appraiser and 30 year veteran collector/dealer does not want "long bull stories" but does want to know where you got your item(s) and any history you can provide. You must include a photo and your asking price, and will be expected to ship for inspection. He does not make offers.

Pierre Bovis
The Az-Tex Cowboy Trading Co.
PO Box 460
Tombstone, AZ 85638
(602) 457-3359

★ **Cowboy equipment and regalia** including:
[1] **Spurs** of all type except English and new military. Especially unusual spurs that are silver and maker marked;
[2] **Cuffs** made of leather, chaps, hats, scarves, and fancy boots;
[3] **Western saddles,** pre-1920, all types, if maker marked, including black military McClellan saddles;
[4] **Saddle bags** with maker's marks;
[5] **Rawhide** riatas, quirts, bridles, etc., that are marked, tooled, or carved;
[6] **Horse bits** more than 50 years old with silver mounts or inlay, although some plain and some foreign are sought, so inquire;
[7] **Prison made spurs,** horse bits, quirts, belts, and lead ropes;
[8] **Saddle maker's catalogs** pre-1936;
[9] **Photographs** of old cowboy scenes;
[10] **Advertising related to the frontier,** especially watch fobs;
[11] **Movie posters** of cowboy movies;
[12] **Books by Will James.**

Especially wants marked spurs authenticated as having been made for some well known personality. Does not want anything made in the last 25 years or made in the Far East. In your description, make certain to mention all marks. Give dimensions and mention all damage or repairs. He prefers if you set the price, but will make offers to assist amateur sellers. No guns! Will buy single items of collections for resale.

Lee Jacobs
Box 3098
Colorado Springs, CO 80934
(719) 473-7101

★ **Fine quality cowboy clothing and gear.** Also other Western ephemera, including trail maps, brand books, wanted posters, and other items. Also wants photos of cowboys, badmen, and peace officers.

Johnny Spellman, DVM
10806 North Lamar
Austin, TX 78753
(512) 258-6910 eves
(512) 836-2889 days

Politics, Politicians & Political Symbols

★ **Political buttons, tokens, and ribbons from any election before 1925.** From before 1910, he will buy tokens, medals, ribbons, glass, china, paper, canes, figures, silks, etc. The only buttons after 1925 that he wants are those that catalog for more than $20 in Ted Hake's book on buttons. Consignments to his auction are invited.

Rich Hartzog
World Exonumia
Box 4143 BID
Rockford, IL 61110
(815) 226-0771

★ **Presidential campaign memorabilia made of paper or cloth,** from any campaign before 1976. *All* candidates are wanted including third party or those who lost in primaries, but **Lincoln** is a particular favorite. Small paper items from the 19th century are generally worth from $5-$15 and include pamphlets, posters, tickets, sample ballots, and cards of any kind. Cloth items such as bandanas, flags, ties, ribbons, and handkerchiefs are wanted, as long as they were used in a presidential campaign. He'll pay $75-$250 for bandanas picturing candidates. **He does not buy** buttons, bumper stickers, or daily newspapers, and prefers to buy piles of paper rather than single pieces, unless the items are early or unusual. When writing to him, indicate the candidate, the year (if you know), the size, any slogans or messages, and what's pictured.

Charles Hatfield
1411 South State St.
Springfield, IL 62704

★ **Election memorabilia of all types, 1780-1960,** for resale, especially higher quality items (not paper). Wants china, ribbons, plates, mirrors, clocks, boxes, glass, paintings, textiles, etc., that are **political or patriotic** in content. "I'll pay from $500-$5,000 for small historical medallions with pewter rims and lithographed portraits of military and political figures." Rex is not interested in doing free appraisals. Please don't contact him unless you want to *sell*.

Rex Stark,
49 Wethersfield Rd.
Bellingham, MA 02019
(508) 966-0994

★ **Abraham Lincoln presidential campaign memorabilia** including items related to his various opponents: Douglas, Bell, Breckinridge, McClellan, and Jefferson Davis. Will buy flags, banners, posters, broadsides, tokens, ribbons, and photographic badges. A photographic Lincoln/Johnson badge would be worth "several thousand dollars" to this 27 year veteran collector/dealer if you can find one. He does not want books, memorial items or commemoratives of any sort. "I'll only buy items issued during an election or for Lincoln's two inaugurations." He wants a Xerox© or photo, or a sketch with dimensions and information about material, inscriptions, and all defects. "I will require to see the item before I purchase it."

Donald Ackerman
149 E. Joseph Street
Moonachie, NJ 07074
(201) 807-0881

★ **Presidential memorabilia** including glass, china, campaign buttons and ribbons, posters, White House gift items, inauguration medals, invitations, Xmas cards, etc. Will pay $4,000 for a mint condition Theodore Roosevelt inaugural medal. This expert dealer is author of *Collectors Guide to Presidential Inaugural Medals and Memorabilia* available for $8.95.

H. Joseph Levine
6550-I Little River Turnpike
Alexandria, VA 22312
(703) 354-5454

★ **Political campaign items of all kinds.** "I'll buy buttons, badges, ribbons, banners, tintypes, portrait flags, and three dimensional objects. Unless unusual, generally not interested in items later than the election of 1960, with top priority given to better 19th century items, especially those associated with **Abraham Lincoln** and his contemporaries in the Civil War period." This 25 year veteran dealer /collector is not interested in buttons later than 1960 or in commemorative items that were not actually issued as part of a campaign. The one exception is **political quilts,** which he does buy. A Xerox© or photo is of "great help."

Cary Demont
PO Box 19312
Minneapolis, MN 55419
(612) 922-1617

★ **Presidential political items of all sort.** Will buy buttons, banners, ribbons, and paper material, especially from the candidates of the 1920's, Coolidge, Davis, Harding, LaFollette, Cox, Hoover, Smith, and Debs, with a strong interest in **Calvin Coolidge.** Please don't send him any *Kleenex* or other reproduction buttons, or anything that is in poor condition. This well known collector/dealer has been active for nearly 30 years. He requests a Xerox© copy and thorough description. The amount you'd like is appreciated, but "I will make an offer if you have no idea of an item's value."
Larry L. Krug, Americana Resources
18222 Flower Hill Way, #299
Gaithersburg, MD 20879
(301) 926-8663

★ **Victoria Woodhull memorabilia.** Anything in any condition is wanted about this spiritualist, feminist, and Presidential candidate, from 1865 to her leaving for England in 1877. Wants portraits, photos, programs, flyers, handbills, booklets, personal effects, and any newspaper or magazine stories by or about her that were written prior to 1900. Materials from **her 1872 Presidential campaign for the Equal Rights Party** are especially sought.
Ronald Lowden, Jr.
314 Chestnut Ave.
Narberth, PA 19072
(215) 667-0257 anytime

★ **Women's suffrage and political campaign** items, especially buttons, ribbons, posters, and pennants.
Ken Florey
153 Haverford
Hamden, CT 06517
(203) 248-1233

★ **William Jennings Bryan memorabilia** including campaign items, letters, banners, autographs, newspapers, photos, items owned by him, etc. Also books by or about Bryan.
Francis Moul, Wordsmith Books & Art
Box 81066
Lincoln, NE 68501
(402) 477-2665

★ **William Jennings Bryan and Tom Dewey memorabilia.**
Rich Hartzog, World Exonumia
Box 4143 BID
Rockford, IL 61110
(815) 226-0771

★ **Personal and other memorabilia related to Harding, Coolidge, Hoover, FDR and Al Smith.** If offering personal items, documentation will be requested.
Michael Graham
345 Cleveland Ave.
Libertyville, IL 60048
(312) 362-4808 days

★ **Illinois and Chicago politicians of the 1920's.** Wants posters, pamphlets, photographs, and buttons from Chicago politicians of the prohibition era such as Mayors William Thompson, William Dever, and Anton Cermak. Also Illinois Governor Len Small, US Senator Charles Deneen, and Cook County States Attorney Robert Crowe. Especially wants items related to prohibition and gangsters. If offering personal items, documentation will be requested.
Michael Graham,
345 Cleveland Ave.
Libertyville, IL 60048
(312) 362-4808 days

★ **Richard M. Nixon collectibles.** "I'll buy campaign collectibles, anti-Nixon items, and Watergate related ephemera including, but not limited to, buttons, jewelry, textiles, glassware, medals, coins, games, novelties, pens & pencils, pocket knives, keychains, stamps, stickers, caricatures, matchbooks, post-cards, puzzles, headgear..almost any-thing picturing or referring to Nixon." **He does not want** magazines, posters, bumper stickers, and newspapers. He is interested in Nixon's entire history as a public figure. Please send a "crisp Xerox© or photo of the item along with a description of all flaws such as foxing, chips, scratches, fading, etc. Include the price you'd like (although he will make offers to amateurs) and an SASE if you want photos returned. His book on Nixon collectibles may be ordered for $60 postpaid.
Eldon Almquist
975 Maunawili Circle
Kailua, HI 96734
(808) 262-9837 eves

141

★ **Tennessee political campaigns.** "I'll buy buttons, posters, postcards, and other souvenirs of Tennessee political campaigns, especially for governor." Also buys U.S. presidential campaign items. Xerox© copies and SASE, please.
  Peggy Dillard
  Box 210904
  Nashville, TN 37221
    (615) 646-1605

★ **North and South Carolina political buttons and ephemera** with a special interest in locating items from Taft's 1909 visit to Charlotte. Asks that you Xerox© and describe.
  Lew Powell
  700 East Park Ave.
  Charlotte, NC 28203
    (704) 358-5229 or (704) 334-0902

★ **Canadian election memorabilia** especially pinback buttons and badges from political campaigns prior to 1965, especially material about John MacDonald and Wilfred Laurier. Small items may be sent on approval. If Mike does not buy them, he will reimburse your postage.
  Michael Rice
  Box 286
  Saanichton, BC V0S 1M0, CANADA

★ **Statue of Liberty** items. What have you? Send a photocopy of what you have to this well known stamp dealer.
  Harvey Dolin & Company
  5 Beekman St., #406
  New York, NY 10038
    (212) 267-0216

★ **Statue of Liberty.** Wants French bronzes of the statue, books from before 1890, advertising items depicting or satirizing the statue, tin signs or containers, bottles, thimbles, lamps, medals and tokens, and other 19th century items related to Liberty or Auguste Bartholdi, its sculptor. Wants US Committee models from early 1880's created to raise money for the pedestal. These pot metal figures come in 6" and 12" sizes and have a tin base. If you have the genuine early ones (they're not all that rare), he's willing to pay from $300 to $1,000. Wants the early ones only. Photos or Xerox copies are requested. Not interested in postcards, or centennial items.
  Mike Brooks
  7335 Skyline
  Oakland, CA 94611
    (415) 339-1751

★ **Flags.** Wants European, African, and all other obsolete foreign or domestic flags. Also buys some current U.S. state flags and all city flags. "I will consider just about any real flag, military, yachting, naval, or other, as long as it is priced appropriately, but I don't want 48 star flags or decorative banners and other tricolor bunting." Although rare flags exist, most flags bring $5 to $100. To sell your flag, provide dimensions, a guess at the material, any info about the flag's history, photo, Xerox©, or sketch. As a point of interest, he notes, "Family oral history to the contrary, 13 star flags seldom date from the Revolution. Most were Centennial Souvenirs dating from 1876, or they were Naval flags."
  Jon Radel
  PO Box 2276
  Reston, VA 22090

★ **American flags.** "I'll buy cloth hand held size (smaller than 3') American flags with 47 stars, 43 stars, and all others with less than 39 stars. I especially like those with unusual star patterns and any flags with advertising printed on them. Larger ones will be considered. Description should include the size, condition, and star pattern. No repros or pictures of flags.
  Mark Sutton
  2035 St. Andrews Circle
  Carmel, IN 46032
    (317) 844-5648

★ **White House memorabilia** including china, dinnerware, silverware, jewelry, and anything else that authentically came from the White House, including pieces of the building itself.
  Paul Hartunian
  127B East Bradford Ave.
  Cedar Grove, NJ 07009
    (201) 857-7275

Scouting

★ **Boy Scout memorabilia and patches**, especially World Jamboree items pre-1951, National Jamboree patches pre-1940, Order of the Arrow items pre-1940 and anything "old and rare." Pays $1,000 each for 1924 World Jamboree patch or Lodge 219 Order of the Arrow pocket flap. Other World and National events can be worth $100 each. Ron has a reputation for paying very well for Scouting items, and encourages comparison.

Ron Aldridge
14908 Knollview
Dallas, TX 75248
(214) 239-3574

★ **Boy Scout, Girl Scout and Lone Scout items from the early years**, especially:

[1] Uniforms, badges, and pins. Patches with WWW from Order of the Arrow lodges, and badges from Senior Scout & Explorer groups particularly needed;

[2] Rank and Honor medals: lifesaving medals, medals for wartime service, Eagle and Golden Eaglet medals, Ace, Ranger, Silver, and Quartermaster medals, and World Jamboree medals. Note: some medals are worth $500+;

[3] Soft and composition Girl Scout dolls of various sizes if reasonably complete. *Kenner* Steve Scout dolls from 1975, if mint in original box. All Steve Scout accessories, such as a summer uniform;

[4] Scout toys and games, including figures, board games, etc.;

[5] Scout table model Bakelite radios from the late 1930's, in various colors;

[6] Official books and other literature including manuals and magazines before 1930, merit badge pamphlets and Cub Scout literature from before 1940, and "all Air Scout stuff;"

[7] Historical items related to founders of Scouting, including Baden-Powell, Juliette Low, Seton, Beard, West, Boyce, and Robinson.

"A photocopy is worth 1,000 words."
Cal Holden
257 Church St.
Doylestown, OH 44230
(216) 658-2793

★ **Boy Scout items of all sorts** including toys, posters, photos, badges, Order of the Arrow, magazines, Rockwell plates, etc. *Boy Scout Handbook* pre-1940, *Patrol Leader Handbook* pre-1945, and many other pre-1945 fiction and non-fiction Scouting books including *Every Boy's Library* with original dust jackets. Buys Cub, adult, and Air Scout uniforms pre-1940 and all pins and medals before 1960. Offers up to $750 for a 1924 World Jamboree patch. Also items from the founders of Scouting.

Doug Bearce
Box 4742
Salem, OR 97302
(503) 399-9872

★ **pre-1960 Boy Scout memorabilia.** "I will buy official and semi-official items, including toys, card games, pins, patches, uniforms, etc., especially National and International events. Handbooks before 1940 are wanted as are books by Baden-Powell, J.E. West, E.T. Seton, Dan Beard, and other Scouting authors." Sayers wrote *Value Guide to Scouting Collectables.* Sayers buys outright or sells on consignment.

Rolland Sayers
PO Box 629
Brevand, NC 28712

★ **Boy Scout items,** patches, pins, medals, Jamboree souvenirs, neckerchiefs with patches, Eagle awards, and Order of the Arrow patches (marked O.A., Lodge, or W.W.W.). "I'll pay from $1 to $100 for most items, though some very scarce items may bring $1,000 or more. I need a Xerox© copy of the item, although you may send what you have for sale to me and if we can't agree on a fair price, I will return and pay shipping costs both ways." He does not want handbooks printed after 1915, first aid kits, neckerchief slides, belt buckles, knapsacks, tents, or camping gear.

Greg Souchik
Box 133
Custer City, PA   16725
(814) 362-2642   Fax (814) 362-7356

*Girl Scouts
are on the next page*

★ **Girl Scout memorabilia.** "Try me for anything that says or means Girl Scout, including calendars, magazines, story books, sheet music, records, song books, membership cards, Senior Round-Up items, badge sashes, loose badges, pins, postcards, first day covers, etc." She especially wants very old items, such as 1913 blue uniforms, 1914 khaki uniform with bugle and drums, 1916 uniform with bloomers, pre-1920 adult uniforms, Mariner and Wing Scout items, Senior Girl Scout items, all pre-1938 items, World's Fair items, War time items, and pre-1945 items from Camp Edith Macy, Our Chalet, and Our Ark. Since she will buy so much **it is important to note she does not want the following:** handbooks after 1918, 1940's green covert uniform, 1960's green cotton or Dacron Brownie and Intermediate uniforms, 1960's forest green two piece senior uniform, 1970's or 80's uniforms, any mess kits, canteens, back packs, sleeping bags, and other big camping gear after 1925. Tell her what you have, and its date if possible. Make certain to note condition and whether anything is missing. Asking price is appreciated.
> Phyllis Palm
> PO Box 5272
> Mt. Carmel, CT 06518

★ **Girl Scout memorabilia.** Wants to buy pre-1960 catalogs, postcards, magazines, uniforms, handbooks 1912-1920, equipment, and other items. Send a list of what you have along with a photo or Xerox©. Do not send items without prior arrangement.
> Jerry King
> 8429 Katy Freeway
> Houston, TX 77024
> (713) 465-2500

★ **Girl Scout memorabilia.** Wants only items before 1963. Handbooks must be before 1920 to be of interest.
> Mary Degenhardt
> 85-37 109th St.
> Richmond Hill, NY 11418
> (718) 847-6518

Famous People

★ **Samuel Gompers ephemera** pre-1886, but please inquire about any Gompers item.
> Tony Hyman
> Box 3028
> Pismo Beach, CA 93448

★ **Lillie Langtry memorabilia** including postcards, photos, cigarette cards and silks, trade cards, letters, programs, posters, tickets, costume or set sketches, and cosmetics issued under her name. Also a wine label or bottle produced on Langtry Farms, 1889-1906, worth up to $500. Langtry was also known as Langtree, the Jersey Lily, Lady Lillie de Bathe, Mr. Jersey, and Emilie Charlotte Le Breton. Also wants material on **Edward Langtry and Freddie Gebhard(t).**
> Orville Magoon,
> Box 279
> Middletown, CA 95461
> (707) 987-2385 days

★ **Carrie Nation memorabilia** including vinegar bottles in her caricature, souvenir hatchet pins, photos, tickets to lectures, *The Hatchet*, newspaper articles about her, *anything* else.
> Steve Chyrchel
> Route #2 Box 362
> Eureka Springs, AR 72632
> (501) 253-9244

★ **John "Johnny Appleseed" Chapman memorabilia** including books and personal items.
> Frederic Janson, Pomona Book Exchange
> Rockton PO
> Ontario L0R 1X0, CANADA

★ **Commodore Matthew Perry material** including autographs, letters, and manuscripts, especially related to his expedition to Japan.
> Jerrold Stanoff, Rare Oriental Book Co.
> Box 1599
> Aptos, CA 95003
> (408) 724-4911   Fax: 9408) 761-1350

★ **Frank Lloyd Wright material** including drawings, furniture, letters, photographs, books, smaller publications, and other ephemera.
> J.B. Muns' Fine Arts Books
> 1162 Shattuck Ave.
> Berkeley, CA 94707
> (510) 525-2420

★ **Stalin, Hitler, and Mussolini** especially during the 1920's and 1930's. Wants documented personal effects, autographs, letters, photos, and selected magazine and newspaper accounts.
> Michael Graham
> 345 Cleveland Ave.
> Libertyville, IL 60048
> (312) 362-4808 days

★ **Personal effects from Al Capone and other Chicago prohibition era figures,** both good guys and bad guys, including gangsters, police chiefs, State attorneys, FBI men, Elliott Ness, etc. Particularly interested in Capone and will pay from $50 to $1,000, depending on what you have, its condition, and its documentation. If offering personal items such as clothing, guns, jewelry, letters, etc., you should phone him.
> Michael Graham
> 345 Cleveland Ave.
> Libertyville, IL 60048
> (312) 362-4808 days

★ **Richard Halliburton ephemera** including books, films, photos, manuscripts, and personal effects of this 1920's-30's author and adventurer. He wants signed first edition books and some foreign editions. Also seeks anything associated with the 1933 Halliburton film *India Speaks*, including a print of the film. Selected items from the 1949 re-release are also wanted. Also news clippings, and magazine articles by or about Halliburton. Also personal items from his home in Laguna Beach or anything related to the U.S. Navy ship *Richard Halliburton*. Also wants anything relating to his associate **Paul Mooney.**
> Michael Blankenship
> 5320 Spencer Drive SW
> Roanoke, VA 24018
> (703) 989-0402 eves

★ **L. Ron Hubbard collectibles** such as books, photos, documents, pulp magazines, and other ephemera. This friend of the author will buy anything in fine condition, "even duplicates and triplicates," she says. She does not want ratty condition pulp magazines or books reprinted after 1960 unless autographed. Send photocopy of smaller items and standard bibliographic information on books. Some autographed books are worth as much as $5,000 each.
> Karen Jentzsch Barta
> 245 W. Loraine #208
> Glendale, CA 91202
> (818) 243-0125 fax: (818) 507-5702

★ **Things by, about, or related to author John Steinbeck** including signed limited editions, first editions, first printings by subsequent publishers, appearances in anthologies, spoken word records and tapes, film and theater memorabilia, and things owned by him. Does not want book club editions, items in poor condition, or fakes. If a book had a dust jacket, slipcase, box, wrap-around, etc., as originally issued, then these items should still be present. Be specific about what you have for sale, giving complete bibliographic information and a full description.
> James Dourgarian, Bookman
> 1595-A Third Avenue
> Walnut Creek, CA 94596
> (415) 935-5033

★ **Jack London memorabilia, books, and personal effects.**
> Russ Kingman, Jack London Bookstore
> Box 337
> Glen Ellen, CA 95442
> (707) 996-2888

★ **Queen Victoria.** Buys a variety of items associated with the Monarch and her era. "Anything small" (no furniture).
> J. Markowitz
> 964 Hillside Blvd.
> New Hyde Park, NY 11040

★ **Sherlock Holmes** items, particularly the rare and unusual. Wants pre-1930 books, early magazines, games, pamphlets, non-books, and "curious items." If items are very rare, they may date after 1930 and still be of interest. John is a Baker Street Irregular, owns 12,000 Holmes items, and is well known as a Holmes authority.
> John Bennett Shaw
> 1917 Fort Union Dr.
> Santa Fe, NM 87501
> (505) 982-2947

★ **Sherlock Holmes.** Wants "anything related to Sherlock Holmes or Sir Arthur Conan Doyle" including figurines, drawings, autographs, posters, photos, etc. Wants first edition books only. Also wants ephemera from actors who have played Holmes including Basil Rathbone, Nigel Bruce, and William Gillette.
> Robert Hess,
> 559 Potter Blvd.
> Brightwaters, NY 11718
> (516) 665-8365

Religions & Cults

★ **Crucifixes, medals, Stars of David, and other symbols from any religion.** Wants a wide variety of items...interesting, unusual, precious, sentimental...anything you'd like preserved or displayed. Religious items don't bring much money, but this avid collector is looking for all the religious artifacts he can find. Donated crosses and other items are preserved with your family name or other identification of your choice. He buys postcards decorated with crosses. He's looking for an "angel" to subsidize a museum of religious artifacts and symbols. Send a stamped self addressed envelope if you'd like an offer, response to a donation, an answer to a question regarding crosses, or simply more information about his goals.
>   Ernie Reda
>   3997 Latimer Ave
>   San Jose, CA 95130

★ **Catholic First Communion books.** "I'll buy small celluloid, mother of pearl, or ivory First Communion books and Catholic missals from the late 1800's to 1950, although earlier are preferred. As long as the condition is fine, will buy them in any language. Send photo and description with your asking price."
>   Monica Murphy
>   Savannah's Antiques
>   1419 Fern
>   New Orleans, LA 70118
>   (504) 866-2221

★ **Catholic Holy Cards (religious cards) from pre-1940.** Holy cards are small decorated cards similar to trade cards, depicting various religious figures and events, usually beautifully printed, often decorated with lace. "The older the better." Wants steel engravings and other quality pieces. Hand made ones particularly sought. "Some of my best cards have come from little old ladies who have treasured them for ages. They give them to me, because they know I'll preserve and take care of them. I don't resell. I do take donations of cards." Xerox© what you have. If you have large lots of pre-1940 cards, you may ship on approval without calling first.
>   Mary Jo O'Neil
>   618 Riversedge Ct.
>   Mishawaka, IN 46544
>   (219) 259-0357

★ **Catholic religious paper** such as holy cards, prayer cards, Infant of Prague materials, and illustrated prayer books, religious school books, and visual aids, as long as they are before 1963. He does not want Bibles, postcards, items not made of paper, items after 1963, or paper goods that are not illustrated. Please, no Old Testament pictures or stories. Give the age, description, publisher, and condition. Xerox© helpful.
>   Joe Flynn, Wah To Wah Park
>   PO Box 1473
>   Greenwood Lake, NY 10925
>   (914) 477-9373

★ **Catholic art calendars, 1938-1969.** "Over $100 paid for certain issues. No *Messenger* calendars, please." SASE for more information.
>   Joe Speciale
>   2353 Pruneridge Ave., #2
>   Santa Clara, CA 95050

★ **Jewish ephemera** including business-related items such as signs, advertising, letterheads, and the like, but also photos, family documents, books, cookbooks, tins, bottles, postcards, Judaica, chatchkelas, and what have you. Also interested in **anti-Semetic material**. Please send a Xerox© copy of what you have.
>   Peter Schweitzer
>   5 East 22nd St., Apt. 21A
>   New York, NY 10010
>   (212) 677-6939

★ **New Testaments** before 1820 in any language printed anywhere in the world. They may be in any condition. Also interested in **any and all books with the words "Holy Spirit" in the title**. "You may ship for an offer and I will respond within three days."
>   Miles Eisele
>   4417 Chase Park Court
>   Annandale, VA 22003
>   (703) 642-6639

★ **Sacred books, including Bibles before 1800, Books of Common Prayer, The Koran,** and other unusual, beautiful or early sacred book.
>   Ron Lieberman, Family Album
>   RD #1, Box 42
>   Glen Rock, PA 17327
>   (717) 235-2134

★ **Paper ephemera about Mormons,** pre-1900.
>   Warren Anderson
>   Box 100
>   Cedar City, UT 84720

★ **Russian religious icons,** especially those with silver covers. Also **enameled bronze crosses** (wall size), icon lamps (*lampadki*) especially with "cut to clear" glass, and other pre-revolutionary religious items. Prices depend upon rarity, authenticity, and condition. Wants a full description but a good clean color photo is probably necessary. Phone to discuss your piece; He'll probably request that you ship for inspection and will tell you how to best ship. What you know of the item's history could be important.

David Speck
35 Franklin St.
Auburn, NY 13021
   (315) 252-8566 eves

★ **Shaker artifacts and ephemera.** "I specialize in Shaker books, pamphlets, photographs, and ephemera. I also buy and sell small Shaker artifacts such as bottles, sewing boxes, baskets, seed boxes, and the like. Four times a year, I publish a catalog of Shaker items for sale. If you have something to sell me, generally all I need is a photo or Xerox© copy."

Scott DeWolfe
Box 1283
Saco, ME 04072
   (207) 282-4773

★ **Watchtower Society publications and ephemera** including *Golden Age, Consolation,* and *Awake* magazines, Millenial Dawn books, Watchtower books before 1927, items related to Pastor Russell, and any pre-1940 Jehovah's Witness literature.

Mike Castro
Box 2817
Providence, RI 02907

★ **Phrenology items** including heads showing trait lines, or numbered zones on the head, posters, and wall hangings. No books.

Donald Gorlick
Box 24541
Seattle, WA 98124
   (206) 824-0508

★ **Mystical arts, crystal balls, tarot cards,** and ephemera related to astrology, spiritualism, pyramids, palmistry, Yoga, numerology, psychic research, Atlantis, Tibet, UFO's and the like.

Dennis Whelan
PO Box 170
Lakeview, AR 72642

Odd & Morbid

★ **Anything odd, unusual, or morbid,** especially **two headed calves and other freak animals,** natural or man-made, alive or mounted and preserved. Also buys:
[1] **Mummies;**
[2] **Skeletons and human skulls;**
[3] **Shrunken heads;**
[4] **Headhunter and cannibal items;**
[5] **Funeral equipment,** coffins and coffin
    plates, caskets, embalming kits, and
    tombstones;
[6] **Torture and execution devices** and
    photos of executions;
[7] **Mounted reptiles, trophy heads, and
    uncommon animals** (like kangaroos);
[8] **Man-made mermaids** he'll pay to $300;
[9] **Merchant Marine memorabilia**
    including photos, uniforms, medals;
[10] **Medicine show photos and literature;**
[11] **Tattoo equipment,** tattoo photos, and
    tattooed skin;
[12] **Voodoo and black magic ephemera;**
[13] **Flea Circus** props and photos;
[14] **Reward posters** and crime photos;
[15] **Human oddity photos and artifacts.**
For 50+ years, this wheel chair bound vet has been buying odd, unusual, and bizarre items for public exhibit in his traveling and stationary museums. He does not buy furniture, clothing, plates, or jewelry. If you have something you think he might want, send a photo, a description, a statement of condition, and your lowest price. When driving through Wilson, NC, drop in and see The Palace of Wonders. You'll find it on Route 4.

Harvey Lee Boswell
Palace of Wonders
PO Box 446
Elm City, NC 27822

★ **Human skeletons and skulls.**
Steve DeGenaro
Box 5662
Youngstown, OH 44504

★ **Animal trophies and skulls.** Please give your phone number with your description.
David Boone's Trading Company
562 Coyote Rd.
Brinnon, WA 98320
   (206)796-4330 Fax: (206) 796-4511

★ **Skulls, skeletons, tusks, teeth, fossils, shrunken heads, and mounted insects.** This relatively new dealer in oddities does not make offers and insists you price what you have.
Ronald Cauble
The Bone Room
5495 C Claremont
Oakland, CA 94618
(510) 652-4286

★ **Steer horns, cow skulls with big horns, mounted steer heads, and old buffalo horns.** "I want the real thing, and **do not want** horns wrapped with the wide, tooled, tapered leather center, nor those wrapped in vinyl and rope." Send photo or sketch with dimensions.
Alan Rogers
1012 Shady Dr.
Gladstone, MO 64118
(816) 436-9008

★ **Funeral related ephemera.** "I'll buy things having to do with funerals such as funeral parlor advertising, mirrors, ribbons, trays, badges, and other items issued by funeral parlors. I am not interested in caskets, funeral or embalming equipment, or cemeteries."
Rich Hartzog
World Exonumia
Post Office Box 4143 BID
Rockford, IL 61110
(815) 226-0771   Fax (815) 397-7662

★ **Cemetery ephemera.** "I'll buy books, maps, magazines, photos, catalogs, deeds, etc., related to the cemetery business, especially:
[1] Sales catalogs for mausoleums, pre-1940;
[2] Maps of cemeteries, pre-1900;
[3] Magazines like *The Cemetery Beautiful*;
[4] Photos and real photo postcards of mausoleums;
[5] Cemetery advertising from before 1920;
[6] Burial society certificates, pre-1940;
[7] Cemetery deeds, 1700-1900.
Since these are paper items, it is simple to include a Xerox© and description of condition. Do not confuse cemeteries with funerals. I am interested in land, monuments, memorials, vaults, and mausoleums, not funerals and embalming. The only funeral item I want is *The American Funeral Gazette* from the early 1880's." Not interested in colored photo postcards of famous tombs or cemeteries.
Steve Spevak
PO Box 3173
Winchester, VA 22601

★ **Caskets.** "I'll buy wicker or wooden caskets. Wicker ones were used for display of bodies at wakes and funerals. The bodies were removed and buried in plain pine boxes. Wooden caskets are also wanted, especially those that are dovetailed, made of odd woods, tapered, or with face plates." Describe as best as you can, giving dimensions. Also buys **photos of caskets with bodies on display.**
Steve DeGenaro
PO Box 5662
Youngstown, OH 44504

★ **Tattoo memorabilia and information.** What do you have?
Marvin Yagoda
28585 So. Harwich Dr.
Farmington Hills, MI 48018

★ **Human hair mourning pieces.** Human hair jewelry with black "beads" worked in, or human hair woven into wreathes, mounted in frames with photos worked in.
Steve DeGenaro
PO Box 5662
Youngstown, OH 44504

★ **Leper colony tokens and other ephemera.**
Rich Hartzog
Box 4143 BID
Rockford, IL 61110
(815) 226-0771

Social Movements

★ **Immigration memorabilia.** "I'll buy documents, photos, passports, pre-1920 naturalization certificates, books, postcards, and other material related to immigrants, Immigrant Aid Societies, Immigrant Social and Political Clubs, Ellis Island, Castle Garden, and ethnic festivals before 1950." Also Immigration and Naturalization Service pre-1930. Xerox© please.
    K. Sheeran
    Box 520251
    Miami, FL 33152

★ **Immigrant and ethnic stereotypes** of Jews, Orientals, Scandinavians, French, Poles, Russians, and other immigrants printed before 1920. Wants stereotypes on prints, photos, valentines, postcards, magazines, posters, sheet music, trade cards, and what have you. Wants Blacks only if shown with immigrant characters. Subject matter can include life in their country of origin, arrival, settlement, assimilation, etc. Not interested in reproductions, native costume, *Harper's Weekly* material, or general articles on immigration. Prefers Xerox© of priced items. Don't send unsolicited material, please.
    John and Selma Appel
    219 Oakland Dr.
    East Lansing, MI 48823
    (517) 337-1859

★ **Chinese immigration memorabilia.** Wants anything to do with Chinese movements to U.S. prior to 1950, including items related to Chinese laundries, and Chinese social and political clubs.
    K. Sheeran
    Box 520251
    Miami, FL 33152

★ **Ku Klux Klan** paper, documents, photos, and small items.
    Steve DeGenaro
    Box 5662
    Youngstown, OH 44504

★ **Items related to Ku Klux Klan activity in the U.S. during the 1920's.**
    Michael Graham, Roaring 20's
    345 Cleveland Ave.
    Libertyville, IL 60048

★ **Socialism and Communism in the U.S. before 1940.** "I'll buy anything pre-1940: books, magazines, leaflets, brochures, buttons, postcards, pennants, etc., that were produced by radical groups such as the Communist Party, Socialist Party, I.W.W. (Industrial Workers of the World), Socialist Labor Party, etc. Would especially like to find the magazines *Masses, New Masses,* and *International Socialist Review.*" Mike will purchase items written in Yiddish, Italian, and other foreign languages, but "I'm really not too interested in material not written in the U.S.A." What does Mike consider important? "Condition Condition Condition!"
    Michael Stephens
    2310 Valley St.
    Berkeley, CA 94702
    (415) 843-2780

★ **Labor union and Socialist material** "I'll buy just about everything relating to organized labor, unions, and working people" including dues buttons, pins, convention and parade ribbons and badges, photographs of workers or Unions, programs, contracts, dues books, labor trade cards, union magazines, books, and most any type of labor collectibles. "I'd like to find the old and unusual from groups like The Knights of Labor, I.W.W., Railroad Brotherhood, AFL, and CIO. Also items about labor leaders. I'll consider almost anything but most interested in items before 1960."
    Scott Molloy
    550 Usquepaugh Rd.
    West Kingston, RI 02892
    (401) 792-2239 or 782-3614

★ **Cigar Maker's Union and Sam Gompers.** "I'll buy almost anything from the Cigar Maker's Union or any of its top officers, including stamps, pamphlets, regulations, photographs, and letterhead." Does anyone have a letter by Samuel Gompers on CMIU stationery or a copy of the papers that dissolved the Union? Please include photocopies and price or ask for offer.
    Tony Hyman
    Box 3028
    Pismo Beach, CA 93448
    (805) 773-6777 Fax (805) 773-0117

★ **All items depicting Blacks:** dolls, folk art, sewing items, walking sticks, miniature bronzes, jewelry, paintings, valentines, playing cards, games, children's books, cookie jars, string holders, small advertising items, souvenir spoons, Golliwogs, linens, jigsaw puzzles, candy containers, Christmas ornaments, and items associated with the Our Gang Comedy's Farina. No postcards, sheet music, tradecards, photos, outhouse figures, ads, large signs, damaged items, or reproductions. NO OFFERS.
Jan Thalberg
23 Mountain View Drive
Weston, CT 06883
(203) 227-8175

★ **Black memorabilia that is exaggerated, comical, insulting or derogatory** made between 1800-1960. Images of mammys, chefs, Uncle Tom, picaninnies, Aunt Jemima, butlers, Topsy, etc., are all wanted in almost any form:
[1] **Folk art** and primitives including rag dolls, whirligigs, etc.;
[2] **Figural kitchen items,** tea pots, pitchers, sugar bowls, etc., especially large faced items and Black cookie jars;
[3] **Mammy and chef salt shakers** with matching stove grease jars and mammy tea pots with wire handles;
[4] **Ceramic jugs** by *Weller*;
[5] **Plastic cookie jars,** sugar bowls, syrup jugs, etc., from *F&F Die Works* or marked *Luzianne*;
[6] **Humidors and bisque figurines** from Europe or Japan;
[7] **Papier mache,** composition and glass **figurals** such as candy containers and Xmas ornaments depicting Blacks;
[8] **Advertising** on paper or tin, trade cards, die-cuts, packaging, and cereal boxes such *Cream of Wheat* and *Korn Kinks*, and all Aunt Jemima products and ads;
[9] **Games of all types,** card and board, with Blacks even if pieces missing.
Needs a detailed description, colors, size, condition, place of origin or manufacturer's name. Clear close up photo or photocopy is strongly urged. Describe all damage, chips, stains, tears, faded spots, repairs, or missing pieces. Wants to know the color of skin and expression on face. Prefers black to brown. On pottery pieces, describe whether surface is shiny or matte (flat).
Mary Anne Enriquez
651 So. Clark
Chicago, IL 60605
(312) 922-1173

★ **Black memorabilia** including cookie jars, older dolls, toys, kitchen items, prints, tins, historical items, Black folk art, Uncle Remus, advertising items, Aunt Jemima, *Cream of Wheat*, Amos 'n Andy, and "all items relating to Blacks in America. Will buy one piece or a collection."
Judy Posner
Box 273 W
Effort, PA 18330
(717) 629-6583 anytime

★ **Black memorabilia** including cookie jars, plates, lamps, clocks, salt and pepper shakers, stringholders, table cloths, towels, plaster or ceramic items, and other kitchen or household items depicting Blacks. "I also buy advertising pieces of all kinds that depict a Black person on the label or logo, including biscuit tins, candy packaging, coffee tins, peanut butter pails, peanut cans, stove cleaner, whiskey advertising, beer signs, Aunt Jemima items, *Cream of Wheat* packs, *Uncle Ben's Rice* memorabilia, etc." Also wants punchboards and other items featuring Blacks.
Diane Cauwels
3947 Old South Road
Murfreesboro, TN 37129
(615) 896-3614

★ **Black memorabilia** including cookie jars of mammys or chefs, string holders, teapots, toys, advertisements, humidors, sugar and creamer, salt & peppers, etc, "one piece or a whole collection." Will pay from $100 to $4,000 for useful items, but no outhouses, sheet music, post cards, or trade cards. Describe condition.
Mike Kranz
659 Oneil Rd.
Hudson, WI 54016
(715) 386-7333

★ **Malcolm X ephemera** such as letters, copies of speeches, autographs, and personal items. Send a Xerox© of what you have for an offer.
Eric Mizrahi
11 Forest Ave.
Framingham, MA 01701

★ **Racism and the civil rights movement.** "I'll buy buttons, posters, and other ephemeral items having to do with Martin Luther King, but no newspapers, magazines, or damaged items."
Peggy Dillard
Box 210904
Nashville, TN 37221
(615) 646-1605

★ **Atomic bombs, nuclear war, and the anti-nuclear movement** from the 1950's to mid 60's. Wants all information, official and anti-bomb, including stuff on CONELRAD, civil defense, government pamphlets on atomic survival, books, comic books, and anything else from that period on atomic bombs and survival, including postcards of the bomb tests. Would love to find *How to Build an Atomic Bomb in Your Kitchen* by Bob Bale. Also "funky" atomic stuff from the 1950's and mid 60's.
>   Edy Chandler
>   Box 20664
>   Houston, TX 77225
>   (713) 531-9615 eves

★ **Paper ephemera about radical movements** from the Tories of the American Revolution, the social and political radicals of the 1800's, the labor unionists, women's suffrage, etc., right down to and including the Black activists, Peace movement, and other "hippies" of the 1960's. Wants letters, documents, posters, broadsides, books, and pamphlets.
>   Ivan Gilbert
>   Miran Arts & Books
>   2824 Elm Ave.
>   Columbus, OH 43209
>   (614) 236-0002

★ **British Royalty.** Buys souvenirs, tins, plates, mugs, medals, busts, postcards and programs from various ceremonies and events involving British royalty from Queen Victoria to Queen Elizabeth Reign. Also wants commemorative souvenirs from special events involving Prince Charles and Princess Diana. Wants pictorial items. Audrey is the author of *British Royal Commemoratives*. ($24.95).
>   Audrey Zeder
>   6755 Coralite T
>   Long Beach, CA 90808
>   (213) 421-0881

★ **All fraternal order** materials that are small and flat, such as coins, tokens, medals, badges and ribbons. Especially interested in Masonic chapter pennies and hand engraved badges of precious metal. Will consider larger BPOE items or unusual fraternal items. If what you have is pre-1930, simply ship it to him for an offer. Hartzog will send you a check for the lot. He claims to pay higher prices than anyone else.
>   Rich Hartzog
>   Box 4143 BID
>   Rockford, IL 61110

★ **Mafia or organized crime items** including books, magazines, photographs, autographs, videotapes, recordings, documents, government reports, and any other memorabilia or artifacts. "I'd love to find a cigar box from the Yale Cigar Co. of New York and a poster from the Italian American Civil Rights League meeting of June 28th, 1971." Wants nothing fictional.
>   Ron Ridenour
>   Box 6818
>   Santa Barbara, CA 93160

★ **Spy material.** Will consider anything you have related to real spies, any country, any period: documents, signatures, photos, etc.
>   Keith Melton
>   Box 5755
>   Bossier City, LA 71171
>   (318) 747-9616

★ **Slave tags.** These small metal tags worn by slaves to indicate their status or occupation. Pays $200-600 and up for tags reading "servant, porter, mechanic, seamstress, fisherman, fruiterer," etc. Some rare types, dates, styles, or occupations can bring $1,500 or more. Call collect or ship insured for his offer. *Do not* clean tags.
>   Rich Hartzog
>   Box 4143 BID
>   Rockford, IL 61110
>   (815) 226-0771   Fax (815) 397-7662

★ **Everything about the homeless children who sold newspapers to survive** in 19th century N.Y.C. and elsewhere. "I buy photographs, paintings, statues, prints, badges, passes, magazine articles, and newspaper accounts pertaining to them, Printing House Square, Newspaper Row, or Father John C. Drumgoole, founder of Mount Loretto, the largest child care facility in the U.S. at the time." Also material about **Charles Loring Brace and the Children's Aid Society**, especially about their orphan trains to the West.
>   Peter Eckel
>   1335 Grant Ave.
>   South Plainfield, NJ 07080
>   (908) 757-0748

★ **Anything pertaining to statues of newsboys** around the U.S. including photographs of the statues, souvenir figurines, advertising for the figurines, and photos of any statue of a newsboy. Replicas of the statues bring $50+.
>   Gary Leveille
>   Box 562
>   Great Barrington, MA 01239

151

Miscellany

★ **Meteorites.** Many types exist, and he wants them all, rough or smooth, large or small. Look for rocks that are especially heavy, or with signs of melting or with rust. A freshly fallen meteorite often has a thin black skin, called "fusion crust." If you have a rock that attracts a magnet, you may have a meteorite. "A strong magnet on a string will swing towards <u>all</u> meteorites, which makes this one of the best preliminary tests. Other excellent field tests for meteorites include checking for rust, and filing off a tiny corner to look inside for bright metal or metal flakes. If you think you have found a meteorite, please send a small, dime-sized piece for me to examine along with a description and photo of the entire specimen. If you wish to have the sample returned to you, you must enclose return postage. All non-meteorite samples without return post are added to the pile outside the back door. If I suspect your sample is a meteorite, I will contact you, so be sure to enclose your name, address and phone number along with all samples." Rare forms of meteorites can be surprisingly valuable.
    Robert Haag
    PO Box 27527
    Tucson, AZ 85726
        (602) 882-8804   Fax (602) 743-7225

★ **Rationing material from anywhere in the world** for addition to an important research collection. The Library buys only paper items, already owns most American items, and seeks a great many foreign items. No U.S. ration books wanted. He reminds sellers that State Governments are slow but certain payers.
    Ronald Mahoney, Head Special Collections
    Madden Library, Calif. State University
    Fresno, CA 93740
        (209) 294-2595

★ **Ration tokens.** Pays 2¢ each for red tokens and 3¢ each for blue. Over 250, he pays 1¢ each. Pays substantially more for those that are off-center, double struck, or have other errors. Simply ship for his check. Rich is one of world's largest buyers of medals and tokens.
    Rich Hartzog
    Box 4143 BID
    Rockford, IL 61110
        (815) 226-0771

★ **Cave or cavern memorabilia** before 1950, including books, magazine articles, pamphlets, prints, postcards, etc. "Any items that would make a contribution to the history of a particular cave or area such as journal entries, deeds, wills, maps, tickets, and advertising, are of interest." Common souvenirs and chrome postcards are not desired.
    Jack Speece
    711 East Atlantic Ave.
    Altoona, PA 16602
        (814) 946-3155 eves

★ **Caves or cavern memorabilia of all sorts.** "I'll buy anything old or unusual pertaining to caves or caverns worldwide" including photos, brochures, postcards, souvenirs, silver spoons, plates, etc. Does not want anything after 1940, and prefers items from before 1900.
    Gordon Smith
    Box 217
    Marengo, IN 47140
        (812) 945-5721

★ **Propagating material (cuttings) of uncommon tree fruit varieties.** If you have an unusual fruit tree, Fred wants a cutting. This veteran horticultural experimenter wants temperate climate fruits, especially apples, but also pears, plums, quinces and medlars. Also buys **books on fruit propagation** before 1920.
    Fred Janson
    Pomona Fruit Exchange
    Rockton PO, Ontario
    CANADA L0R 1X0
        (519) 621-8897

★ **Objects which depict hands.** Will consider sculpture, vases, carvings, jewelry, posters, as well as old books about hands or palmistry. Would love to find the brass or copper life-size hand from a Buddha statue. No praying hands, milk glass hands, or plastic hands are wanted by this long time hand analyst.
    Geraldine Swigart
    12362 Kensington Rd.
    Los Alamitos, CA 90720
        (213) 431-3705

★ **Wooden hands that have fully articulated fingers** such as glove stretchers and sizers.
    Donald Gorlick
    Box 24541
    Seattle, WA 98124
        (206) 824-0508

Christmas

★ **Christmas decorations from before 1920.**
   [1] **Ornaments:** paper and tinsel die cuts, pressed cardboard animals, cotton batting ornaments, Christmas tree dolls of any material, glass ornaments... basically, anything figural;
   [2] **Santa games:** board games with lithographed boxes depicting Santa;
   [3] **Santa toys:** any toy based on St. Nick;
   [4] **Santa ephemera:** all types of items are wanted, including advertising, banners, greeting cards, paintings, die-cuts, chromoliths, prints;
   [5] **Die cut Children's books** 1880-1900 about Santa;
   [6] **Litho on tin candle holders** for Christmas trees;
   [7] **Victorian toys:** jack-in-the-boxes, animals on rolling platforms, nine pins, and other traditional toys, especially those with nursery rhyme tie-ins.
He does not want anything made after 1920. There are many reproductions of Santa items, some of which are quite good and require an expert to authenticate. This 25 year veteran requests a photo or photocopy of what you'd like to sell.
   Dolph Gotelli
   Father Christmas
   Box 8009
   Sacramento, CA 95818
      (916) 456-9734

★ **German glass Christmas ornaments,** pre-1920, in the shape of animals, people, and cartoon characters. Also wants painted cotton ornaments, paper Dresdens, and **old candy containers,** especially Santas. Also buys pre-1930 **postcards and photos of Christmas** events.
   Jim Bohenstengel
   Box 623
   Oak Park, IL 60303
      (312) 524-8870 or 386-5319

★ **Early handmade folk art Christmas decorations.**
   Louis Picek
   Main Street Antiques
   Box 340
   West Branch, IA 52358

★ *Matchless Wonder Stars* **Christmas lights.** "I'll buy all stars, working, dead, or broken. Boxed sets are particularly desirable, but even empty boxes have value, especially those with attractive decorations." This historian of the industry wants all factory wholesale literature and price sheets, as well as store display stands." He also buys other *Matchless* products plus lights by *Paramount, Sylvania, Alps, Royal, Peerless, Mazda, Majestic* and others. Especially interested in nice boxed light sets by *Propp* and *Clemco.* If you have any old light sets, especially those that twinkle, bubble, or whatever, drop him a line. He wants a good description and if you still have the box, the information on it. "I generally avoid plastic items, and Christmas lights later than the mid 1950's. I don't need any more common *NOMA* or *Royal* bubble lights." Although he buys dead bulbs (except *Sylvania* fluorescents), he requests return privilege if things aren't as described.
   David Speck
   35 Franklin St.
   Auburn, NY 13021
      (315) 253-8495 days

★ **Christmas tree ornaments.** Buys a variety of antique ornaments including Kugel ornaments; glass birds with spun glass wings, tails, or crests; Czech beaded ornaments with satin glass rings; birds perched in satin glass rings; unusual strings of glass beads; spun glass and paper decorations; chandelier or fantasy ornaments (where two or three small bells, pine cones, or other items hang from a larger ornament); and other delicate and unusual figural ornaments. Also buys catalogs and manufacturer's sales literature from ornament manufacturers in any language.
   David Speck
   35 Franklin St.
   Auburn, NY 13021
      (315) 252-8566 eves

★ *Hallmark* **figural ornaments** from 1973-1986. Excellent condition only. In original box preferred. No ball ornaments.
   Sharon Vohs-Mohammed
   Box 14192
   Tallahassee, FL 32317
      (904) 385-3595

★ **Holiday decorations from Christmas, Easter, Halloween, or other holiday.** "I'll buy a wide range of fine condition attractive holiday decorations made between 1890 and 1930, for any season. Items such as candy containers, celluloid pieces, papier mache, cotton batting tree ornaments, Halloween pumpkins, centerpieces, displays, etc., are all wanted." Of particular interest are **German china figurines of Santa** engaged in various activities, which she buys in excellent condition and full paint only, paying $40-$100+ apiece. "I pay fair asking prices."
Linda Vines
PO Box 721
Upper Montclair, NJ 07043
(201) 746-5206

Easter

★ **Russian Easter eggs** made of solid glass, silvered hollow glass, porcelain, and other materials. They are characterized by the letters "XB" which stands for "Xhristos Voskrece" (Christ is risen) in paint, enamel, or other material. Value depends upon rarity, authenticity, and condition.
David Speck
35 Franklin St.
Auburn, NY 13021
(315) 253-8495 days 252-8566 eves

★ **Papier mache or composition Easter rabbit candy containers** of rabbits wearing clothes.
Dolph Gotelli
Box 8009
Sacramento, CA 95818
(916) 456-9734

★ **High quality Easter decorations** of all types in fine condition, but only dating from 1890 to 1930. Great old Easter Bunnies are especially sought. No modern items.
Linda Vines
PO Box 721
Upper Montclair, NJ 07043
(201) 746-5206

Valentine's Day

★ **Fine Valentines,** including handmade valentines from before 1940, interesting mechanical valentines, and any unusual ones. Evalene especially likes lacy 8 x 10's and large fan shaped cards from the 1800's, particularly if they say "A token of love". Pays $25-$50 for folding ships, planes, and better fans. She asks that you send a photocopy of what you wish to sell. She does not want children's penny valentines from any era. Evalene no longer has a shop, but runs an extensive mail auction of valentines. She is available for talks and displays of valentines.
Evalene Pulati
Valentine Collector's Association
Box 1404
Santa Ana, CA 92702
(714) 547-1355

★ **Valentines.** Wants early die-cut and elaborate valentines made before 1910, but buys others "if reasonable."
Madalaine Selfridge
Forgotten Magic
33710 Almond St.
Lake Elsinore, CA 92330
(714) 674-9221

★ **Valentines, 1889-1920,** but only the three dimensional fold-out stand-up type.
James Conley
2405 Brentwood Rd.NW
Canton, OH 44708
(216) 477-7725

Halloween

★ **Halloween.** "I'll buy older paper items, Dennison Boogie books, Halloween pins, jewelry, decorations, etc, **if before 1945.** Nothing new, please."
Stuart Schneider
Box 64
Teaneck, NJ 07666

★ **Halloween.** "I'll buy a wide range of fine condition attractive decorations made between 1890 and 1940. Pumpkins, centerpieces, etc., are all wanted. I pay fair asking prices."
Linda Vines
PO Box 721
Upper Montclair, NJ 07043
(201) 746-5206

★ **Candy containers in glass or plastic** especially scarce glass items and early 1950's figural headed plastic *PEZ* dispensers. Pays to $300 for pumpkin headed witches, goblins, or a pop-eyed Jack-0-Lantern. No paper or tin items.
Ross Hartsough,
98 Bryn Mawr Rd.
University of Manitoba,
Winnipeg, R3T 3P5 CANADA

★ **Halloween candy containers in glass, composition, or papier mache.**
Dolph Gotelli
Box 8009
Sacramento, CA 95818
(916) 456-9734

4th of July

★ **Fireworks related items,** especially American and Chinese made. "I'll buy boxes, labels, advertising, catalogs, salesman's samples, display boards, company letters, patents, and posters." Colorful labels are worth from $5-$50 each. Hal does **not** want those marked "DOT."
Hal Kantrud
Route 7
Jamestown, ND 58401
(701) 252-5639 eves

★ **Anything with a fireworks company name** on it including:
[1] **Firecracker packs and labels;**
[2] **Fireworks catalogs** from before 1969 (many bring $100+);
[3] **Fireworks boxes** that held salutes, torpedoes, and other fireworks;
[4] **Sparkler and cap boxes;**
[5] **Salesmen's display boards** and samples;
[6] Rockets, Roman candles, and **fireworks;**
[7] **Paper goods:** stock certificates, posters, banners, photos, letters, billheads, magazine articles, and other paper about American fireworks companies.
Would like to hear from former employees of U.S. fire works companies. Include your phone number when you write.
Barry Zecker
Box 1022
Mountainside, NJ 07092
(908) 232-6100 from 8 to 8

★ **Firecracker labels.** "I'll buy pre-1940 labels with aviation, space, atom bomb, animals, and Americana themes." Also fireworks catalogs. Send photocopy. No modern labels.
Stuart Schneider
Box 64
Teaneck, NJ 07666
(201) 261-1983

★ **Fourth of July fireworks, firecrackers, and firecracker labels.** Wants "anything prior to the early 1970's, especially packs of *Golliwog, Picnic, Tank, Oh Boy, Typewriter, Atlas, Evergreen, Lone Eagle, Spirit of 76, Minute Man, Columbia, Crab, Blue Dragon, Golden Bear, Green Jade, Boa, Santa Claus, Watermelon, Dwarf, Rochester Special, China Clipper,* and many others." He wants most of these badly enough to pay $50 or more per pack! NOTE: if your package or label contains the letters "DOT" and/or "Contents do not exceed 60 mg," he's probably not interested. He eagerly buys catalogs of fireworks too, so send a Xerox© of the cover if you have one.
William Scales
130 Fordham Circle
Pueblo, CO 81005
(719) 561-0603

Pets & Other Animals

★ *Royal Doulton* flambe animal figurines. There are hundreds of different animals, both wild and domestic, to be found in these attractive red pottery figures which range from 2" to 14" in size. They are still made today, so it's the older figures that are most sought after and bring the best prices from this 20 year veteran collector. Have the figure(s) in front of you when you call, or send a good description.
Ed Pascoe
Pascoe & Co.
545 Michigan Ave.,
Miami Beach, FL 33139
    (800) 872-0195   Fax (305) 532-8543

★ **Dog figurines** in ceramics or porcelain that are made by one of the following makers: *Boehm, Hutschenreuther, Mortens Studio, Royal Doulton, Nymphenburg,* or *Anri-Wood*. A few others will be considered. Will pay $175 for a *Boehm* cocker spaniel made from 1980-83. "I do not want Japanese porcelain animals, cloisonne made in China, or small metal dogs. Give the breed if you know it, the manufacturer's marks and numbers, the dimensions, and the condition. A photo is helpful.
Jeffrey Jacobson
6424 Jefferson Ave.
Hammond, IN 46324

★ **Great Dane items** including prints, lithographs, bronzes, calendars, magazine covers, and porcelains (especially *Boehm*). pre-1940 only, nothing newer. Give the material, size, color, markings, condition, and approximate age if you can.
Leon Reimert
9 Highland Dr.
Coatesville, PA 19320
    (215) 383-6969

★ **Greyhounds and whippets.** "I'm interested in paper, porcelain, pewter, wood, and ceramics. But not in recent pottery, reproductions, or damaged items. Give the marks on your item."
June Mastrocola
W137 N9332 Hwy 145
Menomonee Falls, WI 53051
    (414) 251-8347

★ **Borzoi, Russian wolfhound, and greyhound collectibles.** Will also buy some items from other breeds as well, for resale, as long as they are purebred ("no mutts"). Wants "everything from old postcards to bronzes, but antique porcelain figurines are a favorite, as are all *Morten Studio* and *Erphila* dogs." Give her the breed, the dimensions, the material and list any damage. Photo or photocopy is helpful. She prefers you price what you have. SASE gets her catalog of items for sale in your favorite breed.
Denise Hamilton
2835 Carson Drive
Elmira, NY 14903
    (607) 562-8564

★ **Pekingese, Japanese spaniel, and pug dog collectibles** including Vienna bronze figures, doorstops, and books. Will also buy quality **paintings depicting small dogs,** and **dog show medals** with any breed of dog on them. Give condition and approximate age.
Elenore Chaya
4003 S. Indian River Dr.
Ft. Pierce, FL 34982
    (407) 465-1789

★ **Bull terrier dog material** including books, manuscripts, photos and relevant ephemera.
Frank Klein, Bookseller
521 W. Exchange St.
Akron, OH 44302
    (216) 762-3101

★ **Bull terriers and dog fighting.** Especially wants prints, paintings, and statuary. Books on dog fighting also wanted.
Ron Lieberman
Family Album
RD #1, Box 42
Glen Rock, PA 17327
    (717) 235-2134

★ **Labrador retriever books, art, figurines, and cigarette cards.** He is not interested in repros, fakes, reprints, or common items, nor is he interested in any other breed of dog. Please provide a detailed description of what you have.
Bill Eberhardt
682 Ranch Wood Trail
Orange, CA 92669
    (714) 639-0882

★ **Cat items of any sort** including porcelain, carvings, prints, Orientalia, needlework, pottery, jade, jewelry, cookie jars, calendars, art deco, advertising, steins, medals, doorstops, bronzes, crystal, postcards, playing cards, prints and fine art, ivory, etc. Buys some cartoon cats (**Felix the Cat**, Sylvester, Kliban cats) but no Garfield, chalk figures, or anything broken or damaged.
   Marilyn Dipboye, Cat Collectors
   31311 Blair Dr.
   Warren, MI 48092
      (313) 264-0285

★ **Horses.** Everything related to work or recreation horses including polo, horseback riding, carriage driving, sidesaddle, draft horses, **horse-shoeing, veterinary**, etc. Wants posters, prints of riding and recognized horse breeds, books (1st editions in d/j only), magazines, stud books, and breed registers. "I don't buy common books still in print, book club editions, *Diseases of the Horse,* or books on horse betting. Everything must be in fine condition for resale."
   Barbara Cole, October Farm
   Rt. 2, Box 183-C
   Raleigh, NC 27610
      (919) 772-0482

★ **Zebras in many different forms,** including porcelain, carvings, paintings, folk art, etc. To be of interest, an item must be of a zebra, not just zebra striped. Please, no hides or parts of dead zebras.
   Dave Galt
   302 W. 78th Street
   New York, NY 10024
      (212) 769-2514

★ **Musk oxen figurines, prints, book plates, and other small ephemera,** 1750-1930. Especially wants postcards, cigarette silks, trading cards, pottery, stamps and other small paper items. Will pay up to $100 each for illustrations from *History of Quadrupeds* (1781) or *Arctic Zoology* (1784) both by Thomas Pennant.
   Ross Hartsough,
   98 Bryn Mawr Rd.
   Winnipeg, R3T 3P5, CANADA

★ **Pigeon related items** including books, magazines, postcards, and prints, pre-1960.
   Stan and Monty Luden
   11908 Abingdon St.
   Norwalk, CA 90650
      (310) 863-0123

★ **Owls.** Donna buys owls, but only (1) owls made by American Indians, (2) owls on postcards, (3) *Sclarrafia* owls, (4) *Zsolnay* owls, (5) *Meissen* owls, or (6) owl decoys. She does not want anything current or produced for the mass market. You must include a detailed description of all damage, plus a photograph. "We will not respond to offers that do not indicate the price wanted." She publishes a bimonthly newsletter for owl collectors. Sample copy $3.
   Donna Howard
   PO Box 5491
   Fresno, CA 93755
      (209) 439-4845

★ **Wild boar ephemera.** "I'll buy paintings, bronzes, ceramics, advertising, anything featuring the wild European boar or its American counterparts, the peccary or javelina." Describe condition.
   Henry Winningham
   3205 S. Morgan St.
   Chicago, IL 60608

★ **Worms and caterpillars.** "Not real ones," she hastens to add, "but just about any figural in any material. I prefer small ones that can fit on a shelf, but I'll buy cookie jars, bookends, figurines, books, toys, dolls, novelties...any worm or caterpillar I don't have. I'm especially looking for a *Lowly Worm* in a car figure based on the *Lowly Worm* books." Give size, material, and general description.
   Nita Markham
   529 Wave St.
   Monterey, CA 93940

★ **Oyster memorabilia.** Got anything related to oysters? Cans, figurines, what have you?
   Sheldon Katz
   211 Roanoke Ave.
   Riverhead, NY 11901
      (516) 369-1100

★ **Antique tropical fish tanks, equipment and ephemera.** Wants books, magazines, catalogs directly related to tropical fish, as well as "pet shop" or turtle magazines and paper. Xerox© what you have. Priced items preferred but will make offers.
   Gary Bagnall
   1615 E. St. Gertrude
   Santa Ana, CA 92705

★ **Snakes and other reptiles made of wrought iron.** Wants wrought iron snakes and other reptiles created by blacksmiths as whimsies or useful items (such as pot or watch holders, for example). Can depict one snake or several, or other reptiles such as alligators and turtles. **Other figural animal and human whimsies made of iron** are also sought, especially weird forms of dogs. Most of these iron figures are under 9" high. A photo or drawing and description are necessary. Please don't contact her unless your item is for sale.

Linda Campbell Franklin
2716 Northfield Rd.
Charlottesville, VA 22901

Pet Licenses

★ **Pet license tags, rabies tags, and all other metal tags related to animals.** Especially interested in Illinois tags. Especially wants tags pre-1900 for which he pays $15 and up.

Rich Hartzog
Box 4143 BID
Rockford, IL 61110

★ **Dog license tags** including: (1) tags from any state if they are shaped like the date of issue; (2) tags from anywhere in the world pre-1910; (3) all NY tags issued before 1918; and (4) NY Conservation Dept. tags, 1917-35, which are worth from $10-$40. pre-Civil War tags can bring up to $150, and pre-1900 tags start at $5.

James Case
RR #1, Box 68, Crane Rd.
Lindley, NY 14858

★ **Dog and cat licenses,** especially colored ones or those cut into shapes. Will pay $8 each for all dog tags older than 1910 and will buy all cat tags in any quantity.

George Chartrand
Box 334
Winnipeg, MB R3C 2H6, CANADA
(204) 774-1186

pet publications

Canine Collector's Companion,
a 20 page bimonthly.
$20 a year from
PO Box 2948
Portland, OR 97208.

Cat Talk,
a 16 page bimonthly.
$15 a year from
31311 Blair Drive
Warren, MI 48092.

The Owl's Nest,
a 20 page bimonthly.
$15 a year from
PO Box 5491
Fresno, CA 93755

transportation

If it rolls, floats, flies

or travels in any other way imaginable it probably has the attention of collectors. That means it can put money in your pocket.

Transportation collectors love to find the rare and short-lived, but often have fairly narrow specialties.

Don't overlook paper items, catalogs and company brochures. Letters about experiences aboard early trains, planes, ships, and automobiles are also of interest. Many small tokens, badges, pins, and the like are worth your time to sell when you find them.

Your description should include:

[1] What it is;
[2] What it is made from;
[3] Its size, shape, and color, especially of glass;
[4] All markings embossed (raised) or incised (stamped in);
[5] Patent dates and maker info.

License plate collectors want to know the number of chips and cracks on old porcelain plates. Set your Xerox© style photocopy machine to legal size, lay the plate gently down on the glass, and make a photocopy. Wash the plate in mild soap and water (no abrasives!), if needed.

Most transportation collectors do not want damaged items, those with questionable (possibly fake) markings, and things that have been altered or known to have been reproduced.

tony hyman

Railroads

★ **Railroad items** including dining car china, silverware, lanterns and lamps, stock certificates, engine builder's plates, ticket dating machines, depot signs, advertising, postcards of depots, brochures and timetables pre-1940, historical documents, hat and cap badges, wax seals, Express Company signs, annual passes from before 1920, and books, manuals, and guides. Nothing newer than 1959, no letters, receipts, or minor paper. This 30 year veteran requests your phone number.
Fred Arone, The Depot Attic
377 Ashford Ave.
Dobbs Ferry, NY 10522
(914) 693-1832

★ **Almost anything related to American Railroads** especially dining car china, silverware, glass, marked lanterns, and marked brass locks. Pays $20-85 for sugar tongs or spoons marked with railroad names. Make certain your description includes dimensions and all marks and logos. Rick does not want date nails, books, or model trains. This 25 year veteran says he'll be helpful and answer questions from amateurs, with or without things to sell.
Richard Wright
West Coast Rick's
Box 8051
Rowland Heights, CA 91748
(714) 681-4647

★ **Railroad books** of all types, fiction, biographies, histories, etc. Seeks *Poor's Manual of Railroads*, pre-1920. **Also other items, especially from Colorado and New Jersey,** such as pre-1920 annual passes, uniform buttons, pins, and brass padlocks with raised letters. Especially would like anything from Central RR of NJ (*The Blue Comet*).
Dan Allen
Box 917
Marlton, NJ 08053
(609) 953-1387 eves

★ **All railroad, airline, and shipping timetables,** passes, brochures, and other paper.
Ken Prag, Prag's Paper Americana
Box 531
Burlingame, CA 94011
(415) 566-6400

★ **Railroad and Express Company memorabilia** including dining car china, silverware, ashtrays, playing cards, paperweights, brass lamps and lanterns (including unmarked ones), locks, badges, switch keys, builder plates, steam whistles, caps pre-1960, uniforms pre-1920, railroad pocket watches if in perfect condition, pre-1916 timetables, posters, and calendars. Also Cyclopedias or dictionaries or other reference books published by *RY Gazette*, *Simmons-Boardman, Moody*, or *Poors* pre-1950. No large tools, large oil cans, spikes, low value paper, junky or damaged items, or material other than U.S. or Canadian. No "overly cleaned" or replated items. This 15 year veteran dealer carries an extensive list of items for sale so always needs new merchandise.
Scott Arden
20457 Highway 126
Noti, OR 97461
(503) 935-1619   (9 to 9)

★ **Canadian railroad memorabilia** pre-1950, especially *White Pass and Yukon Railway, Grand Trunk Railway,* and *Canadian Pacific,* among others.
Michael Rice
Box 286
Saanichton, BC V0S 1M0, CANADA
(604) 652-9047 eves

★ **Railroad dining car memorabilia** including china, silver, glassware, menus, and anything else. Items without markings as to the railroad are "worthless" to him.
Charles Goodman
636 W. Grant Ave.
Charleston, Il 61920
(217) 345-6771

★ **Railroad memorabilia** such as dishes, silver, lanterns, keys, locks, books, etc. "I'll pay at least $300 for the 10 1/2" china plates used· on the trains." Especially interested in items from Southern roads. **Also wants pre-1930 postcards** showing exteriors of small town depots or trains, and cards of any era showing depot or train interiors. Please include your phone number. Does not make offers, but claims he is "willing to pay your price."
Les Winn
Box 80641
Chamblee, GA 30366
(404) 458-6194 eves

★ **Chesapeake & Ohio Railroad memorabilia** of all sort, as long as it features the two cats, "Chessie" and "Peake." A Xerox or photo is appreciated. No repros. SASE please.
Charles Worman
PO Box 33584 (AMC)
Dayton, OH 45433
(513) 429-1808 eves

★ **Memorabilia from Arkansas railways** including Eureka Springs Railway, St. Louis and North Arkansas Railroad, Missouri and Arkansas Railroad, and the Missouri and North Arkansas Railroad. "I'll buy advertising, passes, china and silver, photos, switch locks and keys, lanterns, tickets, bills of lading, stock certificates, etc."
Steve Chyrchel
Route #2 Box 362
Eureka Springs, AR 72632
(501) 253-9244

★ **Railroad date nails and other small railroadiana items** such as lanterns, locks, and keys. Will buy almost any date nails (nails about 4" long with a date on the head). If you describe the shape of the head, the number, and whether it is incised or raised, he says he's glad to tell you what you have. Dick is a collector with limited storage so is interested only in small fine items.
Dick Gartin
619 Adams
Duncanville, TX 75137
(214) 296-8742 anytime

★ **Date nails** used by railroads, telephone, telegraph, and power companies to record when their ties or poles were placed in service. Most, but not all, have either round or square heads and have numbers (or other symbols) either raised or indented on the head. Nails may be steel, copper, or aluminum. Although there are many common nails, there are also nails worth $50 up so describe what you have and Jerry will make an offer. Jerry is editor of *Nailer News* a brief bimonthly newsletter for nail collectors.
Jerry Waits
501 W. Horton
Brenham, TX 77833
(409) 830-1495

Airplanes

★ **Antique airplane memorabilia** including entire airplanes, parts, early flight equipment, books, magazines, photos, etc., are sought by the 6,000 members of The Antique Airplane Association. Write what you have for sale in the way of early air memorabilia, and President Taylor will forward your letter to a member who is looking for what you have to sell. The Association is the parent organization of the Airpower Museum and Bob is empowered to accept tax deductible donations of significant and interesting items from the history of air flight.
Bob Taylor
Antique Airplane Association
Box 172
Ottumwa, IA 52501
(515) 938-2773 days

★ **All early airplane memorabilia** including propellers, instruments, badges, flight awards, tools, manuals, emblems, accessories, checks, bonds, and virtually any good quality early item.
Joseph Russell
455 Ollie St.
Cottage Grove, WI 53527
(608) 839-4736 eves

★ *Pan Am's China Clipper* and all Chinese airline memorabilia, 1925-45, including caps, uniforms, medals, photos, diaries, badges, posters, and what have you.
Gene Christian
3849 Bailey Ave.
Bronx, NY 10463
(212) 548-0243

★ *Ford* tri-motor airplane memorabilia. Will pay $100 for Ford Airplane Co. employee badge.
Tim O'Callaghan
46878 Betty Hill
Plymouth, MI 49170
(313) 459-4636

★ **Wooden airplane propellers.**
Charles Martignette
PO Box 293
Hallandale, FL 33009
(305) 454-3474

★ **Commercial aviation memorabilia, American or foreign, 1919-50** including books, letters, magazines, photographs, and miscellaneous small artifacts. Especially interested in uncommon items. No books on how to fly, radio, or navigation. Book club editions or defective books are not wanted.
> Ron Mahoney
> Air Age Book Co
> Box 40
> Tollhouse, CA 93667
> (209) 855-8993

★ **Commercial airline memorabilia** including pilot and stewardess wings and hat emblems, display models, anniversary pins, playing cards, postcards with airplanes, buttons, flight schedules, kiddie wings, and almost anything else old and unusual from the airlines. Especially seeking ephemera from *Northeast Airlines, Delta, Chicago and Southern*, and *Western Airlines*.
> John Joiner
> 245 Ashland Trail
> Tyrone, GA 30290
> (404) 487-3732

★ **Airline models from travel agencies.** Buys all types of planes, from 1920 to 1990. Photo probably best, but give the airlines and type of plane if you can.
> Charles Martignette
> PO Box 293
> Hallandale, FL 33009
> (305) 454-3474

★ **Airline pilot and stewardess wings and hat badges** pre-1970. Also stewardess uniforms pre-1965 *if they are complete*. Looking for pilot and stewardess wings from the 1940's and 50's from airlines such as *Mohawk Airlines, Northeast Airlines, Inland Airlines, Pioneer Air Lines, Empire Airlines, Colonial Airlines, Chicago and Southern Airlines, Mid-Continent Airlines*, and others. Also **metal desk models of airliners** (travel agent type) from the 1940's, 50's and 60's. No military items. Xerox© copies are very helpful.
> Charles Quarles
> 204 Reservation Dr.
> Spindale, NC 28160
> (704) 245-7803 eves

★ **Desk display models of aircraft and weapon products** from various manufacturers such as *Convair, General Dynamics, Vultee, Douglass, Lockheed*, and others. Models created by Topping are preferred but all are considered. All models should have their original stands.
> Bob Keller
> Starline Hobbies
> Box 38
> Stanton, CA 90680
> (714) 826-5218 days

★ **China and silverplate used by any airline.**
> Les Winn
> Box 80641
> Chamblee, GA 30366
> (404) 458-6194 eves

★ **Zeppelin, blimp, and dirigible memorabilia** including virtually anything shaped like, or about, the giant gas bags such as photos, paper ephemera, postcards, china marked "LZ," stereocards, timetables, books, souvenirs, stamps and covers, training films, tokens and medals, toys, games, and Christmas ornaments. Especially wants pieces and parts of zeps. No repros, repainted or restored items, homemades, or fakes. "I am a historian not a dealer."
> Zeppelin
> PO Box 2502
> Cinnaminson, NJ 08077
> (609) 829-3959

★ **Aviation magazines, pilot's handbooks, and overhaul manuals** before 1970.
> Alan C. King
> PO Box 86
> Radnor, OH 43066

Space Program

★ **Memorabilia of all early rocket research** including "newsletters, journals, books, magazines, reports, studies, correspondence, blueprints, drawings, photographs, films, and any other documentation from France, Germany, UK, USSR, USA, or any other nation regarding speculation, research and development, experimentation and implementation conducted by any amateur, military, or civilian group or any individual pertaining to the history and development of rockets and missiles and eventual space travel from the period of 1900-1960." He especially wants "any material from WWII pertaining to work done at Peenemunde, Germany, carried out by Wernher Von Braun, which led to the development of the V-2 and other rocket weapons. Also any material having to do with Robert H. Goddard and the experiments he conducted in Worcester, MA, and Roswell, NM, during the 1920's through 1940's." He is not interested in science fiction or pop culture figures like Buck Rogers but does want speculative articles that are scholarly or serious in intent.
> Randy Liebermann
> 211 E. 43rd St., #705
> New York, NY 10017
>   (212) 972-2061

★ **Space shot memorabilia** including souvenirs such as commemorative magazines, buttons, autographs, etc. Especially wants "internal" souvenirs such as special coins, medallions, mission patches, models, etc., produced for people directly involved with some aspect of a space "event" such as a launching or completion of construction. Also internal documents such as manuals, flight plans, charts, and so on. Also hardware, pieces of spacecraft, and other items discarded as part of mission preparation or completion. Also video tapes of launchings or reports from space. Does not want recent items which NASA still sells such as slide sets, T-shirts, etc.
> Mike Smithwick
> 25215 La Loma Drive
> Los Altos Hills, CA 94022
>   (408) 244-8987 eves

★ **NASA and space program items**, including anything produced or distributed by NASA, authentic patches, manuals, medallions, space shuttle tile samples, pieces of spacecraft or spacecraft construction materials, and items owned or carried into space by astronauts.
> Paul Hartunian
> 127B East Bradford Ave.
> Cedar Grove, NJ 07009
>   (201) 857-7275

★ **Space age memorabilia** including souvenirs issued to commemorate various launchings, U.S. or Soviet. Buys glasses, coasters, ashtrays, cards, plates, paperweights, jewelry, and other trinkets as well as books, coloring books, magazines, and albums of newspaper clippings. He requests that you price what you have.
> Barry Burros
> 160 East 48th St.
> New York, NY 10017
>   (212) 688-1581

★ **Apollo XI moon landing souvenirs.** No magazines or newspapers. NO OFFERS.
> Bernard Passion
> 3517 1/2 Kinney St.
> Los Angeles, CA 90065
>   (213) 256-8291

Ships & the Sea

★ **Fine marine antiques of all types**, including but not limited to:

[1] **Paintings and prints** of boats, ships, and the sea of all types in original or good condition, from 1700 to 1900;

[2] **Navigational instruments** from the 19th century, octants, sextants, tripod mounted telescopes, exceptional compasses, marine clocks (especially those by Chelsea & Howard);

[3] **Marine photographs**, especially oversize whaling, yachting, launchings, identified ports, from the 19th century or early 20th century;

[4] **Marine journals, logs, and out-of-print books**, pertaining to whaling, yachting, clippers, etc., but only if in fine resalable condition;

[5] **Carvings** such as pilot house eagles, figureheads, tailboards, name boards, etc.;

[6] **Scrimshaw teeth** and sailor's whimsies such as inlaid boxes, bone swifts, crimpers, and tools but only genuine old pieces;

[7] **Paper and other ephemera** such as deck plans, broadsides, early ship china, etc., as long as it is rare, interesting, and in fine condition.
He does not buy reproductions, fakes, or items which have been altered or restored. Generally buys only 19th century items, with exceptions as noted. He does not want contemporary scrimshaw, compass in a box, or telegraphs unless they are small, very early, or important historically. Your description should include all repairs and restoration, dimensions, age, history, and price (if you can). He specializes in forming and liquidating collections, issues catalogs at whim" and is available for consultations for fee.
Andrew Jacobson Marine Antiques
PO Box 2155
South Hamilton, MA 01982
(508) 468-6276

★ **Model sailboats.** "I'll buy wooden models that are at least 18" long, made of wood, with rigged canvas sails. May be up to 8' high. I prefer them to have stands. I'm looking for their decorative value so am not particularly looking for famous boats, ship builder's models, and other high ticket items. Send a picture of what you have, please." Should be in fine or readily restorable condition.
Joan Brady
834 Central Ave.
Pawtucket, RI 02861
(401) 725-5753

★ **Ship models**, particularly identified 19th century American, English, or French vessels. "I also deal in 20th century high quality models of all types: sail, steam, transition, liners, yachts, and pond models." Also buys **builder's half models**, including 19th century American or British hulls, exceptional 20th century hulls, and all yacht models. Does not want reproductions, or items which have been heavily "restored" or otherwise altered. Please give the dimensions, age, condition, history, and price. "If you want an appraisal, I must examine the object personally, and there is a fee, although I will give 'ball park' verbal estimates on routine items, with the understanding there is no legal responsibility or liability."
Andrew Jacobson
Marine Antiques
PO Box 2155
South Hamilton, MA 01982
(508) 468-6276

★ **Steamship memorabilia** including china, silver, ashtrays, playing cards, brass whistles, locks, lanterns, paperweights, badges, signs, uniforms and caps, calendars, posters, route maps, and numerous similar items. **Does not want** paper ephemera after 1910, low value paper goods, fake or altered items, or big heavy tools. Nor does he buy items that are shabby or missing important parts. Scott is a major national dealer who issues regular catalogs.
Scott Arden
20457 Highway 126
Noti, OR 97461
(503) 935-1619 (9 to 9)

★ **Ocean liner memorabilia from all lines and companies** especially paper items such as deck plans, menus, booklets, and passenger lists from Cunard, French German, White Star, Italian, Canadian, Dutch, and all others. "We do not buy reproductions or items that are strictly 'travel' interest, such as brochures describing Paris. You are invited to send items on approval as we cannot make offers based only on your description."
Alan Taksler
New Steamship Consultants
Box 30088
Mesa, AZ 85275

★ **Ocean liner memorabilia,** deck plans, post cards, paintings, posters, and anything relating to passenger ship travel especially from "disaster ships" such as the *Titanic* or *Andrea Doria.* After 1945, only maiden voyage items are wanted. Ken produces a large illustrated catalog for $15/issue.
    Ken Schultz
    Box M753
    Hoboken, NJ 07030
        (201) 656-0966

★ **Canadian steamship memorabilia** including all pre-1950 ephemera such as calendars, stock certificates, bonds, fancy letterheads, deck plans, envelopes, etc. Seeks Canadian Pacific Steamships, BC Coast steamships, and others.
    Michael Rice
    Box 286
    Saanichton, BC V0S 1M0, CANADA

★ **Alaskan steamship ephemera** such as post-cards, letterheads, photos, from all companies especially the Alaskan Steamship Co.
    Nick Nickell
    102 People's Wharf
    Juneau, AK 99801
        (907) 586-1733

★ **Steamship ephemera collections** dating pre-1960, including menus, programs, deck plans, posters, etc., either American or European. Promises a quick answer to all inquiries.
    George Theofiles, The Miscellaneous Man
    Box 1776
    New Freedom, PA 17349
        (717) 235-4766 days; (717) 235-2853 fax

★ **Great Lakes ships and shipping.** "I'll buy photos, documents, fiction and non fiction books, technical and statistical reports, anything old, new, or historic having to do with Great Lakes shipping."
    James Baumhofer
    Box 65493
    St. Paul, MN 55165
        (612) 698-7151

★ **Wooden motor boat memorabilia** especially items related to Gar Wood, the man and his boats, 1923-47. Also *Chris Craft, Hacker, Old Town*, and others. Buys sales literature, catalogs, magazines, etc. Give date and condition.
    Tony Mollica
    Box 6003
    Syracuse, NY 13217
        (315) 433-2643 days

★ **Outboard motors.** "I'll buy outboard motors, boat and sales literature, and engine manuals from before 1940. Also boating magazines, nautical books, and other ephemera including information about marine engines, outboard motors, yachts, canoes, treasure hunting, Arctic voyages and exploration, and boat building." Nothing after 1940 please. Condition must be described carefully. When describing outboard motors, give the serial number and indicate whether the engine is frozen or will still turn. Offers wants list and catalog of items for sale.
    Robert Glick
    Columbia Trading Co.
    504 Main St.
    West Barnstable, MA 02668

★ **Nautical instruments by American and foreign makers** including brass sextants, wood octants, spyglasses, pocket sundials, and cased navigating devices for charts and globes, as well as map drawing tools. Must be made before 1890.
    Jonathan Thomas
    Scientific Americana
    1208 Main Street North
    Southbury, CT 06488
        (203) 227-2622

★ **Lighthouses, U.S. Coast Guard, and rescue services at sea.** All ephemera pre-1940.
    Robert Glick
    Columbia Trading Co.
    504 Main St.
    West Barnstable, MA 02668

★ **Lighthouses and Life Saving Service.** High quality items are sought by this prominent dealer for resale. If what you have is interesting, rare, and in fine condition, he'd like to hear from you. Give dimensions, history, and condition.
    Andrew Jacobson
    Marine Antiques
    PO Box 2155
    South Hamilton, MA 01982
        (508) 468-6276

Bicycles

★ **Bicycles and bicycle memorabilia,** generally before 1900, although some items are wanted to 1930. Wants all material about high wheelers and velocipedes ("bone shakers") including posters, advertising, trophies, photos, prints, toys and other representations or depictions, especially ephemera created by the Pope Mfg Company. He does not want anything related to balloon tire bicycles.
Pryor Dodge
Box 71 Prince St. Station
New York, NY 10012
(212) 966-1026

★ **League of American Wheelman memorabilia** is sought by this expert 20 year veteran collector who buys pins, medals, ribbons, magazines, etc., from 1880-1955. You might try him for general **early bicycle memorabilia** as well. Not interested in anything after 1955.
Walley Francis
Box 6941
Syracuse, NY 13217
(315) 478-5671

★ **Bicycling before 1910,** with an emphasis on **League of American Wheelmen (LAW) memorabilia.** Artifacts include medals, pins, awards, ribbons, photos, and figurines made of glass, porcelain, silver, etc. Small items or large. Especially interested in high wheeler items.
Charlie Stewart
900 Grandview Ave.
Reno, NV 89503
(702) 747-1439 mornings

★ **Bicycle memorabilia** including paper ephemera, sales literature, catalogs, advertising, and small objects such as pins, medals, and give-away trinkets. Jay specializes in mail order sales of transportation memorabilia of all types and always needs good fresh new stock. He accepts boxes of good clean items sent on approval and "makes immediate offers."
Jay Ketelle
3721 Farwell
Amarillo, TX 79109
(806) 355-3456

★ **Balloon tire bicycles** made between 1934-1960 in new or mint condition only, especially *Schwinn, Shelby, Monarch, Columbia,* or *Elgin* (Sears Roebuck). Please include a photo.
Gus Garton
Garton's Auto
5th & Vine
Millville, NJ 08332

★ **Balloon tire bicycles** from the 1930's to 1960 are wanted. The most desired are boys' bikes with tanks, lights, horns, springs, and other accessories. "The more gaudy features, the better." Look for brands like *Schwinn, Road Master, Elgin, Shelby, Evinrude, Hiawatha* and *Western Flyer.* Bikes will usually have tires sized: 26x1.125, 24x2.125 or 28x1.5 and are especially desirable if colored. Will buy in any condition, but the value is determined by condition and accessories. Mike also buys parts, signs, shop fixtures, and literature relevant to this period of bicycles. No racing bikes, middleweights with 26 x 1.75 tires, or plain bikes. **Photographs and complete description important.**
Michael Brown
260 19th Ave. N.
Clinton, IA 52732
(800) 383-0049

★ *Whizzers* **and balloon tire bicycles** are wanted. *Whizzers* are motordriven bicycles, some of which were factory built, others made from kits with belt drive to rear wheel. Bike tires should be 20, 24, or 26" by 2.125". Especially wants a 1933 *Schwinn Aerocycle* or a 1938-39 *Shelby Speedline Airflow.* "The longer and weirder the tanks are, the more I want them." Also buys signs and shop fixtures, including old brake parts cabinets, literature, and advertising. He does *not* want middleweight bikes with 1.75" tires with lights in the tank, or plain bikes with no tanks. Send a photo and complete description. Include the *Whizzer* serial number.
Alan Kinsey
318 NE Grant
Ankeny, IA 50021
(515) 964-5472

★ **pre-1930 bicycle license tags,** often called "sidepath licenses," from any state. Value ranges from $5-40 depending on age and place of issue.
James Case
RR #1, Box 68, Crane Rd.
Lindley, NY 14858

Motorcycles

★ **Motorcycle memorabilia** including awards, pins, clothing, signs, postcards, trade cards, racing trophies and memorabilia, motorcycle toys, and any unusual items. Also buys American motorcycles and racing cycles from before 1950.
   Chris Savino
   Box 419
   Breesport, NY 14816
      (607) 739-3106

★ **Motorcycle memorabilia** including advertising, giveaway trinkets, watch fobs, and other items. Both foreign and domestic, pre-1960. "I will accept boxes sent to me on approval and will make immediate offer to buy." Promises to reimburse your postage if his offer not accepted.
   Jay Ketelle
   3721 Farwell
   Amarillo, TX 79109
      (806) 355-3456

★ **American made motorcycles and motorcycle parts.** Describe what you have, giving markings and numbers when appropriate. "I pay all shipping costs. I'm in the parts business and will travel to pick up large lots."
   Robert Fay
   Star Route Box AF
   Whitmore, CA 96096
      (916) 472-3132

★ *Can-Am* **motorcycle parts and ephemera** including *Rotax* motor, brochures, decals, gloves, leathers, goggles, and anything else marked "Can-Am." This motorcycle is made by *Bombardier* of Canada.
   Don Schneider
   Box 1570
   Merritt, BC, Canada V0K 2B0

★ *Cushman* **motorscooters** and related ephemera, especially signs and sales literature. Also **pre-1965 motorcycle** photos, postcards, sales literature, manuals, and magazines.
   Don Olson
   Box 245
   Humboldt, IA 50548

Automobiles

★ **Classic American and foreign automobiles.** One of the nation's largest auctioneers of high quality foreign and old domestic automobiles. If you have anything fast, sleek, limited production, or unusual, give Cole a call and discuss putting it up for sale in California's lucrative automobile market. Also *Corvettes, T-Birds,* older convertibles, and selected other American cars of the 1950's and 1960's. Don't sell your old car for too little.
   Rick Cole Auctions
   10701 Riverside Dr.
   No. Hollywood, CA 91602
      (818) 506-6533

★ **Automobiles made between 1940 and 1969.** Want any well maintained low mileage auto, especially a *Cadillac* convertible from the 1950's or 60's. "I'd keep it as long as I live!" Also buys **automotive related signs**: auto sales and service, gasoline, motor oil, etc. Also **auto toys**.
   Gus Garton
   Garton's Auto
   5th & Vine,
   Millville, NJ 08332

★ *Dan Patch* **automobile** or parts and other ephemera from that brand. Call collect if you know of one of these cars for sale.
   Donald Sawyer
   40 Bachelor St.
   West Newbury, MA 01985
      (508) 363-2983

Automobile Ephemera

★ **Paper ephemera, advertising, and promotional items associated with automobiles,** trucks, buses, campers, taxis, auto racing, police cars, ambulances, and hearses. Jay operates a large mail order business selling **transportation memorabilia of all sorts** and always needs clean old items such as catalogs, promotional items, emblems, promotional models given away by car dealers, auto company service pins, owners manuals, and other small items associated with any form of vehicle. Will buy U.S. and foreign items, and multiples of some things. Will accept boxes sent on approval and "will make immediate offers to buy." Requests you include your phone number. Does not want shop manuals, parts lists, and magazine ads.
Jay Ketelle
3721 Farwell
Amarillo, TX 79109
(806) 355-3456

★ **Automobile related memorabilia** including promotional giveaways, **owner's manuals,** repair manuals, radiator emblems and caps, dial type tire gauges, fancy gear shift knobs, car clocks, **spark plugs,** horns, dash panels, brass speedometers, **DAV keychains, automobile magazines,** plant employee badges, canceled checks from auto companies, **stocks and bonds,** porcelain or leather license plates, driving awards and anything you can imagine having to do with automobiles except magazine ads.
Joseph Russell
455 Ollie St.
Cottage Grove, WI 53527
(608) 839-4736 eves

★ **Books, magazines, and factory literature about cars, trucks, motorcycles, and bicycles.** Also buys newsletters and magazines produced by automobile clubs devoted to one particular make of vehicle or another. Documents related to vehicle history 1895-1990 also purchased.
Ralph Dunwoodie
5935 Calico Drive
Sun Valley, NV 89433
(702) 673-3811

★ **Automobile and truck dealers' showroom brochures,** 1900-1970, for any makes, American or foreign. **Also** buying selected automobile owner's manuals, shop manuals, and parts manuals issued by the companies themselves. Not interested in reproductions, reprints, magazines, clipped ads, *Motor's* or *Chilton's* manuals, and items not issued by the auto company. Also **auto dealer promotional items,** including signs, banners, date books, etc., that were originally in a car dealer's showroom. This 25 year veteran collector and dealer says a good description includes measurements, color, number of pages, and condition, listing any visible flaws. Xerox© appreciated but not essential. Please include your phone number.
S.E. Penning
PO Box 16171
Fresno, CA 93755

★ **Books, catalogs, and owner's manuals.** Books may be on automobiles, auto history, racing, biography, auto travel, etc. Not interested in technical and repair manuals. Give standard bibliographic information, and note condition of cover, pages, spine, binding, and dust jacket. Also buys some photos of cars.
David King's Automotive Books
5 Brouwer Lane
Rockville Center, NY 11570
(516) 766-1561

★ **Automobile sales catalogs, brochures, owner's manuals, and repair guides** printed by the auto company. Wants material for all cars and trucks, American or foreign, especially pre-1970. No magazines, clipped ads, *Motor's Manuals, Chilton's Manuals,* or books not printed by the auto company. Also buys **auto dealer promotional items** including signs, salesman's awards, and the like. "Please send me a list of each item by year and make. If a list is not practical, give me a count by decade, such as 'so many brochures from 1950 to 1959,' etc."
Walter Miller
6710 Brooklawn Parkway
Syracuse, NY 13211
(315) 432-8282

★ *Ford* **Motor Company memorabilia** from before 1955, including books, coins, badges, pins, postcards, and literature.
Tim O'Callaghan
46878 Betty Hill
Plymouth, MI 48170
(313) 459-4636

★ Advertising literature for the *Chevrolet Corvette*, 1953 on, including newspaper and magazine ads, sales brochures, direct mailings, race programs, sports programs, and auto show literature. Also "related *Corvette* memorabilia," including promotional giveaways. No reprints.
David Facey, Auto-Ads
7015 Klein Rd.
Lakeland, FL 33813
    (813) 644-8369

★ 1932 *Chevrolet* parts, accessories, go-withs, and paper ephemera including ads, showroom literature, catalogs, repair manuals, and what have you. Will buy nearly any original parts, but especially needs dash clock, heater, various switches, tools, defroster, and many other items. If you regularly come across parts, send for his wants list.
Reed Fitzpatrick
9925 SW 178th St.
Vashon, WA 98070
    (206) 463-3900 days

★ *Buick* promotional items.
Alvin Heckard
RD 1, Box 88
Lewistown, PA 17044
    (717) 248-7071

★ *Mercedes* and *Rolls-Royce* radiator mascots and other parts, accessories, manuals, and literature made before 1960.
Joseph Weber
604 Centre St.
Ashland, PA 17921
    (717) 875-4401 3-5 pm

★ *Rolls Royce* advertising, pamphlets, cards, toys, and other information. Has particular interest in all models from the years 1957 through 1962, Princess through Silver Cloud.
Richard Melcher
1206 Okanogan St.
Wenatchee, WA 98807
    (509) 662-0386

★ *Cunningham* Auto Company ephemera. "I want anything regarding this 1920's Rochester, NY, auto maker. Priced approvals are requested. Your postage will be reimbursed."
David Lamb
48 Woodside Dr.
Rochester, NY 14624

★ Parts and ephemera for *Gardner* and other autos made in St. Louis such as *Moon, Diana, Ruxton*, and *Windsor*. Buys parts, hubcaps, mascots, owner's manuals, and the like. Will pay $75 for a single brochure on the front drive of a 1930 *Gardner*.
Robert Owen
Box 204
Fairborn, OH 45324

★ Odd looking spark plugs. "I'll buy as many as you have, the odder looking the better." He especially wants those with priming cups. No *AC* or *Champion* plugs.
Joseph Weber
604 Centre St.
Ashland, PA 17921
    (717) 875-4401 3-5 pm

★ Factory original automobile AM radios 1926-1962. Only AM-FM from 1963-77. Wants brand and model number. Also auto wheelcovers (*not hubcaps*), 1950 to the present. Tell him the make, model, condition, and quantity. Include your price, phone number and hours to reach you.
John Sheldon
2718 Koper Dr.
Sterling Heights, MI 48310
    (313) 977-7979 days fax (313) 977-0895

★ *Firestone Tire Company* promotional items especially those shaped like tires including tire ashtrays, clocks, penholders, cigarette cases. Also radios shaped like batteries, and other figural selling aids. List everything printed on the tire and on the insert. Does not want domestic ashtrays made after 1950. Pays $20-$35 for most items.
Wayne Ray
10325 Willeo Creek Trace
Roswell, GA 30075
    (404) 998-5325

★ Tire company promotional items especially tire ashtrays, tire clocks, penholders, radios, globes, *Tires* magazines, tire catalogs, and other literature and promotional items. "Will pay $50 for any original *Michelin* or *Overman* rubber tire ashtray." Also want foreign tires, tires with commemorative inserts, and other unusual promotional tires. Long priced wants list available.
Jeff Mc Vey,
Box 50091
Billings, MT 59105

License plates

★ **Ordinary license plates** such as you find in auto wrecking yards and garage sales. Will pay 25¢ each, up to $5 each for harder to find ones. Must be in nearly new condition. Will accept shipments of up to 200 plates; write first if you have more than that. List the type of item, place of origin, date, classification number, condition, quantity, and price (if possible). George is editor of *License Plate Corner*, a Canadian newsletter for collectors.
George Chartrand
Box 334
Winnipeg, MB R3C 2H6, CANADA
    (204) 774-1186

★ **Porcelain license plates** from U.S. and Canadian cars, trucks, and motorcycles before 1923. Also wants early **photos and photo postcards of vehicles clearly showing readable plates**. Pays especially well for plates from Southern and unpopulated Western states. Does not buy painted metal plates. Photocopies suggested.
Rodney Brunsell
55 Spring St.
Hanson, MA 02341

★ **All types of old license plates.** "I buy license plates from anywhere issued to any type of motor vehicle at any time. My number one find would be a 1905 VT porcelain plate, for which I'd pay $1,500 if in good condition." Describe all chips, bends, repainting, rust, etc.
Andy Bernstein
154 Murray Drive
Oceanside, NY 11572
    (516) 764-0273 or (516) 536-3635

★ **pre-1920 license plates**, especially undated plates made of leather, brass, or porcelain. Will buy old collections or accumulations. Describe condition carefully, including damage, chips, and crazing. He offers to answer questions about license plates and says "If I don't want your plates, perhaps I can find someone who does." Gary is secretary of the Automobile License Plate Collector's Association and a valuable source of information.
Gary Brent Kincade
Box 712
Weston, WV 26452
    (304) 842-3773 eves

★ **Extraordinary license plates, especially un-dated** or those made of porcelain, leather, or wood. Also all license plates issued on or for Indian reservations. Also U.S. pre-1915; all motorcycle pre-1950; all foreign pre-1950; all Southern and Southwestern plates pre-1935; New Mexico, Alaska, and Hawaii pre-1950 in good condition and pre-1920 in any condition; and personalized plates "with cute names or phrases." Also any pictorial plates. Will buy any good condition pre-1935 plate plus collections or accumulations of plates. "Plates from populated states like NY, OH, and PA are worth little even if they date as far back as 1915 whereas Alaskan, Hawaiian, and Puerto Rican plates are desirable even in poor shape." George also buys **miniature plates from DAV,** *Goodrich, Wheaties,* or *Post* cereals. Also car club emblems such as AAA, especially foreign ones or those before 1925. Also all **pre-1940 chauffeur's badges** in good original condition. Will make offer on any item if two loose stamps are sent. "If you don't like what I offer for your license plate, I'll let you run a free ad in my license plate magazine so you can try to sell it for more."
George Chartrand
Box 334
Winnipeg, MB R3C 2H6, CANADA
    (204) 774-1186

★ **License plates from vehicles other than trucks and automobiles** such as motorcycles, bicycles, snowmobiles, etc. George will also buy **city auto plates** from before 1920, and pay $40 to $1,000 for them, depending on rarity. List the type of item, place of origin, date, classification number, condition, quantity, and price (if possible).
George Chartrand
Box 334
Winnipeg, MB R3C 2H6, CANADA

★ **License plates and license plate related items**, chauffeurs badges, hack (taxi) badges, Disabled Veterans key chain tags, *B.F. Goodrich* key chain tags, dashboard discs, registration windshield stickers, inspection windshield stickers, early drivers licenses and auto registrations.
Dr. Edward Miles
888 8th Ave.
New York, NY 10019
    (212) 765-2660

★ **License plates from Southern states pre-1958,** and other states pre-1935. Wants *only* automobile plates except from Mississippi, a state from which he will buy all types and classes of plates. 1912 and 1913 Mississippi plates are worth up to $1,000 each. Wants first year of issue plates from all 50 states, as well as any undated or handmade plates.

Eugene Gardner
10510 Rico Tatum Rd.
Palmetto, GA 30268
(404) 463-4264

★ **British Columbia license plates** before 1922 purchased in any condition. Later BC plates that are unusual will be considered, as will Yukon plates before 1960, all Canadian motorcycle plates, and BC chauffeur's badges and key tags.

Don Schneider
Box 1570
Merritt, BC
Canada V0K 2B0

★ **License plates from Missouri, Kansas, and Colorado.** Also wants other states from the years 1936, 1976, and 1989. Also miniature key chain license plates produced by BF Goodrich or the DAV. Provide a list of the items you have and the price you'd like.

George Van Trump Jr.
Box 260170
Lakewood, CO 80226
(303) 985-3508

★ **License plates from Washington and Alaska.** Very early leather and porcelain plates are wanted, but "I'll buy any Washington State plates 1915-1959 in most any condition, and 1960 to 1991 plates in good condition. All Alaska plates are of interest. Unusual plates such as mobile home, taxi, trailer, state representative, and the like are particularly welcome." Also buys old printed matter about vehicle licensing, including titles, certificates, tonnage slips, etc. Also buys license plate frames with Washington and Alaskan car dealership names, and piggyback plates that carry an advertising message and fasten just above or below a license plate. Brass plaques, auto club insignias, and the like are of interest too. "When you contact me, I want to know the state, year, type of plate, whether you have a single plate or matched pair, condition (including rust, extra holes), and the material. I'll also consider plates from other states that are suitable for trading."

Reed Fitzpatrick
PO Box 369
Vashon, WA 98070
(206) 463-3900

★ **B.F.Goodrich and DAV keychain license plate tags.** Pays 50¢ to $1 each, depending on age and state. The older the better.

Dennis Schulte
8th Ave., NW
Waukon, IA 52172
(319) 568-3628 before 10pm

★ **Aluminum license plate attachments.** "I'll buy unusual and attractive licence plate attachments which promote cities, states, turnpikes, or special events. I don't need any more Florida cities, but would like to hear from anyone with any other decorative aluminum bracket designed to fit above a license plate."

Peter Capell
1838 West Grace Street
Chicago, IL 60613
(312) 871-8735 eves

Public Transportation

★ **Horsedrawn streetcars and pre-1920 electric railways.** "I'll buy bells marked with the name of a streetcar line, car gongs, car maker's plates, wall mounted and hand held fare registers, signs reading "Have fare ready," "Pay at rear," etc., hat badges, motorman's and conductor's certificates, and photos of early cars.
Jonathan Thomas
Trolley Fare
1208 Main Street North
Southbury, CT 06488
(203) 227-2622

★ **Memorabilia from buses, taxis, hearses, ambulances, and any other public conveyance** before 1960 including emblems, badges, licenses, license plates, advertising, promotional giveaway trinkets, operator's manuals, sales literature, etc. May be foreign or U.S. as long as they are old, genuine, and small. Will accept items sent on approval.
Jay Ketelle
3721 Farwell
Amarillo, TX 79109
(806) 355-3456

★ **Bus, trolley, and streetcar memorabilia** pre-1940 including photos, artifacts, driver's badges, caps, bus emblems, route maps, and advertising. Has particular interest in Florida companies but says "I will consider any items" if the seller describes them well and attaches a price. Sam has done a book on Coral Gables postcards.
Sam LaRoue
5980 SW 35th Street
Miami, FL 33155
(305) 347-7466

★ *Greyhound* and *Trailways* **bus memorabilia.** Wants wide range of items, such as cap badges, driver awards, etc., but mostly interested in toy *Greyhound* and *Trailways* busses, and *Greyvan Moving* truck toys. Prefers a picture or photocopy. No magazine ads, timetables, postcards or posters, but he does want internal company data like garage locations, driver assignments, and organizational directories..
Eugene Farha
PO Box 633
Cedar Grove, WV 25039
(304) 340-3201

★ **Taxi cabs.** "If it pictures an American taxi cab, I'll buy it," says Henry, who seeks a wide variety of taxi related items. If you have something that is in any way related to taxis, give him a call.
Henry Winningham
3205 S. Morgan St.
Chicago, IL 60608
(312) 847-1672

★ **Transportation tokens.** Will buy in any quantity from any years. Prices vary widely depending on value. "Most modern pieces with cut-out letters are very common. We sell a nice mixed collection of 2,500 tokens for $99, so you can see modern tokens aren't worth a great deal." There are a few common old tokens, but some can be worth $1,500+ each if they picture a ship, trolley, horse car, ferry, or stage coach. Look for the words DEPOTEL, HOTEL, BAGGAGE, OMNIBUS, DRAYAGE, DEPOT TO HOTEL, etc. Simply ship your tokens if you want this well known dealer to make an offer. Lots of 25,000 or more are especially wanted.
Rich Hartzog
World Exonumia
Box 4143 BID
Rockford, IL 61110
(815) 226-0771   Fax (815) 397-7662

★ **Transportation or toll tokens** for bridges, toll roads, ferries, horsecars, depot hacks, and early streetcars. Tokens *must* be made of metal or plastic. Cardboard tokens are wanted *only* if round, *not* square or rectangular. HOTEL TO DEPOT or TRANSFER LINE tokens are worth $25-$100, more if pictorial. A token reading I GIBBS BELLEVILLE & NEW YORK USM STAGE//GOOD FOR ONE RIDE TO THE BEARER would be worth $1,500 in nice condition.
Rev. John Coffee
Box 1204
Boston, MA 02104
(617) 277-8111

business

America has been

a land of builders and inventors, commerce and farming, trade and manufacture. A land of doers....

Unfortunately for historians, few of those doers took the time to sit down and record what they did and how they did it.

Serious collectors who want to learn about the manufacture and marketing of items which interest them today often find it difficult to obtain information about what went on 30 years ago. You can imagine how hard it is to obtain information from before the turn-of-the-century!

Collectors gladly buy products, advertising, business records, letters, bills, posters, store displays, and the like. The fact that many of these items are quite difficult to find does not necessarily make them valuable, although large illustrated company catalogs from the turn of the century usually sell for more than $100 and signs made of tin often bring $500+.

Collectors also buy tools, uniforms, instruments, signs, badges, emblems, and other three-dimensional items.

The history and artifacts of some industries is being preserved by fewer than a half dozen people. In some cases, *I'll Buy That Too!* will put you in touch with the *only* person in the country willing to buy what you have!

tony hyman

Business

★ **Banking ephemera** such as old bank safes, money bags, bullion and stage coach boxes, *Wells Fargo and Co* or *Railway Express* locks, assay office items, scales, and three fingered lock boxes (which cut off your fingers if you put them in the wrong holes to open the box). Wants things before 1900 rather than paper.

Larry Franklin
3238 Hutchison Ave.
Los Angeles, CA 90034
(310) 559-4461

★ **Decorative resalable things found in the office of doctors, dentists, undertakers, blacksmiths, watchmakers, gunsmiths, locksmiths, opticians, jewelers, saloons, hotels, brothels, police stations, firehouses, asylums, mines, prisons, roadhouses, arcades, breweries, boat wrights,** etc., including furniture, cash registers, glass counters, tools, and the like. "I will respond to any honest inquiry for help to identify an item for sale." He requests a complete description indicating all wear or broken parts. If you know the item's history, it is helpful. Photos of larger items and Xerox© of smaller ones are recommended. "I'd rather buy a whole store or business than a single item."

Larry Franklin
3238 Hutchison Ave.
Los Angeles, CA 90034
(310) 559-4461

★ **Bookbinding tools and equipment.**
Frank Klein
The Bookseller
521 W. Exchange St.
Akron, OH 44302
(216) 762-3101 days

"Readers should not expect to get rich from decorator items. It is expensive for dealers to buy, transport, restore, and then try to find buyers for items. If I can resell their item quickly, the offer will be more than if if I must warehouse the item."

Larry Franklin

★ **Fire service and fire insurance items** such as badges, histories of insurance companies, pre-1900 fire insurance policies, firemarks, signs, advertising, postcards, stamps, and envelopes with pictorial return addresses. Doesn't want anything except fire related items, and nothing modern. Please quote books that are fire related.

Glenn Hartley
2859 Marlin Dr.
Chamblee, GA 30341
(404) 451-2651

★ *State Farm Insurance Company* **memorabilia**, 1922-52. He wants all items marked with their 3 oval emblem depicting a car, fire helmet, and cornucopia. Also selected items marked with the home office or an old Buick. He buys signs, ashtrays, pocket knives, pencils, tape measures, stationery, and everything else **except** bumper plates that are not made of brass. He **does not want** anything marked with the three ovals and the words *auto, life,* and *fire.*

Ken Jones
100 Manor Dr.
Columbia, MO 65203

★ **Anything relating to fire insurance companies** before 1940. Wants fire marks, illustrated policies, advertising, signs, and giveaways. Does not make offers, so price what you have.

Ralph Jennings
301 Fort Washington Ave.
Fort Washington, PA 19034
(215) 646-7178

★ **Cigar factories and stores.** Everything associated with the manufacture and sale of cigars before 1920 including cigar maker's mechanical tools, catalogs, advertising, cigar boxes, cigar labels, signs, company records, and related items having to do with cigar taxation. This includes items related to the Cigar Makers' International Union and its leaders, Strasser, Perkins and Gompers. Please send a Xerox© copy of what you have, whenever possible.

Tony Hyman
Box 3028
Pismo Beach, CA 93448
(805) 773-6777   Fax (805) 773-0117

★ **Coal company scrip, stocks and bonds, and cap lamps worn underground.**
"Tip" Tippy
22 Cottonwood Lane
Carterville, IL 62916

★ **Mining company memorabilia,** primarily Pennsylvania and the Western U.S. Buys books, stocks and bonds, sheet music, photographs, and selected artifacts.
Jeffrey Viola
475-B Eltone Rd.
Jackson, NJ 08527
(201) 928-0666

★ **Colorado mining memorabilia 1859-1915** including photos, paper ephemera, stocks, maps, stereoviews, advertising, and small souvenirs, especially from towns of Cripple Creek, Victor, Central City, Leadville, Breckenridge, Idaho Springs, Telluride, etc. Also books about Colorado mining and any city directories pre-1915. No interest in "flatland cities" like Denver or Colorado Springs, nor in Colorado tourist attractions and parks. No photos of mountains unless a mine or mining town is featured.
George Foott
6683 S. Yukon Way
Littleton, CO 80123
(303) 979-8688

★ **Mining ephemera, especially paper goods from Arizona and Colorado mines.** Interested in buying stock certificates and other paper pertaining to mining other than coal. Buys books on mining and gems, catalogs of mining equipment, photographs, etc.
Russell Filer, Mining
Box 487
Yucaipa, CA 92399
(714) 797-1650

★ **Tin can manufacturing ephemera and artifacts.** Also want ephemera related to commercial stone lithography (label printing and box making) before 1925, especially the printing of packages, labels, tin cans, and advertising. Will buy examples of fine printing and tin can making associated with any product if they are in fine condition and interesting subject matter.
Tony Hyman
Box 3028
Pismo Beach, CA 93448
(805) 773-6777   Fax (805) 773-0117

★ **Pre-1900 electrical devices** manufactured by *Stanley Electric, Edison General Electric, Thomson-Houston, Weston, Westinghouse, Crocker Wheeler* and *Sprague.* "I want small open frame bipolar motors and generators, switchboard voltmeters and ammeters, carbon arc lamps, **electric fans with brass blades,** and watt-hour meters. I also want catalogs, photographs and paper related to these companies printed before 1905." Provide all nameplate data including patent dates and numbers. Prefers the seller to set the price, but will make offers.
William F. Edwards
State Road
Richmond, MA 01254
(413) 698-3458

★ **Electrical apparatus, tubes, test equipment, open frame motors, generators,** switch board meters, knife switches, **neon signs, fans,** Tesla coils, **quack medical devices** (Violet Ray, etc.), **unusual clocks,** etc., as well as books on radio and electrical theory and practice. Give info from the item's ID plate, and include a sketch or photo.
Hank Andreoni
504 W. 6th
Beaumont, CA 92223
(714) 849-7539

★ **Early electrical meters, gauges, and other apparatus** made by *Thompson-Houston,* or of the 133 cycle type. Also early direct current watthour meters, type CS, manufactured by GE. Any very old unusual electrical items will be considered by the veteran collector and electrical museum owner. Give info from the item's ID plate, measurements and weight. "I prefer the seller to set the price. I may need to see the item before buying."
Tommy Bolack
3901 Bloomfield Highway
Farminton, NM 87401
(505) 325-7873

★ **Lumber company and store tokens, scrip, stocks and bonds.** Xerox©.
"Tip" Tippy
22 Cottonwood Lane
Carterville, IL 62916

Business Machines

★ **Unusual antique typewriters.** Want items dating between 1870-1920. Look for typewriters with odd designs, curved keyboards, no keyboards, pointers, or more or less than the standard four rows of keys. The most desired machine is a *Sholes & Glidden,* worth as much as $5,000 in outstanding condition. Give the make and model number if shown on the machine, the serial number, and "an in-focus photo." Rehr will provide you with a checklist to help you describe your machine to him. Send an SASE.
Darryl Rehr
Early Typewriter Collectors Association
11433 Rochester Ave. #303
Los Angeles, CA 90025
    (213) 477-5229

★ **Pre-1925 American typewriters and ephemera** including ribbon tins, ribbon, accessories, tools, oilers, advertising, catalogs, instruction manuals, shipping cases if they are imprinted with the name of a typewriter, catalogs for business schools if they picture early typewriters, cardboard or metal signs, paperweights, blotters, clocks, rulers, or any other item imprinted with the name or illustration of a typewriter. "If in doubt, write or call anyway." Also early typewriter tables with fancy cast iron frames or legs (they usually have two drop leaves and a center drawer). Also typewriting instruction books pre-1910. **Some small very early hand held adders and calculators** are of interest. "If the machine is not one that I want, but may be wanted by another collector of early typewriters, I will help you find a buyer. I am not a dealer and do not buy typewriters for stock. I'll happily answer any inquiry rather than risk missing something I would like to hear about," but common brands are not of interest to anyone. Name, model, type of lid and base, and condition. Photocopy accessories. "Never ship a typewriter until a deal is made. I have to provide shipping and packing instructions first." His 280p book, *American Typewriters: A Collector's Encyclopedia* is available from the author for $40.
Paul Lippman
1216 Garden St.
Hoboken, NJ 07030
    (201) 656-5278 eves Fax (201) 714-9350

★ **Typewriters** pre-1910, especially those with fancy or strange mechanisms, such as the *Sholes & Glidden* from 1870's which strikes from below so the typist can't see her work. "I'm always willing to give an opinion about a machine if you send a picture or good description." This 13 year veteran promises, "I will never try to buy your machine for less than it's worth."
Joseph Weber
604 Centre St.
Ashland, PA 17921
    (717) 875-4401 3-5 pm

★ **Check writers and check protectors,** pre-1910 in working condition. May be home, office, or hand held models. No machines by *Todd, F & E Lightning, Hedman, Paymaster,* or *Safeguard.*
William Feigin
45 W. 34th Street, #405
New York, NY 10001
    (212) 736-3360

★ **Calculating devices before 1915** and associated ephemera including catalogs and advertising. Wants mechanical calculators such as arithmometers, generally in wooden cases. Brand names to look for include *Autarith, Baldwin, Calculmeter, Grant, Madas, Rapid, Spalding, Thomas,* but interested in anything odd. Also rotary machine, heavy devices operated by a crank, and other types of calculators including **slide rules,** but *only* slide rules that don't have patent numbers. He buys comptometers with wooden cases as well as **planimeters,** devices for measuring area on maps. Give a photo or sketch of what you have plus describe all markings, serial numbers, etc. Weight and dimensions are helpful. Xerox© paper goods.
Robert Otnes
2160 Middlefield Road
Palo Alto, CA 94301
    (415) 324-1821 eves

★ **Unusual calculators and adding machines.** "I am very eager to purchase unusual and scarce calculators and adding machines, and prepared to pay well for information leading to them. I will travel anywhere in the world in search of these machines, and will pay immediate cash without fuss or bother for the right items. I am happy to buy single items or entire collections."
Peter Frei
Box 500
Brimfield, MA 01010
    (800) 942-8968 (413) 245-4660 in MA

★ **Cash registers made of brass or wood,** especially early wooden registers with inlaid cabinets, dial registers, or multiple drawers. Also registers that ring only to $1. He also buys "Amount purchased" signs that were seen on top of registers, and literature about registers. Machines can be in any condition since he uses damaged machines for parts. Give both the brand name and model number of your machine and include the serial number. Provide your phone number so Ken can make arrangements to pick up your machine. Nothing after 1917.
   Ken Konet
   849 Oak Hill Rd.
   Barrington, IL 60010
      (708) 382-7799   Fax (708) 382-7803

★ **Display cases and lighting fixtures,** especially from old drugstores. Wants early counter-top display cases with original glass, especially revolving cases, bow-front cases, and double tower cases. Also **lighting fixtures** of early wrought iron or tin, especially from commercial buildings. List all damage. Nothing after 1900. Give all numbers or data on maker's plates.
   Jerry Phelps
   6013 Innes Trace Rd.
   Louisville, KY 40222
      (502) 425-4765

★ **Stock market tickers, books, and other memorabilia** having to do with speculation, panics, commodities, cycles, and other activities pre-1940. Also turn of the century prints depicting the stock market, and **stock market magazines** pre-1935.
   R.G. Klein
   Box 24A06
   Los Angeles, CA 90024

★ **Stock market tickers.** "I'll pay $2,000 for Edison glass domed tickers and $1,500 for those made for *Western Union*."
   Frank Guarino,
   Box 89,
   DeBary, FL 32713

★ **Mimeograph memorabilia.** Advertising, instructions, service manuals, etc. If it's very *old* and about mimeos, he may be interested.
   Walley Francis
   Box 6941
   Syracuse, NY 13217
      (315) 478-5671

★ **Microcomputer literature and computers** including just about anything, machines, literature, catalogs, you name it, if it's from the pre-*Apple* pre-*Radio Shack* days (before 1977). Names to look for include *Mark-8, Sphere, Scelbi, Intel* and other machines originally created for hobbyists and do-it-yourselfers.
   Harold Layer
   SF State University-AV
   1600 Holloway Ave.
   San Francisco, CA 94132

★ **Time clocks.**
   Steve Chyrchel
   Route #2 Box 362
   Eureka Springs, AR 72632
      (501) 253-9244

If you recognize the brand name on your typewriter, collectors probably don't want it.

Remington, Underwood, Smith-Corona & Oliver are common.

Business Paper

★ **Business cards of all type.** "We buy business cards of all types with particular interest in cards 1700-1960. We even buy cards that are damaged or written upon. We also buy other paper items such as **photos, letters, and bill heads related to business cards.** We will pay postage both ways on items sent to us on approval." Few business cards have much monetary value, but Jack will pay well for Mathew Brady and Benjamin Franklin. Jack emphasizes that chromolith cards were stock items issued in large quantities. Photocopies are the best description. Jack edits *The Business Card Journal.*
  Jack Gurner
  116 Dupuy St.
  Water Valley, MS 38965
    (601) 473-1154

★ **Business cards.** "I'll consider buying business cards that are unique, unusual, or have an interesting story. Cards from exotic or unlikely materials such as stainless steel, plastic, papyrus, tin, etc., and cards from celebrities. Looks for creativity, which is "timeless," so will consider anything imaginative in shape, color, message, or material. "I love cards that make you laugh." Xerox© if possible, otherwise describe as best you can. Some **trade card collections** will be considered if they are suitable for resale or auction. Avery is President of The American Business Card Club.
  Avery N. Pitzak
  PO Box 460297
  Aurora, CO 80046
    (303) 690-6496

★ **Envelopes with color advertising for products,** pre-1940.
  Gordon McHenry
  Box 1117
  Osprey, FL 34229

★ **Trade catalogs and piles of business letters,** pre-1920, from manufacturers, wholesalers, and retailers. "The earlier the better," says Jim. Most common catalogs bring $5-$10, but "we have paid as high as $400 for some." Please check that all pages are present as you list the company, type of products, size and number of pages, and the type and number of illustrations (Xerox© copies are helpful). Mention *I'll Buy That Too!* for a free copy of Jim's catalog of catalogs.
  Jim Presgraves
  Bookworm & Silverfish
  Box 639
  Wytheville, VA 24382

★ **Trade catalogs** for consumer products. "These are exciting peeks into their time, giving the unvarnished truth about their era. Prices vary from two figures (most) to over $10,000."
  Ivan Gilbert
  Miran Arts & Books
  2824 Elm Ave.
  Columbus, OH 43209

★ **Employee photo ID passes.** All photo ID badges are wanted, especially the celluloid buttons with a pin back. Pays $2 each except for older ones. Don't bother to inquire, just drop it in the mail. "I'll pay immediately."
  Rich Hartzog
  Box 4143 BID
  Rockford, IL 61110

Telephone & Telegraph

★ **Old telephones, parts of phones, and select phone company memorabilia** especially signs and pre-1900 magazines with telephone ads. No modern or electronic phones. They offer the *History and Identification of Old Telephones* with 6,000 pictures of old phones for $58.
Ron and Mary Knappen, Phoneco
RR #2, Box 590
Galesville, WI 54630
(608) 582-4124

★ **Telephones made before 1930,** especially unusual or early pay phones. Ask for his wants list and parts catalog since its handy numbered illustrations will help you describe what you want to sell. Also buys **telephone books** pre-1950, the earlier the better. A *History of Old Telephones* with price guide is available for $6. Correspondence in Spanish or French welcome.
Gerry Billard, Old Telephones
21710 Regnart Rd.
Cupertino, CA 95014
(408) 252-2104

★ **Telephones made before 1905,** porcelain signs featuring phones, telephone watch fobs, telephone pocket mirrors, and similar quality phone related items. **Also spring driven telegraph registers and fire station bells.** No interest in paper. "A photo is worth 1,000 words" to this 25 year veteran collector/dealer.
Paul Engelke
Key Telephone Company
23399 Rio Del Mar Drive
Boca Raton, FL 33486
(407) 338-3332

★ **Rare glass insulators** especially in rare colors. Wants you to describe the color, dimensions, embossing, whether or not it has threads, and its condition. He prefers you describe your insulators using the standard numbering found in Milholland's *Most About Glass Insulators*, available from Linscott with the latest price guide for $39. No damaged insulators are wanted.
Len Linscott
3557 Nicklaus Drive
Titusville, FL 32780
(407) 267-9170

★ **Rare glass insulators.** With over 3,000 already in his collection, Bolack's wants are restricted to 100 or so of the most rare colors and shapes, generally North American pin types. You can send a photo and SASE and description of its color and all embossing, or send an SASE for his wants list, but only if you have access to a book to translate the Standard Consolidated Design code numbers into pictures you can compare to your insulators.
Tommy Bolack
3901 Bloomfield Highway
Farminton, NM 87401
(505) 325-7873

★ **Telegraph instruments and related ephemera pre-1900** including keys (worth $50-$100), sounders, relays, signs, catalogs, and stationery. Especially wants instruments marked with initials of a railroad. Names to look for include *L.G. Tillotson, Patrick and Carter, Greeley, Chester, Clark, Davis, Redding, Jones, Williams, Pope,* and about 100 others. Wants registers (clockwork driven devices that inscribe dots and dashes on a paper tape) and will pay to $800-1,000 for them. Also seeking linemen's sets of very small portable keys in a hard rubber case. Items do not need to be in perfect condition. No *Boy Scout, Western Electric, Signal,* or *Menominee* equipment or post 1900 paper or telegrams, but loves to find signs advertising pre-1890 telegraph companies. Photo or even a crude sketch is most appreciated.
Roger Reinke
Brasspounder
5301 Neville Court
Alexandria, VA 22310
(703) 971-4095

★ **Telegraph instruments** if old, complete, and professional quality, especially from railroads.
Scott Arden
20457 Highway 126
Noti, OR 97461
(503) 9935-1619 (9 to 9)

★ *Western Union* and *Postal Telegraph* instruments, books, and anything else. List every marking found on items you wish to sell. No cracked or damaged pieces.
Charles Goodman
636 W. Grant Ave.
Charleston, Il 61920
(217) 345-6771

Architecture & Building Trades

★ **Architectural antiques,** including large chandeliers, wall sconces, statuary, gargoyles, gates, large quantities of iron fencing, stained glass windows and doors, and the like. Please send complete details and measurements. Collect calls OK if you're a serious seller.
Architectural Antiques,
801 Washington Ave. North
Minneapolis, MN 55401
(612) 332-8344

★ **Architectural antiques.** If you have mantles, stained glass windows, chandeliers, iron fencing or gates, garden statuary, and other architectural relics, give this giant dealer a call.
United House Wrecking,
535 Hope St.
Stamford, CT 06906
(203) 348-5371

★ **Items related to building and architecture pre-1930** including books on architecture, building, carpentry, and surveying. Also manuals and catalogs of cast iron, steel, plumbing, hardware, paint, and other building materials. Also **blueprints, architects renderings,** drafting instruments made of brass, early drafting or drawing machines, slide rules, and watercolor boxes.
Robert Des Marais
618 West Foster Ave.
State College, PA 16801
(814) 237-7141

★ **Blueprints for buildings or machines.**
Jim Presgraves
Bookworm & Silverfish
Box 639
Wytheville, VA 24382

★ **Catalogs related to architecture and building materials, 1850-1960.** Will consider anything informative, including architects' publicity books, house designs, catalogs of plaster ornaments, metal ceilings, roofing materials, signs, store fronts, paint, etc. Send a Xerox©.
Herbert Mitchell
Avery Library
Columbia University
New York, NY 10027

★ **Architect's renderings** and other paintings of skyscrapers, houses, and other buildings.
Charles Martignette
PO Box 293
Hallandale, FL 33009
(305) 454-3474

★ **Antique surveying instruments,** including compasses, transits, levels, wire link measuring chains, circumferentors, semi-circumferentors, railroad compasses, and solar compasses. Tools may be wood, brass, or wood and brass. "Also have interest in **mathematical and philosophical instruments** of the past." Give all names and numbers found on the body or lens.
Michael Manier
Box 100
Houston, MO 65483
(417) 967-2777 24 hours

★ **Old tools of the trades and crafts** especially those used by woodworkers: wooden and metallic planes, folding rulers, chisels, levels, saws, plumb bobs, scribes, spokeshaves, hammers, squares, axes, trammel points, measuring devices, drills, bit braces, marking gauges, wrenches, fancy tool boxes, and hand or foot powered machinery. Also wants advertising items and hardware store displays, catalogs, and documents. "I'll pay $200+ for *Stanley* tool catalogs from before 1900. I also especially want tools made in Ohio, although they're not worth as much as tools from New England." Does not want mechanics tools, electric tools, agricultural and farm tools, or any that have been "reconditioned." Give all markings. Keep your eyes open for an ivory plow plane made in Ohio, because "I'll pay $10,000 for one." Will accept select consignments at 10% commission for inclusion in his good looking quarterly newsletter on tools. John has a $25 book out on *Stanley* tools.
John Walter, The Tool Merchant
208 Front St.
Marietta, OH 45750
(800) 542-1993   (614) 373-9973

★ **Joiner's planes and other tools.** "I'll buy planes or any pre-1900 paper ephemera about them. I'll also buy, and pay retail prices for, fancy old woodworking hand tools."
Richard Wood
Alaska Heritage Books
Box 22165
Juneau, AK 99802
(907) 586-6748

Builder's Supplies

★ **Sidewalk or paving bricks** marked with the name and or address of a maker. "They're hard to mail, but fun to collect." No fire bricks.
Ken Jones
100 Manor Dr.
Columbia, MO 65203

★ **Ornate doorknobs and other builder's hardware** including knockers, hinges, escutcheon plates, doorbells, push plates, bin pulls and any other fancy Victorian hardware. I'll pay up to $200 for some knobs. No plain porcelain or common octagonal glass knobs are wanted. Sets of knobs routinely bring $20-$30, but get my offer before you sell. Send SASE for my illustrated wants list. Xerox© copies speed offers."
Charles Wardell
Box 195
Trinity, NC 27370
(919) 434-1145

★ **Antique doorknobs.** Loretta is editor of the club's newsletter and can put you in touch with collectors all over America who are interested in antique doorknobs and other door hardware. Send a good close up photo or a Xerox® copy.
Loretta Nemec
Antique Doorknob Collectors of America
PO Box 126
Eola, IL 60519
(312) 357-2381

★ **Pieces of famous buildings, structures, monuments, aircraft, etc.**, such as the Statue of Liberty, Independence Hall, The Eiffel Tower, etc. "These must be legally acquired pieces and **not vandalized items**. They must be well documented for me to purchase them."
Paul Hartunian
127B East Bradford Ave.
Cedar Grove, NJ 07009
(201) 857-7275

★ **Parts from buildings** including cornices, gargoyles, arches, fireplaces, mantels, anything unusual. Nothing after 1930. No material not related to building.
Robert Des Marais
618 West Foster Ave.
State College, PA 16801
(814) 237-7141

Barbershop

★ **Decorated shaving mugs depicting the owner's occupation, trade, or hobby** above or below his name. Also hand painted personal occupational barber bottles. Since each was custom made, they must be evaluated individually. Also **salesman's sample barber chairs** made in porcelain or wood. No Japanese reproductions or "Sportsman's Series" mugs from the 1950's.
Burton Handelsman
18 Hotel Drive
White Plains, NY 10605
(914) 761-8880

★ **Shaving mugs depicting occupations**. Must have both a picture and a man's name. "I'll buy those with photo portraits for $500 and up and will pay $500-$1,500 for athletes (especially a high jumper), $400-$1,200 for automobile related professions, $500-$750 for an undertaker, $500-$1,000 for a tugboat worker. Will also buy some mugs with emblems of fraternal organizations. Please give any maker's name on the bottom of the mug and indicate any damage, hairline cracks, or chips no matter how small.
Robert Fortin, Barber Shop
459 S. Main St.
North Syracuse, NY 13212
(315) 458-7465

★ **Barbershop memorabilia of all types** including any good quality item associated with barber shops such as decorated shaving mugs, barber bowls, bottles, waste jars, catalogs, straight razors with scenes or names engraved on the blades, barber's emblem pins, barbershop trade or business cards, salesmen's samples of barber chairs, and much more. Powell both collects and deals so buys a wide range of fine items or accepts them on consignment. Names to look for include Koken, Kochs, Kern, Archer, Buerger, and others. Include a tracing or close up photo. New shaving mugs are not wanted. This well known historian is the only member of the Barber's Hall of fame who isn't a barber.
Robert Powell
Box 833
Hurst, TX 76053
(817) 284-8145

Food & Lodging

★ *McDonalds* **memorabilia** including:
- [1] **Uniforms,** employees, with the M logo;
- [2] **Paper goods** including boxes, place mats, napkins, flyers;
- [3] **Displays** such as signs, decals, posters;
- [4] **Premiums and promotions;**
- [5] **Anything in foreign languages;**
- [6] **Not for public items** such as ID cards, newsletters, worksheets;
- [7] **Fixtures, signs, and lights.**

No items currently available in all restaurants.
Matt Welch
Box 30444
Tucson, AZ 85751
(602) 886-0505

★ *McDonalds* **happy meal counter displays.**
Mike Dyer
230 Eldon Dr. NW
Warren, OH 44483

★ *Bob's Big Boy, Kentucky Fried Chicken,* **and** *Coon Chicken Inn* **restaurant memorabilia** such as ceramic ashtrays and salt & peppers, cups or dishes with logos, lunch boxes, gameboards, toys, comics, figurines, and other unusual pieces. If you have any of these items, please write or fax with a description, noting all repairs. Dealers must set price; amateurs may request offers. Vinyl doll banks are not wanted.
Glen Grush
8400 Sunset Blvd., #3A
Los Angeles, CA 90069
(213) 656-4758   Fax: (213) 656-4158

★ *Bob's Big Boy* **and** *Kentucky Fried Chicken* **premiums.**
William Hamburg
Box 1305
Woodland Hills, CA 91365
(818) 346-9884

★ *Bob's Big Boy* **items,** especially menus, lamps, matches, ashtrays, salt & pepper shakers, and nodders. No plastic banks.
Steve Soelberg
29126 Laro Dr.
Agoura Hills, CA 91301
(818) 889-9909

★ *Coon Chicken Inn* **memorabilia** of all kinds that features Blacks.
Diane Cauwels
3947 Old South Road
Murfreesboro, TN 37129

★ **Items associated with famous Chicago hotels** and their shops. Wants furniture, menus, stationery, fixtures, signs, etc., from places like the *Lexington, Metropole, Hawthorne Inn, Hawthorne Smoke Shop,* and *Scholfields flower shop.*
Michael Graham
345 Cleveland Ave.
Libertyville, IL 60048
(312) 362-8531 eves

★ **Fast food kid's meal toys and boxes** from before 1988. Also crew pins, displays, and other fast-food related items that are odd or unusual. Want *Wendy's, Sonic Drive-In, Arby's, Burger King, Roy Rogers, Hardees, Carls Jr., What-a-Burger,* and other similar chains.
Ken Clee
PO Box 11412
Philadelphia, PA 19111
(215) 722-1979

★ **Swiss hotels paper ephemera** if it shows a picture of the hotel before 1930. Will buy illustrated bills, letterheads, wine lists, rate cards, envelopes, postcards and anything else pictorial showing Swiss hotels.
Ronald Lowden, Jr.
314 Chestnut Ave.
Narberth, PA 19072
(215) 667-0257 anytime

★ **Tourist courts, tourist camps, and motel ephemera.** Wants *Tourist Court Journal* magazine and other pre-1950 ephemera related to motor travel lodging.
Kevin Regn
2127 15th St., NW
Washington, DC 20009

★ **Youth hostel ephemera** such as handbooks, pins, magazines, etc.
Walley Francis
Box 6941
Syracuse, NY 13217
(315) 478-5671

Oil Companies

★ **Gasoline and service station advertising and promotional items** from local, regional and independent dealers including banks and salt & pepper shakers shaped like gas pumps, 4 ounce oil can banks, thermometers, radios shaped like oil cans or gas pumps, and full size original gasoline pump globes. He does not want shakers from national brands, or reproductions of gas pump globes. Give him a description, the brand name, and its condition. Price if you can.

    Peter Capell
    1838 West Grace Street
    Chicago, IL 60613
      (312) 871-8735 eves

★ **Oil company memorabilia from the 1920's** including advertising of all sorts, from giveaways to stationary, point of purchase advertising, signs, pump globes, etc. Also seeking informative material such as early station photos, **trade publications**, and the like, from any company, as long as its generally from the 1920's era. This 20+ year veteran collector does not want reproductions of any sort. Give him the name of the company, and a description of the form and colors of the item you have.

    Bill Allard
    1801 Fernside
    Tacoma, WA 98465
      (206) 565-2545

★ **Oil company memorabilia 1859-1939.** Wants "virtually anything" connected to specific companies, wells, or famous oil pioneers including pre-1900 books about oil and oil exploration, oil stocks especially early with engraved views of oil fields, sheet music (from the 1860's), newspapers from early Pennsylvania oil towns, clippings, photos, deeds, and engravings.

    Jeffrey Viola
    475-B Eltone Rd.
    Jackson, NJ 08527
      (201) 928-0666 eves

★ **Oil cans from Canada**, especially British Columbia oil in tin cans, and any quart oil cans related to motorcycles.

    Don Schneider
    Box 1570
    Merritt, BC
    Canada V0K 2B0

★ *Gulf Oil* **memorabilia** including signs, cans, maps, advertising mailouts, magazine ads, blotters, postcards, ash trays, key chains, and anything else marked *Gulf*, especially older correspondence, paper items, and signs. This retired petroleum geologist also wants postcards which depict oil fields and wells. Prefers items to be sent on approval after first contacting him.

    Charles Roach
    3212 Tudor
    Oklahoma City, OK 73122
      (405) 942-4520

★ *Mobil Oil* **memorabilia** including "*anything* picturing the red horse." Also collecting service pins given to Mobil employees. Also buys porcelain signs from *Gargoyle, White Eagle,* and *Magnolia* gas and oil. No repros...and Billie says she has enough globes. She insists that the seller set the price wanted as she and Bob do not make offers for additions to their herd.

    Bob and Billie Butler
    1236 Helen St.
    Augusta, KS 67010
      (316) 775-6193

★ **Oil cans in all sizes, all types, and all materials,** including brass, aluminum, glass, tin, granite-wear, or plastic. Wants everything from small sewing machine size up to and including railroad oil cans, advertising cans, novelty cans. Pays $10-25 for a graniteware can especially with the name "White" on it, $10-15 for most others, more for railroad cans. Not all desirable cans have names on them. Make a sketch. If it is a pump can, tell whether the pump works.

    Robert Larson
    3517 Vernal Court
    Merced, CA 95340
      (209) 723-7828

★ **Oil company road maps**, particularly those from the 1920's and 30's. "I like city maps, state maps, and regional maps, foreign or domestic." Must be in good condition. Mass quantities wanted. Also will buy old Official State Highway Department maps, the earlier the better. Other oil company items such as credit cards, and pocket calendars are also purchased. Send items for immediate offer and check.

    Noel Levy
    Box 595699
    Dallas, TX 75359
      (214) 987-3513

Farms & Horses

★ **Antique farm equipment**, horse drawn vehicles, and "tools of all type" that are unusual, suitable for museum display.
Harvey Lee Boswell
The Palace of Wonders
Box 446
Elm City, NC 27822

★ **Wagons, carriages, and commercial horse drawn vehicles, in whole or in part.** Buys carriage lamps, dashboard clocks, wagon tools, nameplates, wheel making machines, coachman's and groom's clothing, jacks, tack room fixtures, whip racks, wagon odometers, hitching post statuary, rein clips, wagon seats, wagon poles, veterinary tools, lap robes, life size harness makers horses, zinc animal heads, and anything else related to carriages and wagons. Offers up to $500-$2,500 for lamps marked *Studebaker, Brewster,* or *Healey.* **Also buys goat carts and dog carts**. If your item is old, genuine, and in good condition you may ship on approval. No harnesses. Don will send you a large illustrated wants list if you send an SASE with four stamps.
Don Sawyer
West Newbury Wagon Works
40 Bachelor St.
West Newbury, MA 01985
(508) 346-4724 days (508) 363-2983

★ **Everything related to work or recreation with horses** including polo, horseback riding, carriage driving, sidesaddle, draft horses, **horseshoeing, veterinary**, etc. Wants horse farm catalogs, brochures, posters, prints of riding and recognized horse breeds, books (1st editions in d/j only), magazines, postcards (if horse is named), stud books, and breed registers. "I don't buy common books still in print, book club editions, *Diseases of the Horse,* books on horse betting, or books with highlighting or underlining in the text. Everything must be in fine condition for resale."
Barbara Cole
October Farm
Rt 2, Box 183-C
Raleigh, NC 27610
(919) 772-0482

★ **Windmill ephemera**, especially cast iron windmill weights, display model windmills and salesman's sample windmills. He does not want reproductions, damaged or repaired items, items with new paint, or "short tail horse" windmill weights. Please send a color photo, your phone number, and the price range you'd like to get.
Richard Tucker, Argyle Antiques
PO Box 262
Angyle, TX 76226
(817) 464-3752

★ **Tractor memorabilia** including all sorts of paper ephemera and small trinkets given away as advertising promotion, such as watch fobs, pens, cigarette lighters, etc. You may ship on approval if it's old, original, and clean.
Jay Ketelle
3721 Farwell
Amarillo, TX 79109
(806) 355-3456

★ **Tractor, farm machinery, and gasoline engine paper ephemera** including pre-1970 manuals, catalogs, parts books, in-house publications, and sales literature. Also buys farm magazines such as *Implement Record, Farm Machinery & Hardware,* and *Farm Mechanics.* Also buys "giveaways" such as signs, ashtrays, buttons, etc. associated with any farm machinery. No textbooks or reprints. Please indicate the color of the item and the price you'd like.
Alan C. King
PO Box 86
Radnor, OH 43066

★ *J.I. Case* **Tractor Company memorabilia** including tractors and implements, toy tractors, advertising signs, catalogs, books, and anything else marked *JI Case.* Where is item located?
Ed and Carla Schuth
RR 2 Box 6
Wabasha, MN 55981
(612) 565-4251

★ **Horse bits.** "I'll buy old iron, fancy, or strange horse bits as well as foreign military, and medical bits. I also buy reference material about horse bits, including catalogs. I'd like to find Civil War bits and cowboy bits decorated with buffaloes. Draw what you have."
Jean Gay, Three Horses
7403 Blaine Rd.
Aberdeen, WA 98520
(206) 533-3490

★ **Poultry raising** Wants books, magazines, and paper ephemera, from before 1930.
W.L. Bill Zeigler
10 Lincolnway West
New Oxford, PA 17350
  (717) 624-2347

★ **Everything about fruit and vegetable growing, packing and canning**, such as labels, photographs, postcards, magazines, matchbooks, buttons, ribbons and giveaway trinkets of all types. Wants all sorts of paper ephemera from various organizations and events promoting fruit and vegetable growing and packing. Buys **orange juicers, reamers and extractors** from major packers, if company name is impressed.
T. Pat Jacobsen
437 Minton Court
Pleasant Hill, CA 94523
  (415) 930-8531

★ **Everything about fruit raising and varieties before 1900,** including illustrated books, magazine articles, ceramic tiles depicting fruit, postcards, prints, folders, and greeting cards depicting apples. Especially books and paper with color plates or descriptions of fruit varieties. May be in any language. No tropical fruit, or anything later than 1940.
Fred Janson
Pomona Book Exchange
Rockton PO, Ontario,
CANADA L0R 1X0

"You can never give
too much information
in a description,
particularly when you
are detailing condition.

List _all_ flaws, tears,
scratches, chips or cracks.

I can give you
a good appraisal
only if you give me
a good description."

Ralph Riovo

Dairy

★ **Milk or dairy industry items marked with the name and address of a dairy** including old and unusual bottles, advertising, toys, and signs, especially from institutional bottlers such as prisons, colleges, railroads, hotels, and the like. Any bottles with character endorsements (sports, Hopalong Cassidy, etc.) are wanted with cartoon characters particularly desirable (Disney bottles bring $100+ each). Bottles and posters with WWII slogans are also sought. Unusually shaped bottles with faces or heads or those made of colored glass are always wanted, as are creamer size bottles marked with name of dairy, hotel, or restaurant. Bottles with glass lids, tin handles or lids and pour spouts can go as high as $300. **Anything related to _Borden's_ or their Elsie the Cow trademark is wanted, especially their ruby red bottles which can bring from $700-$1,000. "I'll Buy catalogs of bottle makers which show design variations offered." Large items like cream separators, churns, milk cans, and the like are not wanted. "If in doubt about authenticity, feel free to call or send a photo and I will verify and answer questions, if you include an SASE. List all flaws, scratches, tears, chips or cracks. I can give you a good appraisal only if you give me a good description."
Ralph Riovo
686 Franklin St
Alburtis, PA 18011
  (215) 966-2536

★ **Round milk bottles with dairy names** embossed or printed on them. Square bottles OK if amber or from Western states. Nothing worn, cracked, or chipped.
Leigh Giarde
Box 366
Bryn Mawr, CA 92318
  (714) 792-8681

★ **Dairy creamers** made of glass with the names of dairies embossed or printed on. Do not want ceramic creamers or those without names. Also **milk bottles** with cop tops, baby tops, or war slogans, in excellent condition only.
Ken Clee
PO Box 11412
Philadelphia, PA 19111
  (215) 722-1979

Advertising

★ **Motion display advertising**, especially by Baranger. These are fairly small pieces, under 3' high, usually with animated people advertising watches from the 1930's and 40's, but other products are also found.
Frank Novak
7386 Beverly Blvd.
Los Angeles, CA 90036
(213) 683-1963 Fax (213) 683-1312

★ **Colorful tin cans, signs and trays** advertising beer, whiskey, soda pop, medicines, tobacco, and food such as peanuts, peanut butter, tea, coffee, and the like. Especially likes rare peanut butter pails and one-pound coffee cans from New York companies. Nothing rusty or damaged. Describe colors. Photocopy please.
Burton Spiller
49 Palmerston Road
Rochester, NY 14618
(716) 244-2229

★ **Pre-1920 advertising** including tin, porcelain, and cardboard signs and posters, tin cans and trays, calendars, syrup dispensers, and other advertising for candy, gum, groceries, soft drinks, ammunition, tobacco, beer, and the like. No magazine or newspaper ads. "We pay the highest prices but **do not make offers**. Let us know what you have and your price."
Don Stuart
4751 N.E. Ocean Blvd.
Jensen Beach, FL 34957
(407) 225-0900

★ **Coffee cans with pictures printed onto the tin** are wanted, especially the tall one pound cans with slip tops. No vacuum (key open) cans are wanted. $500 to $1,000 each will be paid for *Army & Navy, Blue Parrot, College Town, Convention Hall* (green or yellow only), *Festall Hall, Mayflower* or *Town Crier*. Most paper label cans are not as desirable, but some are collectible, but bring a substantially smaller selling price. Send the name of the tin, height and diameter, and state whether the condition is like new or scratched and worn. The pictorial can *Luzianne* is common, worth about $15-20.
Tim Schweighart
1123 Santa Luisa Dr.
Solana Beach, CA 92075
(619) 481-8315

★ **Porcelain enamel advertising signs** made between 1880-1950 advertising any U.S. automobiles, motorcycles, bicycles, gasoline, oil, soda pop, food, soap, clothing, telephones, telegraph, money orders, etc. Likes all types of porcelain signs, including those with **neon trim, thermometers**, and the like, especially interesting figurals. Prices are always best for those in multiple colors which depict animals, people, products, or fancy logos. Condition is very important. He is not interested in reproductions (look for brass grommets in the hanging holes). No signs bigger than 8 feet long or high. "I want a close up photo, dimensions, and any information the seller has on the item's background. Make certain to include home phone."
Robert Newman
10809 Charnock Rd.
Los Angeles, CA 90034
(213) 559-0539

★ **Cigar boxes, labels, tins, and advertising from the cigar industry** in fine condition, pre-1920, especially boxes featuring nudes, sports, gambling, comic characters, transportation, and other colorful scenes. Also **gambling devices, trade figures, or signs related to cigars**. Also tin **tobacco cans** and boxes. Photocopy the inside lid of boxes you'd like to sell. Long SASE will bring you a priced illustrated wants list. Don't want items covered with cigar bands, please, except as donations. Nothing in poor condition. Will pay $400+ for *Asthma Cure, Cheez It* or any xxx rated box. Hyman wrote *Handbook of American Cigar Boxes*, an illustrated autographed numbered limited edition for $14.95 with price guide.
Tony Hyman
Box 3028
Pismo Beach, CA 93448
(805) 773-6777

★ **Fruit crate labels and other advertising from the packing, canning and bottling trades** such as posters, tin signs, sales displays, letterheads, magazine ads, and other promotional items. He says he'll buy fruit and vegetable labels, American or foreign, but especially West Coast. Will consider singles, bulk quantities, and labels on crates. Especially interested in *Sunkist, Del Monte, Libby's*, etc.
T. Pat Jacobsen
437 Minton Court
Pleasant Hill, CA 94523
(415) 930-8531

★ **Southern advertising for products.** Wants decorative advertising in any form (signs, posters, labels, paper bags, cloth sacks, bottles, boxes, etc.) for any product or company located in the South. Items may be old or new, but "we prefer unused stock." Buys only in quantity. Does not buy or do appraisals on single pieces. Photocopies helpful. Publishes *The Southern Label Collector's Newsletter*.
> D.W. King & Associates
> Box 24811
> Tampa, FL 33623
> (813) 888-8057

★ **Florida citrus labels.** Also ads and other paper related to pre-1940 Florida citrus industry.
> Jerry Chicone
> Box 547636
> Orlando, FL 32854
> (407) 298-5550

★ **Old salmon can labels.** Singles, samples, or collections from any state. Also buys postcards, letterheads, and views of canneries, fish traps, etc. Only pre-1960 items are wanted. You may send approvals.
> W.E. Nickell
> 102 People's Wharf
> Juneau, AK 99801
> (907) 586-1733

★ **Advertising for medicine and whiskey companies.**
> Robert Daly
> 10341 Jewell Lake Ct.
> Fenton, MI 48430
> (313) 629-4934

★ **Neon advertising clocks and signs,** 1920-50. Buys those entirely of neon as well as those with "reverse painting on glass" that are lit by neon. Prefers smaller sizes that can be safely shipped via UPS. His favorite clocks and signs are "point of purchase" which sit on countertops, although he buys wall models, too. He is particularly interested in signs with neon glow tubes made by AMGLO. Also buys **signs that bubble, create optical illusions, or are animated.** Value is based on visual appeal so a photo is essential. Does not want new neon beer signs, plastic signs of any sort, or signs lit by fluorescent tubes.
> Roark Vane
> 6839 Havenside Dr.
> Sacramento, CA 95831
> (916) 392-3864

★ **Popcorn memorabilia** including boxes, cans, crates, brochures, catalogs, old machines, parts of machines, *Creator's* Steam Engines, and everything else related to popcorn.
> Jack Cory,
> 3395 W. Pinks Place
> Las Vegas, NV 89102
> (702) 367-2676

★ *Cracker Jack* **prizes, advertising** and related items, including tins, jars, store advertising, point of sale, and dealer items from any of the following companies: *Checkers Confections, Angel Marshmallows, Shotwell Mfg. Co., Rueckheim Bros.* and *Eckstein Co.* He does not want plastic *Cracker Jack* toys and prizes. Note any obvious signs of wear. Price if you can.
> Edwin Snyder
> PO Box 156
> Lancaster, KY 40444
> (606) 792-4816

★ *Planters Peanut* **memorabilia.** "I'll buy all rare and unusual items" with particular interest in any and all figural, 3-D, Mr. Peanuts such as:
> Wooden jointed doll;
> "Blinker" with lighted eyes;
> "Tapper" which taps on a window;
> Scale of cast iron and aluminum, 4' high;
> Rubber squeeze toy about 8" tall;
> Mr. Peanut hand puppet;
> Fence sitter, cast iron, 42" high;
> Parade costume;
> Anything papier mache;
> Any tin displays;
> Unopened key wind tins of peanuts;
> Cardboard display boxes peanuts came in;
> Wooden shipping boxes;
> 5# and 10# peanut tins;
> Old jars with peanut finials.

Does not want reproductions or anything from the 1970's or 80's. Does not want plastic items, or tin nut dish sets, except World's Fair (worth about $20). No broken or incomplete items. Send a photo and complete description, including condition of the surface and paint. Enclose an SASE for picture return. Richard is author of *Planter's Peanut Advertising and Collectibles*.
> Richard D. & Barbara Reddock
> 914 Ilse Court
> North Bellmore, NY 11710
> (516) 826-2032 eves

★ **Elsie the Cow and other** *Borden's* **ephemera** including games, toys, cookbooks, comic books, cups, glasses, Xmas cards, employee magazines, neon signs, milk bottles, and trade cards. Would especially like an Elsie string puppet and a *Borden's* Good Food Line train. No Elsie postcards or charms. Also buys milk bottles and advertising from Du Page County, IL. Describe and price your items.
    Ronald Selcke
    Box 237
    Bloomingdale, IL 60108
      (312) 543-4848 eves

★ *Royal Doulton* **advertising china** of all types including ashtrays, jugs, mugs, bottles, ginger beers, display signs. Old and rare pieces do not have to be in perfect condition to be considered for purchase, but you must indicate any flaws in your description. Make sure to mention the item, the product being advertised, size, color, condition, and any markings.
    Diane Alexander
    20834 San Simeon Way #70-C
    North Miami Beach, FL 33179
      (305) 770-4422

★ *Speedy Alka Seltzer* **dolls, toys and ephemera** wanted.
    Jim Frugoli,
    960 N. Northwest Hwy.
    Park Ridge, IL 60068

★ **Advertising depicting cowboys, cowgirls, or cattle.** Any product considered, but particular interest in products with Western orientation. Also wants all **original art for gun and ammunition company ads.** Please send color photo.
    Johnny Spellman, DVM
    10806 North Lamar
    Austin, TX 78753
      (512) 258-6910 eves
      (512) 836-2889 days

★ **Gun and ammunition related advertising.** "I buy posters, calendars, envelopes with ads, cardboard shotshell boxes, gunpowder cans, pinback buttons, glass target balls, catalogs, etc." Buys only items produced by a gun or ammunition maker (not secondary vendors) before 1940.
    Ron Willoughby
    0172 Route 171
    Woodstock, CT 06281
      (203) 974-1226

★ **Items associated with the** *Larkin Soap Company.* "We're primarily interest in catalogs and other historically interesting paper ephemera pre-1920." Larkin is also known as *Larkin Mfg., Larkin, Inc., Larkin Co.,* and *People' Mfg. Co.* Ayars and his wife wrote and published *Larkin Oak* ($16) and are working on *Larkin China and Pottery.* "Readers who have questions about Larkin are welcome; there is no charge for our research." Include title, year, issue number, or a photocopy of the cover.
    Walter Ayars III
    PO Box 279
    Summerdale, PA 17093
      (717) 732-9886

★ **Items associated with the** *Larkin Soap Company.* "I'll buy items made by or relating to the *Larkin Company,* including products, trade cards, catalogs, advertising, calendars and other paper items. If the Item says LARKIN, I'm interested. I want info about the *Larkin* administration building designed by Frank Lloyd Wright and would love to find dedication programs, etc." Please make sure you describe condition.
    Jerome Puma
    78 Brinton St.
    Buffalo, NY 14214
      (716) 838-5674

★ **Everything associated with the** *Larkin Soap Company.*
    Thomas Knopke
    1430 E. Brookdale Pl.
    Fullerton, CA 92631
      (714) 526-1749

★ **Bottles and other items from West Virginia food companies,** including *Flaccus, Hunter, Exwaco,* and *Mc Mechen.* Pays up to $200 for stoneware Flaccus & Elliot water cooler.
    Tom & Deena Caniff
    1223 Oak Grove Ave.
    Steubenville, OH 43952
      (614) 282-8918

★ *Dixie* **ice cream cup picture lids** and other memorabilia 1930-54 including premium pictures and offers, albums, scrapbook covers, ads, and company literature. Also buys some non-*Dixie* pictorial ice cream cup lids such as Tarzan or American Historical Shrines series.
    Stephen Leone
    94 Pond St.
    Salem, NH 03079
      (603) 898-4900

★ **Typewriter ribbon tins.** "I'm interested in any typewriter tin in good condition. I especially want tins made to hold ribbon wider than 1/2" and boxed sets of tins. Large quantities eagerly accepted. I do not want cardboard boxes of any type." Please send a description, sketch, or Xerox©.
> Darryl Rehr
> 11433 Rochester Ave., #303
> Los Angeles, CA 90025
> (213) 477-5229

★ **Celluloid advertising mirrors** and other small advertising items such as bookmarks, pinback buttons, blotters, stamp cases, etc. "I run auctions of these items, so buy anything, but you may also consign your items to my auction, as long as you call first." Especially likes advertising pocket mirrors with colorful pictures of women, children, nudes, or pictures of the product. Send a Xerox© copy of your mirror, along with notations as to color and any imperfections.
> John Andreae
> 51122 Mill Run
> Granger, IN 46530
> (219) 272-2337   Fax (219) 271-1146

★ **Advertising mirrors of all types**, both pocket and paperweight. Higher prices paid for anything from Illinois, Florida, or Michigan. Better prices paid for those with a product or female or both. Condition of the advertising side is very important; the mirror (unless missing or broken) is not. Spots, rips, brown areas, foxing, etc., in the celluloid will lower the value substantially. Please ship or send Xerox© copy for offer. Particularly wanted are any mirrors with words "Good for 10¢ in trade" or similar variation for which he pays from $35-2,000. "I consider paperweight mirrors to be less desirable than pocket mirrors, and seldom pay over $20."
> Rich Hartzog
> Box 4143 BID
> Rockford, IL 61110
> (815) 226-0771

★ **Advertising buttons** from North Carolina and South Carolina products, companies, or any topic at all, including politics, meetings, etc. Make a Xerox© of what you have.
> Lew Powell
> 700 East Park Ave.
> Charlotte, NC 28203

★ **Advertising trade cards** for chewing gum and insert cards, 19th or 20th century, issued by candy, gum, bakery, beverage, cereal, or other food or tobacco companies. Xerox© and price, or "I welcome approvals, pay all postage and respond within 48 hours of receipt. Condition is important as I do not collect trimmed cards, badly creased or otherwise battered items."
> William Nielsen
> 1379 Main Street
> PO Box 1379
> Brewster, MA 02631
> (508) 896-7389

★ **Salesmen's sample and toy stoves.** Wants salesmen's sample stoves, particularly made by *Majestict, Quick Meal, Engman-Matthews* and , *Home Comfort*. Also wants *Dolly's Favorite* and all models of *Buck's Jr*. Also wants toy cooking utensils that accompany these stoves (skillets, Dutch ovens, and especially tea kettles up to 4" high) by such makers as *Wagner Ware* and *Griswold*. Dimensions and condition are helpful but a "picture is usually all I need."
> Ed Hullet
> 5200 No. Lorraine
> Hutchinson, KS 67502
> (316) 662-9381

★ **Salesmen's sample stoves.** "I'll buy salesmen's sample stoves finished in porcelain enamel such as those made by *Beauty Banquet, Monarch, Qualified,* and *Home Comfort*. Especially seeking a miniature *Monarch* range which is 32" tall to the top of the warming ovens and comes in green, yellow, and white." Says she would like to correspond with other collectors or owners of miniature stoves.
> Marilyn Wren
> 9073 Weidkamp
> Lynden, WA 98264

★ **Damaged, bent, or rusty tin cans or signs** which are difficult to sell. They aren't worth much but Ron's the only person we know who buys them at all.
> Ron Knappen
> RR #2, Box 590
> Galesville, WI 54630

Soda Fountain

★ **Ice cream and soda fountain memorabilia:**
  [1] **Postcards** depicting ice cream or soda fountains, ice cream trucks, factories or any other ice cream topic (any year);
  [2] **Photographs** of soda fountain interiors;
  [3] Letterheads, envelopes, fans, and all other **paper** with ice cream images;
  [4] Soda Fountain and ice cream trade **magazines** pre-1930;
  [5] **Trade cards** picturing ice cream parlors, freezers, or soda fountains;
  [6] **Catalogs** pre-1920 (except Mills #31);
  [7] **Advertising** giveaways, fobs, buttons, tape measures, etc.
Allan buys a wide range of ice cream related items, but says his focus for the last few years has been on postcards with historical photos. He buys nothing damaged or made after 1945. He does not make offers, and requests you price what you have.
Allan "Mr. Ice Cream" Mellis
1115 West Montana
Chicago, IL 60614
(312) 327-9123

★ **Soda Fountain memorabilia** and historical ephemera related to soda fountain operations such as trade catalogs, bill and letter heads, recipe and formula books, trade magazines (like *Soda Dispenser* and *Soda Fountain*), photographs, supply catalogs, and the like. Also wants 19th century soda fountain items such as hand crank milk shakers, tumbler holders, root beer mugs, etc. 20th century wants include unusual straw dispensers, glasses marked with a product name, *True Fruit* advertising from the J. Hungerford Smith Co. of Rochester, hand held advertising fans showing ice cream or with a soda fountain theme, pink ice cream soda glasses, and banana split dishes. The favorite find of this 20 year veteran collector is catalogs showing equipment and supplies from before 1870. **He does not want** syrup well inserts for later fountains, nor does he want match book covers, or trinkets related to the ice cream industry. "Please give as much reasonable detail as possible. A photo is helpful." Dealers should price your goods. Amateurs may request offer.
Harold Screen
2804 Munster Rd.
Baltimore, MD 21234
(410) 661-6765

★ Pre-1945 *Coca-Cola* memorabilia including fancier *Coke* items with pretty girls and lots of color especially cardboard cut out signs and back bar decorations. He will pay up to $5,000 for pre-1900 calendars. Pays well for metal tins, trays, and signs. Magazine ads from before 1932 only. No commemorative bottles, please.
Randy Schaeffer, C-C Trayders
611 N. 5th St.
Reading, PA 19601
(215) 373-3333

★ *Coca-Cola* advertising of all type before 1940. Will pay premium prices for all advertising for *Coca-Cola* chewing gum. Also other cardboard cutouts, festoons, and calendars. Most interested in small items such as watch fobs, openers, pocket knives, and the like. Thom says he "will be glad to help you evaluate the worth of your *Coca-Cola* items."
Thom Thompson
123 Shaw Ave.
Versailles, KY 40383
(606) 255-2727 days (606) 873-8787 eves

★ *Coca-Cola* advertising. "I'll buy pre-1960 calendars, trays, small signs, syrup bottles, clocks, thermometers, menu boards, ashtrays, playing cards, lighters, and just about anything else free of rust or wrinkles that says *Coca-Cola*. Loves to find salesman's sample coolers and dispensers. Does not want repro trays, bottles of any sort including commemorative, or magazine ads. Describe condition carefully.
Terry Buchheit
Rte. 7 Box 62
Perryville, MO 63775

★ *Coca-Cola, Pepsi-Cola* and *Chero-Cola* advertising. Wants smaller pieces such as trays, tip trays, smaller signs, door pushes, match strikers, etc., especially porcelain on tin. No paper.
Dick Shay
514 Stevenson Ave.
Worthington, OH 43085

★ *Coca-Cola* ephemera. Wants pre-1960 signs, clocks, calendars, bottles and carriers, dispensers and machines, uniforms, etc. "I'll consider anything" except those that read "enjoy *Coca-Cola*" as they are too new. Older items read "drink *Coca-Cola*." Include your phone number.
Marion Lathan
Rt. 1, Box 430
Chester, SC 29706
(803) 377-8225

★ *7-Up* **memorabilia.** "I'll buy almost any American made item advertising *7-Up*, especially items from the 1930's to 50's. I want historical items, company memos, photos of store displays and the like. The older the better. Watch for ads or items from Howdy Company's *Bib-Lable Lithiated Lemon-Lime Soda* which later became *7-Up*. Your description should include the shape of the *7-Up* logo (round, oval, square, or rectangular). Not interested in foreign items or most stuff after 1960. "I'm a collector not a dealer and will try to help you find a buyer."
　　Don Fiebiger
　　1970 Las Lomitas Dr.
　　Hacienda Heights, CA 91745
　　(310) 693-6484

★ *Dr. Pepper* **memorabilia** and advertising such as signs, trays, posters clocks, and other items from before World War II. Describe what you have thoroughly, emphasizing condition.
　　Ed Royse,
　　Box 33489
　　Fort Sill, OK 73503
　　(405) 357-8000

★ *Hires Root Beer* **memorabilia** pre-1930 in fine to mint condition. Wants trays, dispensers, and signs. No syrup extract bottles or reproductions of any *Hires* items.
　　Steve Sourapas
　　1413 NW 198th St.
　　Seattle, WA 98177
　　(206) 542-1791

★ **Root Beer advertising** such as bottles, mugs, signs, caps, cans, syrup dispensers, and paper items. It *must* have the words "root beer" on the item. "If you don't recognize the brand name, or if it was sold only in a limited area, I'll probably be interested. For many of the 400 makers of root beer, only bottle caps survive. Love to find a *Dr. Swett's* root beer mug in majolica with a false bottom half way up the mug and will pay $200 for a perfect one. I pay $3 each for bottle caps I don't have." Doesn't want anything from brands sold on the market today or any *A&W* mugs except those that say 5¢. No picture needed if you give complete info.
　　Tom Morrison
　　2930 Squaw Valley Dr.
　　Colorado Springs, CO 80918
　　(719) 598-1754

★ *Moxie* **memorabilia.** Wants signs, fans, toys, advertising posters, metal trays, and other pre-1940 items associated with this old time soft drink. Will buy *Moxie* bottles only if the name of a town is part of the inscription. Bowers is the author of *The Moxie Encyclopedia*, a 760 page illustrated history available for $19.95.
　　Q. David Bowers
　　Box 1224
　　Wolfeboro, NH 03894
　　(603) 569-5095

★ **Soda pop cans pre-1965,** especially local brands. Will buy quantities of rare cans, but no rusty cans are wanted by this ten year veteran collector-dealer, but "some light spotting and aging is natural. I do require cans be sent before a final purchase offer is made because condition so greatly affects the value and I need to examine cans closely."
　　Tony Steffens
　　615 Chester
　　Elgin, IL 60120
　　(800) 443-8712

★ **Soda pop bottles with painted labels from New England.** If offering for sale, pay particular attention to describing all colors and wording.
　　Steve Daniels
　　Box 218
　　Medfield, MA 02052

★ **Soda pop bottles with painted labels** (sometimes called applied color labels "ACL") from minor bottling companies anywhere in North America. Would be interested in hearing from people with foreign soda pop bottles, too. "I like to think that I have West Virginia well covered, but I'm buying bottles from anywhere." Other ephemera related to local and regional bottlers including photos and advertising is also wanted. Would like to find a three colored *Uncle Tom's Root Beer* from California. Please describe all wording and colors on the bottle.
　　Gary Brent Kincade
　　Box 712
　　Weston, WV 26452
　　(304) 842-3773 eves

Bottles

★ **Antique American bottles**, both glass and pottery, especially old beer and medicinals from the Buffalo, area. Also wants mineral waters, poisons, barber shop bottles. Buys trade cards, advertising, billheads, and other items associated with makers or users of bottles in Western NY. Sven publishes the newsletter of the Western NY Bottle Collectors Association.
   Sven Stau
   Box 437
   Buffalo, NY 14212
      (716) 825-5448 or (716) 822-3120

★ **All types of bottles and ephemera from bottle companies** including calendars, signs, brochures, and promotional giveaways. Gayner Glass Company is of interest, as are Salem squats, a type of soda bottle made in Salem, NJ. "I am glad to help anyone out however I can."
   Charles McDonald, Old Bottle Museum
   4 Friendship Dr.
   Salem, NJ 08079
      (609) 935-5631

★ **Early American bottles.** Buys a wide range of glass bottles, including campaign bottles, bitters, figurals, whiskey flasks, **and glass jugs with handles.** Wants glass bottles with agricultural symbols, flags, sunbursts, portraits of national heroes, and the like, or bottles in the shape of log cabins, cannons, lighthouses, pigs, etc. Many of these items are worth in excess of $1,000. **Pottery pig bottles** are also wanted, but no *Jim Beam* type whiskey bottles.
   Robert Daly
   10341 Jewell Lake Ct.
   Fenton, MI 48430
      (313) 629-4934

★ **Patent medicine bottles.** "I'll buy pontilled, embossed bottles, especially colored and labeled ones, and will pay from $500 to $6,000 for fine ones. Also buys patent medicine advertising.
   Jerry Phelps
   6013 Innes Trace Rd.
   Louisville, KY 40222
      (502) 425-4765

★ **Early American bottles and historical flasks.** Wants hand blown figural bottles or those with embossed figures and portraits. Will pay $3,000 for *"The American System"* flask depicting a paddlewheeler. Also wants **figural bitters bottles** and hand-blown, pontil marked, **colored ink** and **medicine bottles**. Burt also buys **rare fruit (canning) jars** complete with lids, round and **colored milk bottles** and mineral water bottles. No cracks, chips, or bad stains are acceptable. Burt advises reading McKearin's *American Glass* to see bottles which attract top dollar. No machine made bottles or repros.
   Burton Spiller
   49 Palmerston Rd.
   Rochester, NY 14618
      (716) 244-2229

★ **Bottles from California and the Old West.** "I'll buy whiskey, medicine, food and other bottles from the days of miners, loggers, and cowboys in the West. I especially like bottles with the names of California towns and companies on them." He wants **whiskey bottles with pictures** embedded in the glass, which can bring from $100 to as much as $2,500 for a *California Club* bottle. If your bottle says "Federal Law forbids the resale..." it isn't old enough to be of interest. Bottles without names or designs embossed in the glass are generally valueless to collectors as are most cracked or chipped ones. Tell him what it says on your bottle, what color it is, and what condition it is in.
   John Goetz
   Box 1570
   Cedar Ridge, CA 95924
      (916) 272-4644

★ **Early bottles and jars with colorful food labels**, pre-1910. Has special interest in food jars, bottles, and crocks from Flaccus, Hunter, EXWACO, and McMechen of Wheeling, WV, but will buy **any jars marked as being made or used in Wheeling or Wellsburg, WV.** There's $200 waiting for you, if you have a Flaccus stoneware water cooler. Give the color of the glass and its size. Report *exactly* what is written or embossed on the jar or crock, and note any cracks, chips, dings, or unwashable stains.
   Tom & Deena Caniff
   1223 Oak Grove Ave.
   Steubenville, OH 43952
      (614) 282-8918

Health & Medicine

★ **Unusual medicines and healing devices.**
"I'll buy pills, liquids, mixtures, devices and
things promoted to cure ills or bring on better
health. I'll consider items whether they work or
not, whether scientific or crackpot, drab or
colorful, sincere, absurd, or ridiculous. I'll even
buy brand new items if they are odd or come
with an interesting story."

[1] **Bottles and other containers**, whether
full of pills and powders, or empty;

[2] **Bottling and filling materials;**

[3] **Ads, flyers, signs, trade cards,** and
other advertising for medicines;

[4] **Medical catalogs;**

[5] **Health devices, real or quack,** such as
vaporizers, electric gadgets, etc.,
the more unusual the better;

[6] **Any item that makes a health claim**
such as tobacco, mineral water, etc.;

[7] **Books and booklets** of all types, from
serious to humorous, on medicines;

[8] **Medical teaching devices.**

"I'd like as complete a description as possible,
including the item's age, condition, price, and
what you feel to be its unique characteristics."

August Maymudes
10564 Cheviot Dr.
Los Angeles, CA 90064
(310) 839-4426 eves   fax: (310) 481-8169

★ **Pre-1900 medical and apothecary (drug
store) equipment** including **doctor's instruments,** bleeding bowls, leech jars, apothecary
tools, colored and pontil marked **patent medicine** bottles, patent medicine tax stamps 1860-
80, and all patent medicine advertising in *any*
form especially signs, clocks, tins, and 3-dimen-
sional papier mache figures. A 26 year veteran
collector dealer, he'll pay from $150 to $3,000
for leech jars and up to $1,500 for figures.

Jerry Phelps
6013 Innes Trace Rd.
Louisville, KY 40222
(502) 425-4765

★ **Stethoscopes.** "I'll buy antique and unusual
physician's stethoscopes, both monaural and
binaural." Give all markings, patents, etc.

Chris Papadopoulos
1107 Chatterleigh Circle
Towson, MD 21204
(301) 825-9157 eves

★ **Medical books and ephemera.** Wants
quality items including books from before 1840,
medical broadsides, pamphlets, hand colored
illustrations, stereo views, letters, documents,
and catalogs. "I'll pay well for quality material,"
he states.

Ivan Gilbert
Miran Arts & Books
2824 Elm Ave.
Columbus, OH 43209
(614) 236-0002

★ **Pre-1910 medical and drug store items**
including trade cards, catalogs, advertising,
calendars, journals, ledgers, photos, and other
similar ephemera. Also interested in **patent
medicines, instruments, and quack devices.**

Doug Johnston
529 W. Encanto
Phoenix, AZ 85003

★ **Medical instruments such as monaural
stethoscopes, ear trumpets and conversation
tubes,** brass anesthesia masks from the drop
ether days, all bleeders especially mechanical,
and old dental instruments if made from wood or
ivory.

Lucille Malitz
Lucid Antiques
Box KH
Scarsdale, NY 10583
(914) 636-3367

★ **Microscopes and other medical or scientific instruments.** "I'll buy pre-1900 microscopes
by the following makers: *Zentmayer, Grunow,
Bullock, McAllister, Gundlock, Tolles, Queen,
Pike* and *Charles Spencer.*" Give the maker's
name and serial number. Describe overall condition of the instrument, case, and accessories.
"Don't clean or polish anything," he warns.

Dr. Allan Wissner
Box 102
Ardsley, NY 10502
(914) 693-4628

★ **Embalming tools and bottles.** Embalming
kits and tools are often in black bags and can be
recognized by long aspiration needles. Many
tools and bottles are marked with skulls and
crossbones. Look for *Dioxin* brand, and others.
"I have enough embalming tables unless they're
priced at $20 or less."

Steve DeGenaro
Box 5662
Youngstown, OH 44504

★ **Enema and douche equipment.** Wants a variety of rubber fountain syringes, sinus fountain syringes, bulb syringes, etc, especially in different colors. Especially interested in the *Buckingham* and *Boots* enema syringes, both of which come in a metal box. Also buys books and catalogs related to the subject, from any maker. "No new type fountain syringes with white plastic hoses." Items must be made of rubber, not plastic, and have black not white fittings. Do you have the original box?
Helen Roman
115 Baldwin St.
Bloomfield, NJ 07003

★ **Electric and pre-electric vibrators and hand held massagers.** "I especially like those with metal casings rather than plastic, those with hand-cranks, and vibrators with wooden handles or parts. Not interested in battery operated devices. You won't make a fortune selling to me, but your item could reside in the world's only vibrator museum and will be happier than in your attic." No *Oster* vibrators which are worn on the back of the hand. Describe, give numbers, and indicate whether the box and any attachments or instructional inserts are present. Will buy items which do not work but are not physically broken.
Joani Blank
Good Vibrations
PO Box 2086
Burlingame, CA 94011

★ **Pre-1960 chiropractic equipment and books** especially electronic diagnostic gear or items from the Palmer College/School.
Mel Rosenthal
507 S. Maryland Ave.
Wilmington, DE 19804
(302) 322-8944

★ **Dental cabinets, instruments, and catalogs,** but only before 1920, please.
Peter Chu, DDS
5470 Folkestone Dr.
Dayton, OH 45459
(513) 435-6849

★ **Dental trade cards.** "I'll buy trade cards from dentists, dentifrices, pain medications, dental parlors, breath fresheners, and the like." Will consider any dental related paper.
Ted Croll, DDS
East Street and North Main St.
Doylestown, PA 18901

★ **Ephemera and information about twins, multiple births, and freak parasitic twin births.** This dedicated nurse, historian, and archivist wants photos, newspaper clips, souvenirs, personal information, and *anything* statistical, scholarly, or informative. If there was ever a twin in your family, or you are one of a multiple birth, this is the lady who will preserve the experience. She always wants first hand information from multiples about their life. *She does not want* undated clippings or items that have been damaged by pinning, pasting, or taping. When describing scrapbooks, make certain to note whether the clippings are dated. "My collection is not a hobby but a full time job in research, internationally recognized for its accuracy and extent, a source of factual information for physicians, researchers, and news media of all types." She has been at it since 1939, but Miss Helen always appreciates help, especially people sending clippings from local papers and obscure magazines about twins (as long as you tell where it came from and the date). **Especially wants photos and Dionne quints** memorabilia.
"Miss Helen" Kirk
Multiple Birth Museum
Box 254
Galveston, TX 77553
(409) 762-4792

★ **Medically related advertising and memorabilia** especially tin containers, trays, signs, match holders, trade cards, advertising envelopes, calendars, old corked and labeled bottles, pinback buttons, mirrors, instruments, and the like. Among tins, he wants medical, dental, veterinary, talcums, prophylactics, etc. Fine condition items only.
Eugene Cunningham, MD
152 Wood Acres Drive
E. Amherst, NY 14051
(716) 688-9537

★ **All human glass eyes** in any size or color, rights or lefts.
Donald Gorlick
Box 24541
Seattle, WA 98124
(206) 824-0508

★ **Veterinary medicine ephemera,** pre-1900.
Barbara Cole
October Farm
Rt 2, Box 183-C
Raleigh, NC 27610

★ **Drug store memorabilia** including apothecary bottles with glass labels and stoppers, show globes, all **related advertising, and catalogs**. No scales or mortar and pestle sets are wanted.
Mart James
8269 Scarlet Oaks Cove
Cordova, TN 38018
 (901) 757-0214

★ **Patent medicine advertising.** "I'll buy 19th century advertising, trade cards, almanacs, booklets, postcards, posters, sheet music, tokens, and giveaway items related to any patent medicine. I have a particular interest in *Hadacol* items, and will purchase them as late as 1950. In trade cards, I am looking for "private" cards, made for one manufacturer, not stock cards with overprints. Please send Xerox© or send the item on approval." Walker has a new book forthcoming on the history of patent medicine advertising.
A.Walker Bingham
19 E. 72nd St.,
New York, NY 10021
 (212) 628-5358

★ **Patent medicine bottles**, especially from G.W. Merchant of Lockport, NY.
Sven Stau
Box 437
Buffalo, NY 14212
 (716) 825-5448 or (716) 822-3120

★ **Dark blue bottles which contained medicine or poisons.** Bottles must be cork tops, not screw tops. Particularly looking for bottles which held various types of "salts" by John Wyeth and Bro. that have dose caps, contents, and paper labels.Also want *Warner's, Mulford's*, and other cobalt blue and green bottles complete with contents and labels.Pays $60+ for *Kickapoo* bottle with original stopper. No bottles marked "Taiwan" or "Wheaton" or modern milk of magnesia. Give the color, size, and embossed letters or designs, and note existence of chips, cracks, labels, screw threads, etc.
Adrienne & David Escoe
PO Box 342
Los Alamitos, CA 90720

★ **Old quack medical devices** which shock, spark, buzz, vibrate, or do nothing at all. Most devices were built into fancy boxes with dials, wires, hand electrodes, plated terminals, coils, and levers. Other devices consisted of therapeutic gloves, brushes, charms, and the like. There is an extensive list of brand names he seeks but he does not want common massage vibrators, violet rays, and *Electreat* devices. He also buys books, catalogs, pamphlets, and other paper ephemera promoting quack electrical items or other therapeutic gimmicks. Keller prefers you price your item but will make offers.
Leland Keller
1205 Imperial Dr.
Pittsburg, KS 66762

★ **Almanacs published by patent medicine companies, between 1840-1920.** Many of these pay $20-$30. If you have many of them to sell it is advisable to have his detailed wants list. No Almanacs by *Swamp Root, Nostetters*, or *Ayers*. No foreign language editions. No post 1920. No medical booklets, pamphlets, cookbooks, etc.
Rodney Brunsell
55 Spring St.
Hanson, MA 02341

For faster response include a Stamped Self Addressed Envelope.

Law Enforcement

★ **Law enforcement memorabilia** such as badges, patches, nightsticks, handcuffs, and restraints from all types of law enforcement officers including fish and game, railroad security, sheriffs, marshals, constables, Indian police, city police, and other. Also likes studio **portraits of law enforcement officers.** Make a Xerox© of the front and rear of your badge or photo and give its history if you can. No security company, college police, or "gun show" brass badges. Include any wording or numbers you find on handcuffs or leg irons.

Gene Matzke, Gene's Badges
2345 So. 28th St.
Milwaukee, WI 53215
(414) 383-8995

★ **Western peace officer's badges,** especially from Oklahoma and the Southwest. "I am especially interested in suspension badges (which hang from a bar by chains), stars, circles with cut out stars, shields, and some others, depending on age and appearance. I will also buy some contemporary badges, depending on their hallmark and where they are from. Indian police badges from anywhere are also wanted, as is a genuine Arizona Ranger badge. Note there are a lot of fake badge #11 on the market; a genuine one is made of sheet silver and hand engraved. I am not interested in reproductions, phonies, fakes and cheap brass badges." This 30 year veteran collector and author warns that lots of fake badges exist, and that it is important to have any badge authenticated by someone who really knows what he's doing. If you write him, he wants to know the style of badge, the wording, who wore it and where, any hallmarks, and what you think the age of the badge is. "If in doubt, send the badge insured and I will inspect it, make an offer, or return it."

Ron Donoho
PO Box 13170
Las Vegas, NV 89112
(702) 458-7731

★ **Handcuffs, leg irons, torture and execution devices, and electric chairs,** both authentic or reproduction. Also wants photos of these devices in use.

Harvey Lee Boswell's Palace of Wonders
Box 446
Elm City, NC 27822

★ **Any pre-1950 items connected with the Northwest Mounted Police,** Royal Northwest Mounted Police, the Royal Canadian Mounted Police, the BC Provincial Police, or the Alberta Provincial Police. Especially awards and medals, cap badges, collar badges, uniforms, and law enforcement items marked with the initials of one of these agencies.

Michael Rice
Box 286
Saanichton, BC V0S 1M0, CANADA
(604) 652-9047 eves

★ **Law enforcement memorabilia from prohibition era Chicago** including photos, police bulletins, warrants for arrests, court transcripts, police uniforms (1920's only), badges, and personal items from police chiefs Garrity, Fitzmorris, Collins, Hughs, and Russell. Only well documented personal effects, please, with value in part dependent upon the authenticity and story accompanying the item. If offering personal effects, tell how you obtained them and provide your phone number.

Michael Graham, Roaring 20's
345 Cleveland Ave.
Libertyville, IL 60048
(312) 362-4808 days or 362-8531 eves

★ **All items related to imprisonment, locking and restraint** including handcuffs, shackles, ball & chains, leather restraints, straight jackets, prison uniforms, and **antique or unusual padlocks.** Also wants magician's escape locks, lock picks, and books about lock picking. These well known dealers in magic and escape devices offer a catalog for $2.

Joe and Pam Tanner, Tanner Escapes
Box 349
Great Falls, MT 59403
(406) 453-4961

★ **Prison, jail, or penal colony related memorabilia** including items from juvenile detention centers and reform schools. Items include coins, tokens, uniforms, weapons, badges, letters about prison life, restraint devices, photos of prisons, items made by prisoners, postcards, and "just about anything at all." His prime interest is in **scrip,** the paper money used in institutions as a medium of exchange. If you have genuine prison material you may send it for his offer.

"Jailhouse Jerry" Zara
2414 Mark Place
Point Pleasant, NJ 08742
(908) 899-1016

★ **Old handcuffs, leg irons, and other police or prison restraint devices.** Also police department badges, photos, and histories especially from Ohio. Make certain to mention whether your item works and has a key.
    Stan Willis
    6211 Stewart Rd.
    Cincinnati, OH 45227
        (513) 271-0454 days

★ **Jail, prison, and law enforcement memorabilia,** with emphasis on all types of restraints, including U.S. or foreign military, third world, and Eastern European. Wants handcuffs, ball and chains, manacles, leg irons, thumb screws, nippers, iron claws, and comealongs. Also wants literature from manufacturers, copies of *Detective*, a peace officer trade magazine, and patent information on locks and restraints. Wants to find magician's key rings as well as restraint keys marked with the maker's name. "Pricing on this stuff has gone crazy lately," he says, so it's time to sell.
    Larry Franklin
    3238 Hutchison Ave.
    Los Angeles, CA 90034
        (310) 559-4461

★ **San Quentin and Folsom prison and prisoner memorabilia, 1890-1915** with special interest in Ed Morrell, Donald Lowrie, Jake Oppenheimer, Sir Harry Westwood Cooper, Jack Black, Christopher Evands, and George Sontag. Know or have anything about these people? He wants it.
    Jack Fleming
    1825 Vine #2
    Berkeley, CA 94703

★ **Fingerprinting equipment.** "I'll buy old police fingerprinting equipment including Bertillon equipment, fingerprint cameras, microscopes and especially books and magazines concerning fingerprinting." Also buys WANTED posters and police mug shots.
    Michael Carrick
    1230 Hoyt St. SE
    Salem, OR 97302
        (800) 852-0300

Other Gov't Services

★ **School, teacher, and student memorabilia** from before 1920, especially diaries, postcards, photographs, teaching certificates, teacher souvenirs, rewards of merit, report cards, letters, student assignments, and books having to do with teaching or operating schools. No student textbooks except pre-1860. Has particular interest in ephemera associated with Samuel Read Hall (1795-1877), a New England educator and textbook author.
    Tedd Levy
    Box 2217
    Norwalk, CT 06850

★ **Civilian Conservation Corps (CCC)** memorabilia from the 1930's such as belt buckles, scarves, uniforms, sweetheart pillows, china, etc., which run $15 and up. Items marked with the unit camp number are the most desirable, especially the sleeve unit patches designed by the individual camps, worth $25 up. Honor awards will bring $150 each, more if found complete with original ribbon in good condition. Send photo, sketch or Xerox© of what you have.
    Tom Pooler
    Box 1861
    Grass Valley, CA 95945
        (916) 268-1338

★ **Civilian Conservation Corps (CCC)** memorabilia from the 1930's.
    Ken Kipp
    Box 116
    Allenwood, PA 17810
        (717) 538-1440

★ **Obsolete U.S. Post Office memorabilia** including steel postmarking devices, locks and keys, uniform badges and buttons, scales, marked handguns, and postcards depicting post offices. Many other items are also wanted, but not postage stamps. His large illustrated wants list can be had if you send first class postage on a large self addressed envelope. If you have a postmarking device, make an imprint.
    Frank Scheer
    12 E. Rosemont Ave.
    Alexandria, VA 22301
        (703) 549-4095 eves

Fire Fighting

★ **Fire fighting and fire insurance ephemera** including, but not limited to, fire grenades, awards, helmets, buckets, axes, badges, **toys**, fire marks, fire insurance signs, advertising items, nozzles, apparatus parts, alarm equipment, photos, lanterns, **extinguishers**, postcards, books, salesmen's samples, models, etc., especially pre-1900. Nothing after 1940.
Ralph Jennings, Jr.
301 Ft Washington Ave.
Fort Washington, PA 19034
(215) 646-7178 eves

★ **Wood cased fire station gongs.** "I'll buy any wood cased fire station gong, working condition or not, made by *Gamewell Fire Alarm Telegraph Co., Star Co., Moses Crane Co.*, or other manufacturer. Gongs have wooden cases, glass doors, and key wind movements." Also wants literature describing gongs or photos of fire station watch desks showing a wall gong.
Gary Carino
805 W. 3rd St.
Duluth, MN 55806
(218) 722-0964

★ **Fire and casualty insurance company memorabilia**, especially reverse on glass signs, and automobile tags for bumper or grill that have an insurance company's name. Your description should include the name of the insurance company, size, material, and condition. "Best to send a photo, along with size." If possible, he will give you the name of another collector who might be interested in what you have. **No life insurance.**
Byron Gregerson
Box 951
Modesto, CA 95353
(209) 523-3300

★ **Fire fighting antiques and collectibles,** especially fire alarm boxes and wood cased gongs in any condition and quantity (would like to buy entire systems or collections). Will also buy extinguishers, nozzles, bells, lanterns, helmets, badges, **fire grenades, fire related toys,** and catalogs. Your description should give all markings, dimensions, and any history of the piece you know. Make sure you include your phone number and best time for this Director of the California Fire and Safety Museum to call.
Stan Zukowski
1867 Ellard Place
Concord, CA 94521
(415) 687-6426

★ **Fire fighting antiques** such as early leather fire helmets, leather fire buckets with paintings on them, speaking trumpets with fancy engraving, early fire nozzles from hand operated pumpers, fire department lanterns that burn kerosene or whale oil and have two color glass globes, gold or silver presentation badges, etc. **Anything from the Chicago Fire Department** from before 1940. Very old fire alarm boxes, wood cased fire gongs, fire alarm registers, and other old equipment marked Gamewell, Star, Moses Crane, American, or U.S. Police & Fire is wanted by this veteran fire fighter.
Larry Meyer
4001 Elmwood Ave.
Stickney, IL 60402
(708) 749-1564

weapons and war

Souvenirs & relics from any war interest collectors.

Choice items from the Civil War continue to turn up in the hands of readers. Letters, guns, and relics of every sort are wanted, especially items from the Confederacy.

Among the most valuable newer items are Japanese swords, some of which are worth $10,000. One of our readers owned a sword worth over $25,000. It hung on her rec room wall for forty years. She almost sold it for $50 before getting my advice.

This edition of *I'll Buy That Too!* showcases new buyers of items from 20th century wars. The Korean and VietNam war items are now starting to sell. Interest grows in home front items from WWII, and from the peace movement associated with the VietNam era.

When offering guns for sale, make certain to include all the information found on the barrel or breech. Pay attention to serial numbers. If they do not match from one part to another, make certain to note that fact. When describing the condition, note all changes, modifications, and repairs.

Knives and swords should be measured. Include a tracing or photocopy of any designs on the blade. Many military insignia and other small items are easily photocopied.

tony hyman

Guns & Weapons

★ **Napoleonic arms and armor.** This 30 year veteran collector/dealer in Western ephemera does not make offers. Requires you to send a photo and complete description including information about where you got it, and your asking price. No fakes or reproductions are wanted.
Pierre Bovis
The Az-Tex Cowboy Trading Co.
PO Box 460
Tombstone, AZ 85638
(602) 457-3359

★ **Antique and modern firearms.** "I'll buy a wide range of items, from Civil War carbines, Indian wars guns, trap doors, rolling blocks, cap and ball, etc., to early *Winchester, Marlin, Savage,* and *Remington*. This 25 year dealer also buys some *Colt* handguns. If your gun or rifle is pre-1964 and all wood and metal surfaces are original and unrestored, it might be worth a call. Although he buys *Krag, Springfield* and others for parts, he does not want reworked guns or reproductions. Offers catalog of guns for sale.
Rudy Dotzenrod
Rt #2 Box 26
Wyndmere, ND 58081
(701) 439-2646

★ **American guns from before 1900,** especially those with historic association. No interest in reproductions. If possible, please send a clear photo of the item and write down all markings found anywhere on it. If it is a pistol, please make a Xerox© copy, or draw a pencil outline. Be sure to mention any broken or missing wood, metal that is pitted, parts missing, etc. Does it work? Worman has written a two volume book on firearms of the American West and was firearms editor of *Hobbies* magazine for sixteen years. SASE please.
Charles Worman
PO Box 33584 (AMC)
Dayton, OH 45433
(513) 429-1808 eves

★ **Guns and gun collections** of all types. "I'm always searching for Gattling guns."
Ed Kukowski, Ed's Gun House
Route 1
Minnesota City, MN 55959
(507) 689-2925

★ **Black powder antique guns** made in Western New York State. Makers of interest include *Artis, Cutler, Ellis, Gardner, Lefever, Marsley, Miller, Plimpton, Southerland, Walker, Wood* and several others. Antique guns only.
Alan Stone
Box 500
Honeoye, NY 14471
(716) 229-2700

★ **American percussion and early cartridge firearms,** both long guns and revolvers, 1840-1920. "I'll buy guns by any maker, but especially *Colt, Winchester, Remington, Marlin, Smith & Wesson, Manhattan, Sharps, Stevens,* and *Bacon*. I like to buy derringers of all types, especially those that are particularly small or short barreled, those that are very large caliber (.41 cal. up), or those which take metallic cartridges. I also like finding any pocket size pistols made by *Colt, Remington, Bacon, Marston, Moore, National, Reid, Star, Terry, Warner,* and *Williamson*." Pays $300 to $3,000 for these guns. Wants photos or photocopies of both sides of the weapon and all markings and numbers found anywhere on the gun.
Steve Howard
Past Tyme Pleasures
101 First St., #404
Los Altos, CA 94022
(415) 4844488 eves

★ **High grade shotguns,** fine sporting rifles, and English double rifles. "I'll pay up to $5,000 for pre-1964 *Winchester* Model 70 rifles, and up to $250,000 for *Parker* shotguns, and $100,000 for English double rifles and shotguns. I do not want old worn guns showing little or no original finish. Give the make, serial number, caliber/gauge, and condition if you'd like an offer."
Alan Phillips
Box 7852
Laguna Niguel, CA 92607-7852
(714) 499-4196

★ **Old double barrel shotguns** are wanted in any condition. "I will buy any kind of double barrel made before 1940 that is worth $300 or less. I especially want old side plate *Lefevers, L.C.Smith,* and most English or Belgian guns. Describe the condition, amount of bluing, rust, missing parts, engraving, butt plates, etc.
Charles Black, The Gun Doctor
Rt. 6 Box 237D
Athens, AL 35611
(205) 729-1640

★ **German pistols, parts and accessories** such as holsters, stocks, magazines, etc. This 30 year veteran dealer buys and stocks parts for *Luger, Mauser, Walthers*, and many others. He wants to buy mismatched *Lugers* for parts (at $200 up) and will sell perfect matched pistols on consignment in the $500 to $2,000 range. He is willing to buy in quantity from other dealers, police departments, veterans groups, etc., including nonworking guns in volume. If you have a captured WWII pistol with an interesting story, he'd love to hear from you. He does not want reproduction parts or accessories. If you wish to sell a gun, he wants you to tell him the name of the manufacturer, the model number (usually on the slide), the caliber, the serial number, and anything else printed or stamped anywhere on the pistol. He will give free verbal appraisals over the phone, but charges for formal written assessments. He also sells accessories for most European pistols from 1900 to the present and a selection of books on guns.
> Tom Heller
> Heller Arms, Ltd.
> PO Box 578
> San Bruno, CA 94066
> (415) 3592290

★ *Colt* **pistols with factory engraving.** "I'll buy single action *Colts* in 95% or better original condition, if they predate WWII and have factory engraving." Give the serial number when you write, and if possible, a good close up photo of the artwork. Some newer single actions are also wanted. Also wants guns from outlaws and lawmen if they have proper documentation. All early memorabilia from the *Colt* company, including posters, advertising, and literature are also wanted, including *Coltrock* brand products.
> Johnny Spellman, DVM
> 10806 North Lamar
> Austin, TX 78753
> (512) 2586910 eves (512) 8362889 days

★ *Iver Johnson* **products and memorabilia** including **guns, bicycles, catalogs,** etc. Special wants include "engraved presentation guns and awards and any other unusual *Iver Johnson* item." This 30 year veteran collector does not want "common handguns in less than mint condition." Send a complete description, including a sketch or photo. Prefers seller to price, but will offer.
> Charles Best
> 6288 So. Pontiac
> Englewood, CO 80111

★ *Colt* **Patent Firearms Manufacturing Company ephemera** including:
> [1] All correspondence on factory letterhead;
> [2] Pamphlets and brochures by *Colt*;
> [3] Empty black and maroon boxes that *Colt* guns were packed in;
> [4] Instruction sheets and manuals, and "anything else pertaining to *Colt* products."
John wants *Colt* factory catalogs, 1888-1910, for which he pays from $40-$500. 1910-1940 catalogs bring $20-$75. John also buys plastic and electrical items marked *Coltrock* as well as *The Book of Colt Firearms* by Sutherland and Wilson, 1971, for which he'll pay over $100.
> John Fischer
> 7831 Peachtree Ave.
> Panorama City, CA 91402

★ *Newton Arms Co.* **guns and other memorabilia** from this progressive 1916-18 gunsmith. "I'll buy rifles, catalogs, loading tools, letters, stock, cartridges, and any other paper or memorabilia from the *Newton Arms Co.* or the *Chas. Newton Rifle Corp.* I will pay $5,000 for a .276 Newton rifle or a rifle in .280, .33 or .40 (.400) calibers if in mint condition, and will consider all other *Newton* guns at lesser prices. Also want these and other unusual *Newton* cartridges. I will gladly pay a finders fee for *Newton* guns I buy. I'll take anything signed by Chas. Newton but nothing marked *Buffalo Newton Rifle Co.* Items must be original condition.
> Bruce Jennings
> 70 Metz Road
> Sheridan, WY 82801
> (307) 6746921

★ **Junk guns and gun parts** in any condition. "I'm in the parts business and will travel to pick up large lots." Wants nothing having to do with current guns. Describe, including all markings and numbers. Bob is available for insurance appraisals of fire damaged gun collections.
> Robert Fay
> Star Route Box AF
> Whitmore, CA 96096
> (916) 472-3132

★ **Primitive weapons from around the world.** Also trade beads from various cultures.
> David Boone
> Trading Company
> 562 Coyote Rd.,
> Brinnon, WA 98320
> (206) 796-4330

Heavy Weapons

★ **Tanks, artillery, armored vehicles and machine guns and their parts and accessories.** "We are a Federally licensed machine gun manufacturer and dealer, and seek to buy registered operational machine guns and other military equipment, including **muzzle loading cannon** and **Gattling guns.** We buy machine gun parts and accessories including, but not limited to, barrels, buttstocks, magazines, clips, feeding devices, drums, bi-pods, tri-pods, mounts, loading machines, linkers, armorer's kits, etc. We are particularly interested in mounts for *Maxim* machine guns and will pay $150+ for them. We will buy most anything made in the 19th or 20th centuries. Parts and guns do not have to be in perfect condition. We will look at all items." **Not interested in toys, miniatures, stolen firearms, or U.S. Army manuals.** "Clear photos are a must. A VHS video would be even better. Include dimensions and condition of accessories. Copies of any accompanying paperwork, registrations, or manuals are extremely helpful. We will accept UPS shipments of accessories, parts, or mounts up to 70 pounds, and will send a check by return mail. If the offer in unacceptable, I will pay shipping both ways and return your item."
Greg Souchik
T.M.P. Company
Box 133
Custer City, PA 16725
(814) 362-2642 Fax (814) 362-7356

★ **WWII era halftrack** parts, uniforms, insignia, accessories, manuals, and anything else associ-ated with WWII halftracks. "The boys and I are trying to rebuild one, and can use a lot of different things. Call with what you have."
Charles Eberhart
33616 Seward
Topeka, KS 66616
(913) 235-1016

★ **Half tracks, armored cars, tanks,** Gattling guns, howitzers, and cannons, especially a FT-17 Renault (M1917) tank in any condition, worth $10,000 minimum. Larry will arrange for transporting what you have. Also wants
[1] **U.S. women's uniforms** and accessories from WWI or WWII in fine condition only;
[2] **military diving** equipment and related items including sales catalogs;
[3] *Mercedes Benz* **500K** or 540K autos from between 1930-40 (will pay to $150,000);
[4] **German military staff cars;**
[5] **Military aircraft** pre-1940.
Provide all information on the machine's data plates. A photograph is recommended.
Larry Pitman
Zanzibar War Museum
5424 Bryan Station Rd.
Paris, KY 40361
(606) 299-5022

★ **Ammunition and exploding devices** such as grenades, mines, bombs, and fuses. Wants all ages and types, from the beginning of time to the present day. "We buy everything from stone cannon balls to the smart weapons used in operation Desert Storm. Also want books, films, reports, and videos about ordnance in any format or language." Schmitt's family has been making ammo since 1849, so he particularly wants things marked with the Crittenden name. He is willing to pay $2,000 for a single .69 caliber Crittenden and Tibbals Rimfire cartridge. He wants the measurements, condition, and all markings on what you have, preferring you also include a photo. He has no interest in store stock items. Schmitt is a contributing editor of two gun magazines, and involved with cleaning up explosive ordnance from the Iraq/UN war.
Dr. J. Randall Crittenden Schmitt
Court House Station
PO Box 4253
Rockville, MD 20849

★ **Brass military shell casings.** "I want to buy the casings for shells and projectiles in 37mm and larger sizes. Particularly wants an 8" Navy shell. I'll buy shell casings of all weapons, all nations."
Charles Eberhart
33616 Seward
Topeka, KS 66616
(913) 235-1016

Edged Weapons

★ **American swords from 1789-1902.** "We especially want swords with presentations or inscriptions to military persons with dates, rank, etc., either etched/engraved on the blades or on the metal part of the scabbard. Inscribed Civil War swords are particularly desirable. The best makers marks are *Ames, Starr, Roby, Rose, Widman, Horstmann,* or *Glaze*. It is most important for sellers to send a very good drawing or photo of the hilt handle (guard and grip) of the sword. List all markings on the blade. Indicate the type of metal the guard is made from (brass, iron, aluminum), the type of grip/handle (ivory, bone, metal, wood, leather covered wood, or plastic). Note whether the scabbard/sheath is included, and the condition of the sword and scabbard, as to rust, pitting, etc., and whether the scabbard is dented. Indicate the width of the blade at the handle, the length of the blade, and any engraving/etching. This 30+ year collector/dealer is interested in most items, including early fakes and reproductions as long as the seller knows that the price will be considerably less than for an original. Common original swords are also purchased for resale. We do not buy or appraise nonmilitary swords such as Masonic lodges, Knights of Columbus, Knights Templar, etc." Ron is author of two books on swords and active in gun and sword societies.
Ron Hickox
Antique Arms & Militaria
PO Box 360006, Dept. T
Tampa, FL 33673
(813) 933-0902

★ **American swords and large knives** from before 1900. Please describe thoroughly, including any numbers or writing found on the weapon. Make a Xerox© of the knife and of the sword handle if you can. Otherwise photograph or make a good sketch. No lodge, fraternal, or ceremonial swords, please. SASE requested.
Charles Worman
PO Box 33584 (AMC)
Dayton, OH 45433
(513) 429-1808 eves

★ **U.S. and German bayonets and daggers,** either standard fighting issue or dress type. Other countries also purchased. He prefers to buy directly from the veteran or family, and would like information about your weapons' history. Free appraisals of all military swords and edged weapons are available to private parties from this 25 year expert and appraiser.
Hank McGonagle
26 Broad St.
Newburyport, MA 01950
(508) 462-2354

★ **British and American military knives** of WWI and WWII especially British Commando daggers, *Wilkinson Sword* fighting knives (marked FS FIGHTING KNIFE), and American special unit fighting knives. Value ranges from $50 to $1,500 depending on rarity, condition, and its scabbard. It is very important for you to copy every word and symbol on the blade, handle, guard, and scabbard. John does not want bayonets that attach to the end of a rifle.
John Fischer
7831 Peachtree Ave.
Panorama City, CA 91402

★ **German swords and daggers** from the Nazi era (1933-1945). Will buy both common and rare variations, with etched or with plain blades. Especially wanted are swords and daggers with presentation inscriptions giving name, date, and military unit etched on the scabbard or blade. Make a drawing or Xerox of the item, noting all rust, pitting, scabbard dents, etc.
Ron Hickox
Antique Arms & Militaria
PO Box 360006, Dept. T
Tampa, FL 33673
(813) 933-0902

★ **Japanese swords**, daggers, armor and Samurai items, especially fine swords and daggers, and sword and dagger parts. No other guns, bayonets, or non Japanese items. Ron will send you a checklist to help you describe a sword for sale. Ron has been treasurer of the Japanese Sword Society and editor of its newsletter for ten years. Ron appeals, "Many of these items were brought back to America after WWII and now rust away in basements and attics. It is important that these items be preserved by placement into a collection."
Ron Hartmann
5907 Deerwood Drive
St. Louis, MO 63123

★ **Italian daggers** from WWI through the Fascist era up to and including WWII. Premium prices paid for those with white handles or engraved blades. When writing, please include your phone number and best time to call. I guarantee postage both ways if you send a dagger for my inspection. I will help you identify any Italian dagger free of charge if you send an SASE with your inquiry, or call me after 7pm East coast time. Be prepared to describe the handle style, crossguard, color of grips, style of the blade, all markings, the length, and what the scabbard looks like. Not interested in swords, bayonets, or daggers that have been shortened, filed, or otherwise damaged.
Joseph Venanzi
46 Wolfpack Rd.
Trenton, NJ 08619
(609) 586-3414

*Gun List
150+ page tabloid
12 times a year for $17.
700 E. State St.
Iola, WI 54990*

Military Artifacts

★ **French and Indian War, the Revolutionary War, or the War of 1812** in northern New York especially the Lake Champlain, Lake George, or Ft. Ticonderoga area. All ephemera about the campaigns or the men involved, especially Benedict Arnold and Rogers' Rangers.
Breck Turner
With Pipe and Book
91 Main St.
Lake Placid, NY 12946

★ **Mexican War** (1846-48) photos and documents are sought.
Johnny Spellman, DVM
10806 North Lamar
Austin, TX 78753
(512) 258-6910 eves (512) 836-2889 days

★ **Civil War artifacts** of all types including guns, knives, canteens, uniforms, documents, swords, and prisoner of war items. Reproductions are not wanted. It is important to indicate any markings on the item. SASE requested.
Charles Worman
PO Box 33584 (AMC)
Dayton, OH 45433
(513) 429-1808 eves

★ **Confederate Civil War letters**, envelopes, paper money, posters, pardons, passes, and other ephemera. Also, some other Civil War items, and Lincoln photos and manuscripts.
Gordon McHenry
Box 1117
Osprey, FL 34229
(813) 966-5563

★ **Civil War regimental histories** and first person narratives.
　　Jim Presgraves
　　Bookworm & Silverfish
　　Box 639
　　Wytheville, VA 24382

★ **Civil War, especially Southern Unit histories**, battle accounts, biographies,and personal memoirs. He can provide a detailed wants list to those who regularly deal in Civil War material. No books published by Grosset & Dunlap.
　　James Baumhofer
　　Box 65493
　　St. Paul, MN 55165
　　　(612) 6987151

★ **G.A.R. china, mugs, and spoons.** Any pieces marked G.A.R. (Grand Army of the Republic).
　　Don McMahon
　　385 Thorpe Ave.
　　Meriden, CT 06450

★ **French or British military forces** overseas, British Indian Native States forces, Spanish or French Foreign Legion, Abraham Lincoln Brigade, Camel Corps, Free French & Vichy forces, French forces in China, Devil's Island, White Russian forces, Chinese Customs Service, Chinese bandits or pirates, China Navigation Company, international settlements in China, Chinese airlines, and similar topics. Wants badges, banners, medals, photos, certificates, headdresses, souvenirs, etc. Material about American volunteers or **famous soldiers of fortune** of any nationality is particularly welcome. No souvenir items produced by the Foreign Legion Veteran's Home or repros of Devils Island folk art.
　　Gene Christian
　　3849 Bailey Ave.
　　Bronx, NY 10463
　　　(212) 548-0243

★ **Trench art brass vases and lamps** made from shell casings. "I am only interested if they are engraved or embossed." No plain casings are wanted. Make a sketch or take a photo and include dimensions.
　　Al Lanzetta
　　Box 2082
　　New York, NY 10185

★ **Nazi notables** especially Heinrich Himmler, commander of the SS and Gestapo. Wants items given by or to Hitler, Goering, Hess, Goebbels, Ribbentrop, etc., including promotion and award documents, letters, silver or porcelain trophies, uniforms or medals. "I would particularly like to hear from veterans who brought back collections of material and are interested in selling the lot. I am generally not interested in any item you or a member of your family did not personally bring back from overseas." He prefers you to call him while you have the item in hand. Otherwise write, describe what you have with enough information so Tom can make an offer, or make a Xerox© of it, and include your phone number. Tom will pay $10,000 cash for some Nazi documents.
　　Thomas Pooler
　　Box 1861
　　Grass Valley, CA 95945
　　　(916) 2681338

★ **German and Japanese military** wanted, especially daggers and dagger parts, medals, badges, spike helmets, swords and flagpole tops. Pays $50 each for German WWII helmets complete with liner. Will also buy flags, "but the bigger the flag, the less they're worth." You may write, giving me your phone number. Take a photo or send insured for cash offer. This is a hobby for Dick, so he says that he's happy to help people if they send him a SASE. Makes offers only on items for sale.
　　Dick Pankowski
　　Box 04421
　　Milwaukee, WI 53204
　　　(414) 421-7056 days (414) 421-5212 eves

★ **Army Air Force A2 flight jackets**, AAF pocket insignia, sterling military aviation wings and WWI enlisted man's round collar discs. Nothing later than the Korean War.
Jerry Keohane
16 St. Margaret's Court
Buffalo, NY 14216

★ **WWII leather or cloth aviation jackets** with squadron patch and or painted artwork on the back. "I'm interested in jackets from any branch of the service (Army, Navy, or Marine Corps) and any branch of aviation (fighter, bomber, transport, etc). I am also interested in any squadron patches, escape flags, squadron history books, and photos of any airplane nose art. I don't want any currently made flight jackets with antiqued paintings or patches. If the seller did not acquire the jacket from the veteran or his family, it is probably not old. I need any label information in the jacket, a statement of condition of both the jacket and its patches or art, plus details about the art itself. Photos are extremely helpful. I also buy documented **Flying Tiger memorabilia**."
Gary Hullfish
16 Gordon Ave.
Lawranceville, NJ 08648
(609) 896-0224

★ **Photos and bits and pieces of WWII aircraft.** It doesn't matter whether allied and axis, crashed or operational, Ken wants single snaps, albums, or negatives of photos of any aircraft used in WWII. Also wants instruments, gauges, fabric, fittings, data plates, unit or group insignia, and miscellaneous bits and pieces of the combat aircraft of any nation.
Ken Francella
Box 234
Granite Springs, NY 10527
(914) 2488138

★ **WWI aviation relics and memorabilia from all nations**, especially log books, diaries, awards, certificates and medals, aircraft insignia and maker's plates, trench art made from aircraft parts, and **anything belonging to WWI aces.** He requests a detailed description, sketch or photo and "your lowest acceptable price." Also buys **pulp magazines with air war themes**, but he does not want photos, books, or other mags.
Kenneth Smith
345 Park Ave., 42nd Floor
New York, NY 10154

★ **Airplane identification models**, 1940-1970. Also promotional models, travel agency models, and **squadron and bomb group unit histories**. When writing, copy all info printed on the plane.
John Pochobradsky
1991 E. Schodack Rd.
Castleton, NY 12033
(518) 477-948

★ **Military newsreel and training films** from WWII on any military, naval, or aviation subject will be considered. May be British, American, Canadian, German, or Russian, but must be 16mm sound films shot during 1939-45. Films may be training, propaganda, or documentary. "I'll buy military aviation related films from 1903-1985, especially World War One, the Korean Conflict, and Vietnam. Give the complete title, producer, running time, and a list of defects. If you don't know the running time, measure the diameter of the reel and the diameter of the film on it. If you can, give a brief summary of contents. Nothing damaged. Also buys **military magazines.**
Edward Topor
14313 South Marshfield Ave.
Chicago, IL 60609
(312) 8476392

★ **Military unit histories** from any branch of the service, American or British. Collects all eras, but especially needs Korean and Viet Nam wars. Guarantees "highest prices" for WWII fighter or bomber groups, paratroopers, tank units or units of Black soldiers. "I am not interested in reprints or later editions. I also collect unit photos, military postcards, holiday menus, distinctive unit insignia, shoulder patches, medals, guidons, scrapbooks, berets and **toy soldiers**. If you have an item for sale and want an offer, send it for my examination. I will pay all postage, both ways."
Lt. Col. Wilfred Baumann
PO Box 319
Esperance, NY 12066
(518) 875-6753

★ **Photos or photo albums taken or collected by soldiers** during WWI or WWII. Please set the price you'd like.
Ted Fonseca
785 So. Bryant
Denver, CO 80219

★ **Military items from the Coldstream Guards.** The museum wants to buy uniforms, equipment, badges, and miscellaneous items used by the British Coldstream Guards before 1900. Other British Army ephemera from before 1900 may also be of interest. A full description includes dimensions, materials, and age. Indicate anything you believe to be unique. Donations acknowledged. No U.S. items.

Ernest Klapmeier
Coldstream Guards Living History Museum
PO Box 334
Wayne, IL 60184
(708) 584-1017　(604) 652-9047 eves

★ **Military items of Great Britain or Commonwealth nations.** This well known military author says "I'll buy hat, collar or shoulder badges, headdresses, uniforms, field equipment (belts, packs, pouches, etc.), edged weapons, and other items too numerous to mention, particularly Scottish items such as bagpipers' headdress and badges, kilts and sporrans (leather kilt purses), dirks, and knives. This 45 year veteran collector will consider 1910-1945 items, especially cloth patches, from other countries. No fakes or repros. Describe what material the item is made from, colors, etc. Note if anything seems to be missing, and all chips, dents, nicks, cracks, moth holes, stitch marks, corrosion, fading, stains, polish wear, etc. Please Xerox©.

Charles Edwards
Pass in Review
PO Box 622
Grayslake, IL 60030
(708) 223-2332

★ **Canadian military medals and cap badges.** "I'll buy all cap badges with the initials CEF on them, or badges with a number and the words "overseas battalion" and CANADA or CANADIAN on them. I'll buy any war or period. Look for the name rank and military unit on the rim of medals as some can be worth $1,000 or more." Will answer all inquiries.

Michael Rice
Box 286
Saanichton, BC V0S 1M0, CANADA

★ **Cloth shoulder insignia** of divisions, regiments, brigades, and other units. Wants Civil War to Vietnam. WWI U.S. and German insignia are of special interest. Complete uniforms welcome. He prefers to buy directly from the veteran or family. Condition is important, and a Xerox© requested. This 25 year veteran does not want fakes or reproductions.

Hank McGonagle
26 Broad St.
Newburyport, MA 01950
(508) 462-2354

★ **Military medals and decorations** from all countries and periods. Also any documents or certificates related to military awards, medals and decorations. He prefers to buy directly from the veteran or his family, and would like all associated paperwork and any information about the medals' history. Condition is important, and a Xerox© requested.

Hank McGonagle
26 Broad St.
Newburyport, MA 01950
(508) 462-2354

★ **Medals, Decorations, and Orders** for military gallantry and other campaign medals of the U.S. and British Empire, 1780 to the present. Especially wants U.S. Medals of Honor and British Victoria Crosses and U.S. Purple Hearts for WWII officially named to the Navy and Marines. Does not want reproductions. A Xerox© of both sides of the medal is helpful.

Alan Harrow
2292 Chelan Dr.
Los Angeles, CA 90068

★ **Small U.S. military relics and photographs** including ribbons, awards, paperwork, letters, buttons, canteens, knives, insignia, flags, etc. Rex operates one of the largest mail auctions of Americana in the country and is always looking for new stock, especially 19th century items. Do not bother him if "fishing for free information" or if your items are in poor condition or not for immediate sale.

Rex Stark
49 Wethersfield Road
Bellingham, MA 02019
(508) 966-0994

★ **General Douglas MacArthur memorabilia** of all types is wanted. "I'll buy books, scrapbooks, autographed items, pictures, documents, paintings, toys, dolls, medals, coins, any item with "I shall return" or "I have returned" on it, matchbooks, buttons, statues, and any item that can be documented as having belonged to MacArthur." Please send a Xerox© if you'd like an offer.
Gaal Long
Route 1, Box 40
Sardis, MS 38666
(601) 487-2457

★ **Regimental and Battalion unit flags** from all nations and periods of history. "I'll also buy flag related items such as U.S. Army spear pole tops, color woven flag cords and tassels, engraved battle honor rings and battle streamers, canvas issue flag cover bags, and close up or parade photos showing unit flags." No national flags or reenactment group flags. Please make a sketch of the flag, noting size and material. Ben can provide information about unit flags if you send an SASE with your inquiry.
Ben Weed
Box 4643
Stockton, CA 95204

★ **U.S. Navy memorabilia** including postcards, ship or station postmarks, documents, and what have you. Describe. Pricing appreciated.
Frank Hoak III
PO Box 668
New Canaan, CT 06840

★ **Anything related to the U.S. Navy ship Richard Halliburton.**
Michael Blankenship
5320 Spencer Drive SW
Roanoke, VA 24018
(703) 989-0402 eves

★ **U.S. Marine Corps memorabilia** of all kinds including recruiting posters and materials, books, photos, sheet music, belt buckles, cigarette lighters, steins, mugs, documents, autographs, art work, postcards, trench art, bronzes, novelties, and John Phillip Sousa ephemera. Also buys toy soldiers, trucks, and planes with Marine markings. Describe or make a Xerox© copy.
Dick Weisler
5307 213th St.
Bayside, NY 11364
(718) 428-9829 eves 626-7110 days

★ **U.S. Marine Corps everything.** Anything used and or worn by Marines from 1776 to 1946, such as uniforms, medals, helmets and weapons. Also buys unit histories, documents and recruiting posters. Wants photos of Marines at war, work, or play, especially amateur photos. Also wants trench art created by Marines and souvenirs of war brought home by Marines. When you write, tell what you know of the item's history. Make certain to describe the condition.
Bruce Updegrove
RD5, Box 546
Boyertown, PA 19512
(215) 3691798 eves

★ **Home Front and anti-fascist collectibles** from World War II especially those related to important events or phenomena including the holocaust, resistance, women during war, chaplaincy, soldier benevolent funds, etc. All items, from paper to pottery, considered if made during the period 1939-1946 and related to allied war effort or to anti-Semitism. Items directly related to military occupation of Germany or Japan through 1955 considered. Interested in the rare or unusual. He does not want military uniforms, weapons, medals, or insignia nor does he want souvenirs from Germany or Japan other than those related to anti-Semitism. No magazines, newspapers, or damaged items. Requires some items be sent on approval. Will reimburse postal costs.
Richard Harrow
8523 210th Street
Hollis Hills, NY 11427
(718) 740-1088 D:

*Shotgun News,
250+ page tabloid
36 times a year for $15.
Box 669,
Hastings, NE 68901*

coins & currency

Amateurs over-estimate condition

of their coins and currency, whereas pros grade collectible money severly.

The two most used price guides to coins are called "The Red Book" and "The Blue Book" of coins (one's wholesale, one's retail). They can be purchased at book, coin, or stamp stores or borrowed from most libraries.

Coins with values listed as only a few cents will find few if any takers. Dealers will tend to pay from 30%-50% of prices listed. If you own anything that catalogs over $100, you have a good item and should be extra careful about its dispersal.

There are far too many dishonest people in the world of coins. *Never sell your coins, watches or jewelry* to *someone buying out of a motel room.* More times than not, you will get less than you would be paid elsewhere.

So many tokens and medals exist, that 400 books are currently in print on the topic! Most tokens sell for 25¢ to $3, but it's important to have an expert evaluate your tokens because a few can be worth $500 or more. They usually photocopy beautifully. Set the copier to make "lighter" copies.

Medals are issued by governments, civic and athletic organizations, charities, schools, and other groups. Military valor awards bring the most money, especially those with original paperwork. Many other medals sell for bargain prices (under $20). Buyers of medals and tokens will be found throughout this book.

tony Hyman

Money

★ **Ancient Greek and Roman coins** of high quality. He also buys clean used copies of books related to ancient Greek and Roman coins and history. In business for twenty years, he issues frequent sales catalogs and holds quarterly auctions of coins and related books.
Thomas McKenna
Box 1356
Fort Collins, CO 80522

★ **Ancient coins, especially Biblical, Greek, and Roman.** Also other ancient artifacts including Egyptian, Greek, Roman, and Biblical pottery, glass, and relics. This well known expert is author of *Guide to Ancient Jewish Coins* and other books. A twenty year veteran collector/dealer, he issues periodic catalogs.
David Hendin
Amphora
Box 805
Nyack, NY 10960

★ **Spanish pieces of eight.** Wants *reales* minted in Spanish or South American mints. Seeks coins with globe and pillars known as "pillar dollars," "pieces of eight," or "pirate dollars."
Sven Stau
Box 437
Buffalo, NY 14212
(716) 825-5448 or (716) 822-3120

★ **Coin collections of all types,** "from pennies to gold." Also individual gold coins, medals, and artifacts. Also pre-1930 U.S. banknotes and commemorative coins. No pennies after 1955, nickels after 1939, dimes, quarters, and halves after 1964, or silver dollars after 1936.
Ron Aldridge
14908 Knollview
Dallas, TX 75248
(214) 239-3574 eves

★ **Silver and gold coins from any country** but especially wants perfect proof U.S. silver dollars. "No junk coins."
Robert Hiett
Maple City Coin
Drawer 80
Monmouth, IL 61462

★ **Paper money.** "I buy all U.S. paper money issued before 1929, all Confederate paper money, all Southern states money from 1861-65, and all broken bank notes from any state. I especially want to find **novelty items made of ground up paper money** before 1930, and will pay 60% of retail for them. I recommend making photocopies of bills you'd like to sell."
William Skelton
Highland Coin
Box 55448
Birmingham, AL 35255
(205) 939-3166 ex#3

★ **Paper money.** "We'll buy any foreign and obsolete U.S. and Confederate banknotes. We will buy currency in any condition and quantity in order to supply fellow collectors in all parts of the world. We deal by mail only but telephone calls are welcomed. We will buy collections as well as single notes, but **we do not want U.S. currency after 1928.**" A description should include the date, denomination, and the country of issue. A Xerox© copy is the best way to describe currency. With his available research library, he is "able to identify and appraise any banknote ever issued."
Josef Klaus
World Wide Notaphilic Service
PO Box 5427
Vallejo, CA 94591
(707) 644-3146 or (707) 643-8616

★ **Paper money.** "I'll buy collections, accumulations, and individual items of U.S. and foreign paper money. Send clear Xerox© copies of both sides. Please understand that much of what I look at will not be of interest because of poor condition or lack of collector demand." Over thirty years' experience.
Douglas Swisher
Box 52701
Jacksonville, FL 32201
(904) 448-6214

★ **All foreign paper money.** "I'll buy collections, accumulations, dealer's stock, hoards, rarities, **notgeld,** specimens, printer's proofs, banknote presentations, sample books, and **numismatic libraries.** Will travel. Have been buying since 1964."
AMCASE
Box 5376
Akron, OH 44334
(216) 867-6724

★ **U.S. Coins and paper money.** Wants estates, collections and accumulations of early **U.S. silver and gold coins**, paper money, and all other U.S. coins from 1793-1900. This nationally known dealer has been around for 40 years, and will travel to see large lots and better collections. Send a list and description. Xerox© OK.
  Littleton Coin Co., THCC
  253 Union St.
  Littleton, NH 03561

★ **German coins.**
  Ronald Selcke
  Box 237
  Bloomingdale, IL 60108
    (312) 543-4848 eves

★ **Printed or manuscript items relating to coins, currency, medals, tokens, or counterfeiting.** Especially scholarly books on coins from any period or language. Also scholarly **numismatic periodicals** and catalogs of coin auctions pre-1940 in any language. A Chapman Brothers Auction catalog between 1870-1920 will bring $50-$2,000. Also **counterfeit detectors and bank note reporters** issued in the U.S. between 1820 and 1900. No modern works, or general surveys of numismatics. Will make offers on better items.
  George Frederick Kolbe
  Drawer 3100
  Crestline, CA 92325
    (714) 338-6527

★ **Mis-strike and error coins created by the U.S. Mint.** Under most circumstances, it is best to send a good clear pencil rubbing or photocopy for his inspection and evaluation if you wish an offer. **Also paper money of 1929 issued by banks.** Send photocopy with your inquiry. Don't forget your Self-Addressed Stamped Envelope (SASE) if you want an appraisal of your coin.
  Neil Osina
  Best Variety Coin Center
  358 W. Foothill Blvd.
  Glendora, CA 91740

★ **Error coins** created by the U.S. mint. Send a photo or a rubbing of the coin.
  George VanTrump, Jr.
  Box 260170
  Lakewood, CO 80226

★ **Elongated coins pre-1960.** Also **machines to make them.**
  C. Meccarello
  Elongated Coin Museum
  228 Vassar Rd.
  Poughkeepsie, NY 12603

★ **Elongated coins.** If what you have is pre-1930, ship it to him for an offer, but *do not* ship COD. Hartzog will send you a check for the lot. Pays $1-5 and up for elongates before 1940. Large collections especially wanted.
  Rich Hartzog
  Box 4143 BID
  Rockford, IL 61110
    (815) 226-0771   Fax (815) 397-7662

★ **Any machine or device used to detect counterfeit coins or currency** including coin scales, coin detectors, scanners, grids, reporters, magnifiers, Detectographs, Laban Heath Detectors, and any other device to check weight, thickness and diameter of coins. Also any scale with markings in amounts, such as "20 dol."
  Donald Gorlick
  Box 24541
  Seattle, WA 98124
    (206) 824-0508

★ **Coin scales, coin detectors, and counterfeit detectors.** Will buy the devices and/or books about them and the processes. Will buy outright or accept on consignment for auction. Rich is one of the world's largest dealers in tokens, and has a large auction following.
  Rich Hartzog
  Box 4143 BID
  Rockford, IL 61110
    (815) 226-0771   Fax (815) 397-7662

*A periodical to know
is Coin World,
a 100+ page weekly
found at better newsstands.*

★ **Items made from macerated (ground up) currency** by the U.S. mint, including statues, plaques, plates, postcards, animals, shoes, hats, etc., have a small tag affixed which reads "This item made of U.S. greenbacks redeemed and macerated by the U.S. Government." Don buys them. Describe carefully, noting damage.
> Donald Gorlick
> Box 24541
> Seattle, WA 98124
>   (206) 824-0508

★ **Credit cards.** "I have collected credit cards for over ten years an am seriously interested in buying both the older metal charge cards and modern plastic cards. Please ship any quantity of used or new cards. I pay $4 up for older metal charge cards and will pay *at least* $15 for any metal one I need for my own collection. pre-1980 plastic cards bring $1 up, and those before 1970 average $2. More paid for local businesses, unusual types, etc. Post 1980 cards are worth 50¢ each, a few bring more. I will also reimburse your postage. Please ship for my check."
> Rich Hartzog
> Box 4143 BID
> Rockford, IL 61110
>   (815) 226-0771   Fax (815) 397-7662

★ **Credit cards.** "I'll pay a flat $2 each for credit cards, charga-plates, and charge coins made of celluloid, metal, paper or plastic, U.S. or foreign, as long as they are not abused. Ship what you have, for prompt payment." ATM and sample credit cards are only worth 25¢ each.
> Lin Overholt
> PO Box 8481
> Madeira Beach, FL 33738
>   (813) 393-5397

★ **Credit cards from any source,** paper or plastic, are desired. Send items for immediate offer and check. "I pay postage both ways."
> Noel Levy
> Box 595699
> Dallas, TX 75359
>   (214) 987-3513

Financial paper refers to all documents having to do with money, including stocks, bonds, checks, scrip, mortgages, IOU's, revenue stamps, and the like.

Collectors buy fiscal paper for the elaborate pictorial engravings.

Fiscal paper is also sought if signed by famous people or if it is pre-1830.

The value range is huge, from a dollar to $500+. Most sells for less than $30.

Financial Paper

★ **Elaborately illustrated stocks and bonds,** All are wanted but have particular need for pre-1920 railroads, mining, telegraph, aviation, oil, and automobiles. Also stocks from unusual companies, like life rafts. Items pre-1870 given special consideration. Especially want western items with autographs of important people in financial history, like Rockefeller, Carnegie, Gould, James Hill, U.S. Presidents, and other recognizable people. "Send a Xerox© copy and SASE for fast payment."

David Beach
Paper Americana
PO Box 2026
Goldenrod, FL 32733
    (407) 657-7403   Fax: (407) 6576382

★ **Stocks and bonds from any industry** but especially mining, railroads, automobile companies, expositions, and aviation. Also all other stocks if they are well illustrated and pre-1900. Stocks signed by famous people can be worth as much as $1,000. Please include your phone number.

Ken Prag, Prag's Paper Americana
Box 531
Burlingame, CA 94011
    (415) 566-6400

★ **Fiscal paper** including **rare currency (U.S. and foreign)**, checks, stocks and bonds, certificates of deposits, books on money, other items. He is particularly expert in **California currency, national currency, Mexican currency,** etc. Doesn't want items after 1935 or any kind of reproduction. A photocopy will often do, but "I'll usually request to see the item in person."

Lowell Horwedel
Box 2395
West Lafayette, IN 47906
    (317) 583-2784

★ **Stocks and bonds** before 1910, especially mining, railroads, or unusual companies. *Must be signed and have a company seal.*

Phyllis Barrella
Buttonwood Galleries
Box 1006, Throggs Neck Station
New York, NY 10465

★ **U.S. and Canadian stocks and bonds,** especially railroads, mining, oil, shipping, automotive, aviation, expositions, and others. Also documents with a printed revenue stamp. Also stocks or bonds signed or owned by someone famous. This past president of the Bond & Share Society also wants all pre-1800 certificates from any company.

Bob Kluge's American Vignettes
Box 155
Roselle Park, NJ 07204

★ **Pre-1930 stocks, bonds, checks,** drafts, and warrants from Western states.

Warren Anderson
American West Archives
Box 100
Cedar City, UT 84720
    (801) 586-9497

★ **All paper items printed with fancy engraved illustrations by security printers,** including railroad passes, semi-postals (advertising stamps), souvenir cards, and annual reports. Security Printers include the Bureau of Printing & Engraving, U.S.P.S, American Bank Note Co., Canadian Bank Note Co., and Homer Lee Bank Note Co. Wants to find *Annual Reports* of American Bank Note Co. & other security printers and engravers.

Robin M. Ellis
Box 8468
San Antonio, TX 78208

★ **Fiscal paper from South Carolina** pre-1910, especially from Charleston.

Bob Karrer
Box 6094
Alexandria, VA 22306

*To sell financial paper
a Xerox© copy
is almost essential.*

Medals & Tokens

★ **All types and quantities of tokens, medals, ribbons, badges, and related items.** He buys trade tokens, medals of all sort, hard times tokens, Civil War tokens, transit tokens especially with pictures on them ($10-$750), amusement tokens, telephone tokens, sales tax tokens, **any token or medal that is made from another item,** medals related to medicine or the arts and humanities, **love tokens,** Worlds Fair medals and elongated coins, **G.A.R. badges** and tokens, **Indian peace medals** ($1,500 up), slave tags, all **Canadian** tokens and medals, counterstamped coins, and just about everything similar to the above including advertising mirrors and **Franklin Mint token sets.** There are literally millions of varieties, and condition plays an important role in value. If what you have is pre-1930, simply ship it to him for an offer, but *do not* ship COD. Hartzog will send you a check for the lot. "We cannot make individual offers on a long list of material. Our offers are for the entire lot as we want to purchase everything. We are not interested in pricing your material for you to sell to others, sorry!" He claims to pay higher prices than anyone else. **If your collection is very early, very large, or very valuable,** phone collect and Hartzog will make arrangements to see what you have. Hartzog can also auction your materials for you if you prefer. A sample of his auction catalog is available for $3. Hartzog's lengthy wants list shows prices paid and is highly recommended.
   Rich Hartzog
   World Exonumia
   Box 4143 BID
   Rockford, IL 61110
      (815) 226-0771

★ **Medals and tokens of all sorts** are wanted by this 22 year veteran dealer. Identify what the token or medal is made from, and provide a photocopy or a good rubbing. Buys them all.
   William Williges
   Box 1245
   Wheatland, CA 95692
      (916) 633-2732

★ **Tokens and medals of all kinds and countries** including transportation tokens, advertising tokens, gambling tokens, merchants'' "good for" tokens, and the like. All old coin-like items are purchased as well as related items such as elongated or encased coins, engraved coins, pre-1900 dog tags, advertising pocket mirrors, political buttons, and stage or movie money. **Also wants "hobo nickels"** which are buffalo nickels with the Indian head re-engraved into another face. Steve will pay $10 to $35 each for these. Commemorative and award medals from Fairs are also wanted. Photocopies are usually the best way to describe what you have to sell. No large modern fantasy tokens are wanted. No Franklin Mint medals. No modern arcade tokens. Steve runs mail auctions of tokens and medals and has written books on U.S. tokens, amusement tokens, Scouting tokens and "lucky" souvenir coins, all of which are available from the author at very reasonable prices.
   Stephen P. Alpert
   Box 66331
   Los Angeles, CA 90066
      (213) 478-7405

★ **Medals and medallions from Canada, Britain, and other English speaking countries** issued for coronations, jubilees, town celebrations, victories, fraternal groups, achievement, and athletic competition. Especially military valor medals awarded to Canadians. Also **love tokens** engraved with names, initials, dates, pledges, and the like from around the world especially pre-1900. Also **merchant's "good for" trade tokens from Canada,** Britain, and English speaking countries. Also buys **Canadian paper money,** singles or collections, but only from pre-1937.
   Michael Rice
   Box 286
   Saanichton, BC V0S 1M0, CANADA
      (604) 652-9047 eves

★ **Medals, decorations, and orders,** especially military gallantry awards from U.S. and England, but will consider all governmental awards from any Western nation. No Asian awards, please.
   Alan Harrow
   2292 Chelan Dr.
   Los Angeles, CA 90068

★ **Military awards, orders, and decorations,** especially for valor. If what you have is pre-1930, ship it to him for an offer, but *do not ship COD*. He will send you a check for all you have.

Rich Hartzog
Box 4143 BID
Rockford, IL 61110
(815) 226-0771

★ **Official presidential inaugural medals.** Levine, who has been a dealer for twenty-five years, will pay $4,000 for the Teddy Roosevelt inaugural medal.

H. Joseph Levine
6550-I Little River Turnpike
Alexandria, VA 22312

★ **Medals commemorating or depicting Black Americans.** "I'll buy medals, medallions, badges, or tokens relating to, or depicting, Afro-Americans or including the words "Negro," "colored," or "Black-American." Articles may be positive or negative in tone. "I'll pay $1,200 for the Franklin Mint set of 70 American Negro Commemorative Society medals." Tell him the material (silver, bronze, or aluminum), the size in millimeters, and inscriptions on both sides.

Elijah Singley
2301 Noble Ave.
Springfield, IL 62704
(217) 546-5143 eves

★ **Animal rescue, school attendance, heroism or truant officer's** medals and badges.

Gene Christian
3849 Bailey Ave.
Bronx, NY 10463

★ **Medals, especially foreign,** related to medicine, photography, printing, cycling, railroads, aviation, Judaica, ships, Olympic Games, Africa, Australia, West Indies, Far East, Monaco, or New Zealand. No badly worn items.

Hedley Betts
Box 8122
San Jose, CA 95155
(408) 266-9255

★ **Masonic chapter pennies** all varieties and countries, but especially from Maine. Indicate the chapter name, number, and location. Storck will pay from $3-$40 each. No modern coins counterstamped with Masonic emblems.

Maurice Storck, Sr.
775 W. Roger Rd., #214
Tucson, AZ 85705

★ **U.S., British, and Soviet valor decorations** and war medals. Foreign awards given to Americans are of great interest, especially Soviet World War II orders and decorations. All items *must* have supporting documentation of the award to U.S. personnel. Hlinka also buys all letters, certificates, or documents pertaining to valor awards. Will pay $2,000-$2,500 for U.S. Medal Of Honor awarded 1917-1970. He encourages you to photocopy both sides of medals and supporting paperwork. Hlinka has been dealing in medals for 40 years and has been an officer in various collectors societies.

Peter Hlinka
PO Box 310
New York, NY 10028
(212) 409-6407

★ **Tokens, medals, and exonumia (non money coinage) from Georgia** including "good for" tokens issued by merchants, saloons and lumber companies, encased and elongated coins, advertising and commemorative medals and tokens, including those issued for the 1895 Atlanta Cotton States Exposition, and any agriculture awards and medals from Georgia state fairs. "Top prices paid for collections or single items."

R.W. Colbert
4156 Livsey Rd.
Tucker, GA 30084

★ **Franklin and other private mint issues.** "I will purchase all bronze, silver and gold singles, sets and other items such as plates, bronzes, etc., in any quantity. Many silver or gold pieces are worth substantially above issue price. Bronze tokens and medals are worth less than their issue price, most of them under 25¢ apiece. I pay reasonable prices for all modern mint items. Since I do not specialize in *Franklin Mint* items, do not ship them without inquiring first. State the price you want, or request my offer. If my offer is not accepted, I do not pay return postage on modern mint medals that have been shipped." There is little market for *Franlin Mint* items, so it's best to contact Rich first by phone or letter so you fully understand their value or lack of it. Rich is the nation's largest dealers in exonumia (coins that aren't legal money).

Rich Hartzog
Box 4143 BID
Rockford, IL 61110
(815) 226-0771

stamps

If you own a few stamps

you can look them up in *Scott's Catalog of Stamps* a book found in almost all public libraries. If you own many stamps, you are facing many hours of tedious work.

Only a few 20th century U.S. stamps have substantial value, but you should watch for stamps on envelopes or folded letters before 1900.

Letters dating before the Civil War can have surprising value, from as little as a few dollars, to many hundred. Value is affected by the condition, the stamp, the cancellation, the carriers, and where it was mailed from and to. Although empty envelopes sell, an enclosed letter with interesting contents can also affect value.

When looking for stamps, look for letters about business or trade which give prices or other information about local areas. Personal tales of travel, Indians, mining, war, colorful people, famous events, disasters, and other activities are often worth money. It was someone looking for stamps who paid $20 for a box of envelopes at a Beverly Hills yard sale and later resold the letters for $500,000.

Buyers of early letters are often interested in postmarks. You should examine them with an eye toward historic places, vanished cities, and the like.

tony hyman

Stamps

★ **Collections and accumulations of foreign and United States stamps.** Buys
[1] Albums, any country or mixed;
[2] Stockbooks and unsorted boxfuls of duplicate stamps;
[3] **Old envelopes** with stamps from any country;
[4] Mint sheets and blocks;
[5] Old **revenue (tax) stamps** on documents of all kinds;
[6] **Duck hunting** and fishing permit stamps, mint or used, especially on licenses;
[7] Stamp-like labels and seals of all kinds;
[8] **Postal-related souvenirs** including booklets, cards, and stamp announcements;
[9] **Philatelic reference books** from any period or country in any language;
[10] **Stamp magazines** pre-1945;
[11] **Worldwide stamp catalogs** pre-1925;
[12] **Philatelic auction catalogs** pre-1945;
[13] Photos or real photo postcards of mail carriers, mail trucks, post offices, etc.
This 35 year veteran collector/dealer says, "If in doubt, <u>include it!</u> I must be one of the last people who collect EVERYTHING in stamps and stamp-related items." He says stamp collecting is a highly specialized hobby, and that even the most common looking items (especially envelopes with unusual markings) may have value. "Because of their nature and sheer numbers, stamps have to be sent for my personal inspection. Call first, because I can give you clear shipping instructions and help you eliminate unwanted items like newer stamp catalogs, 3-ring notebooks, and empty albums. I can give guidance on how to ship stamps to prevent damage and preserve value. Return postage normally required, but negotiable."
Douglas Swisher
Box 52701
Jacksonville, FL 32201
(904) 448-6214 eves

★ **U.S. and foreign stamps and covers** (envelopes) have been purchased for resale for over 30 years by this veteran dealer.
Bill Colby
Kenrich Co.
Box 248T
Temple City, CA 91780
(818) 286-3888

Don't make these THREE COMMON ERRORS

(1) Cutting stamps off older envelopes and documents;

(2) Improperly storing and handling mint stamps;

(3) Forgetting that labor costs of preparing stamps for resale will affect how much you are paid.

★ **Stamps from any country in any quantity.** "We'll buy everything you have," says Harvey, who has been dealing through the mail since 1934! He wants collections of singles, plate blocks, sheets, covers, and rarities. If you have a large or valuable collection, Harvey Dolin & Company will come to your home. Smaller collections may be shipped to them for their cash offer. "Your satisfaction is always guaranteed," say their ads. Dolin buys **stampless (pre-Post Office) letters, Confederate stamps and envelopes, Wells Fargo envelopes, and Duck Hunting stamps.**
Harvey Dolin & Company
5 Beekman St., #406
New York, NY 10038
(212) 267-0216

★ **Various stamps and envelopes.** McHenry has been in business for 30 years and provides a long list of covers (envelopes) he wants, including Presidential free franks, letters mailed without stamps, color advertising on envelopes, expositions, pioneer flights, and more. You should request his list if you have early or unusual envelopes for sale. In addition to covers, he buys **revenue stamps, Confederate stamps and letters, precancels,** and **stamps from U.S. possessions.**
Gordon McHenry
Box 1117
Osprey, FL 34229
(813) 966-5563

★ **U.S. or foreign stamp collections.** This well known Southern California dealer has been buying and selling stamps for more than 40 years in San Bernardino. Call first.

Fred E. Coops' Stamps
115 Central City Mall
San Bernardino, CA 92401
    (714) 888-1025

★ **U.S. or foreign stamp collections,** pre-1960.
Ron Aldridge
14908 Knollview
Dallas, TX 75248
    (214) 239-3574

★ **U.S. Internal Revenue special tax stamps,** licenses and permits for making and selling beer, liquor, wine, tobacco, cigars, margarine, firearms, opium and marijuana. Also for businesses as brokers, pawnbrokers, dentists, lawyers, etc., No stamps from between 1873 and 1885 with punched holes are wanted. Also want state stamps and licenses for any business, activity, or product including hunting and fishing. **USDA export stamps** and certificates for meat and meat products are also sought. **Ration coupons** for gasoline, fuel oil, sugar, etc., are wanted, but no war books (1,2,3, or 4) or any red/blue tokens. "Photocopies are very helpful."

Bill Smiley
Box 361
Portage, WI 53901
    (608) 742-3714 eves

★ **Federal and state revenue and special tax stamps** including document stamps and all stamps used to show that taxes had been paid on a product. Special tax stamps are large and look like licenses to engage in various occupations, such as liquor dealer, cigar salesman, wine maker, etc. Photocopies are strongly urged by this 30 year veteran buyer.

Hermann Ivester
5 Leslie Circle
Little Rock, AR 72205
    (501) 225-8565 eves

★ **Stamps, covers, and postal stationery from Hong Kong and Macao.** Covers are decorated or embellished envelopes, and among philatelic items sought by this Hong Kong postcard/stamp dealer, who requests you Xerox© and price what you have.

Kin Leung Liu
1517 South Angeline St.
Seattle, WA 98108
    (206) 767-3025

★ **Envelopes with stamps mailed in the Orient.** Buys nearly all envelopes with stamps mailed in China, Tibet, Korea, Hong Kong, Nepal, Mongolia and Japan. Advisable to first phone or send a Xerox copy by mail or fax. Pledges to pay post on items sent on approval.

Bridgewater Onvelopes Collectibles
680 Route 206 North
Bridgewater, NJ 08807
    (201) 725-0022 (201) 707-4647 fax

Always leave stamps on envelopes and documents. They're worth more.

*Linn's Stamp News
70+ page weekly tabloid
of articles and ads for $28.
Box 29
Sidney, OH 45365.*

Available at most newsstands

art

Paintings and prints

usually have little value, but a few turn up each year worth $10,000 and more.

If you are not an art critic, trained to recognize valuable art, get expert advice. Paintings and prints that look sloppy or amateurish to you can be snapped up by buyers for big dollars.

If you own an original painting which has been passed down in your family for two or more generations, check the current value of that artist's work. Many painters whose work cost $100 or less at the turn of the century are worth 100 times that today.

When searching for valuable prints, look for those signed and numbered in pencil, as they often have value. Some inexpensive like Currier & Ives, Sarony and Knapp, and a few others have developed cult status and dollar value. Be particularly careful about signed prints from the 1930's, as prints of that period are "hot" right now.

To sell paintings, a sharp 35mm photo is essential. You must also give the dimensions of the painting or art. Selling prints requires the dimensions of the image and of the border. Xerox© prints if possible. List all signatures and dates on paintings and prints.

Folk art is another area where amateurs should not make judgments about value. Take good quality 35mm slides or prints of any handmade items.

tony hyman

Paintings & Prints

★ **Paintings by listed artists of all types and periods,** including 20th century. This first rate auction house regularly handles works of art from $100 to $100,000 and may be the perfect outlet for your better quality paintings. Send a photo, five the dimensions, describe any damage and note any signature.

    James D. Julia Auctions
    Box 830
    Fairfield, ME 04937
       (207) 453-7904 Fax: (207) 453-2502

★ **Paintings, prints, and photographs made by artists in** *Who Was Who in American Art.* Primarily interested in American Impressionism, Peter will consider a wide range of works from 1800-1950, as long as the artist is listed. Among special interests are:

    [1] Prints and paintings about the sport of **competitive rowing** ($500-$1,500);
    [2] **Color woodblock prints,** particularly the *White Line* prints of the Provincetown, MA, printmaker group ($500-$2,000);
    [3] **Paintings and prints by American women artists** ($500 -$10,000+);
    [4] Vintage **photos of Abraham Lincoln** ($500-$10,000).

No wood engravings from *Harper's, Leslie's,* etc. Send photograph and the dimensions.

    Peter Falk
    206 Boston Post Rd.
    Midison, CT 06443
       (203) 245-2246

★ **Pre-1900 chromoliths and hand colored prints** on topics of natural history (birds, bugs, fish and animals), military, medicine, old West, Indians, costumes and fashion, Negroes, sports, and art Nouveau. Will also buy **advertising art and labels** on similar themes or with other attractive pictures. Describe fully for this major graphics dealer, known for paying high prices for quality items. Joe is author of two books on advertising labels.

    Joe Davidson
    Aaron Industries
    5185 Windfall Road
    Medina, OH 44256
       (216) 723-7172

★ **Old etchings and lithographs worldwide** if before 1900. American etchings and lithographs may be as late as 1950. **Particularly interested in the work of Currier & Ives,** John Sloan, Thomas Rowlandson, Thomas Hart Benson, J.S. Curry, Frank Benson, Daumier, **Audubon,** Goya, A. Horn, Millet, Piranesi, and Rembrandt. "I'll pay from $1,000 to $10,000 for large 19th century lithographic views of Baltimore." He has no interest in 20th century European prints, and is not interested in the work of Parrish, Icart, Mucha, R.A. Fox, or Wallace Nutting. You'll have to tell him the artist, title, subject, size, and condition. "While I do purchase through the mail and will make tentative offers on items before I see them, I cannot commit to purchases until I have personally examined the items. It would be unprofessional to do otherwise."

    Craig Flinner
    Craig Flinner Gallery
    505 N. Charles St.
    Baltimore, MD 21201
       (410) 727-1863

★ **Paintings and limited edition prints** by listed artists, particularly American and Oriental. Give the size and condition. Include photo.

    Ivan Gilbert
    Miran Arts & Books
    2824 Elm Ave.
    Columbus, OH 43209
       (614) 236-0002 eves

Look on the back of paintings for evidence they have been exhibited. Artist signatures and picture titles are often found on the stretcher or on the back of the canvas itself.

★ **Illustrations by well known 20th century illustrators** such as Maxfield Parrish, the Leyendecker brothers, Norman Rockwell, Rolf Armstrong, Vargas, Petty, Rose O'Neill, Mucha, Erte, Grace Drayton, Will Bradley, and Coles Phillips. Wants original art, prints, posters, advertising, calendars, magazines, and books 1895-1930. Especially Maxfield Parrish calendars for *Mazda* and pin up calendars 1920-1960. give him the dimensions and condition of your print, and tell what book, magazine, calendar, etc., it came from. Note the condition. Denis does not want "free appraisals, pen pals, or time wasters." He is the author of price guides for Parrish, Rockwell, Petty/Vargas, and others, and edits *The Illustrator Collector's News*, available for $12 a year. Write for his catalog of books and prints for sale.

　　Denis Jackson
　　Box 1958
　　Sequim, WA 98382
　　(206) 683-2559

★ **Pre-1900 prints, engravings, chromoliths, and woodcuts** on many topics including city scenes of the U.S. and Canada, natural history (birds, bugs, fish, and animals), military uniforms, fashion, the old West, children, Expositions and Fairs, disasters, mining, Indians, and Oriental life in America. These are very difficult to buy by mail, and must be examined under high magnification. If your print is framed, he believes "it is wise to remove the print from the frame in order to find the publisher and date of publication." Indicate the size of the image, and the size of the overall print, including border. Include an SASE.

　　John Rosenhoover
　　100 Mandalay Road
　　Chicopee, MA 01020
　　(413) 536-5542

★ **Paintings of 18th and 19th century American political figures** or historic events. Please send a photo along with a description of the painter's signature if there is one. Only original oils or watercolors in fine condition are wanted. No paper prints, engravings or illustrations torn from books.

　　Rex Stark
　　49 Wethersfield Road
　　Bellingham, MA 02019
　　(508) 966-0994

★ **Woodblock prints by European, American and Canadian artists** (1895-1950) in color or black and white. He buys only pencil signed prints created and signed by the artist whose work they are. Particular interests include:

　　[1] **Landscapes and marinescapes** by the widely traveled artist, **Arthur Wesley Dow**, Ipswitch MA. Signed, but never numbered, his prints are usually 5x7 inches or smaller, often in the popular "pillar print" size of 5x2.5 inches. Can be worth $1,000 and more.

　　[2] **Prints by the Provincetown printers**, especially their "white line prints" characterized by blocks of color separated by white lines. These run in size from 3x4 inches to 16x20, but are mostly from 5x7 to 8x10 inches. Values run from $1,000 to $15,000.

　　[3] **Prints with Oriental subjects**, but only those by Western, often British, artists. People to look for include Bartlett, Hyde, Keith and Lum. He does **not want** Oriental prints from Japan and the Far East.

"I do not want wood engravings from *Harper's Weekly* or other magazines and newspapers. Nor do I generally buy woodblock illustrations from books." If your print is loose and unframed, a Xerox© is quick and accurate. If you feel you have one of these valuable prints, the expense of a color copy may be justified. If your print is framed, try to get a good photograph by shooting it outdoors in open shade. Thomas will make offers *if your item is genuinely for sale*, but is not interested in making free appraisals. In business for 10 years, Thomas issues annual catalogs and will send you an illustrated wants list if you send a #10 (long) envelope.

　　Steven Thomas, Inc.
　　PO box 41
　　Woodstock, VT 05091
　　(802) 457-1764

"Do I have a woodblock?"

Experts describe woodblocks as "very rectangular" with sharply defined borders. When printed in color, a slight registration problem is often apparent. They are usually signed in pencil outside the image.

★ **Paintings and prints depicting smoking.** Buys a wide range of prints, paintings, and other items with a tobacco theme. All sizes, all media, all nationality, all tobacco topics considered but prefer smaller paintings. Buys pre-1930 magazine illustrations, prints, advertising, signs, posters, photographs, and other items. Especially interested in cigars, but anything related to tobacco consumption will be considered. Buying for resale and for personal collection.
>   Tony Hyman
>   Box 3028
>   Pismo Beach, CA 93448
>   (805) 773-6777 Fax: (805) 773-0117

★ **Paintings of the Hudson River or Catskill Mountains.** No modern works. A complete description includes dimensions, condition, and the signature.
>   Edward Sheppard
>   221 Water St.
>   Catskill, NY 12414
>   (518) 943-2169

★ **Paintings of Indians and Eskimos.** Please send a photo for a prompt response. It's helpful if you can read the signature. Dealers price your goods; amateur sellers may request an offer.
>   Barry Friedman
>   22725 Garzota Drive
>   Valencia, CA 91355
>   (805) 296-231859

★ **Paintings and prints depicting boats** including whaling, yachting, racing, working, etc., are sought by this well known dealer in marine antiques. Give the dimensions, history, and a careful account of any damage or restoration. Photo suggested. Will give "ball park" estimates of value on ordinary items, but appraisals are for a fee. Sporadically issues a pictorial catalog for refundable $5.
>   Andrew Jacobson
>   Marine Antiques
>   PO Box 2155
>   South Hamilton, MA 01982
>   (508) 468-6276

★ **Paintings depicting the industrial/machine age.** Wants paintings and signed prints depicting workers in industrial settings. **WPA paintings and prints** are also sought. Send photo.
>   David Zdyb
>   2988 William St.
>   Buffalo, NY 14227

★ **Original paintings for American magazine covers and story illustrations,** 1900 to date. "I'll buy art for magazines and stories in the following genres: aviation, western, fantasy, science fiction, erotica, adventure, detective, mystery, and movie. **Also buys art for pin up calendars, advertising campaigns, and paperback book covers with similar themes.** These covers were generally vividly painted on 24" x 30" canvas. Rough sketches for cover or story art can also have value. "The rule of thumb is don't ever second guess about what is and isn't worth something. Send us pictures and let us evaluate it for you." Sellers should submit a photograph of the art, along with the dimensions and an accurate description of the condition of the surface (any soil, holes, dents, scratches, etc.). Note the signature, in the unlikely event there is one. Make certain to check the back of the painting because exhibit and/or publishing history may be recorded there. Most pulp paintings range from $500 to $2,000 in value, depending upon the artist, subject and condition, although some Tarzan and movie covers can bring up to $10,000. Jim is a popular award winning artist and comic book illustrator who writes extensively on pop culture and art and is author of two books on the history of comics.
>   Jim Steranko
>   Supergraphics
>   PO Box 974
>   Reading, PA 19603
>   (215) 374-7477

★ **Original paintings by American illustrators for magazine covers,** magazine story illustrations, or advertising, 1910-1980, including artists such as Norman Rockwell and all his contemporaries. Also original art for magazine or calendar pin ups, especially by Vargas or Petty, but others as well. Has special interest in sexual or sentimental themes (children, dogs, families, patriotism, etc.).
>   Charles Martignette
>   455 Paradise Isle, #306
>   Hallandale, FL 33007
>   (305) 454-3474

★ **California paintings.** Wants to purchase the work of Edgar Payne, William Wendt, Maurice Braun, Franz Bischoff, Hanson Puthuff, Elmer Wachtel, Ben C. Brown, and Clarence Hinkle.
>   Robert Lewis
>   2940 Westwood Blvd #2
>   Los Angeles, CA 90064
>   (213) 475-8531

★ **Paintings by Cincinnati artists** and others. Buying work of Blum, Twachtman, Hurley, Sawier, Weis, Vogt, Wessel, Selden, Casinelli, Duveneck, Sharp, Farney, Nourse, Potthast, Volkert, and other American and European artists. Please send a good clear photo of items for sale. If in doubt, telephone. Have your work in hand when you do.
> Cincinnati Art Galleries
> 635 Main St.
> Cincinnati, OH 45202
>   (513) 381-2128

★ **Paintings by New Orleans and Gulf Coast artists.** Buys oil paintings from artists of New Orleans and the surrounding area, especially from the 1920's and 30's such as A.J. Drysdale, Clarence Millet and G.L. Viavont among others.
> Sanchez Galleries
> 4730 Magazine St.
> New Orleans, LA 70115
>   (504) 524-0281

★ **Sketches, drawings, and paintings by Philip Boileau and Robert Robinson,** American 20th century illustrators. Boileau is known for his 1900-1917 paintings of attractive women done for private customers and for magazine covers, and other commercial purposes. Robinson worked commercially from 1907-1952 also on magazine covers and other commercial work. Please provide Bowers with a good close up color photograph and as much information about the work as you can. The value of paintings varies greatly, and Bowers will work with you to determine value.
> Q. David Bowers
> Box 1224
> Wolfeboro, NH 03894
>   (603) 569-5095

★ **Wallace Nutting pictures, books and other ephemera,** including furniture, lamps, wooden dishes, post cards, calendars, and greeting cards. "Not interested in recent items, or things that are damaged, broken, or otherwise in less than very good condition," says this five year veteran Nutting dealer.
> James Buskirk
> Eleanor's Hand Tinted Photos
> 312 Starling Way
> Anaheim, CA 92807
>   (714) 998-9615

★ **Wallace Nutting pictures, books, furniture, and other memorabilia.** Collections are preferred, but single pieces will be considered. No size is too large. Mike says he'll travel anywhere to view collections of considerable size and diversity. Among Nutting pictures, Mike particularly wants interiors, scenes with people, animals, and houses. He does not want single pictures of common exteriors of apple blossoms, country lanes, trees, lakes, and ponds, although he will take these as part of a large collection. When describing pictures, give the title, frame size, and condition. When describing books give title, edition, color of the cover. Mike is author of a price guide to Nutting and accepts items on consignment for Nutting auctions.
> Michael Ivankovich
> PO Box 2458
> Doylestown, PA 18901
>   (215) 345-6094

★ **Engraved portraits and photographs of famous people** in all walks of life. Will consider items loose or in books. Photocopies make the best descriptions.
> Kenneth Rendell
> Box 9001
> Wellesley, MA 02181
>   (617) 431-1776   fax (617) 237-1492

★ **Black and white steel engravings** of birds, animals, nature, romance, and fantasy. Interested in most subject matter other than city views and violence.
> Gregory Mills
> Box 2073
> Hollywood, CA 90078

★ **Prints and illustrations,** including **yard longs, calendars,** and prints of flowers, children, beautiful women etc., including calendars and books before 1919. **Also illustrations by** Harrison Fisher, Francis Brundage, Newton Wells, Catherine Klein, Maud Humphrey, and others. Also wants **magazines** with fashion prints and color pictures of women and children, such as *Ladies Home Journal, Women's Home Companion, Butterick, McCall's,* etc. Buys only color prints. Prefers unframed items. Must send photocopy. Note *all* defects. Will make approximate offers, but must see to determine condition before buying.
> Linda Gibbs, Heirloom Keepsakes
> 10380 Miranda
> Buena Park, CA 90620
>   (714) 827-6488

★ **Prints, American and European.** Buys a wide range of prints. Generally prefers topical prints rather than scenics. Give a complete description, including size of image, size of sheet, colors, and any and all information printed or written at the bottom of the print.
Kenneth Newman
The Old Print Shop
150 Lexington Avenue at 30th Street
New York, NY 10016
(212) 683-3950

★ **Paintings, drawings and original art for advertising** airlines, automobiles, gasoline, tires, soft drinks or whiskey. Especially likes paintings for ads for *Coke*, alcohol, movies, tobacco products, and other culturally significant items and events. If in doubt, call.
Charles Martignette
PO Box 293
Hallandale, FL 33009
(305) 454-3474

★ **Commercial printed art by J.G. Scott** who specialized in cute round faced children. Most of his work is signed "JG Scott" and can be found on women's magazine covers, advertising blotters and calendars from the 1920's and 30's, and on children's greeting cards from the Gibson Co.
Robert Stauffer
3235 Mudlick Road SW
Roanoke, VA 24018
(703) 774-4319

★ **Maxfield Parrish printed art.** "I'll buy prints, books, calendars, cards, posters, etc., especially Edison *Mazda* calendars. If you phone, have the piece in front of you!"
Michelle Ferretta
888 Lasuen Dr.
San Leandro, CA 94577
(415) 522-1823

★ **Maxfield Parrish** calendars (all years), complete books, full decks of playing cards, original prints, autographs and unusual advertising items. Not interested in book fragments or modern reproductions. Describe condition. She offers "thousands of dollars" for an original oil.
Debra Buonaguidi
540 Reeside Ave.
Monterey, CA 93940
(408) 375-7345

★ **Original art and prints by F. Earl Christy** who specialized in beautiful society women. Wants covers from movie and women's magazines, advertising, fans, blotters, calendars, postcards, and anything else illustrated by Christy.
Audrey Buffington
2 Old Farm Road
Wayland, MA 01778

★ **Paintings and prints by R. Atkinson Fox, Maxfield Parrish, and Icart.** Claims she'll pay "top cash."
Christine Daniels
La Petite,
135 E. Shiloh Road
Santa Rosa, CA 95403
(707) 838-6083

★ **R. Atkinson Fox prints wanted.** "I'll buy prints, calendars, postcards, or anything else with artwork by R. Atkinson Fox." Please telephone or send a Xerox©.
Pat Gibson
38280 Guava Drive
Newark, CA 94560
(710) 792-0586

★ **Currier & Ives prints, and chromos published by Prang.** No modern reproductions.
Edward Sheppard
221 Water St.
Catskill, NY 12414
(518) 943-2169

★ **Art Deco color prints,** posters, calendars, from the 1920's and 30's.
R. Bright
Box 449
Noel, MO 64854
(417) 475-6367

★ **Damaged art of all kinds** is wanted. "If people send a good sharp photo I will make an offer on paintings, sculpture, and Currier & Ives prints that have been damaged but are still in restorable condition."
Alan Voorhees
Art Restoration
492 Breesport Rd.
Horseheads, NY 14845

Orientalia

★ **Fine quality Oriental antiques** with special emphasis on Japanese netsuke, inro, lacquer, and fine Chinese porcelains. Marsha buys, sells, and collects all types of Oriental antiques from early ceramics to late 19th century items including furniture, Japanese swords, sword fittings, jade carvings, and jewelry. Many small ivory carvings are worth between $1,000 and $10,000. Modern or reproduction items are not wanted, nor is anything imported since 1960. Marsha is a senior member of the American Society of Appraisers, specializing in Oriental art, and will appraise for a fee. She will also help amateur sellers with fine items genuinely for sale if you make a good photo, give the measurements, and draw or Xerox© all markings or signatures.

    Marsha Vargas
    The Oriental Corner
    280 Main St.
    Los Altos, CA 94022
      (415) 941-3207

★ **Antique Japanese netsuke, inro, and other art** including pouches, pipes and pipe cases, ivory and wooden statues, Japanese lacquer, metalwork, cloisonne, paintings, and ceramics. Will pay $10,000 up for ivory and wood 18th and 19th century netsuke and $500 for netsuke inlaid in various materials. No roughly carved pieces, man made materials, or factory pieces bought in hotel lobbies, airports or gift shops. If you provide clear close up photographs of your netsuke from all angles and an exact drawing of the signature, Denis will make an offer. He is member of the Appraisers Association of America and does formal appraisals for a fee.

    Denis Szeszler
    Antique Oriental Art
    Box 714
    New York, NY 10028
      (212) 427-4682

consider a donation

★ **Obsolete corporate inventory, services, or other assets** can be donated to EAL, who barters your donations with colleges in exchange for tuition scholarships for disadvantaged youth. Donations can range from hard goods such as paint, paper products, office furniture, computers, and lab equipment to such intangibles as catering, conference centers, hotel rooms, transportation, and the like. EAL is a 501(c)(3) tax-exempt organization and run by a bunch of downright nice folks. Call for more information.

    Peter Roskam or Eric Anderson
    Educational Assistance, Ltd.
    P.O. Box 3021
    Glen Ellyn, IL 60138
      (708) 690-0010
      (708) 690-0565 fax

Folk Art

★ **Figures and native carvings made of ivory.** Ivory can be elephant, walrus, whale, hippo, wart hog, or narwhale, but he wants ivory art, not small items like pins, combs, spoons, brooches, toothpicks, and other utilitarian objects. Picture is a necessity, and he prefers you to set a price. Terry also buys **Primitive and pre-Columbian artifacts.**

Terry Cronin
207 Silver Palm Ave.
Melbourne, FL 30901

★ **Ivory items of all sort,** including Eskimo and Oriental carvings, scrimshaw, ivory tusks (elephant, walrus, whale, hippo, etc.), dresser sets, poker chips, dice, and billiard balls. **Dave does not want** ivory jewelry, letter openers, or sewing and crochet tools, nor does he buy bone or synthetic objects. David advises that bone has fine brown specks, and plastic imitations will sometimes have air bubbles or pits, whereas real ivory has grain, somewhat like fine wood. If you are selling tusks, give the length around the outside curve, and the diameter at the large end. He asks you to use a flashlight to carefully inspect for cracks in the hollow end. Follow standard description form. A sample of their lovely illustrated catalog is $1. Please list your phone number and best time of day to call.

David Boone's Trading Company
562 Coyote Rd.
Brinnon, WA 98320
(206) 796-4330   Fax (206) 796-4511
(800) 423-1945

★ **American folk art** such as **carvings, weathervanes,** whirligigs, **duck decoys,** pre-1900 **quilts,** figural 19th century **pottery, fishing decoys,** windmill weights shaped like animals, figural **architectural pieces such as cherubs or gargoyles,** small hand painted boxes, **game boards, handmade dolls,** Indian rugs, baskets, Indian pottery, **folk paintings of children** and animals, and **hooked rugs** with pictorials rather than patterns. No damaged or repaired pieces.

Louis Picek
Main Street Antiques
Box 340
West Branch, IA 52358
(319) 643-2065

★ **American folk art of the 20th century.** "This is a very subjective area of collecting, and not everyone agrees on what's folk art. I like, and will buy, a variety of paintings and sculpture. They have to be well done, but naive in perspective, or quirky in subject. Narrative "story telling" paintings are especially desirable although I don't want anything cute or fakey, and don't want "memory" pictures done recently of some old-timely scene." If you have something you think might be good, and is for sale, send a photo along with a complete history and description. "I prefer people to state what they want for a price," says this 20 year veteran collector and expert, "as too many people have overblown expectations, and are insulted when they get fair offers."

Linda Campbell Franklin
2716 Northfield Rd.
Charlottesville, VA 22901

★ **Mourning pictures in watercolor or embroidery.** In either medium, these are characterized by willow trees, tombstones, birth and death dates, weeping women, etc. These are often for famous people, presidents, generals, etc. Those honoring "no-bodies" are more rare and desirable. Will pay at least $100 and as much as $300-400 for better ones.

Steve DeGenaro
Box 5662
Youngstown, OH 44504

★ **Prisoner of war straw figures** woven or plaited by French prisoners during the early 1800's. Other prisoner art from the 19th century, including **ivory carvings** are sought.

Lucille Malitz
Lucid Antiques
Box KH
Scarsdale, NY 10583
(914) 636-3367

★ **Folk art** including painting, sculpture, weaving, wood, etc., including American Indian, Oriental, African, or Eskimo art. Provide the dimensions, condition, and photos. Condition critical. Special interest in current "outsider art." Contact Ivan only if your item is for *sale.*

Ivan Gilbert
Miran Arts & Books
2824 Elm Ave.
Columbus, OH 43209
(614) 236-0002

★ **Tramp art** items made from cigar boxes or fruit crate wood which has been layered into edge-notched pyramids. Typical items include boxes, picture frames, doll furnitures, banks, wall pockets and small furniture. Especially wants large items like chests of drawers, but will buy those only if they are in fine condition with a minimum of missing pieces. He will consider painted or gilded examples (most are varnished). Original surface is important and information about its origin (such as signatures and dates) is a plus. **He does not want** items made from ice cream sticks, clothespins or matches, nor does he buy items recently repainted or in rough condition. "A photo is almost essential," he advises, "and make sure you include everything you know about the item's history." Inspect closely for signatures and dates.

    Michael Cornish
    Cigar Box Antiques
    195 Boston Street
    Dorchester, MA 02125
      (617) 282-3853

★ **Wax carved portraits, paper cuttings, and pinpricked pictures** of scenery or groups of people. Give a good description of what you have and set the price you want.

    Laurel Blair
    Box 4557
    Toledo, OH 43620
      (419) 243-4115

★ **Folk art weavings worldwide,** including rugs, saddle blankets, tapestries, ponchos, and other old, fine, and rare pieces. Will consider Oriental, Middle Eastern, European, Indian, and South American fine quality rugs and other weavings. Also **Eskimo and American Indian weavings.** Also **needlepoint, paisley shawls, and hooked rugs.** Nothing after 1920 or that is machine made.

    Renate Halpern Galleries
    325 E. 79th Street
    New York, NY 10021
      (212) 988-9316

★ **Micronesian, Polynesian, and New Guinea masks, ceremonial bowls, and the like.** Some interest in scrimshaw, but none in items from New Zealand and the Maori.

    David and Cathy Lilburne
    Antipodean Books
    Box 189
    Cold Spring, NY 10516
      (914) 424-3867

★ **African or South Pacific tribal art** including masks, weapons, musical instruments, jewelry, household objects, bowls, furniture, feather work, textiles, and "almost anything else that was made for tribal use and not for the tourist trade." Especially old collections including artifacts with elaborate decoration and animal, human, or spirit figures. Collections of **pre-Columbian pottery from Mexico or Peru** are sought, but *only* if documented and authenticated. High quality tribal art can bring as much as $100,000 so is worth inquiry. **Does not want** items made after 1970, ebony carvings, tourist items, or figures holding spears. A photo is essential and Jones would like to know where the item was collected.

    Charles Jones African Art
    6716 Barren Inlet Road
    Wilmington, NC 28405
      (919) 686-0717

"I prefer people to state what they want for a price. I have had a horrible time with people who have over-blown expectations who accuse me of cheating or insulting them."

This complaint is being heard more and more from listees. Not everything you have is valuable... Buyers know the market.

Figurines

★ **Bronzes and porcelain figures** prior to 1935. Describe all markings and give dimensions and colors. Photo is highly recommended.
Arnold Reamer
Box 26416
Baltimore, MD 21207
    (301) 944-6414 or (301) 486-8412

★ **Bathing beauties and "naughties" figurines.** Wants small bisque or porcelain figurines, 1900-1940, which are nude, in bathing suits, in their underwear, stockings, or dressed in lace. They are finely modeled and in coy poses. Some had actual mohair wigs. Naughties were hollow figurines, often of children or women, intended to be filled with water so they peed or squirted out of their breasts. Other naughties appeared to be an innocent figurines until lifted up or turned over, displaying a risque (often explicit) side. "I am especially interested in finding Black naughties or bathers with a wig, but I am interested in *all* fine examples of bathing beauties and naughties. I am also looking for old catalogs, advertisements, and other information about them. A good wigged naughty is worth from $250-450, depending upon the pose and execution." **No Japanese figures** or reproductions. Generally does not want damaged pieces, but will consider extraordinary figures with minor damage. Size and pose is important so accurate measurements and a sketch, copy, or photograph is almost essential. Include your phone number. Will buy only if you grant right of refusal after inspection. If you collect these, please call. She'd love to meet you.
Sharon Hope Weintraub
2924 Helena
Houston, TX 77006
    (713) 520-1262

★ **Female figurines, especially nudes** in bronze or porcelain in Art Deco or Art Nouveau, 1880-1930. Wants *Dresden, Meissen, Capo di Monte, Royal Dux, Amphora, Teplitz*, and other fine makers. Nothing that has been broken or repaired. No figurines of children or popular limited edition collectibles.
Madeleine France
Past Pleasures for 20th Century Women
Box 15555
Plantation, FL 33316
    (305) 584-0009

★ *Royal Doulton* figurines and character jugs are purchased by this well known dealer who has been in business for 20 years. "No collection is too large or too small," he says, encouraging you to call toll free as long as you have the name and HN number of the figurines and the name and size of the character jugs. They are especially interested in the rarest items, since they maintain a computer list of collectors worldwide who are looking for specific types of figure. Ed lectures frequently in the U.S. and England, and has edited price guides to these popular figures. He is not interested in buying dinnerware, and does not do pattern matching.
Ed Pascoe
Pascoe & Co.
545 Michigan Ave.,
Miami Beach, FL 33139
    (800) 872-0195 Fax (305) 532-8543

★ **John Rogers statuary.** If you have a white or putty colored plaster grouping of figures, check for the signature "John Rogers," often accompanied by "New York" and a date and patent number. These figural groups can be from 12" to 48" high, with most just under two feet tall. Themes are Civil War, Americana, theater, etc., with a few of them comedic. A few are made of material other than plaster. Perfect condition is always best, but he will consider damaged pieces, as he is a restorer of Rogers' work. He needs to know the name of the piece (which is always found on the front of the base) and the condition of the putty colored paint... how badly is it flaked. Prefers you to phone with your statue in front of you.
Bruce Bleier
73 Riverdale Rd.
Valley Stream, NY 11581
    (516) 791-4353

★ *Heubach* **porcelain or bisque figurines and other items** including children's tea sets, trays, religious items, and anything else. Porcelain portraits of the Three Fates, singly or as a group, would be a treat to her and worth hundreds of dollars. Draw a picture of the mark, and give all colors. Frances is cataloging every *Heubach* product made and she'd like to hear from anyone with anything unusual by Gebruder Heubach, even if it is not for sale.
Frances Sanda
5624 Plymouth Rd.
Baltimore, MD 21214

★ *Hummel* **figurines** with full bee and crown markings. Please give complete information concerning condition and all markings on the bottom. He is available to restore *Hummels*.
Dr. Donald Hardisty
Don's Collectibles
3020 E. Majestic Ridge
Las Cruces, NM 88001
    (800) 762-2263 or (505) 522-3721

★ **Pre-1971** *Hummel* **figurines,** especially figurines with the Crown or Full Bee marks. **Also wants** *Goebel* vases, figurines, half dolls, wall plaques, etc., especially monks in red robes. Also *Hummel* calendars from 1950-75. **Also** *Precious Moments* **figurines** with the triangle or hourglass mark or with no mark at all. All *Hummels* must be marked. Please give all marks and numbers and note whether you have the original box. Please don't offer *Hummel* plates, bells, or anything chipped or cracked.
Sharon Vohs-Mohammed
Box 14192
Tallahassee, FL 32317
    (904) 385-3595

★ *Goebel* **figurines of cats.** "I don't want cats other than those made by *Goebel*. I don't want *Goebels* other than cats." Include marks and numbers on the bottom of the figurine.
Linda Nothnagel
Rt. 3
Shelbina, MO 63468
    (314) 588-4958

★ **Nude figurines** in any material, 1900-1990.
Charles Martignette
PO Box 293
Hallandale, FL 33009
    (305) 454-3474

★ **Snow Babies.** "I'll buy any and all clean German "Snow Babies" (little china children in pebbly snow suits), especially jointed Snow Babies and 'action' Babies with animals or engaged in some activity." Doesn't want Babies from Japan, Taiwan, or Dept 56, nor does she want damaged or faded items. Give the size and markings, if any, and note all damage, no matter how minor. "Photo would be great." **Also buys small German bisque Santas.**
Linda Vines
PO Box 721
Upper Montclair, NJ 07043
    (201) 746-5206

★ *Pen Delfin* **rabbits.** This mail order dealer in modern *Pen Delfin* bunnies is always looking for retired rabbits of all types, from the middle 1950's on. Will buy from all of this popular cute English series, including the larger rabbits, houses, etc. Wants undamaged items suitable for resale. Note the figure's name (given on the bottom).
George Sparacio
PO Box 791
Malaga, NJ 08328
    (609) 694-4167 eves

★ **Wade figurines,** whimsies, Disney, circus, friars, animals, fairy tales, party crackers, etc.
Ken Clee
PO Box 11412
Philadelphia, PA 19111
    (215) 722-1979

★ *Noritake* **human and animal figures.**
Tom Burns
109 E. Steuben St.
Bath, NY 14810
    (607) 776-7942

Many collectors want figurines depicting their hobbies: gambling, sports, pipe smoking, etc.

Make certain you check the index at the back of the book and look for buyers in the suggested sections.

★ *Bossons* artware including character heads, wall plaques and figures. These are made of plaster or "stonite," a vinyl/stone mixture. Figures made of the latter are marketed as **Fraser-Art.** "We buy modern figures that are still available, but are primarily interested in obtaining discontinued figures, which can be worth $85 and up, with a few rare ones valued at over $10,000." There are *Bossons* "look-alikes," but only figures with backs marked "Bossons, Congleton, England, copyright" are sought. Slightly damaged figures will be considered, since Dr. Hardisty is a restorer approved by *Bossons*. He is a charter life member of the International *Bossons* Collectors Society, a licensed dealer of modern *Bossons*, and author of the price guide to these popular British figures.

Dr. Donald Hardisty
Don's Collectibles
3020 E. Majestic Ridge
Las Cruces, NM 88001
(800) 762-2263 or (505) 522-3721

★ *Osborne Ivorex* plaques. These are three dimensional plaster composition wall plaques that are hand painted and then waxed. They were made between 1899 and 1968. In addition to plaques, the company made statuary of people and buildings, jewelry boxes, and a few other small items. Subject matter of the plaques included individual characters to large cathedrals. Anne Hathaway's home, and that of poet Robt. Burns were popular subjects, as were other buildings and monuments in the U.S., Canada, and Europe. Sizes range from a few inches to over a foot, with 3"x5" and 6.5"x9" two popular sizes. Values range from $30 up, with a few reaching $200+ because there are relatively few collectors. Some are factory framed in wood, making them premium items. Some poor quality reproductions exist. Most, but not all, *Ivorex* plaques are marked "A/O" (Arthur Osborne) on the lower right or left corner. In the 1930's they began marking them on the back with a three line ink stamp with the company name and copyright. Small vertical oval and rectangular plaques sometimes have markings on the lower rim. Andy wants to hear from other collectors for purposes of starting a club.

Andy Jackson
823 Carlson Ave.
West Chester, PA 19382
(215) 692-0269 fax (215) 272-7040

Collector Plates

★ **Collector's plates.** The Ernst family is one of the nation's larger dealers in collector's plates. If you have a collection of plates to sell, they will help you in one of two ways. If your plates are items they have requests for and can sell promptly and easily, they will purchase some or all of them outright. In the more likely event that you have some plates in less demand, they will sell them for you on consignment. They will price them according to the current market, catalog them, and notify their extensive mailing list that your plates are available. The price they ask is dependent upon how quickly you wish to sell them. They charge 20% of the item's selling price for this valuable service. When you call or write, they will send you complete information plus specific instructions on how to pack and ship your plates safely. The company has been in business for 21 years and is listed in Dun & Bradstreet.

Ross, Ruth, and Ruth Ann Ernst
Collectors Plates
7308 Izard
Omaha, NE 68114
(402) 391-3469

★ **Collector's plates and limited edition figurines** such as *Hummel, Cabbage Patch, Royal Doulton, Bing & Grondahl, Anri,* and *Bumpkins*. The Selesh family deals only in limited edition items, not in antique or commemorative plates, nor in dinnerware. If offering a plate for sale, indicate whether you have the original box, authenticity certificate, and other paperwork. This major dealer and appraisal service will make NO FREE OFFERS but may help you in other ways to dispose of what you have.

Adam Selesh
Tiffany Steven's Collectibles
478 Ward Street Extension
Wallingford, CT 06492
(203) 284-0306

paper

All interesting paper

items will find a buyer, especially paper printed before 1900. You will find buyers of paper in nearly every chapter of *I'll Buy That Too!*

Paper items are collected because of **who** printed it, **when** it was printed, **where** it was printed, **why** it was used, **how** or by whom it is illustrated, or **what** message is printed on it.

Buyers of paper items want you to tell them about creases, tears, fading, discoloration, foxing (little brown spots), trimming, silverfish, or other damage. The amount of damage acceptable varies from collector to collector, topic to topic. No one buys junk or brittle paper items.

Value of paper items varies widely. Although a few very expensive items exist, most paper is modestly priced. Keep your eyes open for catalogs, sales literature, and other paper about business or manufacturing. Historians of various professions and industries eagerly seek these. The index of this book will help you identify a buyer.

Autograph collectors agree that sellers must do two things. **First**, include a Xerox© with your inquiry. **Second**, be prepared to ship your autographed item for inspection. Autographed items are often one of a kind, so every piece must be individually evaluated as to importance and condition. Only after viewing the actual document will most dealers be willing to pay your requested price or make you an offer. Too, there are many fake autographs, particularly of politicians and movie stars.

tony hyman

Miscellaneous Paper

★ **Paper goods of all sorts** if in good condition are sought by one of the West's better known ephemerists. Kenrich Company buys postcards, sports cards, photographs, stamps and covers, philatelic items, posters, stereoviews, menus, letters, timetables, slave documents, brochures, calendars, original artwork, bumper stickers, blotters, book marks, playing cards, pin-back buttons, cookbooks, insurance policies, score-cards, match book covers, napkins, coasters, seed packets, guide books, reward cards, panoramic photos, letterheads, movie lobby cards, scrapbooks, diaries, logs, signs, autographs, souvenirs, games, trade cards, paper dolls, fans, almanacs, directories, and more. If it's paper, collectible, and in fine condition, Bill will probably buy it. Closed Sunday and Monday.
>Bill Colby
>Kenrich Company
>9418T Las Tunas Drive
>Temple City, CA 91780
>(818) 286-3888   Fax: (818) 286-6035

★ **Collections of paper on just about any subject.** Wants any collection of the old or unusual. "Immediate answer if you include your phone number."
>George Theofiles
>Miscellaneous Man
>Box 1776
>New Freedom, PA 17349
>(717) 235-4766 day

★ **Accumulations of paper items from before 1920.** Especially wants stocks and bonds, but also bills, checks, and letters with "pretty vignettes." Buys some **Western, circus, and magic posters** as well. Does not buy anything made after 1940. If you have a large collection, or just boxes of old paper, please call on the phone, with your items in front of you.
>David Beach
>Paper Americana
>PO Box 2026
>Goldenrod, FL 32733
>(407) 657-7403   Fax: (407) 657-6382

★ **Rare documents** from the time of papyrus to the present. Buys collections of letters, manuscript (hand written) material, land grants, photograph collections, diaries, hand colored maps, atlases, and "anything unusual in paper."
>Ivan Gilbert, Miran Arts & Books
>2824 Elm Ave.
>Columbus, OH 43209
>(614) 236-0002

★ **Rare documents in all fields,** from autographs to stock certificates, from song sheets to pardons and passes, including handwritten documents, land grants, maps, and "most any other unusual paper items." Gordon buys lots of all sizes, from single items to entire estates.
>Gordon McHenry
>Box 1117
>Osprey, FL 34229
>(813) 966-5563   Fax: (813) 966-5563

★ **Accumulations of paper items from before 1910.** Prefers Western items, but will consider all collections, especially related to the military, mining, railroads, energy, banking, express companies, law enforcement, etc.
>Warren Anderson
>Box 100
>Cedar City, UT 84720
>(801) 586-9497

★ **Manuscripts and printed documents** with interesting content. These need not be signed by anyone famous. "I particularly like colonial American documents from before the Revolutionary War, but will consider material from all periods. Please describe the contents and why you think the item is unusual enough for me to buy." Xerox© advisable.
>Chris Wilson
>2762 N. Washington Blvd.
>Arlington, VA 22201
>(703) 525-5930

★ **Paper collectibles,** specifically movie memorabilia, autographs, character (pop culture) paper and picture postcards, are sought by this West Coast paper dealer. Not interested in reproductions. Wants all the information you can provide, including how you came by the item. DOES NOT MAKE OFFERS.
>Mike Rasmussen
>Box 726
>Marina, CA 93933
>(408) 384-5460

★ **Items fringed in silk.** Buys Victorian greeting cards from any holiday or event and made in any style from single sheet to little booklets, as long as they have silk fringe. Also wants sachets, menus, advertising, and similar trinkets, as long as they are silk fringed, 1875-1925.
  Ronald Lowden, Jr.
  314 Chestnut Ave.
  Narberth, PA 19072
    (215) 667-0257 anytime

★ **Trade cards**, especially better quality and specialized collections. Especially interested in clipper ships, mechanical banks, Currier & Ives, metamorphic and mechanical, and other better items. Will pay $300 up for fine cards depicting mechanical banks, and $150+ for clipper ships. No interest in damaged common cards or stock cards with no company name. Must actually see an item in person before making offers. Will not do phone appraisals or evaluations of items not for sale.
  Russell Mascieri
  6 Florence Ave.
  Marlton, NJ 08053
    (609) 985-7711   fax (609) 985-8513

★ **Prints, calendars, trade cards, advertising, and magazine covers** featuring the work of name artists such as Frances Brundage, Ida Waugh, Jessie Wilcox Smith, Maud Humphrey, Torres Bevins, Mable Lucie Attwell, Henry Clive, Harrison Fisher, Coles Phillips, Rose O'Niell, Grace Drayton, Charlotte Becker, Maxfield Parrish, and others.
  Madalaine Selfridge
  Forgotten Magic
  33710 Almond St.
  Lake Elsinore, CA 92330
    (714) 674-9221

★ **Collections of labels, stickers, and poster stamps** from before 1960. Wants collections of colorful, smaller graphics of all types, even if there are many duplicates. Immediate answer if you include your phone number.
  George Theofiles
  Miscellaneous Man
  Box 1776,
  New Freedom, PA 17349
    (717) 235-4766 day

★ **Paper puzzles in any printed format.** "I'll buy crosswords, mathematical puzzles, rebuses, tangrams, brain teasers, picture puzzles, etc. The format can be a book, magazine, pamphlet, broadside, trade card, or newspaper, but I do not want 'hidden image' puzzles or those that are too juvenile, intended for small children." In general, he is most interested in items from before 1950, the earlier the better, although value depends on the quality of the puzzle and the rarity of the material. He also wants material about the history of puzzles, directories of puzzles, and "anything with the byline 'Sam Loyd,' a famous turn of the century puzzlist." Give the date and condition, and describe the puzzle or state its objective. **Not interested in jigsaw puzzles.**
  Will Shortz
  Games Magazine
  19 West 21st Street
  New York, NY 10010
    (212) 727-7100 days

★ **Rebus puzzles.** Rebus puzzles are combinations of pictures, syllables, and letters which create a message when decoded. Linda wants hand drawn rebus puzzles in letters or post cards. She only wants noncommercial hand drawn puzzles, not printed ones, but they can be from any period, if they're interesting. Preferably wants pencil or pen and ink rather than paintings, with less sophisticated drawings the most interesting to her. She doesn't care how difficult the puzzle is. Doesn't want trade cards, greeting cards, or puzzles printed in books.
  Linda Campbell Franklin
  2716 Northfield Rd
  Charlottesville, VA 22901

★ **Scrapbooks compiled by children or adults before 1895.** Books can be any size and a variety of contents may be of interest *except* those consisting primarily of newspaper clippings. You must write detailed descriptions of contents, noting materials that are damaged or trimmed. Your alternative is to photocopy pages from the book. He promises to return your materials promptly and unmarked if he invites you to ship it for inspection. Condition is an important factor in value for this 40 year vet.
  Ronald Lowden, Jr.
  314 Chestnut Ave.
  Narberth, PA 19072
    (215) 667-0257 anytime

★ **Scrapbooks and collections of loose die-cut, embossed Victorian paper.**
Madalaine Selfridge
Forgotten Magic
33710 Almond St.
Lake Elsinore, CA 92330
    (714) 674-9221

★ **Scrapbooks of Victorian era trade cards.**
Russell Mascieri
6 Florence Ave.
Marlton, NJ 08053
    (609) 985-7711   fax (609) 985-8513

★ **Passports** and some other travel documents, pre-1940 American or any foreign. Documents must be complete, nothing missing, removed, or torn. Xerox© the page with the owner's description and inside pages that have been used. No overpriced passports belonging to "celebrities."
Dan Jacobson
Box 277101
Sacramento, CA 95827

★ **Consular and foreign service stamps on documents** of any type, 1906-1955. Send photocopy.
H. Ritter
68 Heatherwood
Norristown, PA 19403

★ **Admission tickets of all types.**   "I buy sports, political, theatrical, and social tickets. Must be complete. No stubs or foreign items. No transportation tickets for trolleys, railroads, etc. Please price what you have and ship it on approval."
David Lamb
48 Woodside Drive
Rochester, NY 14624

★ **"Dirty letters"** are purchased. Buyer wants hand written or typed sex or risque letters 1800-1975, ideally with the original envelope if mailed. Even better if any photos or other items mailed with the letters are still there.
Charles Martignette
PO Box 293
Hallandale, FL 33009
    (305) 454-3474

Stamped Self-Addressed Envelopes are a must if you wish an answer.

The phrase "photocopy" refers to a Xerox© or similar machine. It is not the same as a "photograph" which you take with a camera.

★ **Diplomas.**   Will buy college and advanced degree diplomas before 1930.
Bob Hut
Box 1495
New York, NY 10163

★ **Christmas catalogs, 1950's and 60's.** wants *Sears, Montgomery Wards, Spiegel, JC Penny,* and *Alden* catalogs 1958-69 only. "Please contact me with prices and what you have."
David Snow
E. 4217 22nd Ave.
Spokane, WA 99223

Paper Dolls

★ **All types of paper dolls, cut or uncut,** one or a collection as long as they're pre-1960. Will buy commercial, magazine, or newspaper dolls. Sellers should list paper dolls by name, if possible, and indicate whether they are cut or not. Photocopies are helpful. Fran (a collector for 20 years) is available for slide shows about paper dolls.
 Fran Van Vynckt
 7412 Monroe Ave
 Hammond, IN 46324

★ **Paper dolls of all types.** Wants to buy antique paper dolls, 1910-1960 books, greeting card dolls, magazine dolls from adult or children's publications, newspaper comic strip dolls from the 1930's and 40's such as *Flash Gordon* and *Brenda Starr*. Celebrity or not. If neatly done, will buy cut dolls. When describing your doll, give the name, if possible, and include any writing on the front or back of the doll, the box, or the book.
 Madalaine Selfridge
 Forgotten Magic
 33710 Almond St.
 Lake Elsinore, CA 92330
  (714) 674-9221

★ **Paper dolls and paper toys** of all kinds, cut or uncut, from boxed or book sets, newspapers, magazines, cereal boxes, etc. Especially wanted are paper dolls of real people. For 23 years, Loraine has published *Celebrity Doll Journal*, a quarterly, available for $6.25/year. If you really want to sell your dolls, indicate names, dates, and quantity, and whether cut or not. Also indicate condition, mentioning bends, tears, missing parts, and tape. No need to photograph or photocopy any more than the doll (not the whole set). Will buy rare sets even when damaged, and buys some current items, but no Betsy McCall sheets.
 Loraine Burdick
 Quest-Eridon Books
 5 Court Place
 Puyallup, WA 98372

★ **Paper toys, figures, and buildings,** especially toys and models by *Builtrite,* but interested in any paper dolls and soldiers in good condition. In business for more than a decade, Paper Soldier publishes a large and informative catalog for $4.
 Jonathan Newman
 Paper Soldier
 8 McIntosh Lane
 Clifton Park, NY 12065
  (518) 371-5130

Collectors seldom want paper dolls with bent arms and legs or with taped joints, although dolls may be cut out and still be desirable.

Do not mend anything with tape!

Numbers on boxes or dolls are useful info to savvy collectors.

Xerox your dolls.

Autographs

★ **Autographs in all fields** are purchased for resale by this collector/dealer. He buys old letters, envelopes, canceled checks, and various documents and photos signed by famous people.
  Bill Colby
  Kenrich Company
  9418T Las Tunas Drive
  Temple City, CA 91780
    (818) 286-3888   Fax: (818) 286-6035

★ **Autographs in all fields** including presidents and their wives, statesmen, scientists, inventors, entertainers, characters from the old West, and famous people in all walks of life. Especially wants handwritten letters of any president, particularly modern presidents. "Autographs of most politicians are worth little unless they became president or rose to great prominence. Most TV and movie stars since 1960 are worth little, except for a few exceptions such as Marilyn Monroe." Purchase offers are free. Appraisals are for a fee. His sample catalog of autographs for sale is available for a long SASE.
  Paul Hartunian, Autographs
  127B East Bradford Ave.
  Cedar Grove, NJ 07009
    (201) 857-7275

★ **Autographed letters and documents from ancient times to modern days in all fields.** Significant medieval documents and manuscripts are always of interest. This 28 year veteran dealer **does not want** autographs obtained by writing celebrities, modern politicians, or movie stars. A photocopy is suggested.
  Kenneth Rendell
  PO Box 9001
  Wellesley, MA 02181
    (617) 431-1776 fax (617) 237-1492

★ **Handwritten documents and letters of famous Americans.** "We particularly want Washington, Adams, Jefferson, Franklin, Hancock, and Lincoln, and specialize in U.S. Presidents." Famous scientists, inventors, authors, and musicians are also sought. Mention all imperfections in your letter.
  Steve and Linda Alsberg
  9850 Kedvale Ave.
  Skokie, IL 60076
    (708) 676-9850

★ **Letters, signed photos and signatures of famous people** in any category: Presidents, Hollywood, NASA, sports, Civil War, art, music, literary, scientific, historical, rock and roll, theater, aviation, old west. Also interested in old handwritten diaries, collections of letters from the not-so-famous, handwritten recipe books, and anything written while traveling across America. Wants California and New Orleans letters from 1800-1870. Offers $1,000 for signed Buddy Holly photo. Please photocopy what you have. **Does not want** autopen or printed signatures.
  Michael Reese II
  PO Box 5704
  S. San Francisco, CA 94083
    (415) 641-5920

★ **Autographs, signed books, and rare documents in all fields.** Particularly wants U.S. Presidents and first ladies and "investment quality items." Handwritten letters of Presidents while in office, particularly of William Henry Harrison and James A. Garfield, whose letters could be worth as much as $50,000! No facsimile or secretary signatures. "It is usually necessary to see the actual item, particularly in order to make a firm offer." They publish a free monthly catalog of autographs for sale.
  Michael Minor and Larry Vrzalik
  Lone Star Autographs
  PO Drawer 500
  Kaufman, TX 75142
    (214) 932-6050   10-10 CST any days

★ **Historical documents signed by U.S. Presidents.** "I'll buy land grants, military and civil commissions, ship's papers, passports, appointments of judges, postmasters, ambassadors, etc. I search for clean documents with no holes, stains, tape, or trims. I concentrate on quality. I'd love to find a George Washington land survey (to $10,000) or a Supreme Court appointment. Every mark, every fade, every crease or wrinkle *must* be described accurately."
  Richard Lechaux
  HC-60 Box 3712
  Fort Valley, VA 22652
    (703) 933-6305

★ **Autographed non-fiction books.** Will consider any, but is particularly interested in the Soviet Union, Eastern Europe, Asia, Communism, Socialism, and conservative authors.
Edward Conroy
SUMAC Books
RD#1 Box 197
Troy, NY 12180
(518) 279-9638 eves

★ **Autographs in all fields** with a particular emphasis on presidents, political, military, and historical figures. He does not want Hollywood or TV people after 1940. "The more information the better. If it is an autograph of someone famous, describe what it is written on, whether faded or bright, whether written in pen or pencil, and the wording of any inscription."
Chris Wilson
2762 N. Washington Blvd.
Arlington, VA 22201
(703) 525-5930

★ **American and foreign autographs in all fields throughout Western history,** including politicians, Presidents, signers of the Declaration of Independence, music and the arts, literature, the military, and scientists. Will buy one or collections. This 20+ year veteran is not interested in unsigned documents of any sort.
Robert Batchelder
1 West Butler Ave.
Ambler, PA 19002
(215) 643-1430   Fax: (215) 643-6613

★ **Checks autographed by any famous person** are wanted, especially bounced checks. He'll pay from $750-$3,500 for checks he especially wants from Henry Ford, Harry Houdini, Greta Garbo, Buddy Holly, President Taylor, Gerald Ford, Lyndon Johnson, Al Capone, Richard Nixon, Charles Chaplin, president Tyler, and others. "I want to know the condition, the date, whether the check is signed or endorsed, and the color of the check. If the seller has a price in mind, please quote it up front. If the seller has no idea of value, then I will make him a fair quote." He also buys pay orders, certificates of deposit, an other small size financial documents. Send a fax or photocopy.
Olan Chiles
1892 Avenida Aragon
Oceanside, CA 92056
(619) 724-2339 Fax: (619) 726-4964

★ **Famous people's signatures on manuscript documents, land grants, maps, photographs,** and other early paper. Has particular interest in Southern and Civil War figures and in letters signed by James McHenry, Washington's Secretary of War.
Gordon McHenry
Box 1117
Osprey, FL 33559
(813) 966-5563

★ **Historic early American autographed documents,** letters, and ephemera in all fields. Also buys autographed books, maps, prints, stock certificates, and bonds.
Earl Moore
Box 243
Wynnewood, PA 19096
(215) 649-1549 anytime

★ **Composers, musicians, and singers of classical music** including signed photographs, letters, musical notations, and manuscripts. Does not do free appraisals.
J.B. Muns
Books & Fine Art
1162 Shattuck Ave.
Berkeley, CA 94707
(510) 525-2420

★ **Composers, musicians, opera singers, and movie stars** from the late 1800's to the 1950's. Prefers to buy signed photos, letters with important content, or musical quotes. Among the many people they would like to find are Kathleen Ferrier, Conchita Supervia, Maria Galvany, Celestina Boninsegna, Fernando De Lucia, Guilio Grisi, and Marietti Alboni. "We are not interested in the autographs of current performers, but will pay very well for first class older items. Condition is very important. We request Xerox© copies and prefer to see the item in person, especially when large collections are involved." Will make offers for amateurs. Dealers, price your goods.
Bill Safka & Arbe Bareis
Box 886
Forest Hills, NY 11375
(718) 897-7275

★ **Autographs of celebrities and "news-worthy persons"** including photos, letters, checks, or other documents signed by mass murderers, assassins, spies, heads of state, Royalty, rock stars, presidents, and other famous and infamous persons. Examples: Arafat, Jackie Onasis, Madonna, Michael Jackson, David Berkowitz, John Hinkley, etc. Not interested in printed signatures or autopens. Xerox© copies are a must if you want an offer. "If I cannot tell from your Xerox whether the signature is authentic, it will be necessary to ship it for my inspection. Before I buy items, I expect the seller to sign a statement guaranteeing that they own the item in question and that there are no liens against it."

> Sheldon Kamerman
> World Wide Auctioneering Group
> 466 11th Street, #F
> Lakewood, NJ 08701
> (908) 363-6161 weekends

★ **Autographs of Hollywood stars** with a strong interest in young ladies of the screen. Buys some autographs of deceased famous folks in science, politics, military, business and religion. No sports personalities, although "I want *anything* signed by Walt Disney." Tom publishes address directories of famous people (mostly movie stars) and is interested in obtaining home addresses you might know. Tom prefers you to set the price wanted but will make offers. Send a Xerox©. His autograph catalog is $3.

> Tom Burford
> Celebrity Access
> 20 Sunnyside Ave, #A241
> Mill Valley, CA 94941
> (415) 389-8133

To sell posters, give dimensions, country of origin, and a sketch or photo. Condition is critical (as with all paper) so report all trimming, edge damage, soil, water stains, tears, fading, or anything else wrong.

Posters

★ **Old posters of all types.** This 30 year veteran dealer says "I'll pay top prices for any printed poster done before 1960, especially WWI and WWII, film, travel, theater, circus, and transportation (ocean liner, railroad, and air). Also buys poster books, periodicals, postcards, photos of posters being printed or posted. Include phone for immediate answer.

> George Theofiles, Miscellaneous Man
> Box 1776
> New Freedom, PA 17349
> (717) 235-4766 day

★ **Vintage posters 1880-1950, all countries and subjects,** especially U.S. posters from WWI and II and 1890-1910 American advertising. Army recruiting posters by Christy and Flagg from WWI bring $500-$1,500. No reproduction posters. Poster Master offers an illustrated $3 catalog of 800 posters for sale.

> George Dembo, The Poster Master
> 9 Passaic Ave.
> Chatham, NJ 07928
> (201) 655-6505

★ **Original posters 1890-1960** including, but not necessarily limited to, posters for airlines, air shows, automobiles, bars, books, cycles, circus, drinks, fashion, films, food, entertainers, soap, restaurants, sports, opera, theater, and travel. No reproductions. Provide photo, dimensions, and details of damage. NO OFFERS.

> John Campbell Fine Art
> Box 22974
> Nashville, TN 37202
> (615) 385-3303

★ **American posters of World War One.** No foreign, repros, or damaged. Give the main slogan on the poster, the size, the artist if known, and the condition.

> Ken Khuans
> 155 Harbor #4812
> Chicago, IL 60601
> (312) 642-0554

★ **Pre-1940 posters which advertise magazines.** Condition must be excellent.

> Leon Williams
> 467 Portland Ave.
> St. Paul, MN 55102
> (612) 291-1639

famous places

Everywhere you go

people collect memorabilia from various towns, states, regions or countries.

Check all paper, china, glass, souvenirs, advertising, photographs, letterheads, stock certificates, maps, postcards, prints, catalogs, etc. There is a good chance that someone is collecting the area from which they came.

People who collect souvenir china, and other regionally related collectibles, tend to read and advertise in: *Antique Souvenir Collectors News,* a twelve page bimonthly magazine of ads and articles, available for $15 per year from
>Box 562
>Great Barrington
>MA 01230.

If you are interested in selling things related to the history of the region in which you live, you might consider visiting the local historical society. Although local societies almost never purchase things for display, donating to them may have tax advantages.

If you have an item of local interest and can't find a buyer in *I'll Buy That Too!,* you might pay a visit to local antique shops and see if there is a free regional antiques newspaper covering your area. Always try *I'll Buy That Too!* first.

tony hyman

Nationwide

★ **City view books.** Buys city souvenir books which show city and town scenes, 1870-1940. Xerox© the cover, title page, and a sample pictorial page. Describe the condition of the cover, binding, and the contents pages.
Herbert Mitchell
Avery Library
Columbia University
New York, NY 10027

★ **Wooden Adirondack souvenirs.** "I'll buy the weird and the wonderful! I'm seeking items made in the Adirondacks and sold all over America, usually stamped with the name of the place where they were sold." The distinguishing feature of these rustic wood souvenirs is the maker always left some bark on the piece. He wants **lamps, mugs, tankards, picture frames, smoker's stands, clocks, plaques, inkwells, towel racks, wishing wells,** and just about anything else except nut bowls and salt and pepper shakers. Many of these items had decals of Indians on them and better pieces had carvings of big game animals like moose or bears. He will also buy **miniature canoes and canoe paddles** and other birch bark items of all types. All souvenirs must be completely undamaged. Price and describe fully in your first letter, realizing that these are inexpensive items. "You're not sitting on a gold mine with a handful of tourist trade souvenirs," he cautions, promising to answer immediately.
Barry Friedman
22725 Garzota Drive
Valencia, CA 91355
(805) 296-2318

★ **Roadside ephemera.** Wants ephemera from any diners, tourist courts, motels, gas stations, drive-in theaters, and other roadside businesses, with particular interest in those designed to serve the Lincoln Highway traveler between 1920 and 1970. Buys postcards, photos, guidebooks, advertising, roadside signs, and books and magazines having to do with road travel. Especially interested in Pennsylvania items and seeking all ephemera from the S.S. Grand View Ship Hotel.
Brian Butke
2640 Sunset Drive
West Mifflin, PA 15122

The Northeast

★ **New Hampshire ephemera** from before 1900. Please price and photocopy.
Alf Jacobson
Box 188
New London, NH 03257

★ **Great Barrington, Massachusetts, and Berkshire County souvenirs** including pictorial china, plates, pins, shakers, spoons, cups, postcards, photos., etc., especially souvenir china, 1905-1916. Towns to look for are Housatonic, Van Deusenville, Risingdale, Egremont, North Egremont, Stockbridge, and Sheffield.
Gary Leveille
Box 562
Great Barrington, MA 01230

★ **Pennsylvania Turnpike memorabilia** of all kinds. What have you?
J.C. Keyser
12 Springcreek
Westerville, OH 43081

★ **Ocean Grove, New Jersey, memorabilia** including souvenirs, maps, photos, postcards, books, glass, porcelain, and anything else from this camp meeting seaside resort located south of Asbury Park. "I want everything, including beach, hotels, auditorium, etc."
Norman Buckman
Box 608
Ocean Grove, NJ 07756
(800) 524-0632

★ **Hoboken, New Jersey, memorabilia** including paper ephemera, books, photographs, postcards, prints, maps, articles, letterheads, labels, and any manufactured item with the word "Hoboken" molded or printed on the item. "We buy almost everything, no matter how trivial," including **personal reminiscences of early Hoboken residents** for inclusion in various local histories which they are writing. You have the Hans' permission to ship any pre-1949 Hoboken item on approval. They'll pay postage both ways.
Jim and Beverly Hans
Hoboken Historical Museum
Box M-1220
Hoboken, NJ 07030
(201) 653-7392

★ **New Castle, Delaware.** Items of historic value, including books, photos, postcards, etc.
Mel Rosenthal
507 S. Maryland Ave.
Wilmington, DE 19804
(302) 322-8944

★ **Adirondack Mountains memorabilia** including all books, paper ephemera, photos, stereoviews, hotel brochures and registers, transportation timetables, manuscripts, maps, guidebooks, diaries, postcards, sheet music and prints related to any mountain towns and lakes of the Adirondacks. Lake George, Lake Placid, Lake Luzerne, Old Forge, Keene Valley, Plattsburgh, and the counties of Clinton, Herkimer, Essex, Lewis, Warren, St. Lawrence, Franklin, and Saratoga are among the many places which interest him.
Breck Turner
With Pipe and Book
91 Main St.
Lake Placid, NY 12946
(518) 523-9096

★ **Brooklyn, New York, and Long Island ephemera.** Historically interesting paper items are sought, including county and city atlases, city directories, photos, bill and letterheads, trade and business cards and similar items.
Brian Merlis
2569 West 2nd Street, Suite 5B
Brooklyn, NY 112233
(718) 645-3743

★ **Souvenir china and glass from Western New York state,** especially Rochester, LeRoy, and Batavia, but other cities as well.
Burton Spiller
49 Palmerston Rd.
Rochester, NY 14618
(716) 244-2229

★ **Coney Island souvenirs** including Dreamland, Luna Park, or Steeplechase. He particularly wants pitchers, glasses, dishes, and other cream colored diamond and peg pattern custard glass marked "Coney Island."
John Belinsky
84 Day St.
Seymour, CT 06483
(203) 888-2225

★ **Junction Canal between Elmira, NY, and Athens, PA (1856-1872).** Wants photos and all ephemera of any type about this canal. Also items from any branch extensions such as that along the Susquehanna River in Pennsylvania.
F.C. Petrillo
95 Miner St.
Wilkes-Barre, PA 18702

★ **West Point memorabilia.** "I'll buy almost anything made of china or metal, but also want postcards featuring West Point. Send for my list of items I"m especially seeking."
Pat Klein
5 Pasco Hill Road
Cromwell, CT 06416

*Do not send items
without permission.*

*Postal Regulations say
if you do
you are giving it away.*

*The person you send it to
has the right to keep it free!*

The South

★ **Tennessee.** Bookstore owner Snell says "I'll buy Tennessee history, authors, pamphlets, and maps. Also books and documents **by or about presidents Jackson, Polk, and Johnson** and books by Tennessee authors such as Alfred Crabb, H.H. Kroll, and Samuel Cole Williams." Especially wants *Charles Egbert Craddock* by Edd Parks. No library discards.
   William Snell
   3765 Hillsdale Drive NE
   Cleveland, TN 37312
      (615) 472-8408

★ **Southern souvenirs, especially Georgia, Tennessee, and Kentucky.** China, glass, postcards, sterling, pottery, and other items. Send long SASE for wants list.
   Abbie Bush
   PO Box 503
   Elkader, IA 52043
      (319) 245-2128

★ **Charleston, South Carolina, memorabilia** including letters and envelopes, maps, tokens and medals, books, pamphlets, postcards, stock certificates and other fiscal paper. Also any South Carolina item related to the Confederacy.
   Bob Karrer
   Box 6094
   Alexandria, VA 22306
      (703) 360-5105 eves

★ **Georgia, South Carolina, and Florida paper pre-1870** that is related to slavery, the Civil War, indentures, Kings's grants, state grants, wills, or historically interesting topics. Georgia is of particular interest and documents can bring $100-$500 depending upon contents.
   John Parks
   203 Tanglewood Rd.
   Savannah, GA 31419
      (912) 925-6075

★ **Eureka Springs, Arkansas, souvenirs and paper ephemera.** Wants informative or colorful paper, plates, cups, spoons, etc., from Resort Capital of the Ozarks. Pre-1930 in fine condition.
   Janis Watson, Bank of Eureka Springs
   Box 309
   Eureka Springs, AR 72632
      (501) 253-8241

★ **Great Smoky Mountains National Park** in NC and TN. "I'll buy guidebooks, maps, photos, brochures, pamphlets, and similar paper ephemera. Also souvenirs, especially plates and glassware associated with the Park. Also interested in similar items for the towns of **Gatlinburg and Townsend, TN, and the Cherokee Indian Reservation, NC.** Not interested in accordion style color postcards, but do want real photo cards of the park. Pre-1970 items only." Photocopies appreciated.
   Doug Redding
   9129 Turtle Dove Lane
   Gaithersburg, MD 20879
      (301) 926-6158

★ **Eureka Springs, Arkansas, before 1920.** "Anything wanted from souvenirs to advertising, photographs to books, but I'll especially buy any information, maps, lawsuits, newspaper reports, etc., on the early land disputes in Eureka Springs. Also the Eureka Springs railroad. Also have strong interest in **Dr. Norman Baker's Cancer Hospital** in the Springs in the 1930's and will buy all ephemera related to it."
   Steve Chyrchel
   Route #2 Box 362
   Eureka Springs, AR 72632
      (501) 253-9244

★ **New Orleans, Louisiana, and the Gulf Coast.** Wants to buy anything pre-1940 from New Orleans especially *Newcomb* pottery, old **oil paintings** by local artists of the 20's and 30's like A.J. Drysdale, Clarence Millet, and G.L. Viavont among others, **Mardi Gras** favors of all sorts, and **prints and photos** of the people and events of New Orleans and surrounding areas, across the Lake, and the Gulf Coast.
   Sanchez Galleries
   4730 Magazine St.
   New Orleans, LA 70115
      (504) 524-0281

★ **Florida historical paper and memorabilia,** especially items from Fort Jefferson, Florida.
   Gordon McHenry
   Box 1117
   Osprey, FL 34229
      (813) 966-5563   Fax: (813) 966-5563

★ **Orlando, Florida, memorabilia.**
   Jerry Chicone
   Box 547636
   Orlando, FL 32854
      (407) 298-5550

The Midwest

★ **Ohio memorabilia,** especially books, manuscripts, maps, and photographs, pre-1900. Particularly interested in local history prior to the Civil War, especially in the Akron area.
    Frank Klein, The Bookseller
    521 West Exchange St.
    Akron, OH 44302
       (216) 762-3101

★ **Wisconsin china, glass, or** *Red Wing* **souvenir items,** especially from the towns of La Crosse, Fountain City, Waupaca, Reedsburg, and Kilbourn.
    Dana Zimmerman
    1411 Briarcliff Drive
    Appleton, WI 54915

★ **Waukesha, Wisconsin, memorabilia.** Waukesha was noted for its spring waters and a number of food products, so keep your eyes open for all sorts of things marked as being from Waukesha.
    W.E. Schwanz
    45 W22339 Quinn Rd.
    Waukesha, WI 53186

★ **Michigan and the Great Lakes** ephemera and historically interesting paper goods of all types from that region.
    Jay Platt, West Side Book Shop,
    113 W. Liberty,
    Ann Arbor, MI 48104
       (313) 995-1891

★ **Duluth, Minnesota and the Great Lakes.** Wants books, photos, postcards, with particular emphasis on shipping.
    James Baumhofer
    Box 65493
    St. Paul, MN 55165
       (612) 698-7151

★ **Midwest, especially Iowa souvenirs.** "All good items from all Iowa towns, especially Colfax, Clayton and Elkader." Send long SASE for wants list.
    Abbie Bush
    PO Box 503
    Elkader, IA 52043
       (319) 245-2128

★ **Trade tokens and dog licenses from Iowa.**
    Dennis Schulte
    8th Ave., NW
    Waukon, IA 52172
       (319) 568-3628 before 10pm

★ **Iowa souvenirs.** "Always interested in all Iowa souvenirs, especially china. Towns of Colfax, Ackley, and Sibley are particularly wanted."
    Mary Yohe
    6827 So. Juniper
    Tempe, AZ 85283
       (602) 820-7442

★ **Humboldt or Rutland, Iowa,** pictorial postcards and advertising from those two towns.
    Don Olson
    Box 245
    Humboldt, IA 50548

★ **Rockford, Freeport, and Belvidere Illinois, tokens, medals,** buttons, badges, ribbons, and other small flat collectibles. Also banks, early signs, coffee tins, bottles, etc. Loves to find larger items marked as being from Rockford. No paper or cardboard items.
    Rich Hartzog
    Box 4143 BID
    Rockford, IL 61110
       (815) 226-0771

★ **Dakota Territory, South Dakota, North Dakota, Minnesota, Wyoming, and Montana photographs and small ephemera** from before 1930 in any format, including real photo postcards. Wants all historically or pictorially interesting paper ephemera, advertising, letters, books, bottles, and small objects. Especially wants items marked DT, DAKOTA TERRITORY, DAK or SOUTH DAKOTA. Buys single items or collections. Is often as interested in the photographers as the subject matter of the photo. Xerox© copies highly recommended, and approvals of fine condition items are accepted.
    Robert Kolbe
    1301 S. Duluth
    Sioux Falls, SD 57105
       (605) 332-9662

The West

★ **Paper ephemera about the Western U.S.** especially related to the military, early forts, ghost towns, Mormons, railroads, mining, banking, cowboys, Indians, lawmen, cattle, courts, and financial matters. Buys letters about the West, autographs of famous Westerners, and most illustrated pre-1910 Western documents.
>   Warren Anderson
>   American West Archives
>   Box 100
>   Cedar City, UT 84720
>   (801) 586-9497

★ **Dallas ephemera** pre-1915, including pamphlets, letters, documents, postcards, photos, and items related to **the Texas State Fair.** *The Artwork of Dallas* folio will bring $300 or more.
>   Ron Pearson
>   10620 Creekmere Dr.
>   Dallas, TX 75218
>   (214) 321-9717

★ **Maps of Texas** from before 1900. Also trail driving maps.
>   Johnny Spellman, DVM
>   10806 North Lamar
>   Austin, TX 78753
>   (512) 258-6910 eves (512) 836-2889 days

★ **Texas maps and prints.** "The popular image is that people in Texas in wealthy, but they are not. Being a *thing* from Texas does not auto-matically make it worth a lot of money either." Mostly wants pre-1900 prints of Texas industry. San Antonio is the only Texas city she is interested in finding prints and maps.
>   Shirley Sorenson
>   270 Sherri Dr.
>   Universal City, TX 78148
>   (512) 658-2548

★ **Nevada and Death Valley ephemera** including books, newspapers, magazines, diaries, letters, maps, promotional brochures, "and anything else printed or written on paper." Also stereoviews, merchant tokens, dog tags, hunting licenses, photos, postcards and what have you. He requests prices but will make offers.
>   Gil Schmidtmann
>   Route 1, Box 371
>   Mentone, CA 92359
>   (714) 794-1211

★ **Colorado mining memorabilia,** 1859-1915, especially Cripple Creek and all other mining towns and camps and the railroads that served them. Wants photos, stereoviews, advertising, letterheads, billheads, brochures, pamphlets, mining papers, stock certificates, maps, badges, candlesticks, souvenirs, and other small items marked with the name of one of these towns. Photos should be of mining, railroad, or downtown activities, not people or scenery. Albums with numerous photos eagerly sought, as are Business or Mining Directories and books on Colorado mining. Does not want *anything* from the flatland Colorado towns like Denver, Pueblo or Colorado Springs, nor anything from state or national parks. Give info on back of photos.
>   George Foott
>   6683 S. Yukon Way
>   Littleton, CO 80123
>   (303) 979-8688

★ **Colorado and Wyoming memorabilia** (1860-1930). Wants real photo and advertising postcards, souvenirs, "good for" trade tokens, stereoviews, envelopes and letterheads, fancy whiskey bottles, posters, calendars, trade cards, political buttons, ephemera from the Leadville Ice Palace, *any* item from the 1908 Democratic National Convention held in Denver, items from military forts, and items from fairs, rodeos, and Cheyenne Frontier Days. All items *must* be from Wyoming or Colorado and be within the 1860-1930 timeframe. "I do not want items from National Parks, items after 1930, newspapers, or magazines. Please give a complete description. DO NOT send unsolicited items."
>   Edward Marriott
>   9191 East Oxford Dr.
>   Denver, CO 80237
>   (303) 779-5237

★ **Las Vegas, Nevada souvenirs and memorabilia** from before 1970. Buys gambling tokens and chips, casino playing cards, match covers, postcards, stationery, plates, business directories, showroom programs, magazines with stories about Las Vegas history, and photos of interiors of casinos, banks, hotels, motels, and restaurants. Also interested in photos of Las Vegas celebrities. Will consider other ephemera from this desert playground.
>   Marc Weiser
>   Box 28730
>   Las Vegas, NV 89126
>   (702) 871-8686

★ **Nevada ephemera** including mounted photos, pre-1930 postcards, law badges, bottles, railroad ephemera, fire department ephemera, cowboy relics, maps, stocks, Indian artifacts, posters, advertising, mining, military, etc. If it's early and marked "Nev." Ron is interested.
>Ron Bommarito
>Box 114
>Genoa, NV 89411
>(702) 782-3893

★ **All Nevada memorabilia from before 1950** is wanted but especially that relating to banks and finance including bank bags, letterheads, documents, stocks, checks, scrip. Also photos, maps, postcards, stationery, tokens, and other ephemera from or about Nevada, including items related to prostitution.
>Douglas McDonald
>Box 20443
>Reno, NV 89515

★ **Southwest, especially Nevada, Utah, and Wyoming** souvenirs. China, glass, sterling silver, postcards, pottery, and other items. Send long SASE for wants list.
>Abbie Bush
>PO Box 503
>Elkader, IA 52043
>(319) 245-2128

★ **Idaho, Montana, and Washington items** including trade tokens, postcards, letterheads, calendars, buttons, ribbons, wooden nickels, stocks, match holders, calendar plates and other advertising china. Pays $1-$3 each for postcards with postmarks from discontinued post offices. Pays $2-$10 for cards of small towns he can use. Nothing after 1930.
>Mike Fritz
>1550 Stevens St.
>Rathdrum, ID 83858
>(208) 687-0159

★ **Yakima, Washington, memorabilia.** "My primary interest is real photo postcards of Yakima and North Yakima, but I also buy photographs and other ephemera including newspapers, phone books, directories, souvenirs, and promotional booklets that are before 1950. I like Yakima H.S. items from the 1930's and photo postcards taken by Frank Lanternman."
>Ron Ott
>10 N. 45th Ave.
>Yakima, WA 98908
>(509) 965-3385

★ **San Francisco Bay area ephemera** pre-1910, especially related to the 1906 quake. Photos, diaries, letters, family mementos, and the like are wanted with emphasis on unusual. Ron has particular interest in items associated with schools and education before 1906 and to meal tickets and other items related to life in relief camps immediately after the disaster. **No newspapers or postcards.** Ron is Head of the S.F. History Ass'n and can accept tax deductible gifts related to S.F. from any period.
>Ron Ross
>620 Church St.
>San Francisco, CA 94114
>(415) 626-3666 eves

★ **San Bernardino, California, items** from buildings, fairs, and resorts. Wants ceramic souvenirs including cups, plates, sterling silver spoons, badges, ribbons, pins, etc. Particularly interested in items associated with the 1903 Street Fair, 1908 Festival of the Arrowhead, 1910 Centennial, and the National Orange Show, from 1911 to 1920.
>Gary Crabtree
>Box 3843
>San Bernardino, CA 92413
>(714) 862-8534

★ **San Gabriel Valley, CA, items.** Wants pre-1930 items from any San Gabriel Valley town, Arcadia, Temple City, El Monte, San Gabriel, Baldwin Park, Rosemead, Pasadena, Covina, San Marino, Monrovia, Duarte, Azusa, etc. Also wants anything related to **Emperor Norton** and **Lucky Baldwin.** Suggests you ship your items to him via UPS (650 W. Duarte, #309) for offer.
>SC Coin & Stamp Co.
>Drawer 3069
>Arcadia, CA 91006
>(800) 367-0779

★ **San Diego, California, memorabilia** including postcards, pamphlets, and photos.
>Ralph Bowman's Paper Gallery
>5349 Wheaton Street
>La Mesa, CA 91942
>(619) 462-6268

★ **Santa Cruz, CA,** postcards, photos, souvenir plates, and other collectibles.
>Rick Righetti
>219 Olive St.
>Santa Cruz, CA 95060
>(408) 426-3014

★ **Alaskan and Canadian memorabilia** including postcards, trade cards, advertising, labels, letterheads, and photos, especially items pre-1875. Buys for resale. Nothing damaged or after 1950. Approvals welcome.
Nick Nickell
102 People's Wharf
Juneau, AK 99801
   (907) 586-1733

★ **Alaskan memorabilia.** "I'll buy nearly anything old about Alaska, the Yukon, or the Polar Region including books, maps, photographs, letters, souvenirs, china, spoons, and miscellaneous ephemera. One of my specialties is Alaskan postcards around 1910. I buy for resale, and seldom buy items newer than 1945."
Richard Wood, Alaska Heritage Books
Box 22165
Juneau, AK 99802
   (907) 586-6748

★ **Alaskan memorabilia.** Wants embossed bottles with Alaskan product or business names, license plates, post cards (not scenery), Klondike novelty material, brochures from the Alaskan & Canadian Railroad & Steamship lines, and "all very early newspapers, photographs, and printed matter." Also wants *Alaska Sportsman* magazines from the 1930's and selected issues of *Alaska Journal*. **Does not want** Alaska-Yukon Exposition material. Give description, condition, date of origin, and indicate what cities, towns, or regions are featured. **Do not send items unsolicited.** Will send a wants list for SASE.
Reed Fitzpatrick, The Paper Scout
Box 369
Vashon, WA 98070
   (206) 463-3900 days

★ **Hawaiian and South Seas ephemera.** Wants books, printed items, paintings, prints, photos, postcards, and other memorabilia from Hawaii, as long as it's pre-1920. Send insured.
Bernie Berman
755 Isenberg St., #305
Honolulu, HI 96826

★ **Puerto Rico.** Wants pre-1930 books, postcards, and other memorabilia of Puerto Rico. Please price and describe in your first letter.
Frank Garcia
13701 SW 66th St., #B-301
Miami, FL 33183

Foreign Places

★ **Canadian items:** calendars, stock certificates, bank notes, old letters in original envelopes, fancy letterheads, all Canadian railway, merchants' tokens from Western Canada, Canadian military or law enforcement, and postcards of BC, Yukon, NWT, AB, SK, and Newfoundland. Nothing after 1950, please. No road maps, tourist brochures, and postcards of tourist attractions or scenery. Prefers items be sent on approval or Xeroxed©.
Michael Rice
Box 286
Saanichton, BC V0S 1M0, CANADA
   (604) 652-9047 eves

★ **Canada, the Arctic, and the Klondike.** All information wanted including maps, paper ephemera, prints, government documents, and photographs about Canadian immigration, travel, history, fur trade, mountaineering, Indians and Eskimos. NO OFFERS.
Tom Williams
Box 4126, Station C
Calgary, Alberta T2T 5M9 CANADA
   (403) 264-0184

★ **Canadian postcards, stereoviews, and other ephemera** especially from the Province of Ontario. Mainly interested in small town views, events, railroad stations, and transportation. No scenics or items after 1950. "A photocopy of the item is almost essential" to accompany your complete description. Also wants **Canadian made woodworking planes.**
Peter Cox
Box 1655
Espanola, Ontario P0P 1C0 CANADA
(705) 869-2441 wntr   (705) 859-2410 sumr

★ **Panama Canal Zone and the Isthmus of Panama memorabilia** including postcards, letters, stamped envelopes, scrapbooks, tokens, medals, maps, coins, stamps, and everything else including souvenirs. Especially likes pre-1915 picture postcards with cancellations from obscure Panama post offices. "I will probably offer to buy anything Isthmus." Bob is long time editor of the Isthmus collectors' journal.
Bob Karrer
Box 6094
Alexandria, VA 22306
   (703) 360-5105

★ **Pre-1960 Cuban memorabilia** including coins, stamps, money, historical documents, postcards, souvenir spoons, maps, stocks and bonds, lottery tickets, cigar bands, military decorations and insignia, "or any other collectible item including those related to the Spanish domination of the Island." He'll pay from $80-$400 for the 10, 20 and 50 peso bank notes of 1869. There is a 1916 coin and a 1944 banknote each worth more than $50,000, so it could pay you to look.
> Manuel Alvarez,
> 1735 SW 8th St.
> Miami, FL 33135
>   (305) 649-1176

★ **Brazil.** Books, photos, and paper ephemera from the colonial period through 1945. Especially interested in travel and exploration books with early information about Rio de Janeiro and/or the Amazon. Also wants letters and diaries of military personnel who served in Brazil during WWII or in the Joint Brazil-U.S. Military Commission. Material may be in any language. Please include your phone number.
> Lee Harrer
> 1908 Seagull Drive
> Clearwater, FL 34624
>   (813) 536-4029 evenings

★ **Philippine Islands.** "I'll buy postcards, photos, books, magazines, maps, and other paper items, especially real photo postcards from Manila or elsewhere in the Philippines. I don't want coins, stamps, paper money, or books on the Spanish American War. The postcard publisher's name is very helpful."
> Michael Price
> Box 7071
> Ann Arbor, MI 48107

★ **Australia and Antarctica items from before 1920,** including prints, maps, photographs, ship's logs, scholarly ethnographic studies, novels, travel books, children's books, postcards and paper ephemera. No interest in items from New Zealand or the Maori.
> David and Cathy Lilburne
> Antipodean Books
> Box 189
> Cold Spring, NY 10516
>   (914) 424-3867

★ **Antarctic and Arctic ephemera** especially books but also diaries, posters, photographs, letters, pamphlets, and *Aurora Australis,* the Antarctic newspaper 1907-09.
> Jay Platt
> West Side Book Shop
> 113 W. Liberty,
> Ann Arbor, MI 48104
>   (313) 995-1891 days

★ **Greenland, Pitcairn Island, Hudson's Bay, Canada, Mexico, and other country's ephemera** especially tokens and medals, but other small items, especially before 1930 are likely to be of interest.
> Rich Hartzog
> World Exonumia
> Box 4143 BID
> Rockford, IL 61110
>   (815) 226-0771

★ **Micronesia, Polynesia, and New Guinea ethnographic materials,** masks, ceremonial bowls, and the like. Also maps, mariner's charts, voyage books, and ship's logs from vessels traveling in that region, in any language. Some interest in scrimshaw. No items from New Zealand or the Maori.
> David and Cathy Lilburne
> Antipodean Books
> Box 189
> Cold Spring, NY 10516
>   (914) 424-3867

★ **Imperial Russian antiques & memorabilia** whether civil, religious, or military. We buy:
> [1] Russian Orders, decorations, badges, buttons, medals, and other militaria;
> [2] Russian porcelains, bronzes, icons, prints, paintings, and other graphic arts;
> [3] Russian coronation and other commemorative memorabilia.

Items are bought for cash or brokered. "Please send a clear photo or Xerox© copy and details, including price wanted." Mail order catalog and appraisal services available. **No Soviet items.**
> ART Co.
> Box 278183
> Sacramento, CA 95826
>   (916) 366-8850

Dr. Tony's Guide to:

Types of Postcards

Early cards: The phrase used to describe cards from the mid 1870's. There were no pictures on cards, other than advertising, until 1893. You will sometimes hear the earliest cards called **Pioneer era cards.** From 1898-1901 they are called **Souvenir cards.** Cards from this period are collected for their stamps and postmark as much as for the card.

Postcards: In 1901, private printers were allowed to use the word POSTCARD. "Real photo" cards begin to appear at this time. Real photo cards as the most sought after because historians are interested in what is pictured. Cards of this period have the picture on one side and the address on the other. You were not permitted to write messages on the the address side.

Divided back cards: The cards used between 1907-1914 are called "divided back" cards because the message was permitted to be written on the address side. The message written on the left and address on the right. Real photo, greetings, and ads.

White border cards: Starting just before WWI and lasting to the Depression (1915-1930), postcards had a white border around picture.

Linen cards: During the Depression and WWII (1930-45), postcards had a textured surface, like linen. Inks from this period were usually bright. The colored printed photographs were usually of poor quality with little detail.

Chrome cards: Modern brightly colored, slick surface postcards start around WWII and continue today. Their colors are vivid and the details are sharp.

How to Describe Your Postcards

Mint: A perfect card, just as it comes from the printing press.
No marks, bends or creases. No writing or postmarks.
Not seen often.

Near mint: Like mint but very very light aging or very slight
discoloration from being in an album for many years.
Not as fresh looking as mint.

Excellent: Card looks like mint with sharply pointed corners
(no blunt or rounded corners). It may not have any bends or
creases. May be postally used or unused, but the writing and
postmark only on address side, with clean fresh picture side.

Very good: Corners may be just a bit blunt or rounded, or it might
have an almost undetectable crease or bend that does not
detract from overall appearance of picture side. May have
writing only on the address side.

Good: Corners may be noticeably blunt or rounded with noticeable
but slight bends or creases. May be postally used or have
writing, but only on the address side.

Average: Creases and bends more pronounced. Corners more
rounded. Or it may have writing in margins on picture side,
or the postmark may show through from address side but
not on main portion of picture.

Poor: Card is intact, but has excess soil, stains, or heavy creases.
Or it is written on the picture side, or has a cancel that affects
the picture. Salable only if it is a very scarce card.

Space filler: Poor condition, perhaps with torn or missing corners,
or breaks in the picture surface. Neither desirable nor valuable.

*Postcard collecting is
one of the largest hobbies.*

*Postcards are collected for
the photograph, the greeting,
the message, the stamp,
and the postmark.*

*Real photo cards are a
valuable source of historical
information. Often the only
surviving photos
of buildings, parade floats,
and other slices of our past.
Buyers for real photo cards
will be found throughout
this book.*

*Describing a postcard is easy.
Make a Xerox© copy.
Describing the condition
of your cards is difficult
because buyers are very fussy
about condition.*

Postcards

★ **Postcard collections, pre-1930,** especially American street views, disasters, railroad stations, fire departments, and diners. He also buys cards depicting foreign royalty, expositions, snowmen, full length Santas, and pre-jet commercial aircraft. Does not want foreign views, scenery, parks, woods, mountains, lakes, and flowers. Does not want damaged cards or those which have been pasted in albums. "If your cards are not for sale, or if my offer is not accepted, **I will appraise your cards at a cost of only one postcard of my choice for each 100 cards I appraise.**" Cards must be shipped for inspection for purchase or appraisal. John runs auctions, postcard shows, and heads the Postcard History Society. He can supply you with many interesting free or low cost items regarding postcard collecting. For more information send a Self Addressed Stamped Envelope for his "Postcard Opportunity" sheet.
John McClintock
Box 1765
Manassas, VA 22110
    (703) 368-2757 eves

★ **All types of postcards, modern or old,** are purchased for resale. You may ship any quantity up to a shoe box full (about 600-700 cards) together with your telephone number and he will make an offer. If the offer is unacceptable, the postcards will be returned immediately.
Bill Colby, Kenrich Co.
9418-T Las Tunas Dr.
Temple City, CA 91780
    (818) 286-3888

★ **Pre-1940 picture postcards** are sought by this West Coast paper dealer.
Mike Rasmussen
Box 726
Marina, CA 93933
    (408) 384-5460

★ **All pre-1950 postcards, American and foreign,** all subjects, used or unused. "I'll pay competitive prices for better single cards or will buy collections, box lots, accumulations, etc."
Sheldon Dobres
4 Calypso Court
Baltimore, MD 21209
    (301) 486-6569

★ **Postcard albums and collections,** the older the better, in very good condition only. Interested in all topics, but does not want damaged cards. Joan conducts mail auctions and sells on approval. Wants to know the number of cards, condition, and types of subjects pictured. She's been a collector for nearly 50 years!
> Jo Ann Van Scotter
> 208 E. Lincoln St.
> Mt. Morris, IL 61054
> (815) 734-6971

★ **Pre-1950 postcards worldwide,** used or unused, from any country, but especially from the U.S. and Canada. Wants street scenes, buildings, occupationals, sports, transportation, and people. **Doesn't want** water, forests, mountains, deserts, trees, etc. Also buys some pictorial "greetings." Pays 25¢ to $5.00 for most postcards, but a few European cards drawn or painted by famous illustrators can bring $100 up. No quantity too large. Prompt payment if you send approvals, and unwanted cards are returned. All payment is in the currency of the seller.
> Neil Hayne
> Box 220
> Bath, Ontario K0H 1G0, CANADA
> (613) 352-7456

★ **Postcards from the 1920-1950 era** picturing:
> [1] **Art deco or art moderne buildings**
>   typical of those times, such as
>   diners and gas stations;
> [2] **New York World's Fair;**
> [3] **Texas Centennial** of 1936;
> [4] **Houston, Texas;**
> [5] **Advertising products or services.**

Primarily wants "linen" cards with a slightly textured surface. Please photocopy.
> Edy Chandler
> Box 20664
> Houston, TX 77225
> (713) 531-9615 eves

★ **Cards advertising any product or service.** "I'll buy milk, medicine, automobiles, boats, shoes, musical instruments, tourist attractions, bands and singing groups, farm products, home items, clothing, entertainment, trains, auto dealerships, restaurants, highways, sports events... the list is endless. I'll buy one or a box full."
> Jay Ketelle
> 3721 Farwell
> Amarillo, TX 79109

★ **Postcards made of macerated (ground up) U.S. currency.**
> Donald Gorlick
> Box 24541
> Seattle, WA 98124

★ **Cards showing automobiles,** especially convertibles, trucks, used car lots, dealer show rooms, and any card showing a truck or car with clearly readable advertising on the side of it, any era, from anywhere in the world. Also "better grade" **commercial airline cards** showing propellor-driven planes. Only cards issued as advertising by the airlines are wanted. Most cards are purchased for resale, although many are for Jay's private collection. Jay recently released *The American Automobile Dealership,* illustrated with 340 postcards ($25 from the author).
> Jay Ketelle
> 3721 Farwell
> Amarillo, TX 79109
> (806) 355-3456

★ **Postcards illustrated with original drawings by the sender.** Wants pen and ink or pencil sketches more than more elaborate paintings.
> Linda Franklin
> 2716 Northfield Rd.
> Charlottesville, VA 22901

★ **Sexy real photo postcards** of women acting provocatively (such as lifting their skirts, etc.), 1880-1980. Also wants nudes, semi-nudes, and xxx-rated postcards, all periods. Photocopy.
> Charles Martignette
> PO Box 293
> Hallandale, FL 33009
> (305) 454-3474

★ **Scenic views of Colorado, Kansas, and Missouri** before 1930. Also buys early cards of Elks Lodges, prisons, and bowling alleys.
> George VanTrump, Jr.
> Box 260170
> Lakewood, CO 80226

★ **Views of Hong Kong and Macao before 1945.** Please Xerox© and price what you have.
> Kin Leung Liu
> 1517-S. Angeline St.
> Seattle, WA 98108
> (206) 767-3025

photographs

"Instant ancestors"

(unidentified people) have little value, but photos of businesses, workers, famous events, outdoor city scenes, parades, vehicles, officials, uniforms, and the like can always find a buyer among collectors and historians trying to learn more about an industry or era.

To sell a photo, make a Xerox© of what you have. This saves a lot of your effort. Condition of the photo and its mat are both important to a buyer. Note banged corners, stains, and the like. If the photo is faded, make certain you indicate that fact, as a Xerox© makes photos look better than they are.

When reading entries in this chapter you will run across reference to various types of photographs. My glossary on the next page will help you understand them and describe photos you own.

If you come across round photos with square mounts, you may have pictures taken by one of the first *Kodaks*. For that reason, they are an interesting curiosity as they do not exist in great numbers.

Stereoviews are also popular. Of interest are earlier, larger, cards depicting famous events, disasters, important people, and industrial processes, especially related to mining, oil, or transportation. Early stereo cards have colored mounts and were originally flat. After years of being stored with later curved cards, they too are often curved. Don't try to flatten them with pressure as you may crack the photographic emulsion.

tony hyman

Dr. Tony's Guide to:

Types of Photographs

Daguerreotypes: Earliest photo process, 1839-1854, recognizable by its silvery image on glass. The leather and early thermoplastic cases are often worth far more than the photo. Outdoor and city views are rare. Large "Dags" can be valuable. **Do not** try to clean them and do not leave them open and exposed to sunlight.

Ambrotypes: Photos on a glass negative backed with dark paper to make a positive image. Mid 19th Century. Subject matter is the key to value. These too sometimes come in elaborate cases worth more than the photo.

Albumen photographs: Paper prints before 1890 usually used egg albumen in preparation of the image surface. You can't tell the difference looking at the photo.

Tintypes: Cheap popular portraits, 1858-1910, printed on sheets of blackened tin. Also called ferrotypes. Subject matter is the key to value. Pictures not taken in a studio are usually more valuable. Occupationals (photos showing someone with the tools of his trade) are widely sought after, whether studio or on location.

Stereoviews: Cards containing two shots of the same subject to give a 3-D effect when seen through a viewer. Older views are larger, flat, and have colored mounts (pink, yellow, etc.) and generally do not contain descriptions of the subject matter printed on the back. Later views have curved gray mounts (*Underwood* is the most common brand). Because they are often stored together, some older cards become somewhat curved, so don't be fooled. Newest, and almost worthless to collectors, are colored printed stereoviews.

Carte de visites: Photos on card stock measuring 2.5" x 4" popular between 1860-1890. Often found in albums. These are generally abbreviated as "cdv."

Cabinet cards: Photos on 4" x 7" cards, usually with the photographer's name at the bottom. Generally studio shots. These, and cdv's were often sold as souvenirs and memorials and can be found with pictures of celebrities, Presidents, Generals, midgets, and the like, often with printed signatures.

Photographs

★ **Pre-1915 photographs** including tintypes, Daguerreotypes, ambrotypes, cartes de visite, cabinet photos, albumen prints, stereocards, silver prints, platinum prints, cyanotypes, and photo albums. His list of "fine subjects" includes: banjo players, Russians, kids playing marbles, Brooklyn, photographers, auto racing, nudes, military, Civil War, autographed photos, funny photos, Lincoln, John Wilkes Booth, portraits taken in Philadelphia of identified people, unusual photos, Shakers, WWII, mug shots, writers, gunmen, artists, Philadelphia, famous people, Hawaii and Samoa in the 19th century, Puerto Rico, Indians, mining, Orientals, rockets, sports, aviation, and similar topics. **No ordinary studio portraits,** and no photo equipment is wanted. Xerox© both sides of your photo and price what you have for sale.
　Richard Rosenthal
　4718 Springfield Ave.
　Philadelphia, PA 19143
　　(215) 726-5493

If you have photos of events, businesses, industry, or sports, specialists in those subjects are often your best buyers.

It could put $$$ in your pocket to read the chapter in this book dealing with the subject matter of your photo.

★ **Rare old photographs,** cased photos, stereoviews, etc., especially work by important photographers such as Jackson, Curtis, and other Western photographers. Also buys books with actual photos tipped (pasted) in.
　Ivan Gilbert
　Miran Arts & Books
　2824 Elm Ave.
　Columbus, OH 43209
　　(614) 236-0002

★ **Photos and photographic literature.** Wants to buy Daguerreotypes, ambrotypes, tintypes, stereo views, round *Kodak* snapshots, and other interesting photos, from any era. No portraits. Would love to find photos of photographers at work. Buys complete unpicked photo albums, specializing in Pittsburgh and Allegheny County, Pennsylvania. **Also wants early cameras, photographic accessories and literature.**
　Nicholas Graver
　276 Brooklawn Drive,
　Rochester, NY 14618
　　(716) 244-4818

★ **Original photos of Lincoln.** "I'll buy photos of Lincoln taken from life and printed before 1866. Will also purchase the Ayers photos of Lincoln printed in the 1880's and 1890's. I'll also buy photos of Lincoln look-alikes." No photos of prints, statues, or Abe's house. Send a photocopy of what you have. Serious sellers only, please."
　Stuart Schneider
　Box 64
　Teaneck, NJ 07666
　　(201) 261-1983

★ **Stereoview cards,** particularly older Western scenes, transportation, mining, Mt. Lowe, fires, high wheel bicycles, famous people, Civil War, and early California. "However, I buy most common stereos, too," presumably for a lot less. He particularly wants **stereos of Lincoln** published while Lincoln was alive. If you want to sell your cards, Chuck wants to know the subject of the card quite specifically, an accurate description of condition, the publisher. If you have a price you want, say so. He does not want cards *printed* in color or in black and white.
　Chuck Reincke
　2141 Sweet Briar Rd.
　Tustin, CA 92680
　　(714) 832-8563 eves

★ **Photographs of all type (1860-1930's)** from tintypes to large photos mounted on cardboard that show people and/or animals in fake rustic or outdoorsy settings created with painted backgrounds and 3D papier mache props, stumps, fences, rocks, etc. Photos must be clear and in fine condition. Also wants 1930's to 60's department store **photos of kids with Santa.** Please send a Xerox of these inexpensive items for sale, keeping your expectations reasonable.
Linda Campbell Franklin
2716 Northfield Rd.
Charlottesville, VA 22901

★ **Bathing beauties and nudie photos,** pre-WWI.
Steve DeGenaro
Box 5662
Youngstown, OH 44504

★ **Stereoviews showing the development of the early West, 1860-1900:** expeditions, **railroad construction,** freighting through the Sierras, maritime scenes, **Indian portraits** and culture, **mining, logging,** and **early small town scenes** as well as cosmopolitan **San Francisco.** Particular interest in Custer, Teddy Roosevelt, Mark Twain, Bret Harte, John Sutter, artist Albert Bierstadt, and all early photographers and their equipment. The latter will bring "hundreds of dollars" in excellent condition. Also wants paper ephemeral advertising from early western photographers. Not interested in faded views or those with damaged mounts. No lithographed views, only real photos in excellent condition.
Jim Crain
131 Bennington St.
San Francisco, CA 94110
   (415) 648-1092 eves

★ **Stereoviews.** Buys most U.S. black and white views as well as other interesting pre-1920 photos. This large paper dealer buys for resale.
Bill Colby, Kenrich Co.
9418-T Las Tunas Dr.
Temple City, CA 91780
   (818) 286-3888

★ **Old photos of famous people, outdoor scenes and "the odd and the unusual."** Will buy Daguerreotypes, ambrotypes, tin types and cartes de visite in fine condition. Xerox©.
Chris Wilson
2762 N. Washington Blvd.
Arlington, VA 22201
   (703) 525-5930

★ **Bizarre photos,** such as freaks, dwarfs, lynchings, slaves, public punishment, and what have you? Especially interested in photos of **death, especially post-mortem photos, but also mourning photos, executions, lynchings, embalming and medical photos with doctors and cadavers.** Wants all types of photos from Daguerreotypes to 1940. Will take later photos if someone famous. Likes to find old prints of the family gathered around the deceased. Worth from $5 to $75+ for the very early and unusual.
Steve DeGenaro
Box 5662
Youngstown, OH 44504

TONY'S GUIDE TO
ABBREVIATIONS

photo- real photograph
rp - real photograph
b/w - black and white. Postcards are assumed to be in color, photos are assumed to be in b/w, unless noted.
cu - close up
cr - crease
crn - corner
emb - embossed
flat - not embossed
lt - light
tr - tear
m/t - margin tear
unu - unused
wob - writing on back
wof - writing on front
pm - postmarked
cof - canceled on picture side (front) of the card
s/m - stamp missing (on used card)

★ **Photographs and engravings of famous people** in all walks of life. Will consider items loose or in books. Please photocopy.
Kenneth Rendell
Box 9001
Wellesley, MA 02181
(617) 431-1776 fax (617) 237-1492

★ **Provocative or obscene photographs** including nudes, semi-nudes, candids, home made pictures, outdoor frolicking, etc, from teasing to xxx. Also pin up photos of dancers, starlets, and sexy ladies of all ages and periods.
Charles Martignette
PO Box 293
Hallandale, FL 33009
(305) 454-3474

★ **Photos of cowboys, Indians,** and related subjects, including cattle drives, early Texas towns, outlaws, lawmen, the Geronimo expedition (especially those taken by C.S. Fly), and the Mexican War. All types wanted, including stereo. Please send Xerox© copies.
Johnny Spellman, DVM
10806 North Lamar
Austin, TX 78753
(512) 258-6910 eves (512) 836-2889 days

★ **Photos of Indians and Eskimos,** especially the work of Edward S. Curtis. Also buys real photo postcards on the same theme. Please send Xerox© copies for a prompt response. Dealers price your goods, but amateur sellers may request an offer.
Barry Friedman
22725 Garzota Drive
Valencia, CA 91355
(805) 296-2318

★ **Photographs of people with guns.** Has a particular interest in Civil War and Western scenes but wants hunters, soldiers, sailors, Indians, and cowboys. All types of early images are considered, including cdv's, cabinet cards, tintypes, daguerreotypes, ambrotypes, etc. Send a Xerox© of any image you want to sell, except those on Daguerreotypes, the cased photos with a mirror finish. SASE please.
Charles Worman
PO Box 33584 (AMC)
Dayton, OH 45433
(513) 429-1808 eves

★ **Occupational photos,** especially baseball players, firefighters, Civil War soldiers, and other occupations. "I prefer cdv and cabinet card photos, and will pay particularly well for photos of doctors, nurses and other medical topics, especially related to embalming or medical school." Only items from before 1930 are wanted. Please send Xerox© copy.
Steve DeGenaro
Box 5662
Youngstown, OH 44504

★ **Photos taken before 1930** of special events, parades, sports, transportation, people with unusual clothing, people doing "something weird," twins, children with toys and "unusual photos." Is not interested in studio photos of men and women's heads and shoulders. Describe the photo's size, condition and content. A Xerox© is suggested, although this relatively new dealer will ultimately ask to see your photos before making final payment.
Joe Burkart
Antique Photo Art
143 Northwood Drive
Hiawatha, IA 52233
(319) 393 2206

★ **Photos in memorial matts.** These are ordinary portraits mounted in memorial matts after the person died. Memorial matts have printed or embossed angels, doves, Gates of Heaven, etc., and mottoes like "Free at Last."
Steve DeGenaro
Box 5662
Youngstown, OH 44504

★ **Panoramic group photos** taken in North or South Carolina.
Lew Powell
700 East Park Ave.
Charlotte, NC 28203

Watch for revenue stamps on the back of Civil War era carte de visites. Most are common, but a few are valuable.

cameras

Camera buyers want the odd and unusual.

Hidden ("detective") cameras were popular in the late 1800's and bring premium prices today, as do panorama cameras, multi lens cameras, and other early oddities. It is hard for amateurs to recognize early Daguerreotype cameras because they often look like wooden boxes without a lens. They are quite valuable.

When describing a camera, give the brand and model name, as well as any numbers which appear on the body of the camera. Camera buyers want info about the lens. Give the maker's name and all numbers and other information that is printed around the front circumference of the lens.

If you want to sell a camera, provide the following info in your first letter:

[1] Does the camera work?

[2] Does it seem to be complete?

[3] Is the case and camera covered with wood, metal, leather or cloth? What condition is the covering?

[4] Does the camera have a folding cloth or leather bellows? If so, what color is it?

[5] What accessories come with the camera, such as lenses, boxes, instructions, etc.

tony hyman

Cameras

★ **Unusual and early cameras** including panorama cameras, wide angles, sub miniatures, hidden cameras, and oddly shaped or novelty cameras such as those shaped like cartoon or advertising characters. When writing, include all names and numbers found on the lens. If the camera is unusual, make certain to take a picture of it or make a good sketch. Jim is author of *Collectors Guide to Kodak Cameras* and *Price Guide to Antique and Classic Cameras*.
Jim McKeown
Centennial Photo
11595 State Road 70
Grantsburg, WI 54840
(715) 689-2153

★ **Cameras of brass, chrome, or wood** made before 1948. Anything interesting photographic, be it camera, book, or what have you, will be considered, including pre-1930 **photo magazines**, pre-1948 catalogs, and other ephemera. *No Polaroids.* Provide any numbers or names anywhere on the object. Describe condition of wood, leather, or metal. *Must* include SASE.
Alan Voorhees
Cameras & Such
492 Breesport Rd.
Horseheads, NY 14845

★ *Kodak, Polaroid,* **and other cameras.** "I buy the following *Kodak* cameras: Colored (not black) folding cameras in any size or color, Beau Brownie colored box cameras, Super Six-20, Chevron, Bantam Special with black and chrome finish, Gift *Kodak*, and other unusual or deco-looking cameras and projectors." Harry also buys **quality 35mm cameras** by *Canon, Legit, Nixon, Voigtlander,* and *Zeiss.* "An early *Canon* with pop-up viewfinder is worth $3,000+ to me, even in poor condition." He also buys **large format press and view cameras**, lenses, roll-backs, etc. He also buys **8mm and 16mm cameras** by *Angenieux, Arriflex, Beaulieu, Bolex* and *Mitchell* only. Harry will also buy model 180, 190, and 195 *Polaroids*, and any passport *Polaroid* (with more than one lens), but only those models...no others.
Harry Poster
Box 1883
South Hackensack, NJ 07606
(201) 794-9606 weekdays before 7pm

★ *Kodak* **publications,** especially *Kodak* catalogs before 1950, *Kodak* advertisements in color prior to 1900, *Kodak Salesman* magazine, *Kodak* trade circulars, *Kodak* display counter cards, *Kodak* advertising novelties, and *Kodak* postcards. He does not want cameras or equipment from *Kodak* or anyone else.
Wayne Ellis
754 Bob-Bea Lane
Harleysville, PA 19438
(215) 256-6888

★ *Kodak* **cameras, advertising, and memorabilia.** "I'll buy only pre-1930 cameras in near mint condition, especially those with original cardboard or wooden cartons. I'll also buy just the empty cartons!" Frank's list of cameras he seeks is too long to print here, but if you regularly deal in cameras or if you have an old *Kodak*, it might be worth picking up his wants list. He also wants a *Kodiopticon* **slide projector**, and cameras made by companies absorbed by Kodak including *Poco, Columbus, Ludigraph, Kameret* and **Rochester Optical's** *Empire State View* camera. *Kodak* newspaper and magazine advertising before 1930 may also find a buyer, as will countertop advertising, posters, signs, wooden framed pictures of people using *Kodaks*, and any of the the literally hundreds of items with the *Kodak* logo. "If it says '*Kodak*' on it, I want to know about it. That includes books which use *Kodak* as part of the title, advertising in foreign languages, instruction books, stock certificates from any camera company, *Kodak* annual reports, and anything else that is old and in fine condition."
Frank Storey
324 School Lane
Linthicum, MD 21090
(301) 850-5728 eves

★ **Cameras, accessories, and photographic literature.** Wants early or unusual cameras and photo accessories, photography books, catalogs of photo equipment, advertising for cameras and film, and miscellaneous photographic ephemera such as lapel pins, buttons, and *Kodak* items.
Nicholas Graver
276 Brooklawn Drive
Rochester, NY 14618
(716) 244-4818

★ *View-Master* **reels and equipment** made by *Sawyers* or *GAF*, the companies that owned *View-Master* before 1980. Will buy single reels, 3-pack reels, cameras, *Stereomatic 500* projectors, and the blue Model B viewer. Also buys some *Tru-Vue* and other 3-D items. Does not want any cartoon reels or any damaged, broken, or worn items. Give numbers and condition.
>   Walter Sigg
>   Box 208
>   Swartswood, NJ 07877
>   (201) 383-2437

★ **3-D stereoscopic cameras and accessories** including viewers, projectors, manuals, books, by *Airequipt, Realist, Kodak, TDC, Wollensak, Busch, Radex, Brumberger*, and other makers. Books which discuss 3D photography and dealer displays which show any 3D image. "I will pay over $1,000 for some special 3D items such as the Macro Realist outfit by David White."
>   Harry Poster
>   Box 1883
>   South Hackensack, NJ 07606
>   (201) 794-9606 weekdays until 7pm

★ *View Master* **cameras, reels, and dealer displays** wanted. "I will pay over $100 for film punch or close-up lenses, $200 for *Stereomatic 500* 3D projector, $5 and up for Military reels in sets or for advertising reels, and over $50 each for movie preview reels and display from the 1950's 3D movies.. I need clean single reels and 3-packs, often paying over $5 for many newer packs. Send list, or the items themselves, for offer."
>   Harry Poster
>   Box 1883
>   South Hackensack, NJ 07606
>   (201) 794-9606 weekdays until 7pm

★ **3-D cameras, reels, and other** *View-Master* **equipment**, including flash, close up lenses, cases, film cutters, 3-D projectors, library boxes, adjustable viewers, and old order lists from *Sawyers* or *GAF*, the manufacturers of *View Master*. Want early views with blue backs, view reels that look like they're hand printed, Belgian made scenic views, pre-1970 U.S. scenics of other continents. "I don't want children's cartoon reels made after 1950 or any scratched or damaged reels." The reel number and © date are more important information than the title.
>   Robert Gill
>   PO Box 1223
>   Seaford, NY 11783
>   (516) 781-8741

Most Kodak and Polaroid still cameras have little if any value.

Colored, commemorative, and very early Kodak cameras are worth inquiry.

16mm home movie equipment also has little value.

magazines

People are attracted

to magazines for many reasons. Some buy for the covers and illustrations by Norman Rockwell, the Leyendecker brothers, Rockwell Kent, and other famous illustrators.

Other magazine buyers look for industry trade magazines and other publications with early articles about their specialty. Automobile, music, sports, tropical fish, guns, and other specialized magazines can be sold.

Advertising cut from magazines can be sold, but the price per ad is usually so low it doesn't pay the average person to do so. Leave that to the professional paper dealers in most instances.

Science fiction, mystery, and other fiction magazines also have their fans.

To describe items for sale, give the name and date of the magazines and note *all* tears, creases, writing, mailing stickers, or anything else which affects the cover or contents. If you have many issues, list them, counting only those with covers and pictures intact. Give a general condition statement.

If you are offering the magazine to someone because of an article contained in it, give the name and date of the magazine, name of the article, the author, and the number of illustrations. Xerox© copies of the story are helpful.

Ship magazines by "Special 4th Class Book Rate." It is the cheapest way to ship books and magazines.

tony hyman

Magazines

★ **Volume 1, Number 1, first issue magazines,** newspapers, comic books, or miscellaneous publications including newsletters, catalogs, fan publications, etc. Also buys pre-publication issues, proofs, dummies, and premier issues. "When I don't buy, I will try to help the seller find someone else who might."
> Stan Gold
> 7042 Dartbrook
> Dallas, TX 75240
> (214) 239-8621

★ **First issue and dummy issue magazines.** Seeking well known titles from before 1930. All should be in fine condition with especially clean covers and contents intact.
> Leon Williams
> 467 Portland Ave.
> St. Paul, MN 55102
> (612) 291-1639

★ **Most pre-1950 magazines in quantity.** Also most newer fashion, movie, and quality photography magazines. Give quantity per title and a description, and "we will contact you immediately." **Doesn't want** *National Geographic* after 1910, *Reader's Digest* after 1930, *Life* after 1936, *Arizona Highways* after 1940, or *American Heritage* with hardcovers. One of the country's largest dealers in magazines says, "we will pick them up if you have a truckload."
> The Antiquarian Bookstore
> 1070 Lafayette Rd.
> Portsmouth, NH 03801
> (603) 436-7250

★ **Illustrated magazines 1895 to 1930** including women's, children's, movie, pulps, theater, farm, motorcycle, and many more. Titles such as *Colliers, Esquire, Vogue, Saturday Evening Post, Vanity Fair, American* and others are wanted. Will consider movie and men's girlie magazines as late as the 1970's. Tell him the date, condition, and price. He is not interested in giving free appraisals and requests that "pen pals and time wasters" not bother him. Denis is author of inexpensive price guides to magazines, and offers an extensive catalog of prints for sale.
> Denis Jackson
> Box 1958
> Sequim, WA 98382
> (206) 683-2559

★ **Bound volumes of illustrated fashion and other magazines,** including *Grahams, Ladies Repository, Vicks, Petersons, Godeys Ladies Magazine,* and others published before 1880. Wants *Craftsman* (1900-1915), and *Delineator, Ladies Home Journal, Vogue, Womans Home Companion, Designer,* and *Saturday Evening Post* for periods from 1910 to 1922. Also wants *Gentlemans Magazine* published in London pre-1800. Condition is very important. Generally, inexperienced people overestimate the condition of these, often saying "good for its age" when it is in fair to poor condition. Note cracks or tears, foxing, etc. Include SASE for an answer.
> John Rosenhoover
> 100 Mandalay Rd.
> Chicopee, MA 01020
> (413) 536-5542

★ **Old magazines with beautiful covers and illustrations.** "I'm primarily interested in the period from 1910 to 1930, but will buy a few earlier or later. The quality and condition of the artistic illustrations are the key. Mucha is a favorite, but the work of many other illustrators is sought. Titles that are the most interest are *Collier's* (1900-1910), *Delineator* (1910-1924), *Harper's Bazaar* (1900-1960), *Hearst's* (1912-1930), *Inland Printer* (1890-1910), *Ladies Home Journal* (1900-1930), *Ladies World* (1912-1918), *Metropolitan* (1912-1924), *Vanity Fair* (1913-1936), *Vogue* (1900-1960), *Pictorial Review* (1910-1924), and movie magazines 1900-1945). I don't buy much after 1940, and nothing less than excellent condition. I always prefer to buy whole stacks, not single issues."
> Leon Williams
> 467 Portland Ave.
> St. Paul, MN 55102
> (612) 291-1639

★ **Fashion magazines, 1890-1910:** *Harpers Bazaar, Delineator,* and others from 1890-1910 only. Also buys pictures, postcards, and catalogs showing women's fashions of that period.
> Cheryl Abel
> 103 Jacqueline Ave.
> Delran, NJ 08075

★ **Magazines about fashion, costume, textiles,** sewing, beading, and the like. Especially wants pre-1870 fashion magazines like *Godey's Lady's* and others. NO OFFERS.
> Lois Mueller, Wooden Porch
> Rte 1, Box 262
> Middlebourne, WV, 26149

★ **Women's fashion magazines before 1900** including *Lady's Friend, Delineator, Godey's, Peterson's, Grahams,* and others. Please price what you offer.
Annie Nalewak, Shop 4
5515 So. Loop, East Crestmont
Houston, TX 77033

★ **Women's magazines.** "I'll buy women's magazines such as *Better Homes & Gardens, Good Housekeeping, McCalls* and *Ladies Home Journal.* I especially want issues from the 1930's and 1940's but will consider issues from 1900-1950."
Susan Cox
800 Murray Dr.
El Cajon, CA 92020

★ **Men's outdoor magazines.** "We are active and good buyers in need of magazines on hunting, fishing, guns, archery, hunting dogs, and guns. We buy *Stoeger Shooter's Bibles* (1924-1949), *Gun Digests* (1944-1962) and gun and fishing tackle catalogs (1850-1949). We will currently purchase all fine copies, including current years, of *Guns, Man at Arms, Gun Report, Gun World, Arms and the Man, World & Recreation, Rifle, Shooting and Fishing, Shooting Times, American Angler, Handloader, Guns and Ammo* and certain issues of other similar magazines. Special wants include *Chicago Field* (1876-1880), *Forest & Stream* before 1930, *Sports Afield* before 1932, *Field and Stream* before 1920, *Outdoor Life* before 1920 and others. "We need magazines in fine condition, both covers present, and as originally attached, with no bad musty smell, and nothing cut out. We realize you cannot go page by page through each magazine, but if one in a group has things cut out, the chances are that most of them will. Sometimes in the case of very old and scarce magazines we can use them in less than fine condition. Do not ship anything in advance, as our wants do change over time."
Lewis Razek
Highwood Bookshop
PO Box 1246
Traverse City, MI 49684
(616) 271-3898

★ **Men's outdoor magazines** including *Field & Stream, Outdoor Life* pre-1920, and *Sports Afield* before 1932.
Thomas McKinnon
PO Box 86
Wagram, NC 28396

Never send items to anyone without permission. Postal regulations say the person you send to has the right to keep what you send free!

★ *Esquire* **magazine,** 1933-1959. Also buys *Playboy* (pre-1960 *only*), *True,* and complete years or decades of *Cosmopolitan, McCalls, Vogue, Ladies Home Journal, Women's Home Companion, Redbook, Saturday Evening Post, Country Gentlemen,* and *Collier's.* Also buys **sexually oriented pulp magazines** like *Spicy Stories, Snappy Tales, Bedtime Stories,* etc. List years, and condition.
Charles Martignette
PO Box 293
Hallandale, FL 33009

★ **Scandal and exploitation magazines** from 1952-1973 including, but not limited to, *Anything Goes, Behind the Scenes, Blast, Bunk!, Celebrity, Confidential, Dynamite, Exposed, Hollywood Tattler, Hush-Hush, Inside Story, The Lowdown, Naked Truth, Private Lives, Private Story, Rave, Revealed, Secret Life, Sensation, Sh-H-H-H, Suppressed, Top Secret, TV Scandals, Uncensored, Untold Secrets, Untold Story,* and *Whisper.* "I'll pay $35 each for clean complete issues of *Inside Stuff* from the 1930's." Also wants complete copies of *Police Gazette* in good condition from any year, especially bound. Wants nothing current, nothing soiled or with pages clipped or water or sun damage. Give title, date, and volume number.
Gordon Hasse
Box 1543, GC Station
New York, NY 10163-1543
(212) 996-3825 eves

★ **Brewers, saloon, coin-op, and "Police"** magazines pre-1920 including *Brewers Gazette, Champion of Fair Play, Coin Machine Journal, Automatic Age, Spinning Reels, Pacific Coin Machine Review, The Billboard* (1894-1932 only), and *National Police Gazette*. "I'll pay $1,000 per year for *Police Gazette*, 1896-98."
Richard Bueschel
414 N. Prospect Manor Ave.
Mt. Prospect, IL 60056
(708) 253-0791 eves

★ *Cash Box, Coin Machine Journal* and other publications which covered the coin operated amusement business. Particularly wants issues featuring pinball. Also *Billboard* magazine in from any date before 1960, especially quantity purchases of bound volumes. Fine condition only. Give dates and volume numbers.
Gordon Hasse
Box 1543 GC Station
New York, NY 10163-1543
(212) 996-3825 eves

★ *Downbeat, Metronome, Billboard* and movie magazines.
Beverly Hamer
Box 75
E. Derry, NH 03041

★ **Music and song magazines 1920-60** including *Downbeat, Billboard, Disc, Metronome, Bandleader*, and song magazines that print words to songs such as *Song Hits, Hit Parader, 400 Songs, Songs That Will Live Forever*, etc. He will consider those with damage or minor cut outs. "Just ship them for my offer." Also **Movie magazines**, 1920-49. He asks that you double check to make certain *nothing* has been clipped out of the magazine. Indicate whether there is a mailing label pasted on the cover.
Ken Mitchell
710 Concacher Dr.
Willowdale, Ontario M2M 3N6, CANADA

★ **Movie magazines.** "I prefer larger quantities, not single issues, of magazines from 1925-1950. I also want **trade magazines sent to theater managers** with advertising selling films to theaters rather than the public: *MGM Lions Roar, Motion Picture Herald,* and *Boxoffice*."
Buddy McDaniel
2802 West 18th St.
Wichita, KS 67203
(316) 942-3561

★ **Movie and other magazines with movie stars on the cover.** Will buy movie, TV, radio, and other magazines with celebrities on the cover from 1908 to 1950. Magazines must be in fine or better condition, and complete with no cut or missing pages. "Please let me know what you have and what you want for it, or just ship for my immediate offer."
Alan Levine
292 Glenwood Ave.
PO Box 1577
Bloomfield, NJ 07003
(201) 743-5288

★ *TV Guide*, 1948-70, including early local editions. Selected issues from 1971 to 1989 are also purchased. Issues of NY City's *Television Guide* from 1948 are worth $25-$50 each. Jeff wants to know if address label is on the cover.
Jeffrey Kadet
Box 20
Macomb, IL 61455
(309) 833-1809

★ **American humor magazines and newspapers,** 1765 to date. Comic material and ephemera (but *not* comic books). Humorous periodicals included satire, cartoons, or comic sketches in a variety of formats, mostly to a popular audience. Does not want recent national titles such as *MAD* and *National Lampoon*.
David Sloane
4 Edgehill Terrace
Hamden, CT 06517
(203) 624-4206

★ *Humorama* magazine. "I'll always pay $1 and up for this joke magazine." Give dates.
Jeff Patton
3621 Carolina St. NW
Massillon, OH 44646

★ **College humor magazines and covers.** "Buying one and all. Send a Xerox© copy of the cover and indicate the date if it doesn't show."
Lisa Lisciotto
455 Harding Place
Fairview, NJ 07022

★ **Magazines about airplanes, boats, motor-cycles, automobiles, and other vehicles.** Prefers to buy longer runs, rather than single issues. pre-1960 only. Telephone or write first. If interested, he will request items be sent for inspection. Excellent condition for resale only.
Jay Ketelle
3721 Farwell
Amarillo, TX 79109
(806) 355-3456

★ **Magazines about boats, boat racing, yachting, marine engineering, and similar topics.** Buys for resale, but has strong personal interest in small boats, outboards, and canoes.
Robert Glick
504 Main St.
West Barnstable, MA 02668

★ *Sportsman Pilot* magazine. All early issues.
Karen Jentzsch Barta
245 W. Loraine #208
Glendale, CA 91202
(818) 243-0125 fax: (818) 507-5702

★ *British Journal Photographic Almanacs* any year, and **other photo magazines** pre-1930.
Jim McKeown, Centennial Photo
11595 State Road 70
Grantsburg, WI 54840

★ **National Geographic Society publications of all types.** Buys magazines, books, booklets, maps, article reprints, pamphlets, map indexes, atlases, pictorials, school bulletins, news bulletins, advertising brochures, booklets, catalogs, invitations, announcements, autographs, slides, videos, postcards, and calendars produced by the NGS. Also buys materials published by other companies with articles about the NGS, which spoof the NGS, are funded by the NGS, or in any way refer to the NGS. He is particularly interested in magazines before 1913, technical books such as that on Machu Picchu (for which he'll pay $1,000) and the complete advertising brochure sent to prospective members in 1888. He'll pay you $5,000 for a vol. 1, No. 1 magazine. **Not interested in magazines after 1959.** As a service to fellow collectors, Nick buys outright or accepts items on consignment. He encourages correspondence from buyers and sellers.
Nick Koopman
Collectors Exchange
10600 Lowery Dr.
Raleigh, NC 27615
(919) 870-8416

★ **Gaming magazines** including *The General, The Wargamer, Fire & Movement, Games & Puzzles, The Dragon*, and similar magazines in fine condition, any year.
H.M. Levy
Box 197CC
East Meadow, NY 11554
(516) 485-0877

★ **Crossword and other puzzle magazines** before 1970. "It doesn't matter if they're filled in." Give the name, date, and condition. Early issues of *The Eastern Enigma*, a puzzle magazine of the National Puzzlers' League are of particular interest, and he'll pay $1,000 for the missing eighteen issues.
Will Shortz
Games Magazine
19 West 21st Street
New York, NY 10010
(212) 727-7100 days

★ **Packing, canning, bottling and printing trade magazines** from 1880 to 1960, such as: *Modern Packaging, Better Fruit, California Citrograph, Modern Printing, Skookum News, Pacific Bottler*, and *California Farmer*.
T. Pat Jacobsen
437 Minton Court
Pleasant Hill, CA 94523
(415) 930-8531

★ **Military magazines published by U.S., British, or Canadian forces** between 1939-45. "I'll buy *Field Artillery Journal, Air Force, Infantry Journal, Sea Power, The Aeroplane, Coast Artillery Journal, Flight, Ordnance, Impact* and the *Army-Navy Recognition Journal*. No other titles and no damaged, incomplete, or badly soiled magazines."
Edward Topor
4313 South Marshfield Ave.
Chicago, IL 60609
(312) 847-6392

★ **Pipe, tobacco, and smoking magazines of all sorts.** This internationally known tobacco historian wants pipe magazines from 1930's and 40's and tobacco magazines 1860-1900. Prefers long runs. Pays $1-3 per issue, plus all shipping. Nothing after 1950.
Tony Hyman
Box 3028
Pismo Beach, CA 93448

Pulp Magazines

★ **Detective and mystery pulp magazines** such as *Black Mask, Dime Detective*, etc. Can be contacted by modem as stock is computerized.
> Richard West
> Box 406
> Elm Grove, WI 53122
> (414) 786-8420

★ **Pulp magazines.** "I'll buy many different types, the most valuable of which are hero, super-hero and character pulps such as *The Shadow, The Spider, Doc Savage, Secret Agent X, The Secret Six, Operator #5, Captain Satan, Captain Hazard, Captain Zero, the Whisperer, The Wizard, Wu Fang, Dr. Yen Sin* and the like. Also important are aviation pulps like *G-8, Bill Barnes, Dusty Ayres, Battle Aces, Dare-Devil Aces, Battle Birds, Flying Aces* and many similar titles. Other collectible pulp categories are detective, mystery, spicy, horror, terror, and "odd-ball titles" like *Gun Molls* and *Speakeasy Stories*." Not interested in romance or Westerns. Give the title, date, and overall condition of magazines for sale. Include your phone number. Please do not inquire about comic books or family magazines like *Post, Life, Look, Geographic,* or *Reader Digest.* "I also want **pulp related items** such as pins, badges, rings, membership cards, cover proofs, original art, promotional displays, autographs or writers and artists, etc."
> Jack Deveny
> 6805 Cheyenne Trail
> Edina, MN 55435
> (612) 941-2457

★ **Pulp magazines.** "I'll buy nearly 1,000 titles broken down into Adventure, Aviation, Crime & Detective, Hero, Mystery & Menace, Western, Science Fiction & Fantasy and "Miscellaneous." This includes romance, spicy, erotic, sports, confession, and many other types. Give the title, date, and overall condition of each magazine for sale, with emphasis on the cover, following the guide provided below." This award winning artist, prolific writer, and editor also wants **lurid original art for covers and inside stories.** Include your phone number if selling art.
> Jim Steranko
> PO Box 974
> Reading, PA 19603
> (215) 374-7477

★ **Pulp magazines of the 1930's** such as *G-8, Spider, Operator 5, The Shadow, Doc Savage, Black Mask,* and the like. Also, would love to find the October, 1912, issue of *All Story* with "Tarzan of the Apes."
> Claude Held
> Box 515
> Buffalo, NY 14225

★ **Pulp magazines** from before 1950 such as *The Shadow, Doc Savage, The Spider,* and *G-8,* in the genres of aviation, science fiction, spicy, detective, horror, etc.
> Ken Mitchell
> 710 Concacher Dr.
> Willowdale, Ontario M2M 3N6 CANADA

★ **Lurid gangster magazines of the 1920's and 1930's.**
> Michael Graham
> 345 Cleveland Avenue
> Libertyville, IL 60048

How to Describe the Condition of a Magazine
COURTESY OF JIM STERANKO

VF (very fine) = fresh, bright copy without flaws except for minor aging of paper;

F (fine) = bright copy with very minor wear and only minute cover tears or creases;

VG (very good) = some cover and spine wear, tiny tears and creases, minor chipping and browning of interior paper;

G (good) = indicates obvious cover and spine wear, discoloration, water stains pieces missing or tears up to an inch long;

FA (fair) = tight and complete, but longer cover creases, tears, rubbing, fading, and/or store stamps or dates;

P (poor) = many defects, serious damage, referred to as a "reading copy."

newspapers

Even if 100 years old

newspapers seldom sell for a lot of money.

A whole year of the *London Gazette* from 1800 is only worth about $300. Fascinating newspapers and magazines with first hand stories of Daniel Boone and Andrew Jackson can be bought from some dealers listed in *I'll Buy That Too!* for less than $30.

One of our dealers sold a Baltimore paper describing the burning of Washington by the British in the War of 1812 for only $15.

To describe a paper, give the name, city, date, number and size of pages, and an indication of any significant stories. If bound, indicate the type and condition of the binding (leather or boards, loose, split, leather crumbling, etc.). If it is a small town 18th or 19th century paper with a fancy masthead, a photocopy is suggested.

The newspapers that bring the most are illustrated weeklies like *Harper's* and *Leslie's* from 1855-1900. When offering 19th century illustrated papers, make certain they are complete as the value drops significantly when important pictures are missing. Tell the buyer about foxing (brown spots), tears, rips, stains, and cut outs.

If the paper is dry, brown, or brittle, it is seldom of value unless pre-1750 or the only known copy of a title.

Both newspapers and magazines can be shipped "Special Fourth Class Book Rate," which is inexpensive. Ask for the latest rates at your post office.

tony hyman

Newspapers

★ **Newspapers covering any important event before 1945.** Also all half year bound runs of pre-1870 papers, especially from Southern U.S., Confederate States, Early West, or anywhere in the U.S. pre-1800. Wants specialty papers covering the women's movement, labor, railroads, abolitionism, temperance, or the Civil war. Also **illustrated newspapers** like *Harper's, Leslie's, New York Illustrated News, Ballou's Pictorial, Southern Illustrated News, Canadian Illustrated News, London Illustrated News,* etc. Also bound volumes of British newspapers and magazines pre-1700 (although he will buy later issues if historically significant). Also bound runs or single issues of any American magazine published before 1800. Pays $100 an issue for newspapers before 1730 but notes that many reprints exist so they need be authenticated. *No 20th century items* except mint condition reports of important events. *No severely defective papers.* For $5 per year (free to buyers) Phil issues an interesting catalog of historic papers available reasonably. Send $3 for a sample.

> Phil Barber
> Box 8694
> Boston, MA 02114

★ **Newspapers of historical significance** especially relative to Lincoln's speeches or death, George Washington, the Revolution, the Civil War, colonial America, early Illinois and the Chicago fire. Buys individual issues of historical significance or bound volumes. Buys all *Harper's Weekly* and *Frank Leslie's Illustrated*, 1855-1916.

> Steve and Linda Alsberg
> 9850 Kedvale Ave.
> Skokie, IL 60076
> (708) 676-9850

★ **Bound volumes of American and European illustrated newspapers, 1850-1910** including *Harper's Weekly, Leslie's, Illustrated London News, Judge, Vanity Fair, La Vie Parisenne, Das Plachate, Jugend, Puck,* and the like. Condition is important.

> Joe Davidson
> Aaron Industries
> 5185 Windfall Road
> Medina, OH 44256
> (216) 723-7172

★ **Bound volumes of illustrated weekly newspapers** including *Harper's, Leslie's, Puck, Scientific American, London Illustrated News, London Daily Graphic, Judge, Vim, Wasp, Gleason's, Ballou's, Verdict, Inland Printer, Aldine, New York Daily Graphic* (1870-89 only), and others, but before 1890 only. Stacks of loose issues considered, but single copies are not wanted. Fine condition only.

> John Rosenhoover
> 100 Mandalay Rd.
> Chicopee, MA 01020
> (413) 536-5542

★ **Foreign language newspapers published in New York City** during the 19th century. Not interested in any papers published elsewhere or published after 1900.

> Peter Eckel
> 1335 Grant Ave.
> So. Plainfield, NJ 07080

★ **Chicago newspapers which cover gangster activities, 1920-33.** He has more than 60 particular events he wants the papers for and will provide a list upon request.

> Michael Graham
> Roaring 20's
> 345 Cleveland Avenue,
> Libertyville, IL 60048
> (312) 362-4808 days

★ **Modern spicy scandal sheet type newspapers** like *Top Secret, Inside Story,* and *Whisper.*

> Warren Nussbaum
> 29-10 137th Street
> Flushing, NY 11354

collector's periodicals

If you want to read or

advertise in collectibles periodicals, there are hundreds of specialty publications from which to chose. Among the more popular which offer general coverage are:

The Antique Trader Weekly.
100 page weekly tabloid of classified ads for every collectible imaginable. National. $22 a year from Box 1050, Dubuque, IA 52001.

Maine Antique Digest. 300+ page monthly tabloid paper covering art, folk art, furniture, and better antiques. Most scholarly and interesting of antiques publications. Many New England dealer and auction ads. $29 a year from 71 Main Street, Waldoboro, ME 04572.

Antique Gazette. 75+ page monthly tabloid covering the South. $15 per year from 6949 Charlotte Pike, #106, Nashville, TN 37209

NY-PA Collector. 90+ page monthly tabloid covering shows and auctions of that area. $15 per year from Drawer C, Fishers, NY 14453

Paper and Advertising Collector.
34 p. monthly tabloid. Excellent place to advertise for paper things you want. $12 per year from Box 500, Mount Joy, PA 17552.

Paper Collectors' Marketplace.
64 page monthly. $12 per year from Box 127, Scandinavia, WI 54977.

Samples are available for $3 from these publications.

tony hyman

books

You find book buyers

all through *I'll Buy That Too!* If you have non-fiction books on specific historical, technical or scientific topics make certain to check out the appropriate section to find a buyer.

Book buyers look for books on specific topics, the work of specific authors, books published by certain publishers, books illustrated in a particular manner, books from a particular period or country, and books of a specific type, such as leather-bound, miniature, first edition, or autographed.

Give "Standard Bibliographic Information" on all books for sale, remembering that Xerox© copies can save you lots of time. Don't offer people books that are damaged, torn, recent, or not what people say they buy.

A dealer's price for books depends upon his customers, his present stock, the rarity of your offering, the current market, and his mood and cash flow at the moment. If you want an appraisal of your books, hire an appraiser and pay the fee. Understand before you do, however, that most family book collections, except large collections on a single topic, are not worth the expense.

Books may be shipped Special 4th Class Book Rate, which permits three pounds for about two dollars. Remember, books are fragile, and can be damaged in transit. If it's good enough to sell, it's good enough to protect with proper padding.

tony hyman

Fine Books

★ **Large collections of good books,** especially subject collections of Americana, Civil War non-fiction, Michigan history, theology, golf, chess, etc. Also wants books with color plates, leather bound books, and autographed books by famous authors. Catalogs are issued periodically. If you want to sell, give standard bibliographic information. One of the nation's largest used and rare booksellers, John does not buy *Reader's Digest* books, *National Geographics,* book club editions, textbooks of any kind, encyclopedia sets, or anything in poor condition.

John K. King Books
901 W. Lafayette Blvd.
Detroit, MI 48226
(313) 961-0622

★ **Any book, pamphlet, or tract printed in English speaking America before 1800.** "Books need not be complete nor necessarily in good condition. We will purchase damaged books or even fragments." If you own a book without a title page that you believe to be very old you may send them the book for identification. It's always best to write first, though, and if possible send them a photocopy. The Haydn Foundation for the Cultural Arts is a non profit public institution.

Michael Zinman
Haydn Foundation
495 Ashford Avenue
Ardsley, NY 10502

★ **Various fine and early books,** including:
[1] **Books with fore edge paintings;** "Let us hear about all fore edge paintings, no matter the era;"
[2] **Incunabula,** printed before 1501;
[3] **European books** before 1600;
[4] **English books** and manuscripts from before 1700;
[5] **American books before 1800;**
[6] **Books on China or Japan** if scholarly and illustrated;
[7] **Sets of fine leather bindings;**
[8] **Books illustrated in color, especially chromolithographs,** before 1900;
[9] **Books published in Pennsylvania** before 1810 in English or 1830 in German. Especially seek items printed by Benjamin Franklin in Philadelphia, the Brotherhood in Ephrata, or the Saurs (Sower) in Germantown.

Please make a Xerox© of the title page. In business for 20 years, Ron offers a series of fine catalogs. He is a member of numerous historical and professional organizations.

Ron Lieberman
Family Album
RD #1 Box 42
Glen Rock, PA 17327
(717) 235-2134

★ **Fine and antiquarian books,** pamphlets, and original manuscripts, especially dealing with medicine, travel to the old West and photography.

Ivan Gilbert
Miran Arts & Books
2824 Elm Ave.
Columbus, OH 43209

Books worth $100+ turn up regularly.
First edition mystery books (1930's and 40's)
are often worth that and more.
They must have their dust jackets
to bring anything approaching top price.

Standard Bibliographic Information

Title, author, publisher, place and date(s) of publication,
number of pages, illustrator, and approximate number of illustrations.

Give the condition of (1) the binding, (2) the spine, (3) the pages, and
(4) the dust jacket. Note bookplates, writing, and other damage.
A photocopy of the title page will save lots of writing.

★ **Any type of book from art and archery to Zen and zoology.** This important Florida dealer prefers rare books but is interested in a wide variety of topics and subject matter, especially limited edition books by fine presses such as Derrydale, Kelmscott Press, Black Sun Press, Grolier Club, Grabhorne Press and the like. He does not buy school books, encyclopedia, medical texts, book of the Month Club editions, or reprints of famous novels. He feels only tentative evaluations are possible without actually seeing your book, but provide him with complete Standard Bibliographic Information.
Steven Eisenstein
Book-A-Brack
6760 Collins Ave.
Miami, FL 33141
(305) 865-0092

★ **Book collections and libraries of fine items.**
James D. Julia Auctions
Rt. 201, Skowhegan Rd.
Fairfield, ME 04937
(207) 453-9725

★ **Collections or accumulations of rare books, illustrated books or photography books.**
The Antiquarian Bookstore
1070 Lafayette Rd.
Portsmouth, NH 03801
(603) 436-7250

★ **Autographed non-fiction books.** Will consider all, but has particular interest in the Soviet Union, Eastern Europe, Asia, Communism, Socialism, and conservative authors.
Edward Conroy, SUMAC Books
RD#1 Box 197
Troy, NY 12180
(518) 279-9638 eves

★ **Leather bound books.** "I'll buy decorator leather bound books in quantity for $3 to $5 each. Not interested in fine first editions, just old books with little other value. Must have good spines and covers, but can be in any language from any period, as I want them only for their decorator potential. Call if you've got a bunch of them."
Joan Brady
834 Central Ave.
Pawtucket, RI 02861
(401) 725-5753

★ **Books illustrated by Japanese woodblocks.**
Jerrold Stanoff
Rare Oriental Book Co.
Box 1599
Aptos, CA 95003
(408) 724-4911   Fax: (408) 761-1350

★ **Books illustrated with photographs tipped (glued) in,** U.S. or foreign. Also books illustrated by important photographers.
Janet Lehr
Box 617 Gracie Square Station
New York, NY 10028

★ **Books illustrated with full page b/w illustrations,** including steel engravings, etchings, copper plates, or woodblocks. Wants views of the U.S. and Canada, North American Indians, explorations and Western America, animals, art, railway surveys, pre-1880 fairs and Centennials, architecture, Civil War, and pre-1860 Hawaii (Sandwich Islands). Indicate size along with standard bibliographic information. Note tears, foxing, etc. Count the number of illustrations.
John Rosenhoover
100 Mandalay Rd.
Chicopee, MA 01020
(413) 536-5542

★ **Books from before 1890 illustrated with color pictures** depicting plants, animals, birds, fish, Indians, sports, cowboys, medicine, military, buildings, costumes, fashion, or advertising. Provide standard bibliographic data to this major graphics dealer.
  Joe Davidson
  Aaron Industries
  5185 Windfall Road
  Medina, OH 44256
    (216) 723-7172

★ **Atlases with colored plates** as long as they deal in whole or in part with the United States. Wants bound volumes by Colton, Mitchell, Finley, Carey & Lea, Johnson, Copperthwaite, Melish, Tanner, Arrorsmith, Bradford, and Gray & Smith. Others considered. Important that double page plates should not have a white border separating the plate into two sections. Also interested in **commercial atlases prior to 1925** and **books of all types with foldout maps** in black and white or color, but they must be before 1870. Groups of loose color plate maps are also considered. Include dimensions with standard bibliographic information. Note tears, erasures, foxing, etc. Give the number of maps in color and in black and white.
  John Rosenhoover
  100 Mandalay Rd.
  Chicopee, MA 01020
    (413) 536-5542

★ **Atlases with colored plates** a published before 1870. Provide standard bibliographic data to this important dealer.
  Joe Davidson
  Aaron Industries
  5185 Windfall Road
  Medina, OH 44256
    (216) 723-7172

★ **Books illustrated with color plates before 1899**, especially German before 1895, American natural history (plants and animals) before 1870, and Indians. Give standard bibliographic information, noting tears, erasures, foxing, etc. Give the number of illustrations in color and in b/w.
  John Rosenhoover
  100 Mandalay Rd.
  Chicopee, MA 01020
    (413) 536-5542

★ **Books illustrated by** Kate Greenaway, Arthur Rackham, Jessie Smith, K. Neilson, Wyeth, W. Crane, Maxfield Parrish, Pogany, Dulac, Newell, Maud Humphrey, Remington, Erte, or Harrison Fisher. Books must date between 1890 and 1926. Give standard bibliographic information, noting tears, erasures, foxing, etc. Count and indicate the number of illustrations in color and in black and white.
  John Rosenhoover
  100 Mandalay Rd.
  Chicopee, MA 01020
    (413) 536-5542

★ **Large 20th century fiction collections.** If you have many hundreds of hardback fiction books with their original dust jackets, give him a call. No paperbacks.
  James Dourgarian, Bookman
  1595-A Third Avenue
  Walnut Creek, CA 94596
    (415) 935-5033

Standard Bibliographic Information

Title, author, publisher, place and date(s) of publication, number of pages, illustrator, and approximate number of illustrations.

Give the condition of (1) the binding, (2) the spine, (3) the pages, and (4) the dust jacket. Note bookplates, writing, and other damage. A photocopy of the title page will save lots of writing.

Books by Various Authors

★ **Things by, about, or related to author John Steinbeck** including signed limited editions, first editions, first printings by subsequent publishers, appearances in anthologies, spoken word records and tapes, film and theater memorabilia, and things owned by him. Does not want book club editions, items in poor condition, or fakes. If a book had a dust jacket, slipcase, box, wrap-around, etc., as originally issued, then these items should still be present. Please be specific about what you have for sale, giving complete bibliographic information and a full description.
James Dourgarian, Bookman
1595-A Third Avenue
Walnut Creek, CA 94596
(415) 935-5033

★ **First editions and non-fiction titles by Gene Stratton Porter or Zane Grey.** Also all fishing books by Zane Grey. No Grosset & Dunlap books. Wants list available.
James Baumhofer
Box 65493
St. Paul, MN 55165
(612) 698-7151

★ **Books by Harlan Ellison,** U.S. or foreign, hardbacks with dust jacket or mint condition paperbacks, especially 1st editions, numbered editions, and autographed copies. Especially wants copies of *Sex Gang*, written under the pseudonym Paul Merchant.
Edy Chandler
Box 20664
Houston, TX 77225
(713) 531-9615 eves

★ **Books by Jack London,** especially 1st editions. Pays $300-$800 for 1st editions in dust jackets, $100 to $500 without. No paperbacks, unless rare titles or unusual copies. Also all Jack London memorabilia including photos and hand-written manuscripts.
Russ Kingman
Jack London Bookstore
Box 337
Glen Ellen, CA 95442

★ **Books by Joseph Conrad,** *only* if first editions or in nicely bound sets. Also books and ephemera about Conrad. Also **books by George Macdonald** in any edition and condition.
Chip Greenberg, Booksearch
Box 123, Planetarium Station
New York, NY 10024
(212) 362-9336

★ **Thornton W. Burgess and Harrison Cady books and ephemera.** Does not want any of their books published by Grosset & Dunlop.
Stephen Kruskall
Box 418
Dover, MA 02030

★ **Books by or about Victoria Woodhull,** American spiritualist, feminist, and Presidential candidate.
Ronald Lowden, Jr.
314 Chestnut Ave.
Narberth, PA 19072

★ **Autographed books by Richard Halliburton,** especially 1st editions with dust jackets, and all foreign editions. Also paper ephemera, including letters, flyers, photos, etc.
Michael Blankenship
5320 Spencer Drive SW
Roanoke, VA 24018

★ **Books by Samuel Beckett or Franz Kafka.** Wants only English or German 1st editions of Kafka. Will pay $1,000 up for 1st edition or signed works by Beckett.
Breon Mitchell
Peartree Books
Box 1072
Bloomington, IN 47402
(812) 876-4827

★ **First edition books by Southern Appalachian authors,** including Harriett Arnow, Wilma Dykeman, Davis Grubb, and works by ministers and travelers in this area. Also Virginia, West Virginia, South Carolina, Kentucky, Tennessee, Louisiana, Texas, Delaware, and Washington DC, history, bibliography, natural history, and outdoor recreation, if published pre-1900.
Jim Presgraves
Box 639
Wytheville, VA 24382

Books by Various Publishers

★ **Peter Pauper Press books.** First published in 1929, still going strong today, PPP is usually associated with 4.5"x7" illustrated books, but it has done larger ones too. Especially wants fine condition books from the 1930's, 40's, and early 50's. Include the name of the illustrator with the standard bibliographic information. It's important to include the *color of the cover* since these were offered in various colors and she buys variants. Small ones are usually under $5 and large ones under $20 "except something fabulous and unusual."
Mary Mac Franklin
2716 Northfield Rd.
Charlottesville, VA 22901
   (804) 973-3238 before 9pm

★ **Books published by Arlington House.**
Edward Conroy
RD #1 Box 197
Troy, NY 12180
   (518) 279-9638 eves

★ **Rare editions of works published by the Elzevirs.** Provide full bibliographic information and description of condition.
Albert J. Phiebig, Inc.
Box 352
White Plains, NY 10602
   (914) 948-0138   fax (914) 948-0784

★ **Books published by the Limited Editions Club.** "I'll buy all years, all titles, as long as they are in fine condition in a fine box. I'll also buy Club ephemera including monthly letters, prospectus, etc." Only *Lysistrata* and *Ulysses* are acceptable without original box.
Lee & Mike Temares
50 Heights Rd.
Plandome, NY 11030
   (516) 627-8688

★ **Books published by:**
[1] **Neale** in either NY or Washington, DC;
[2] **Henkel** of New Market, VA;
[3] Pennsylvania German **Folklore Society**;
[4] **Any Southern publisher** prior to 1865.
Write or phone, giving Standard Bibliographic information.
Jim Presgraves
Bookworm & Silverfish
Box 639
Wytheville, VA 24382
   (703) 686-5813

★ **Books published in Pennsylvania** by Benjamin Franklin, the Brotherhood in Ephrata, or the Saurs (Sower) in Germantown.
Ron Lieberman
RD #1 Box 42
Glen Rock, PA 17327
   (717) 235-2134

★ **Books published by Roycroft.**
Thomas Knopke
House of Roycroft
1430 E. Brookdale Place
Fullerton, CA 92631

Standard Bibliographic Information

Title, author, publisher, place and date(s) of publication, number of pages, illustrator, and approximate number of illustrations.

Give the condition of (1) the binding, (2) the spine, (3) the pages, and (4) the dust jacket. Note bookplates, writing, and other damage. A photocopy of the title page will save lots of writing.

Books on Various Topics

★ **Art, architecture, music, dance, and photography.** Wants 19th and 20th century scholarly or out-of-print books. Also photographic albums of quality photographs. Buys for resale. Muns issues periodic catalogs in these fields.
J.B. Muns
Fine Arts Books
1162 Shattuck Ave.
Berkeley, CA 94707

★ **Mining, minerals, and gems** especially in Arizona and Colorado. Russ buys old, scarce, or out of print books and paper ephemera. Wants *System of Mineralogy* by James Dana in the first through sixth editions, 1837-1892.
Russell Filer
Geoscience Books
Box 487
Yucaipa, CA 92399
(714) 797-1650

★ **History of mining, telegraph, and railroads,** including Colorado mining directories.
David Beach
Paper Americana
PO Box 2026
Goldenrod, FL 32733
(407) 657-7403   Fax: (407) 6576382

★ **Photography, photographers, photographs,** and selected how-to photographic books, but only those before 1938. Also books with tipped in (glued in) photos.
Alan Voorhees
Cameras & Such
492 Breesport Rd.
Horseheads, NY 14845

★ **Photography books.** Old, out-of-print, or remaindered books on glamour photography, nude photography, or boudoir photography. "I'll buy single titles or collections, but not interested in other photography books." Jack asks you to set your price, but he'll send you a catalog of titles for $1. You might get his catalog and price yours at 50% of what similar books are sold for.
Jack Qualman
Jax Photo Books
5491 Mantua Ct.
San Diego, CA 92124

★ **Books about photography or photographers,** 19th or 20th century, *Camera Work* magazine, and books with photographs tipped in (glued in) and photo albums pre-1900 only. You must price what you wish to sell to him.
Richard Rosenthal
4718 Springfield Ave.
Philadelphia, PA 19143
(215) 726-5493

★ **Crossword puzzle books.** It doesn't matter if the puzzles are filled in, as long as the books are hard cover and before 1955. Give standard bibliographic information.
Will Shortz
Games Magazine
19 West 21st Street
New York, NY 10010
(212) 727-7100 days

★ **Pre-1970 crossword and other word puzzle books,** hard or soft cover, even if written in. Especially wants Simon and Schuster hardcover puzzle books 1924-60. Give the complete title, date, and series number, and tell how much of the book has been filled in. No crossword dictionaries, but does buy **crossword puzzle magazines.** Wants list sent for large SASE.
Stanley Newman
American Crossword
Box 69
Massapequa Park, NY 11762

★ **Checkers or draughts.**
Don Deweber
Checker Book World
3520 Hillcrest #4
Dubuque, IA 52001
(319) 556-1944 let ring

★ **Playing cards, card playing, and card games,** especially bridge and whist.
Bill Sachen
927 Grand Ave.
Waukegan, IL 60085

★ **Electric organ owner's manuals.**
C. Ray Erler
Box 140 Miles Run Road
Spring Creek, PA 16436
(814) 563-7287

Standard Bibliographic Information

Title, author, publisher, place and date(s) of publication,
number of pages, illustrator, and approximate number of illustrations.

Give the condition of (1) the binding, (2) the spine, (3) the pages, and
(4) the dust jacket. Note bookplates, writing, and other damage.
A photocopy of the title page will save lots of writing.

★ **Adirondack mountain communities, events, people, or history** including French and Indian War, Revolutionary War, War of 1812, hunting and outdoor recreation, personalities. Offers $75 each for the **Birch Bark Books**, a series of 19 small volumes bound in simulated birch bark and given by Henry Abbott between 1914 and 1932 as Christmas gifts. Breck publishes both a catalog and wants list of Adirondack materials, available upon request.
  Breck Turner
  With Pipe and Book
  91 Main St.
  Lake Placid, NY 12946

★ **Tennessee or Alabama history**, with some interest in all Southern materials. No textbooks, religious titles, library discards, or items in poor condition.
  William Snell
  The Book Shelf
  3765 Hillsdale Drive NE
  Cleveland, TN 37311

★ **Nebraska history and books related to the Western movement and Western Americana.** Interested almost exclusively in hardback first editions, especially autographed books with dust jackets.
  Francis Moul
  PO Box 81066
  Lincoln, NE 68501

★ **Canadian topics** including travel, history, politics, exploration, fur trade, Indians, immigration, or mountaineering.
  Tom Williams, Books
  Box 4126, Station C
  Calgary, Alberta T2T 5M9, CANADA

★ **Travel and voyages,** pre-1920.
  David and Cathy Lilburne
  Antipodean Books
  Box 189
  Cold Springs, NY 10516

★ **African exploration and development** as well as materials devoted to solutions to problems faced by lesser developed countries today. Also **Arabic studies** including materials relating the spheres of Moslem influence, both ancient and modern. Buys important books in Arabic and related languages.
  Ron Lieberman
  RD #1 Box 42
  Glen Rock, PA 17327
    (717) 235-2134

★ **China, Japan and Korea.** "I'll buy pre-1940 books on China or Japan, pre-1950 books on Korea, and pre-1980 books on Asian art. Also interested in books about Asians in the U.S., Japanese or Chinese Buddhism, Lafcadio Hearn, and Asian travel. Also interested in Far Eastern bibliography, Japanese wood block printing, and maps of those three countries.
  Jerrold Stanoff
  Rare Oriental Book Co.
  Box 1599
  Aptos, CA 95003
    (408) 724-4911   Fax: 9408) 761-1350

★ **Russia, Soviet Union, China, Afghanistan, Mongolia, Tibet, or Eastern Europe** before 1940.
  Edward Conroy
  SUMAC Books
  RD #1 Box 197
  Troy, NY 12180
    (518) 279-9638 eves

★ **Communism, socialism, Marxism** and books by or about **Russian Royalty.**
> Edward Conroy
> RD #1 Box 197
> Troy, NY 12180
>> (518) 279-9638 eves

★ **Urban studies** including material about cities everywhere and in all eras, including architectural, social, and historical aspects. Also **city view books** showing buildings and streets of cities worldwide. Make certain to include count of pages and photos in your description.
> Ron Lieberman
> The Family Album
> RD #1, Box 42
> Glen Rock, PA 17327-9707

★ **Violin making, identification, and repair** in any language from any period. Illustrated works are of particular interest.
> David N. Jones,
> Jones Violin Shop
> 3411 Ray St.,
> San Diego, CA 92104
>> (619) 584-1505

★ **Antique Pewter.** May be in any language. Provide full bibliographic information and a description of condition.
> Albert J. Phiebig, Inc.
> Box 352
> White Plains, NY 10602
>> (914) 948-0138   fax: (914) 948-0784

★ **Fishing and hunting books.** "We are always interested in purchasing "sporting" books on hunting, fishing, bird dogs, archery, guns and gun collecting, game animals and birds, books by the Derrydale Press, and many more. We purchase for stock, so there is no delay. We do ask that if you quote a book to us, you wait until you hear from us. We answer all quotes even if we do not buy them. We are good active buyers and ask that you keep our wants in mind. Among many authors we seek are Frank Forester, Havilah Babcock, Robert Ruark, Archibald Rutledge, Robert Traver and Corey Ford." Provide standard bibliographic info.
> Lewis Razek
> Highwood Bookshop
> PO Box 1246
> Traverse City, MI 49685
>> (616) 271-3898

★ **Fishing and hunting books,** but older, out-of-print titles *only.*
> Robert Whitaker
> 2810 E. Desert Cove Ave.
> Phoenix, AZ 85028

★ **Horses and horse breeding,** including horse history, carriage driving and driving, breed registers, show yearbooks, stud books, and material about the Spanish Riding School, mules, and donkeys. Also veterinary medicine, but **no** *Diseases of the Horse*, books about betting, or books that are still in print.
> Barbara Cole
> October Farm
> Rt. 2, Box 183-C
> Raleigh, NC 27610

★ **Thoroughbred horse racing** books and paper ephemera including KY Derby programs.
> Gary Medeiros
> 1319 Sayre St.
> San Leandro, CA 94579

★ **How to drive and/or care for coaches and teams of horses.**
> Donald Sawyer
> West Newbury Wagon Works
> 40 Bachelor St.
> West Newbury, MA 01985

★ **Fruit varieties before 1900,** including illustrated books, magazine articles, ceramic tiles depicting fruit, postcards, prints, folders, and greeting cards depicting apples. Especially books and paper with color plates or descriptions of fruit varieties in any language. Also information about John Chapman (Johnny Appleseed). No tropical fruit, or anything later than 1940.
> Fred Janson
> Pomona Book Exchange
> Rockton PO, Ontario L0R 1X0 CANADA

★ **Poultry,** but only books published pre-1930.
> W.L. "Bill" Zeigler
> 10 Lincolnway West
> New Oxford, PA 17350

★ **Poultry books.** Wants hardcover books about poultry (chickens, ducks, geese, etc.) that are illustrated, preferably in color.
> Clark Kidder
> 1582 West County Hwy "N"
> Milton, WI 53563
>> (608) 868-2376

★ **Used and rare books, manuscripts, and maps.** "We specialize in books on the military, aviation, lighter-than-air craft, Ohio subjects, and U.S. maps and atlases before 1870."
Frank Klein
The Bookseller
521 W. Exchange St.
Akron, OH 44302
(216) 762-3101

★ **Commercial aviation, U.S. or foreign, 1919-50.** Does not want how to fly books, radio or navigation books or manuals, and no book club editions. Make certain to note condition of dust jacket.
Ron Mahoney
Air Age Book Company
Box 40
Tollhouse, CA 93667
(209) 855-8993

★ **Aeronautics and airplanes.** Buys for resale.
Perry Eichor
Keep 'em Flying
703 N. Almond Dr.
Simpsonville, SC 29681
(803) 967-8770

★ **Boats and boat building, boat racing, yachting, marine engineering, and similar topics.** Buys for resale, but has strong personal interest in small boats, outboards, and canoes.
Robert Glick
Columbia Trading Co.
504 Main St.
West Barnstable, MA 02668

★ **Paddlewheel steam powered river boat books** especially those that give historical or technical information.
Bill Warren Mueller
Rt. 1, Box 262
Middlebourne, WV 26149
Fax: (304) 386-4868

★ **Railroad technical reference books,** cyclopedias, dictionaries, and manuals published by *RY Gazette, Simmons-Boardman, Moody,* or *Poors,* pre-1950. No fiction.
Scott Arden
20457 Highway 126
Noti, OR 97461

★ **Technical books and paper ephemera,** pre-1910. He wants books on trades, machines, manufacturing and technical processes.
Jim Presgraves
Bookworm & Silverfish
Box 639
Wytheville, VA 24382

★ **Occult and mystic science,** astrology, magic, numerology, alchemy, palmistry, spiritualism, pyramids, tarot, Yoga, Atlantis, UFO's, ESP, and anything else metaphysical. "I'll also buy art, posters, cards, games, antique crystal balls, and other mystical and occult ephemera. I'll buy one or one thousand, if in fine condition."
Dennis Whelan
PO Box 170
Lakeview, AR 72642

All possible buyers of books are not listed in this chapter.

Always check the index and the chapter in "I'll Buy That Too!" that covers the topic of your book.

Standard Bibliographic Information

Title, author, publisher, place and date(s) of publication,
number of pages, illustrator, and approximate number of illustrations.

Give the condition of (1) the binding, (2) the spine, (3) the pages, and
(4) the dust jacket. Note bookplates, writing, and other damage.
A photocopy of the title page will save lots of writing.

★ **Various books including**
[1] *Encyclopedia Britannica* published after 1980;
[2] *Encyclopedia Judaica*, any editions;
[3] **Limited Editions Club** books and ephemera;
[4] **Heritage Press** books;
Please describe fully.
Lee & Mike Temares
50 Heights Rd.
Plandome, NY 11030
(516) 627-8688

★ **German books and magazines of all kinds.**
Especially interested in pre-1920 cookbooks, topographical books depicting German and European landscapes and cities, trade catalogs, and children's books. Would love to find bound runs of magazines like *Jugend, Gartenlaube,* etc. Requests that you price what you have as she does not make offers.
Anni Waterman
321 New Street
Colesburg, IA 52035

★ **Coins, currency, medals, tokens, or counterfeiting.** Especially wants scholarly books and auction catalogs on coins from any period or language. Chapman Brothers Auction catalogs between 1870-1920 will bring from $50-$2,000.
George Frederick Kolbe
Drawer 3100
Crestline, CA 92325
(714) 338-6527

★ **How-to books about picking locks and making escapes,** including but not at all limited to those by Houdini.
Joe and Pam Tanner
Tanner Escapes
Box 349
Great Falls, MT 59403
(406) 453-4961

★ **Stock market.** Wants books on Wall Street speculation, the various panics, the commodities markets, market cycles, and biographies of speculators. Will buy U.S. and British editions, especially pre-Civil War. Will also buy old stock market mail order courses. He is most interested in pre-1940 titles.
R.G. Klein
Box 24A06
Los Angeles, CA 90024

★ **Eyes or optics.**
Dr. James Leeds
2470 E. 116th St.
Carmel, IN 46032
(317) 844-7474

★ **All aspects of palmistry or hands,** pre-1940. Buys fine condition only. Will pay $15-$20 for Sorrel's *The Human Hand.*
Geraldine Swigart
12362 Kensington Rd.
Los Alamitos, CA 90720

★ **Teaching or operating schools.** Buys books or paper ephemera, pre-1900.
Tedd Levy
Box 2217,
Norwalk, CT 06850

★ **Sound recording history and technique** published before 1930.
Steven I. Ramm
420 Fitzwater St.
Philadelphia, PA 19147

★ **City Directories and telephone books** published 1860-1960.
George Rinhart
Upper Grey
Colebrook, CT 06021
(203) 379-9773

★ **Bizarre and unusual subjects** are wanted, "such as freaks, torture, executions, swindling, gambling, con games, strange peoples, tribal customs, erotica, and other interesting and unusual subjects. We do not want books that are still in print, and are not interested in recent reprints of old rare books. Please advise me of what you have and what you want for it."
  Alan Levine
  PO Box 1577
  Bloomfield, NJ 07003
    (201) 743-5288

★ **Books on flags, flag history, worldwide.**
  Jon Radel
  PO Box 2276
  Reston, VA 22090

★ **Cartoon books and magazines.** Wants all types of cartoon books, both humorous and political, British or American, 19th century to the present. Also buys original **cartoon art.**
  Bill the Booky
  PO Box 16475
  Chapel Hill, NC 27516
    (919) 942-2834

★ **Trade directories from the tobacco industry, 1860-1940.** Trade directories are hardbound books which list the name, address, and factory number of manufacturers and others involved in the tobacco industry. They come in a variety of sizes and publishers, usually *Tobacco Leaf, Tobacco World,* or *Costa.* Will buy all. Ship any tobacco trade directory in any condition for my prompt check. Will pay from $30-$200 each, even more for a perfect 1887. **Please quote** *all* **tobacco related books, photos, and catalogs from before 1940.** Especially wanted are catalogs of pipe companies, cigar companies, and wholesalers with a large line of tobacco related items and long runs of 19th century tobacco trade magazines.
  Dr. Tony Hyman
  Box 3028
  Pismo Beach, CA 93448
    (805) 773-6777 Fax: (805) 773-0117

★ **Catalogs of Oriental art goods including Japanese ceramics.** Wants to buy all catalogs on this topic published before 1942.
  Gardner Pond
  62 Saturn St
  San Francisco, CA 94114
    (415) 626-9081 Fax (415) 863-7088

★ **Paperback books from the 1940's, 50's and early 60's.** "If it had an original cover price of 25¢ or 35¢ and it's in nice condition, we want to buy it all. We are very competitive for any books, and will travel worldwide to buy complete libraries of these books. We specialize in science fiction, mystery, Western, and slease" but will consider other fiction from this period as well. We will also consider **digest size books and pulp magazines** in these same fields. "Please don't send us badly creased, soiled, water damaged, or destroyed copies, as we buy for resale. We cannot use reprints either." Give standard bibliographic information and include what the original cover price was. Describe condition of cover and binding. Gorgon books issues monthly catalogs of books for sale, sponsors the annual paperback expo, and was a founder of the paperback collector's club.
  Joe Crifo and John Gargiso
  Gorgon Books
  102 JoAnne Drive
  Holbrook, NY 11741
    (516) 472-3504

★ **Detective and mystery 1st editions** in hardcover or paperback. Also biography, reference, and bibliography related to the detective/mystery genre. Wants Dashiell Hammett and Raymond Chandler 1st editions with dust jackets. His wants and stock are computerized for modem access.
  Richard West
  West's Booking Agency
  Box 406
  Elm Grove, WI 53122
    (414) 786-8420

★ **Science fiction and mysteries.** First editions of fantastic adventure novels by authors such as Edgar Rice Burroughs, A.Merritt, Sax Rohmer, and Talbot Mundy with their original dust jackets. He also buys **adventure and detective pulp magazines.** Include publication dates in your description.
  Claude Held
  Box 515
  Buffalo, NY 14225

Children's Books

★ **First editions of children's books** in very good condition. Wants books illustrated by Mabel Lucie Atwell, Jessie Wilcox Smith, Charles Robinson, Maxfield Parrish, Charles Folkard, Maurice Sendak, Edward Gorey, and Ralph Steadman, among others. Also illustrated editions of *Alice In Wonderland* dating from before 1880. Especially interested in editions illustrated by Harry Furniss, in English or in Hebrew. Also wants *Alice* presentation copies, fore-edge illustrated editions, or pop ups. No editions published by Whitman. Can send you a wants list of books.
> Joel Birenbaum
> 2486 Brunswick Circle, #A1
> Woodridge, IL 60517
> (312) 968-0664

★ **First editions of the *Bobbsey Twins* series** published by Mershon or Chatterton-Peck. No Grosset & Dunlop editions. Also wants **Frank Merriwell items**, especially *Frank Merriwell's Book of Athletic Development*, Merriwell postcards, and the Tip Top League badge.
> Audrey Buffington
> 2 Old Farm Rd.
> Wayland, MA 01778

★ **Children's series books.** Must be in dust jacket if originally issued that way. Especially seeking the last 3 or 4 titles in series. Describe condition of dust jacket.
> Lee & Mike Temares
> 50 Heights Rd.
> Plandome, NY 11030
> (516) 627-8688

★ **Editions of *Alice In Wonderland*** illustrated by just about anyone other than Tenniel. All foreign editions are wanted.
> Alice Berkey
> 127 Alleyne Dr.
> Pittsburgh, PA 15215

★ **Children's books,** American or English, from the 1400's to 1925, including educational books such as McGuffey's readers.
> Ron Graham
> 8167 Park Ave.
> Forestville, CA 95436
> (707) 887-2856

★ **Children's early readers** and other early colorful and interesting children's books in fine condition for resale. Wants primers amd pre-primers like the Dick and Jane series: *Look and See, Come and Go, Work and Play, Good Times with our Friends, Happy Days,* and *Fun with Dick and Jane.* Also wants *Our Big Book* , a flip chart version of the readers which stood in the front of a classroom. He'll buy foreign editions, teacher's editions, and Catholic school editions (with John, Jean, and Judy). Other early readers, "dating back as far as you can go," are also wanted by this specialty dealer. Look for Bob and Judy, Jerry and Alice, and "about 200 others" from the 1940's and before. "We'll buy school books other than readers, if fine condition and well illustrated." He also buys *Tom Swift* **and other children's series books.**
> Joe Perry Collectibles
> PO Box 5967
> Garden Grove, CA 92645
> (714) 898-8297

★ **Children's books** that are old, rare and colorfully illustrated.
> Ivan Gilbert
> Miran Art & Books
> 2824 Elm Ave.
> Columbus, OH 43209

★ **Oz books by L. Frank Baum.** Will also consider other **Oz memorabilia.**
> Dennis Books
> Box 99142
> Seattle, WA 98199

★ **Children's coloring books,** from the 1930's and 40's if all uncolored. Movie star coloring books may be from any year up to 1960.
> Fran Van Vynckt
> 6931 Monroe Ave.
> Hammond, IN 46324

If your children's books have cartoon characters, movie stars, or TV personalities, be certain to also check the "Pop Culture" chapter when seeking a buyer.

Late Additions

★ **Globes of the world.** Wants unusual or oversized globes, black globes, and, especially, light up globes. "No ordinary globes, please." Send a photo, SASE, and your phone number. Prefers you to set price wanted, but will make offers to amateur sellers.

Jay Novak
7386 Beverly Blvd.
Los Angeles, CA 90036
(213) 933-0383 fax (213) 683-1312

★ **James Dean memorabilia** including books, magazines, photos, records, sheet music, lobby cards, film programs, posters, scrapbooks, plates, novelties, etc. Description should include the item's size, year, condition, and how much you want for it.

David Loehr, JADE
GPO Box 7961
New York, NY 10116

★ **Marilyn Monroe and other sex symbol movie star memorabilia.** He wants Marilyn, but also Jayne Mansfield, Mamie Van Doren, Diana Dors, Anita Ekberg, and Brigitte Bardot. He asks that you quote prices for any pre 1962 items, including U.S. and foreign magazine covers, in excellent condition.

John Van Doren
60 Wagner Road
Stockton, NJ 08559
(609) 397-4803

★ **Gubernatorial (governor) or U.S. Senate race political buttons.** "I'll pay $25-$50 each for those I can use. Please send a Xerox© or good description."

Dave Quintin
PO Box 800861
Dallas, TX 75380

★ **Whiskey miniatures.** Buys pre-1960 miniature American whiskeys and will pay "top dollar for rare brands." Used as premiums and samples since 1875, and he buys them all. Mike likes the post-prohibition ones best for his personal collection.

Mike Olson, MELO
309 Knopp Valley
Winona, MN 55987
(507) 454-1499

★ **Pub jugs (whiskey pitchers).** They are made in glass, pottery, pewter, and plastic, but "I'm buying only the pottery (ceramic) ones, and pay from $5 to $20 for pitchers I can use." Will make offers if you give an accurate description, including the exact height, shape, color and all the information on the pitcher. "I don't buy jugs with chips or cracks." But he'd love to find copies of a magazine called *The Pub Jug*.

Victor Case
200 S.E. "B" Street
Bentonville, AR 72712
(501) 273-7276

★ **Porcelain signs, clocks, thermometers, and door pushes** for any product, but has special interest in colas. Wants fine condition items with good graphics only. Photograph suggested. Give dimensions. Dealers price your goods, but he will make offers for amateur sellers.

Van Stueart
Route 3, Box 216
Nashville, AR 71852
(501) 845-4264

★ *Walgreens Drug Store* **products and ephemera.** "I'll buy a wide range of products marketed by this national chain between 1901 and 1960, including non prescription drug and health aids, candy, tobacco, coffee, toys and what have you. These items were sold under many different brand names: *Walgreens, Myers, Union Drug, Keller, Valentine, Carrel, Glide, Orlis, Amoray, Ladonna, Olafsen, Triomphe, Hill Rose, CRW,* and others. I'm especially interested in finding *Walgreens* tin cans for coffee and other products. I do not want any product marked with the word "Agency" as in "Walgreen Agency," nor do I want heating pads, water bottles, or ice caps." To sell to this 10 year veteran collector, you need to tell him what you have, and its size, color, and condition. Indicated whether you have the original box or not, and give the original price, if you know it. "There are only ten or so collectors of *Walgreens* items in the country, so there isn't a great deal of competition. On the other hand, some items are quite rare."

Gordon Addington
260 E. Chestnut #2801
Chicago, IL 60611
(312) 943-4085

★ **Magazines about diving and underwater activities.** "I'll buy hundreds of different foreign and domestic magazines on this topic such as *Skin Diver, Aquarius, Diver, Scuba Times, Sport Diver, Ocean Realm,* etc." Give the magazine title and date, as well as a description of condition. Not interested in any books, please, hardcover or soft.

    Thomas Szymanski
    5 Stoneybrook Lane
    Exeter, NH 03833
       (603) 772-6372

★ **Stained or beveled glass windows.** Please include photos and your phone number.

    Carl Heck
    Box 8416
    Aspen, CO 81612
       (303) 925-8011

★ **Coral Gables, Florida, souvenirs and advertising,** especially related to land sales.

    Sam LaRoue
    5980 SW 35th Street
    Miami, FL 33155
       (305) 347-7466

★ **Music boxes.** "I'll buy *Regina* automatic changers, *Orchestrions* by Seeburg and others, Band organs by *Wurlitzer* and others. The larger the better! I'll make immediate decisions and immediate payment. Give me a call if you have one of these for sale."

    Q.David Bowers
    Box 1224
    Wolfeboro, NH 03894
       (603) 569-5095 weekdays

★ **Nippon and *Noritake* china.** "We're seeking large vases, urns, portrait pieces, dolls, chocolate and tea sets, jugs, wall plaques, smoke sets, humidors, and anything else that's quality and perfect. We'll buy Coralene, Moriage, blown-outs, rectangulars, pieces with silver overlay, you name it! We're also in the market for *Noritake* with art deco decorations of men and women. Call or write."

    Mark Griffin and Earl Smith
    1768 Maple Avenue
    Fort Myers, FL 33901
       (813) 334-0083

```
┌─────────────────────────────┐
│                      ▓▓▓▓▓   │
│          Your Stamp  ▓▓▓▓▓   │
│   Your Name                  │
│   Your Address               │
│                              │
└─────────────────────────────┘
```

Self-Addressed Stamped Envelope SASE Include them.

Buyers in "Late Additions" are often people we don't personally know, people with whom we've had no dealings. Sometimes they are old friends who are slow to respond to their mail.

They are all included because their specialties might be helpful to readers.

understanding auctions

I'll buy That Too! is a book on selling. Auctions are generally better places to buy than to sell.

People believe that auctions are a good way to get top dollar for what they have. Sometimes that's true, more often it's not.

The success of an auction depends in part upon the quality of what is being auctioned. Better stuff attracts more and better bidders. High prices go to "fresh" goods. Pieces that have been "shopped around" seldom do well at auction.

There are all kinds of auction houses and auctioneers, from the art galleries of Sotheby's and Christie's where million dollar items are handled, to the country auctions of rural America. In between them are the "mid level" auctioneers found in most major cities who handle prestigious goods and better quality households, and often collect record prices in the tens and hundreds of thousands of dollars. Cities are full of auctioneers of every size, specialty and ability. To select the right auctioneer takes a lot of thought and research.

If you want to know how a particular auction house works, you can look up "auction houses" in the yellow pages, telephone them, and ask them to explain how you sell things at their auction. Most of them are happy to help you. That's how they make their living. This report will help you know what questions to ask and what answers to expect.

When you ask an auction house how much your item might sell for, there is a great temptation for them to over-state the amount. High prices get your business.

Over valuating helps an auction house in other ways. Since value is tied to condition, potential bidders hear of high estimates and believe the items are in better condition than they in fact are. High estimates are believed by some to "psyche" bidders into bidding more. High prices attract media attention.

Top auctions with top merchandise have pictorial bound catalogs. When merchandise is good but not great, catalogs tend to be simple lists. Catalogs may or may not have *estimated selling prices* listed, but when they are, it is usually as a range [eg. $50-75]. Estimated prices will vary from auction house to auction house, and give a clue to where the reserve price might be if the item has one. Other than that, they don't mean too much.

In any business, publicity is the difference between success and failure. If people don't know about the auction, they don't come and bid and you don't get as much money. Simple as that. Before deciding whether auctions are for you, it's important to know and consider how your auction is to be advertised and to whom the ads are aimed.

Your profit is determined by who decides (or remembers) to travel to the auction house or bid by phone. Some important bidders may not be available that day. Many times I would have bid higher than what something sold for at auction. I lost a $3,000 African mask I was bidding on by phone because I forgot the closing time of the auction. The mask sold for $125. Pity me. Pity the seller more.

Even if "the gang's all there" and the room is full of "players" the bid will depend on the economy, whether the bidder has the item pre-sold, how many other things he buys, whether he likes the aesthetics of the piece, how well he knows the item, and how he felt when he got out of bed.

> SOME PEOPLE CONSIDER IT A DISADVANTAGE THAT AUCTIONS ARE A MATTER OF PUBLIC RECORD SO RELATIVES, NOSY NEIGHBORS, AND STATE AND FEDERAL GOVERNMENTS ALL KNOW YOUR PERSONAL BUSINESS. SOME AUCTION HOUSES ARE REQUIRED TO WITHHOLD TAXES ON THE SALE OF YOUR GOODS.

Sometimes the final bid is simply a matter of ego. When two prominent rivals bid against each other at important specialty auctions, money isn't the issue. I've seen $100 items become $1,200 items, and anyone who attends auctions regularly has far worse examples of overpaying than that.

"Well," you say, "if all that overpaying is going on, why not sell my stuff at auction?"

The answer is: What happens when one of those guys isn't there? The price is a lot less. A few years ago, Edgar Alan Poe's first published book of poems sold for $198,000 at auction. Two years later the same book sold for under $150,000. Same book. But different bidders in a different economy. The auctioneer bragged about the first sale. It was on newscasts coast to coast. You didn't hear about the second one, did you?

On the other hand, you could have a hot item in just the right auction with just the right audience and just the right people reading the catalog, and get $15,000 for an item everyone thought would bring $4,000.

If you're willing to take that kind of gamble, auctions may be for you. In all fairness, most auctions aren't quite that big of a gamble. All but the lowest level auction barns will estimate for you what larger lots will bring and be within ±30%.

When you auction better items, you can specify it cannot be sold for less than a certain amount. If your item doesn't reach that amount, you pay the auction house a fee for trying. You get back an item that has negative exposure in the market and you've tied it up for month waiting for the auction.

Another thing to find out if you're considering an auction is how and when you will be paid. In rare cases, consigners are paid the same day or the next day. It can happen. Some houses have dragged feet for months and hanky-pankyed around with the funds in the meantime. It took us more than two months to pay our consigners and we worked at it as fast as we could.

Most auction houses charge a sliding fee. Since overhead is pretty much the same for cheap items and for valuable ones, they have to charge a higher percent on less valuable items. You can find yourself paying as high as 25% and I've heard auctioneers charging 30% for really cheap goods. Sounds outrageous, but if you hire a good auctioneer, you're paying for a lot of work.

Who does the actual auctioneering plays a role in how much you'll get. If you are thinking of an auction, make certain you go to an auction conducted by the auctioneer you are considering. Watch what and how he or she does. Do you want them doing that same thing for you?

At auction, your item is held up described, and sold in 20 seconds.

On the whole auction houses try to do a good job, but don't assume they are going to be paragons of either virtue or knowledge. The art world is constantly astir at some scandal or another in the auction world, misattributions, forgeries, bankruptcies, shills, pools, theft, time payments, money loans to bidders, and what have you.

> *People go to auctions hoping to find bargains. 40% to 70% of bidders at every auction are dealers who will resell what they buy.*

Local "country auctioneers" are great for your junk. You're going to get junk prices. Just make certain you don't give them items you could easily sell for a great deal more to someone else

These auctions are attended mostly by small town antique and second hand dealers who become the third owners of an item which may pass through seven to ten hands before reaching the specialty buyer, which is where good items all ultimately end up. At these auctions, you'll get rid of everything, but will often give things away for as little as $1 for every $100 worth of potential value. This is especially true of better quality specialty collectibles (worth $100-$5,000), where you'd be lucky to get 10-20% of retail value.

Except on potentially very valuable items, auctioneers aren't interested in time consuming research. Houses that produce catalogs are renown for how little they will put in print (some don't even print dimensions!). It's up to the buyer to know what's good and to be ready.

Small estates, and low value items are seldom cataloged. They are sold by local or regional auctioneers, depending on the importance of the items and who got the job.

At uncataloged auctions, the auctioneer's attitude is "let the customer do the research. I'm here to sell."

What it means to consign at any auction can be summed up in our experience with a large, well run country auction barn in upstate New York. It drew a mix of locals, curiosity seekers, and dealers, much like any other auction. We'd bought many a bargain there, so expected only $30 or so for the load we trailered in. When a check for $160 arrived, we quickly loaded up again, this time full of "the good stuff," expecting $350-500. We got a check for $32. That's the risk of auction selling.

I bought two cardboard boxes full of about 25 empty cigar boxes at a country household auction for $15. Had someone written me and asked for an offer, I'd have offered $125 for the lot. If the cartons of cigar boxes were yours, which way would you have preferred to sell them?

```
┌─────────────────────────────────┐
│            WARNING              │
│                                 │
│ BE CAREFUL OF AUCTIONEERS WHO   │
│ MAKE A BUSINESS OF PREYING      │
│ UPON WIDOWS AND WIDOWERS,       │
│ USUALLY DESCENDING A FEW DAYS   │
│ AFTER THE FUNERAL, SUGGESTING   │
│ THAT THEY CAN CLEAR THE         │
│ LOVED ONES' PROPERTY, REMOVE    │
│ PAINFUL MEMORIES, AND HELP      │
│ CLEAN UP. THEY'LL CLEAN UP.     │
│ YOU WON'T.                      │
│ NO MATTER HOW PAINFUL THAT      │
│ TIME OF GRIEF MAY BE, DO NOT    │
│ MAKE DECISIONS ABOUT PERSONAL   │
│ PROPERTY WHILE IN MOURNING.     │
│ YOU WILL LOSE MONEY, AND CAN    │
│ LOSE A GREAT DEAL MORE IF YOU   │
│ SIGN THE WRONG CONTRACT.        │
└─────────────────────────────────┘
```

specialty auctions

if you have a large collection of similar items, "specialty auctions" are often a terrific way to dispose of them

Important collections of anything should go to an auction which specializes in that type of collection, particularly if the owner of the collection is well known, so its dispersal will attract friends and rivals. The auctioneer should be willing to catalog the collection, do proper promotion, and schedule the sale advantageously as to time and place. Specialty auctioneers have reputations and mailing lists of hot bidders.

Collectors seldom have time to attend auctions, but the top money spenders never miss specialty auctions, either in person or by phone or mail. At specialty auctions, more things go to collectors than dealers, because they can outbid them.

Specialty auctions prefer not to sell just one or two items for you, unless the items are very good and worth their time.

Even if a dealer pays a "record auction price," s/he must sell the item to someone else for more money. If that's true, who gets higher prices, private sales or auctions?

auctioneers

Specialty auctions, which the author recommends as an optional way of selling collections of particularly important goods, are conducted by many of our listees. You will find this fact mentioned in their entry if the listee has put us on their mailing list so that we get copies of their auction catalog. A few of them are:

Rich Hartzog (tokens and medals)
Jan Sorgenfrei (Indian items)
Lynn Geyer (beer)
Rex Stark (Americana and pop culture)
Barbara Frasher (dolls)
J.R. Crittenden Schmitt (ordinance)
James Julia (decoys, guns, glass,
    furniture, lamps, art)
Sanchez Gallery (furniture, glass, art),

and many others whom time and space do not permit us to list. If you have a large collection of any significant collectible item, read the appropriate entries in **I'll Buy That Too!** Discuss dispersal with our listees, and ask them if they can recommend a specialty auction, if appropriate.

THIS SPECIAL REPORT IS A SERIES OF OBSERVATIONS AND OPINIONS BASED ON MY 35 YEARS EXPERIENCE ATTENDING AUCTIONS, CONSIGNING AT AUCTIONS, AND WINNING AND LOSING BIDS AT AUCTION IN MANY DIFFERENT STATES. MY WIFE AND I ALSO CONDUCTED THE LARGEST SPECIALTY AUCTION EVER HELD IN THE FIELD OF TOBACCO COLLECTING, SELLING OVER 10,000 ITEMS TO PEOPLE ON FOUR CONTINENTS. THE $40 CATALOG FOR THAT AUCTION WAS HAILED BY THE U.S. LIBRARY OF CONGRESS AS "THE MOST INFORMATIVE AUCTION CATALOG EVER WRITTEN ON ANY TOPIC."

Index: Buyers

Index: Buyers

Index: Buyers

Index: Buyers

Index: Buyers

Index: Things you can sell

Index: Things you can sell

Index: Things you can sell

Index: Things you can sell

297

Index: Things you can sell

Index: Things you can sell

Changes since this book was first printed.
Bold indicates most recent changes

A book involving people is going to change. We learned of an address change the day the first copy of *I'll Buy That Too!* was delivered from the printer. The next day our second change came. Changes of which we are aware on February 1st, 1994 include:

Ackerman, Donald   33 Kossuth Street, Wallington, NJ 07057
Aldridge, Ron   **250 Canyon Oaks Drive, Argyle, TX 76226 (817) 455-2519**
Alpert, Stephen   **Has recently passed away.**
Andreoni, Hank   Phone is now (909) 849-7539
Applebaum, Steve   10636 Wilshire Blvd. #204, Los Angeles, CA 90024 (310) 475-3861
Bailey, David   **Bailey's Antiques, 517 Kapahulu Ave., Honolulu, HI 96815**
Baker, Lillian   Phone is now (310) 329-2619
Barta, Karen Jentzsch   1216 N. Geneva St., Glendale, CA 91207. Same phone/fax
Blank, Joani   **Good Vibrations, 938 Howard St #101, SF CA 94103 (415) 974-8985**
     Fax: (415) 974-8989
Blondy, Mark   **31745 Sheridan, Birmingham, MI 48009 (313) 646-8215**
Breedlove, Michael   Now can be called for free: (800) 858-3267
Bridges, Herb   Phone is now (706) 253-4934
Brooks, Mike   Phone is now (510) 339-1751
Burla, Frank   Phone is now (708) 961-0156
Butke, Brian   Our apologies for the typo to Brian Butko
Cavigga, Margaret   Phone is now (310) 659-3020
Chaussee, Annette   PO Box 22, Calhan, CO 80808 (719) 347-2000 Fax (719) 347-2780
Chaussee, Calvin   PO Box 22, Calhan, CO 80808 (719) 347-2000 Fax (719) 347-2780
Cole, Barbara   **2609 Branch Road, same city, zip, phone. Add Fax: (919) 779-6265**
Coops, Fred   Has passed away. A long time friend and true gentleman.
Corenman, Aaron   **Is no longer in business and has quit collecting.**
Crabtree, Gary   Phone is now (909) 862-8534
Dembo, George   Phone is now (201) 635-6505
Dobres, Sheldon   Phone is now (410) 486-6569
Docks, Les   Phone is now (210) 492-6021
Dougerian, James   Phone is now (510) 935-5033
Eggers, Bryan   Moved, with no forwarding address yet available
Enriquez, Mary Anne   **1741 West Albion St., Chicago, IL 60626**
Ferretta, Michelle   **1314 Oak Street, Alameda, CA 94501 (510) 522-1823**
Filer, Russell   Phone is now (909) 797-1650
Geyer, Lynn   300 Trail Ridge, Silver City, NM 88061 (505) 538-2341
Giarde, Leigh   Phone is now (909) 792-8681
Glick, Bob   Now has a fax machine: (508) 362-3551
Govig, Valerie   Phone is now (410) 922-1212
Graham, Michael   Phone is now (708) 362-4808
Hardisty, Don   Index error Bossons (p. 230, not 236). Phone (800) 827-3721
Hampton, David   Creekside #31, 16425 Dam Rd., Clearlake, CA 95422 (707) 995-1411
Harris, Warren   6130 Rampart Dr., Carmichael, CA 95608 (916) 966-3490
Hickox, Ron   Phone is now: (813) 968-1571 Fax now: (813) 935-0190
Hiett, Robert   PO Box 47, Monmouth, IL 61462 (309) 734-3212 Fax: (309) 734-8083
Hiscox, Mimi   Phone is now (310) 598-5450
Horwitz, Dennis   Phone is now (310) 455-4002
Hyman, Tony   Fax number is incorrect. It should read: (805) 773-0117
Jacobson, T. Pat   Phone is now (510) 930-8531
Johnson, Patricia   Phone is now (310) 373-5262
Joiner, John   **52 Jefferson Parkway #D, Newnan, GA 30263**
Jung, S. Paul   Phone is now (410) 569-8194
Kegebein, Jim   6831 Colton Blvd., Oakland, CA 94611
Kimbell, Joseph   passed away according to acquaintances.
Kolbe, George   Phone is now (909) 338-6527

Changes since *I'll Buy That Too!* was first printed

Konet, Ken	**4470 Westminster Place, St. Louis, MO 63108 (314) 652-7505**
Lewis, Robert	Phone is now (310) 475-8531
Lieberman, Randy	4 Layfayette Station, Fredericksburg, VA 22401
Linn, Kier	2591 Military Ave., Los Angeles, CA 90064 (310) 477-5229
Markowitz, J.	**No longer buying Queen Victoria or Al Jolson**
Marks, Jerome	120 Corporate Woods #260, Rochester, NY 14623 (716) 475-0220
Mattlack, Jack	**Passed away**
McHenry, Gordon	Added Fax: (813) 966-4568
McVey, Jeff	**Is no longer collecting.**
Merlis, Brian	Zip code should be 11223. Our apologies for the typo.
Murphy, Monica	**9337 Lenel Place, Dallas, TX 75220 (214) 352-4137**
Newman, Robert	Phone is now (310) 559-0539
O'Brien, Jim	PO Box 885, Sugar Grove, IL 60554
Papadopoulus, Chris	Phone is now (410) 825-9157
Patterson, Don	Phone is now (706) 738-7227
Pattison, Lee	**6 Christview Drive, Cuba, NY 14727 (716) 968-2458**
Phillips, Alan	**Alan is not actively buying at this time.**
Rann, Rick	Phone is now (708) 442-7907
Reamer, Arnold	Phone is now (410) 944-6414 or (410) 486-8412
Redding, Douglas	16532 Baederwood Lane, Rockville, MD 20855
Rehr, Darryl	2591 Military Ave., Los Angeles, CA 90064 (310) 477-5229
Retskin, Bill	16 Forest View Dr., Asheville, NC 28804 (704) 254-4487
Ridenaur, Ron	PO Box 357, Moorpark, CA 93020
Rinhart, George	Mail being returned as of 3/93
Ross, Ron	**1982-A Fulton Street, San Francisco, CA 94117**
Sachen, Bill	Phone is now (708) 662-7204
Sage, Ed	PO Box 13025, Albuquerque, NM 87192 (505) 298-0840
Sandler, Miles	**PO Box 13028-TH, Shawnee Mission, KS 66282 (800) 235-2866**
Schmidtmann, Gil	Phone is now (909) 794-1211
Seiderman, Jack	1631 NW 114th Avenue, Pembroke Pines, FL 33026 (305) 438-0928
Selcke, Ron	Phone is now (708) 543-4848
Selesh, Adam	**Has stopped collecting and dealing.**
Selfridge, Madalaine	Phone is now (909) 674-9221
Semegran, Mike	Phone is now (310) 373-0464
Senerchia, Steve	91 Tillinghast Ave., Warwick, RI 02886 (401) 821-2865
Sharp, Curtis	232 South Reeves, Beverly Hills, CA 90212
Shochet, Jerry	Phone is now (410) 795-5879
Sorgenfrei, Jan	**Please use the daytime number only. No evening calls.**
Stephens, Michael	Phone is now (510) 843-2780
Storey, Frank	Phone is now (410) 850-5728
Stueart, Van	Correct phone is: (501) 845-4864
Swigart, Geraldine	Phone is now (310) 431-3705
Temes, Irv	Phone is now (410) 882-0580
Thomas, Jonathan	Phone is now (203) 263-2233
Treadwell, TK	quit buying when his wife, the more active collector, passed away.
Trombley, Ken	Added a Fax: (202) 457-0343 and a toll free number: (800) 673-8158
Utley, Bill	Phone is now (310) 861-6247
Vohs-Mohammed, S.	PO Box 7233, Villa Park, IL 60181 (708) 268-0210
Wallerstein, Herb	Phone is now (310) 273-4194
Way We Wore	1094 Revere Ave #A-29, San Francisco, CA 94124 (415) 822-1800
Wright, Richard	PO Box 8051, Rowland Heights, CA 91748 (714) 681-4647
Zecker, Barry	PO Box 217, Martinsville, NJ 08836 (908) 253-3400
Zeder, Audrey	Phone is now (310) 421-0881
Zemenick, Greg	**Phone is now (810) 642-8129**
Zukowski, Stan	Phone is now (510) 687-6426

★ **Buttons**, especially U.S. military, Confederate, military school, and uniform buttons with state seals. He also buys "high quality clothing buttons of porcelain, satsuma, or with pictures." He does not want WWI or WWII buttons or "simple clothing buttons made of plastic or bone." Please describe the design, and note anything stamped on the back. This director of the National Button Society prefers that you ship for inspection prior to final offer.

Warren Tice
PO Box 8491
Essex, VT 05451
(802) 878-3835 phone/fax

★ **Rock, mineral, and fossil collections** are wanted, as are samples of gold, silver, and copper, particularly samples associated with Western mining. Claims he'll pay you in cash in you prefer.

David Crawford
1308 Halsted Road
Rockford, IL 61103
(815) 637-6720

★ **Stereoview cards** "in nearly all categories" are sought. He points out that there are two types of stereo cards, printed and photographic and that he wants only photographic views of:

* Famous people
* Aviation, blimps, balloons, etc.
* Railroads, especially Western
* Ships, sailboats, riverboats, wharfs, etc.
* Automobiles, any early views
* Sports and games, from checkers to football
* Music, bands, theatrical scenes, etc.
* Street scenes from any city or town
* Mining anything
* Western lore, cowboys, Indians, etc.
* Photographers
* Fire fighting anything
* Military, depicting equipment or arms
* Occupationals...people at work

"I want any cards that capture a bygone era, people at leisure, at home, children playing, costumes, furniture, and the like. In addition to U.S. views, I will also buy fine condition photos of Canada and Europe." If your photo has a title, copyright date, or catalog number, please give them. Describe the scene or make a Xerox copy. Tell him the color of the card on which the photos are mounted. Describe any damage.

Steve Jabloner
7380 Adrian Drive, #23
Rohnert Park, CA 94928
(707) 795-3081

★ **Mining items** including safety lamps, oil wick cap lamps, carbide lamps, blasting cap tins and blasting machines, candle holders, and hundreds of other small tools, photos, souvenirs, and advertising items related to mining. Will even buy ore carts and buckets. Claims he'll pay you in cash in you prefer. Also wants ribbons, banners, and badges from the United Mine Workers (UMWA) and the Western Federation of Miners (WFM).

David Crawford
1308 Halsted Road
Rockford, IL 61103
(815) 637-6720

★ *Isaly's* **ephemera** Wants advertising, paper ephemera and souvenirs from this dairy/deli chain from Western Pennsylvania /Ohio. Buys postcards, photos, guidebooks, roadside signs, and what have you.

Brian Butko
2640 Sunset Drive
West Mifflin, PA 15122

★ **Canning machinery, catalogs and tools** of the Ferracute Machine Company of Bridgeton, NJ, are sought by this collector/researcher who also wants anything related to the company founder, **Oberlin Smith,** a local inventor and engineer. The Oberlin Smith Society is particularly interested in advertising, catalogs, small presses, medals, and tokens, but will consider anything related to FMCo or Smith himself. The OSS is a 501(c)(3) organization and seeks donations as well.

James Gandy
Oberlin Smith Society
Box 109, RD #2, River Road
Bridgeton, NJ 08302
(609) 451-5586

★ **Scouting coins, medallions, wooden nickels** and other exonumia (coins that aren't money). He even buys Scouting paper money! These have been issued by Troops and events all over the world. Rudy's $10 book, *Scouting Exonumia* is the guide used by collectors everywhere. For a free appraisal, describe (or make a rubbing or Xerox© of) both sides of the coin. Tell the material from which it's made. Give the diameter. If you know the country and date, tell him.

Rudy Dioszegi
3307 126th Street East
Burnsville, MN 55337
(612) 890-6336
(612) 882-8332 fax

★ **Three-dimensional advertising trademark character displays from stores.** "I buy plaster, composition, plastic and wooden store figures depicting cartoonish advertising characters. Items wanted are store displays and statuettes, and promotional banks, figural ash trays, and bobbing head dolls. I'm particularly interested in items of the 1940's through 1970's. Some character examples include Speedy *Alka Seltzer*, Reddy Kilowatt, Elsie the Cow, *Philip Morris*'s Johnny, the *Esquire* man, Pep Boys figures and other chefs, servicemen, and characters. Please provide a good description, paying close attention to damage. I prefer dealers to price goods, but will make offers to amateur sellers."
Warren Dotz
2999 Regent St.
Berkeley, CA 94705
   (510) 652-1159

★ **Popular portrayals of Black dancers** on sheet music, figurines, post cards, and other media. "I want dancers doing the cake walk, jitterbug, and the like, and will consider all items new to my wife's and my collection."
William Sommer
9 West 10th St.
New York, NY 10011
   (212) 260-0999

★ **Antique glass paperweights,** 1845-1900. "I will buy fine French (Pantin, Baccarat, Clichy, St. Louis), American (Boston Glass Co., Sandwich Glass Co., New England Glass Co., Gillinoer, Mt. Washington), English (Bacchus, Whitefriars), Russian and Bohemian paperweights. I am especially looking for Pantin paperweights from the late 1870's for which I will pay from $2,000 to $35,000. I also seek early Clichy bouquet on a moss background which can be worth as much as $40,000. **I don't want** paperweights with blobs of colored glass or with large bubbles in the design" A close up color photo of your weight is important and should be accompanied by a good description, including the diameter. This well known author and collector does not send out a wants list because, he explains, "I will purchase <u>all</u> top quality weights."
Paul Dunlop
The Dunlop Collection
PO Box 82370
Phoenix, AZ 85071
   (800) 227-1996

★ **Vegetable and oyster people trade cards** are wanted. Please Xerox© what you have.
Linda Mellis
1115 West Montana
Chicago, IL 60614

★ **Lamps and light fixtures** in fine or restorable condition sought by this restoration house.
Helene Hilton
Bright Idea Home Lighting Center
8563 Oswego Rd., Route 57
Baldwinsville, NY 13027

★ *I.C.S. Reference Library* or *I.C.S. Technical Library* books on any topic are sought, as long as they are from the early 1900's and bound in brown or black leather.
Jack Zimmerly
1200 Shypoke
Fairbanks, AK 99709
   (907) 479-3817

★ **Books by Jules Verne** are wanted, but only British and American editions. Most interested in buying first or other early editions, or editions of lesser known titles such as *Clovis Dardentor, Mathias Sandorf* and *Foundling Mick*. But, will also buy many of the G.Monro, Seaside Library paperbacks and "If you find an old edition of any work in good shape, you might send a quote." Eales cautions, "don't bother me with comic books or little books or books in poor condition." Give full title, copyright date[s], publisher, and the type and number of illustrations. Best to Xerox© the cover, as they are generally highly decorated. Give complete statement of condition of cover, binding, and pages. Include your phone number.
Dana Eales
2447 Delta Drive
Uniontown, OH 44685
   (216) 699-5341

★ **Encyclopedias** from any year that are in good resellable condition. She buys and sells encyclopedias of all sort and publisher, including *World Book, Britannica, Americana,* and others. She *sells* for prices varying from 10% to 60% of new cost. Your books will probably be worth from 30% to 50% of that, depending on customer demand.
Kathleen Italiane
Encyclopedias
14071 Windsor Place
Santa Ana, CA 92705
   (714) 838-3643 10-10

★ **Race car "speed equipment"** to hop up automobiles from the 1930's, 40's, 50's, and 60's. Whether factory equipment or aftermarket, if it's designed to make a car go faster, and you want to sell it, give Dale a call. He'd especially like to find early *Ford* flathead engine cylinder heads, intake manifolds, and camshafts. 1955 to '58 *Chrysler* aftermarket intake manifolds or valve covers will bring top prices. He personally does not want complete cars, complete engines, or "any items that can't be shipped U.P.S." But, if you have these things for sale, you might inquire as he adds, "I do have quality buyers for this type item." Describe what you have, including manufacturer and date, when possible. Dale publishes *RPM*, a monthly catalog which includes 30 pages of classified ads for folks buying and selling speed parts. You can subscribe for $20 a year.
Dale Wilch
2217 North 99th
Kansas City, KS 66109
(913) 788-3219 fax: (913) 788-9682

★ **Seal of North Carolina** advertising. Does not want tin cans, only lithographed ads. Fine condition a must. Photos appreciated.
Lisa Van Hook
PO Box 13256
El Cajon, CA 92022

★ **Zippo© lighters**, especially those with Navy and Marine Corps insignia, including ships, squadrons, submarines, etc. Will even buy some imitation Zippo© lighters from military units. Lighters with "Zippo" in block letters and "PAT.2032695" or PAT.2517191" are desirable as well as outside hinge or square cornered Zippoz© even if plain. Personalized lighters with names or dates or places or unusual decoration are sought. Those decorated on both front and back are most desirable. Please send Xerox© copies of your lighter. "We actively buy all quality lighters, lighter combinations, and unusual lighters. Our lighter museum is open to the public."
Jeff Mogilner
Racine & Laramine, Ltd.
2737 San Diego Ave.
San Diego, CA 92110
(619) 291-7833 (619) 6653 fax

★ **Homeopathic medicine.**
Julian Winston
2067 E. Clearfield St.
Philadelphia, PA 19134

★ **Magazines about diving and underwater activities.** "I'll buy hundreds of different foreign and domestic magazines on this topic such as *Skin Diver, Aquarius, Diver, Scuba Times, Sport Diver, Ocean Realm,* etc." Give the magazine title and date, as well as a description of condition. Not interested in any books, please.
Thomas Szymanski
5 Stoneybrook Lane
Exeter, NH 03833
(603) 772-6372

★ **Saxophones made by *Selmer***, especially in the early 1930's in Paris, but also other models through 1980. Serial numbers are found on the neck and on the back bottom, and must match. Look for serial numbers 60,000 through 89,000 on tenor saxes and numbers 50,000 through 120,000 on alto saxes, as they are most desirable. Others will be considered, however. Original finish, even worn, is preferable to refinished instruments. Large dents and heavy scratches will take away some value. "Write or call collect if you want to sell an instrument described above. Other brands of sax considered by this nationally known specialist.
Ed Hakal
10126 Signal Butte Circle
Sun City, AZ 85373
(602) 972-3091 evenings

★ **Sunshine Biscuits ephemera** including tins, boxes, signs, jars, display racks, novelties, games, calendars, pin back buttons, and what have you. Buys items from all brands produced by Sunshine. Make a photocopy of what you have.
Liz and Dick Wilmes
38W567 Brindlewood
Elgin, IL 60123
(708) 697-9679

★ **Tin Plates** from the turn of the century depicting women and/or advertising. Plates were usually printed by Meek, Beech, or Shonk. Plates must be in fine condition. Photos of what you have are almost essential.
Lisa Van Hook
PO Box 13256
El Cajon, CA 92022

★ **Israel, Palestine, and the Holocaust.** What have you? It could be worth an inquiry.
Harvey Dolin
5 Beekman Street #406
New York, NY 10038

Additions for 1993

★ **Revolvers (pistols).** "I'll consider any antique or collectible firearms to build my inventory and enhance my collection, but my special personal interests are:

[1] Serial number one guns, antique or modern;

[2] Antique *Smith & Wesson* large frame top-break revolvers;

[3] Antique engraved revolvers;

[4] Unusual hammerless revolvers;

[5] Guns owned by famous individuals.

"I'll buy an entire collection to get a piece I want. I can travel to buy if needed. Confidentiality assured if you request it. I try to be considerate and helpful in cases of divorce, bankruptcy, and estate liquidation. I can pay immediately or arrange auction or consignment sales. I am not interested in fakes, reproductions or common modern guns. I'm more interested in unusual or oddball older guns that many other collectors avoid. I will consider heavily worn, broken, or refinished items only if they are rare or have documented historical association. Honest wear and alterations from the period of use don't bother me, but do affect the value of the piece.

Any gun buyer wants to know the make, model, serial number, caliber or gauge, type and percent of finish, barrel length, type of stock or grips, mechanical condition, condition of bore, description of all markings (inside and out), any alterations, description of all dings and defects. If offering a gun with historical association, the quality of documentation is very important. Send a photocopy of existing documentation and what you are willing to swear to in a notarized affidavit. A photograph or photocopy is very helpful, but personal inspection is required before final offer can be made on many guns, especially those with fine engraving. Please don't offer me anything stolen or illegal. I won't buy it."

There are specific regulations regarding the shipment of firearms. Jim has the necessary licenses, but check with him for specific shipping instructions. If you don't want to sell your gun but would like an informal appraisal, Jim charges only $1 to appraise most guns.
Jim Supica, Jr.
Old Town Station
PO Box 15351
Lenexa, KS 66285
   (913) 492-3000
   (913) 492-3064 fax

★ **Jigsaw puzzles** by *Tuco, MarMar, Regent,* and other pre-1950 manufacturers. Especially interested in depression era puzzles. No moderns. Complete puzzles in good condition boxes only, please. A photocopy of the box is helpful.
Jim Rohacs
9721 Lomond Drive
Manassas, VA 22110
   (703) 369-5578 from 6-9pm weekdays

★ **Quilts** are wanted for consignment auctions held four to six times each year. Give a call for more information.
Homer Swartzentruber, Auctioneer
PO Box 331
1515 North State Road 5 S.
Shipshewana, IN 46565
   (219) 768-4744

★ **Old Sugar Packets** are wanted. I'll buy wrappers, collections, or accumulations. You can state the price you want or send them for my offer.
Herb Schingoethe
156 South Western Ave.
Aurora, IL 60506
   (708) 892-2173

★ **Pocket knives** over 50 years old, especially those with multi-colored celluloid handles. Celluloid is a synthetic plastic with a variety of colors, usually looking swirly or in some type of pattern, and could resemble stone, wood, horn, pearl, marble, etc., and may be opaque or translucent. To sell your knife, make a photocopy with the blade[s] open. If you don't, it is essential to give very accurate measurements of the knife open and closed. Provide all information stamped on the blades or handle. Include an SASE. If you have a price you'd like, tell him. If not, this 25 year veteran will make offers to amateur sellers. He is not interested in knives that are badly rusted or which have broken blades or handles. Never attempt to clean or sharpen an old rusted or broken knife, as you usually destroy all its possible value. "It's worth more when it looks worthless than when you make it worthless." Cleaning and restoration must be done by a knife expert.
"Mr. T.C."
PO Box 6694
Woodland Hills, CA 91365

★ **Glass knives** are wanted, especially those colored amber, emerald green, opal, and cobalt blue, as well as those with ribbed handles or combinations of clear blades with colored handles. "I would really love to find a 6.5" Westmoreland with a certain type of thumb guard. I'd also love to find a "glass pig," the blob of glass with two of three knives attached, before they were broken off." Buys printed material, catalogs, photos, etc. on all aspects of 1920 to 1940's glass knives. Brands include Kitchen Gadget Company, Kitchen Novelty Company, Buffalo Knife, ES Pease, John Didio, and a number of others. Please describe the size, color, pattern on the handle and the condition. You must price your knife.

Michele Rosewitz
PO Box 3843
San Bernardino, CA 92413
(714) 862-8534

★ **Disneyland souvenirs and memorabilia** "from the California Park" before 1980. Wants maps, guidebooks, tickets, food wrappers, brochures, parking tickets, special event programs, posters, passes, postcards, and what have you. Especially wants a Marx Playset of Disneyland. This serious collector has been to Disneyland more than once a month for thirty years! Nothing from DisneyWorld in Florida is wanted.

Linda Cervon
10074 Ashland St.
Ventura, CA 93004
(805) 659-4405

★ **Salesmen's samples** and other well-made miniatures of real objects. "If your item is in miniature, all parts to scale, and complete, it can be well worth your while to contact me about it. A sample barbers chair, for example, is worth $10,000 to me. So is a Wooten desk sample. Other samples are worth from $300 to $5,000. I'm not interested in doll house miniatures, but want to hear about just about any other small well-crafted items. Since I am writing a book on salesmens' samples, I would like to hear from you even if your piece is not for sale." A photo is almost essential. Include dimensions. Note all repairs. Describe any marks or labels. Describe the case and its condition.

John Everett
PO Box 126
Bodega, CA 94922
(707) 876-3513

★ **Fountain pens, mechanical pencils, and pen and pencil desk sets** are wanted by this aggressive collector. He will do appraisals for free if you mail your item to him and include enough postage for him to return your item(s). He says he'll buy both vintage and modern pens and claims "nobody pays higher."

Steven Alpert
PO Box 6522
Orange, CA 92613
(714) 771-5500

★ **Mechanical pencils with advertising on them** are wanted. Most advertising mechanical pencils are modestly priced $50¢ to $3, with some national ads worth $10, and a few as much as $20. Some non advertising pencils are wanted including brands like *Parker, Conklin, Shaffer, Wahl, Eversharp, Swan* and others. Prices on these can range as high as $200 for rare, high quality pencils. He enjoys finding dual-purpose pencils, such as those combined with knives, magnifying glasses, pliers, etc. "I am also interested in pre-1960 catalogs, brochures, display cases, salesman's samples, sample cases, or signs that relate to mechanical pencils, but no magazine ads, please. I do not want new mechanical pencils or those with Bible verses. I am **not** interested in wood pencils, ink pens or fountain pens unless they are part of a set that includes a mechanical pencil. I will accept shipments up to 50 pencils for immediate response and payment. Please phone first if you have more than 50." He cautions "do not clean dirty or frozen pencils as you are more likely to destroy their value than to help it." He will make offers on collections of mechanical pencils, but only after inspecting them in person.

Tom Basore
715 West 20th Street
Hutchinson, KS 67502
(316) 665-3613 eves

★ **Ceramic flower frogs and candelabra** depicting ladies dancing or posing. "I'm especially interested in those made by the Ohio pottery company called Cowan, but will buy European makers as well." He especially seeks Cowan frogs number 708, 717, 803, 804, 805, 812, and 853 as well as the figural dancing candelabra #752. These can bring from $300 to $600, so are definitely worth your time.

William Sommer
9 West 10th St.
New York, NY 10011
(212) 260-0999

★ **Children's lunch boxes and/or** *Thermos* **bottles,** metal or vinyl, in excellent condition, especially radio, TV and space characters from the 1950's and 60's. "Call about any find condition item as I am always glad to talk to anyone any time about lunch boxes, and will be happy to give a reasonably accurate assessment of the value of your old character lunchbox." Joe has prepared guidelines for describing the condition of your box and information on cleaning them which he will send if you include a long SASE with your inquiry. If you telephone, first inspect your box carefully for a date.
> Mark "Joe Lunchbucket" Blondy
> 121 East Mulberry
> Lebanon, OH 45036
> (513) 897-9421 or (513) 932-4435

★ **Outboard motors, 1940-1960.** "I'm especially interested in motors by *Flambeau, Neptune, Martin 200* and any racing outboards made in the United States, such as *Mercury* and *Champion.* If you send me a photo of your old outboard motor along with a SASE, I'll identify it for you, and if it's something I can use, I'll make an offer." Peter is the author of *The Old Outboard Book.*
> Peter Hunn
> c/o WZZZ Radio
> Lakeshore Road
> Fulton, NY 13069
> (315) 593-1313

★ **U.S. Marine Corps ephemera** including recruiting posters, other artwork, postcards, autographs, letters written by Marines, and "almost anything" in book form. including signed books by or about Marines, personal memoirs, unit histories, campaign histories, biographies, fiction, juveniles, children's books and poetry. "I would especially like a set of monographs written by Marine Major Edwin McClellan in 1925, in book or mimeographed form." He is not interested in book club editions or in books "in questionable condition." To sell your Marine Corps books, give standard bibliographic information, including number of pages, size, and whether or not it has a dust jacket. This 10 year veteran distributes four catalogs a year of military books for sale.
> Stan Clark, Jr.
> Stan Clark Military Books
> 915 Fairview Ave.
> Gettysburg, PA 17325
> (717) 337-1728

★ **Wedgwood dinnerware** is bought and sold, but only discontinued patterns. Send photocopies, please. Her shop is open by appointment.
> Gloria Voss Beyer
> 740 North Honey Creek Parkway
> Milwaukee, WI 53213
> (414) 259-1025

★ **Bells,** especially cast bronze. The country's largest broker in used bells buys and sells a wide range of bells. Write or call for more information.
> Brosamer's Bells
> 207 Irwin Street
> Brooklyn, MI 49230
> (517) 592-9030

★ **Charles M. Russell memorabilia.** "I'll buy just about anything illustrated by Russell: trays, posters, books, magazines, calendars, etc., as well as personal items, autographs, and other Russell memorabilia. Also buys **art by Philip Goodwin** on trays, calendars, posters, and advertising. He can provide a detailed wants list of magazines, illustrations, books, and other items to dealers who send an SASE.
> Jim Combs
> 417 27th Street NW
> Great Falls, MT 59404
> (406) 761-3320

★ **Montana memorabilia** including
> Photos of saloons, cowboys, Indians, etc.;
> Montana tokens;
> Advertising from Montana companies, especially saloons and breweries;
> Books about Montana;
> Paper ephemera from Montana Territory.

Has a particular interest in Great Falls, and especially items associated with its breweries and famous *The Mint* and *Silver Dollar* saloons. This 25 year veteran collector prefers you to set the price, but you may ask for offers if you provide a good description.
> Jim Combs
> 417 27th Street NW
> Great Falls, MT 59404
> (406) 761-3320

SELL-A-GRAM from a reader of Tony Hyman's *I'll Buy That Too!*

TO: _____

FROM: _____

Phone: ( )

I have the following item:

Remember to include the (1) shape, (2) colors, (3) dimensions, and (4) all names, dates, and marks. Re-read pages 10-14 and and any text or entry notes for selling what you have.

It's condition is:

List all chips, repairs, cracks, dents, fading, scratches, rips, tears, creases, holes, stains, and foxing. Note any missing pages, parts, or paint.

CHECK ONE

☐ The item is for sale for $_____ plus shipping.

☐ The item is for sale. I am an amateur seller and would like you to make an offer.

☐ The item may be for sale if the price is sufficient. Would you like to make an offer?

☐ The item is not for sale, but I am willing to pay a fee to learn its value.

To assist you to evaluate the item, I am enclosing a:

☐ Sample ☐ Photocopy ☐ Photo ☐ Tracing ☐ Sketch ☐ Rubbing ☐ Nothing

This is to certify that, to the best of my knowledge, the item is genuine and as described. Buyer has a 5 day examination period during which the item may be returned for any reason.

Signature: _____ Date: _____

☐ Answer Requested (SASE enclosed). ☐ No answer needed.

BUYER'S RESPONSE:

1986 Treasure Hunt Publications, Box 3028, Shell Beach, CA 93448

TREASURE 🎁 HUNT

Free books
special to our valued readers

Send us a true story about a "hidden treasure" you found and sold to one of our listees.

If we use it in print or tell it on the air,
we'll send you a free copy
of our next edition of *I'll Buy That Too!*

We want to know about "junk" that turned out to be good.
★ Odd things you sold
★ Valuable things you sold
★ Very old treasures you sold
★ Anything with an interesting story
★ Things you thought trash, that proved valuable

Save $5/$12/$21
Special to our valued readers

Give *I'll Buy That Too!* to a friend...and SAVE !

SAVE $5...Give this valuable book to a friend...and we'll pay the postage. YOU SAVE $5. Pay only $19.95 postpaid.

SAVE MORE...Send *I'll Buy That Too!* to two friends and save $12! That's right...Order two copies as gifts for only $37.90.

SAVE MORE YET...Send *I'll Buy That Too!* to three people and save $21! That's right...Order three copies as gifts for only $53.85.

YES, I want to help my friends make money.

Send copies of *I'll Buy That Too!* to:

Name_____

Address _____

_____

Name_____

Address _____

_____

I have enclosed (circle) $19.95 for one $37.90 for two $53.85 for three
California residents add state sales tax

MC/VISA_____ Expires _____

Treasure Hunt Publications, PO Box 3028, Pismo Beach, CA 93448

Call about larger quantities: (805) 773-6777